SOTHIS PRESS

Sothis Press aims to completely reimagine the public domain book with an emphasis on universal access to captivatingly designed print editions. We believe that technology will enable every single book ever published to be perpetually accessible in beautiful print form. Sothis is beauty in ubiquity.

www.sothis.press
1 Waterhouse Square, London, ECIN 2ST

Cultural Landscape Report for the Sandy Hook Coastal Defense Batteries

Gateway National Recreation Area, Fort Hancock, New Jersey; Site History, Existing Conditions, Analysis and Evaluation, Treatment

Timothy W. Layton

SOTHIS PRESS

ISBN 978-1-0365-2671-9

This edition is published by
Sothis Press The company
is registered in England and Wales.
The Company Number is 14900389.

Cultural Landscape Report for the Sandy Hook Coastal Defense Batteries

"New York City can be satisfactorily defended, if the outer defenses are placed at Sandy Hook..."

Commander W. T. Sampson, U. S. Navy, *Report of the Board on Fortifications or Other Defenses*, 1886.

Gateway National Recreation Area

Fort Hancock, New Jersey

Site History

Existing Conditions

Analysis and Evaluation

Treatment

Prepared by
Timothy W. Layton, ASLA
Historical Landscape Architect

H. Eliot Foulds
Senior Project Manager

Olmsted Center for Landscape Preservation
National Park Service, Boston, Massachusetts, 2010

The Olmsted Center for Landscape Preservation promotes the stewardship of significant landscapes through research, planning, and sustainable preservation maintenance. The Center accomplishes its mission in collaboration with a network of partners including national parks, universities, government agencies, and private nonprofit organizations. Techniques and principles of preservation practice are made available through training and publications.

Olmsted Center for Landscape Preservation
Boston National Historical Park
Charlestown Navy Yard, Quarters C
Boston, MA 02129
www.nps.gov/oclp/

National Park Service, Denver Technical Information Center Report NPS 646/104869

Library of Congress Cataloging-in-Publication Data

Layton, Timothy W. (Timothy William), 1974-
Cultural landscape report for the Sandy Hook coastal defense batteries, Gateway National Recreation Area / Timothy W. Layton, H. Eliot Foulds.
p. cm. -- (National Park Service, Denver Technical Information Center report ; NPS 646/104869)
"Olmsted Center for Landscape Preservation, National Park Service"--T.p. verso.
Includes bibliographical references.
1. Sandy Hook Unit of Gateway National Recreation Area (N.J.)--Antiquities. 2. Gateway National Recreation Area (N.J. and N.Y.)--Antiquities. 3. Coast defenses--New Jersey--Sandy Hook Unit of Gateway National Recreation Area. 4. Batteries (Ordnance)--New Jersey--Sandy Hook Unit of Gateway National Recreation Area--History. 5. Historic buildings--Conservation and restoration--New Jersey--Sandy Hook Unit of Gateway National Recreation Area. 6. Military architecture--New Jersey--Sandy Hook Unit of Gateway National Recreation Area. 7. Landscape protection--New Jersey--Sandy Hook Unit of Gateway National Recreation Area. 8. Sandy Hook Unit of Gateway National Recreation Area (N.J.)--History. 9. Sandy Hook Unit of Gateway National Recreation Area (N.J.)--Management. 10. Sandy Hook (N.J.)--History, Military. I. Foulds, H. Eliot, 1960- II. Olmsted Center for Landscape Preservation (U.S.) III. Title.
F142.G371.39 2010
974.9'46--dc22

2010033060

Cover Photograph: Detail of a color photograph of Fort Hancock's "Nine Gun" battery in operation, circa 1940s. Gateway National Recreation Area Museum Collection #685.12

Title Page: Hercules missiles at the NIKE launch site, circa 1958. Gateway National Recreation Area Museum Collection #8067

TABLE OF CONTENTS

LIST OF ILLUSTRATIONS

FIGURES

INTRODUCTION

SITE HISTORY

EXISTING CONDITIONS

ANALYSIS AND EVALUATION

TABLES

ANALYSIS AND EVALUATION

TREATMENT

DRAWINGS

INTRODUCTION

SITE HISTORY

EXISTING CONDITIONS

TREATMENT

FOREWORD

Starting in 1893, Sandy Hook represented the first line of defense of America's most important seaport. Large caliber and rapid fire gun batteries, such as Batteries Gunnison, Potter and Mortar, played an important part of an ever changing coastal fortification strategy which kept the United States an arm's length from its enemies. The defensive strategy shifted focus, but continued into the Cold War-era with the installation of a NIKE missile battery at Sandy Hook.

The following report details the present conditions for these significant batteries within Fort Hancock, part of the Sandy Hook Unit within Gateway National Recreation Area. As the park moves forward in developing more comprehensive planning and treatment strategies in preserving these facilities, this plan will keep us headed in the right direction.

The Olmsted Center for Landscape Preservation has done a great job in organizing the details through attainable objectives for the park to build upon in future preservation and rehabilitation efforts. As we move forward in our efforts to fulfill the NPS mission, this document will provide the needed guidance and documentation to reach that goal.

Pete McCarthy
Unit Coordinator
Sandy Hook Unit Gateway NRA

ACKNOWLEDGMENTS

This report represents a collaborative effort between the Olmsted Center for Landscape Preservation and the Sandy Hook Unit of Gateway National Recreation Area. At the Olmsted Center, Lisa Nowak and Allison Crosbie, Historical Landscape Architects, conducted research at the National Archives and the Center for Military History. Timothy W. Layton, Historical Landscape Architect, served as lead author with guidance and contributions from Eliot Foulds, Senior Project Manager. Margie Coffin Brown, Senior Project Manager, reviewed draft documents and Robert Page, Director, provided project oversight and reviewed draft documents.

At the Sandy Hook Unit, Pete McCarthy, Unit Coordinator, and Lou Venuto, former Chief of Interpretation and Cultural Resources, participated in the formulation, coordination, and review of this project. Brian Forseth, Chief of Maintenance, participated in identifying and reviewing treatment tasks. Mike Thomas, Park Ranger, assisted in the on-site documentation of the coastal defense batteries during several bitterly cold January days. Thomas Hoffman, Interpretative Ranger, graciously dialogued with the authors, reviewed draft documents, and shared his wealth of knowledge about the park's coastal defenses. Mary Rasa, former Museum Curator, provided digital copies of images from the park's collection and Mark Christiano, GIS Specialist, shared GIS and orthophoto data.

Additionally, this report was aided by contributions from Wade Myers, Technical Information Specialist at the Harpers Ferry Center, who provided digital copies of images from the center's Commissioned Art Collection. The authors greatly benefitted from conversations with Bolling Smith and Mark Berhow and direction to the Coastal Defense Study Group's e-library of *Report of Completed Works* and NIKE missile documentation. Finally, the *Historic Fortification Preservation Handbook* prepared through a partnership between the National Park Service, the University of Oregon, and the Washington State Parks and Recreation Commission, served as an invaluable guide to preparing treatment recommendations for Sandy Hook's coastal defense batteries.

INTRODUCTION

This report recounts the past, documents the present and prescribes an appropriate future for the essential surviving elements of Sandy Hook's historic coastal defense batteries. Over the course of more than one-hundred years, facilities at Sandy Hook have had major roles in the testing and deployment of weapons systems including nearly every kind of seacoast artillery, harbor mines, searchlights and RADAR systems, of which there is little tangible evidence remaining above ground. The purpose of this report is to provide park managers with preservation measures focused on the surviving and visible coastal defense infrastructure and the associated landscape characteristics and features that since 1975 have been the responsibility of the National Park Service.

To aid in navigation and defend the metropolitan New York area, public and government agencies have been present on Sandy Hook since the late eighteenth century. Most recently, the U. S. Army used the peninsula as a missile defense site until the mid-1970s when the missile system was deemed obsolete and the Army's land was transferred to the National Park Service. Prior to that time, the gun batteries built between 1893 and 1917 had been disarmed and mothballed by the Army following the end of World War II. The Army then briefly took Fort Hancock off-line until the onset of the Korean Conflict in 1950, and soon thereafter used the property to locate missile defenses protecting the New York, New Jersey metropolitan area against bombardment by high-altitude aircraft and intercontinental missiles. When the Department of Defense transferred the property to the National Park Service, the extant missile defense infrastructure remained sound, while the former gun batteries had been deteriorating in obsolescence for nearly thirty years.

Gateway National Recreation Area's Sandy Hook Unit, provides opportunities for outdoor recreation and enjoyment of natural and cultural resources that are unusually accessible to large urban populations (Figure 1.1). The park's successful new Multi-Use Path (MUP) has begun attracting visitors beyond the popular ocean beaches, introducing thousands to the peninsula's diverse natural and cultural environments and broadening the typical visitor experience. As the Sandy Hook Multi-Use Path continues to attract visitors, the park anticipates that many will become interested in learning more of Sandy Hook's military history, and the historic purpose of the coastal defenses arranged along its length.

PROJECT METHODOLOGY AND OBJECTIVES

The scope of this report includes a brief site history, a description of existing conditions, and a landscape analysis based on National Register of Historic Places definitions and criteria. The final chapter of the report concludes with treatment recommendations intending to preserve the characteristics and features of the landscape that give the property historical significance.

As Sandy Hook's complex history has been well examined in research presented by others, the purpose of this report is not to retell the comprehensive history of Sandy Hook's coastal defenses. Rather, the purpose of this report is to supply background information and to organize a logical framework supporting recommendations for the preservation of the most tangible remnants of the former defensive system. Relying on comprehensive histories prepared by others, the preparers of this report have focused new research efforts entirely upon the question of vegetation management. Work has also been focused on providing graphic "period-plans" of the coastal defense system as it developed and evolved, and providing adequate mapping to guide and illustrate treatment recommendations. Given that coastal defense infrastructure is primarily structural, prior National Park Service reports and documents give scant attention to the historic role of vegetation. Yet, the engineering of these concrete structures relied fundamentally on the cushioning effect of sand and soil to absorb the explosive force of munitions. Vegetation was encouraged, even cultivated, on these engineered landforms in order to protect the steep engineered slopes against erosion and to protect the batteries from detection by hostile parties.

As more definitive histories are available elsewhere, this report provides a brief historical overview of the development of the coastal defense system sufficient to provide a sound basis for choosing appropriate preservation treatments. This overview is followed by an inventory and assessment of existing landscape conditions. This in turn is followed by an analysis and evaluation of the historical significance of the military landscape and the relative contribution of its surviving elements in conveying that significance. This analysis provides base inventory data and cultural resource evaluations for use in managing these landscape resources. This report concludes with landscape treatment recommendation. Regarding the NIKE missile battery sites, recommendations include site-planning intending to sensitively accommodate visitation and interpretation. Elsewhere within the various earth-sheltered coastal battery sites, treatment recommendations center upon management strategies for treating the vegetation growing on the earthen slopes integral to the coastal defense sites.

The objectives of this report include the following:

1. To provide additional details needed to both preserve, make accessible, and to interpret Sandy Hook's surviving coastal defense sites. The identification and preservation of significant downrange views and views between rangefinding stations are of particular interest in helping to interpret the coastal defenses as an integrated system.

2. To guide the preservation and accessibility modifications of the Sandy Hook coastal fortifications insuring that proposed alterations to the historic landscape meet the *Secretary of the Interior's Standards for the Treatment of Historic Properties: Rehabilitation.*

3. To organize and present the proposed treatment of the Sandy Hook coastal defenses landscape to facilitate consultation and to satisfy Gateway National Recreation Area's responsibilities under Section 106 of the National Historic Preservation Act of 1966.

PROJECT SETTING AND GEOGRAPHIC SCOPE

Fort Hancock, the historic Sandy Hook Proving Ground, and the accompanying coastal defense batteries are located near the northern tip of the Sandy Hook peninsula at the mouth of New York City's outer harbor. Fort Hancock was established in 1895 as part of a new nationwide system of coastal fortifications proposed in the 1880's by the Endicott Board. Acquired by the National Park Service in 1975 for use as part of the Gateway National Recreation Area, the Sandy Hook Unit is comprised of the greater part of a narrow 2,000 acre peninsula extending north from coastal New Jersey. The park lies at the northern end of the New Jersey barrier island system. More than two million people visit the Sandy Hook Unit each year. While this cultural landscape report documents a dozen military fortifications made up of discontinuous sites, the historic fortification system at Sandy Hook is unified by other surviving base infrastructure, including roads, railroad rights-of-way, and utility corridors. This report does not report upon or make recommendations for coastal batteries that currently lie within the boundaries of the U. S. Coast Guard Reservation at the northern extremity of the Sandy Hook peninsula (Drawing 1.1).

SUMMARY OF FINDINGS

This report has defined working boundaries for each of Sandy Hook's coastal battery sites, excluding Battery Arrowsmith, a structural fragment occupying an unstable site undermined by water. These working battery site boundaries extend beyond the above-ground masonry battery features to include engineered slopes in front of the masonry structures, and battery service areas to the rear of the masonry structures. Originally designed to be indistinguishable at a distance from the surrounding naturalized landscape, it is understandable that park visitors and staff unfamiliar with the historic function of the batteries might mistake the engineered landforms for naturally occurring sand dunes. The battery site boundaries defined in this report are both minimal and reasonable boundaries sufficient to protect and preserve these cultural resources for the enjoyment of future generations. Within these boundaries, cultural resource values, and the preservation of cultural resources should be well understood as fundamental to the National Park Service mission at the Sandy Hook Unit of the Gateway National Recreation Area.

This report recommends that effective management of vegetation growing within each of these working battery site boundaries is critical to both short and long term preservation of the historic resources. A mix of woody and herbaceous vegetation were historically encouraged to grow on the engineered landforms to prevent soil erosion and to conceal the batteries from view. Soil erosion continues to be an issue affecting the preservation of these resources, and the park should avoid the removal of large areas of vegetation from battery slopes without a robust corresponding plan for immediately revegetating cleared areas with plantings known for their ability to protect against soil erosion.

However, the presence of large trees growing on battery slopes presents a threat to the preservation of Sandy Hook's coastal batteries because large trees have the potential to uproot during storm events and displace large volumes of soil that make up the historic engineered landforms. Woody vegetation of any size should also not be permitted to become established in cracks and voids in the historic concrete structures, or otherwise allowed to take root in accumulated organic matter on concrete battery surfaces. Historically inappropriate growths of tall vegetation should not be permitted to block historic downrange views that were critical to the historic operation of the ordnance as well as to a contemporary understanding of the operation of the historic defenses.

Providing park managers with a useful rule-of-thumb, this report presents vegetation management recommendations that might be conveniently remembered as "***4-by-4-by-Fore***." The first of the two "4's" representing the elimination of all trees greater than four-inches, in diameter measured at breast height, growing upon engineered landforms; the second of the two "4's" representing elimination of woody vegetation of any size growing within four-feet of buildings and structures or masonry battery features. The third "Fore" representing the effective management of vegetation forward of battery sites in perpetuation of historic downrange views and enhancing public interpretation and understanding of these sites.

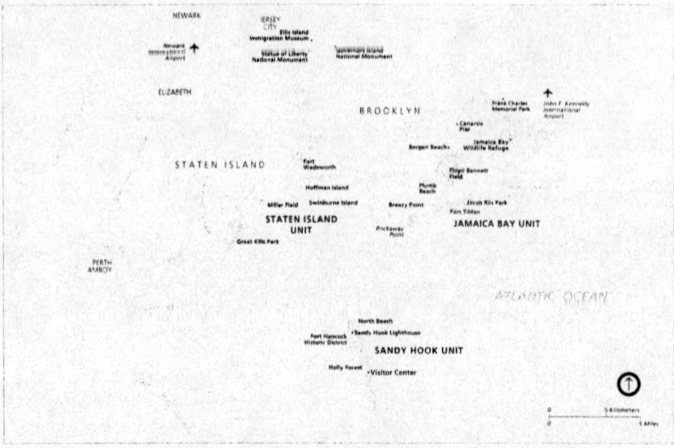

Figure 1.1. Gateway National Recreation Area Location Map. Sandy Hook is one of three units of the Gateway National Recreation Area (Harpers Ferry Center, National Park Service Maps, http://data2.itc.nps.gov/hafe/hfc/carto-detail.cfm?Alpha=GATE#).

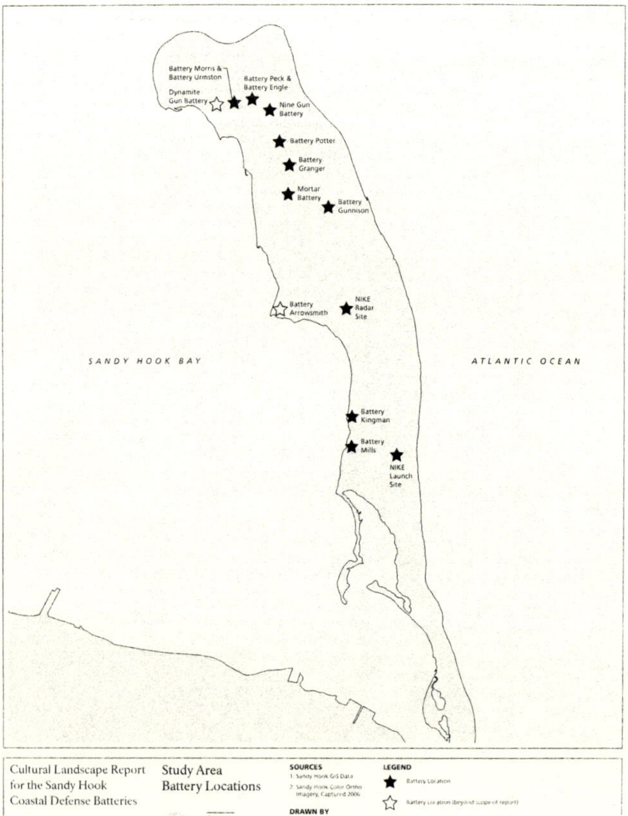

Cultural Landscape Report
for the Sandy Hook
Coastal Defense Batteries

Gateway National
Recreation Area
Sandy Hook, New Jersey

Study Area
Battery Locations

National Park Service
Olmsted Center for Landscape Preservation
www.nps.gov/oclp

SOURCES
1. Sandy Hook GIS Data
2. Sandy Hook Color Ortho Imagery, Captured 2006

DRAWN BY
Tim Layton
AutoCAD 2007, Illustrator CS3, 2009

NOTES
1. All features shown in approximate location and scale

LEGEND
★ Battery Location
☆ Battery Location (beyond scope of report)

0' 825' 1650' 3300'

Drawing 1.1

SITE HISTORY

PRE-HISTORY AND EUROPEAN CONTACT–1859

Located in the northeast corner of Monmouth County, New Jersey, Sandy Hook extends six and a half miles from the town of Highlands into lower New York Harbor. The landform parallels the primary deep water channel into New York Harbor and is nineteen miles south of the southern tip of Manhattan.

Approximately 10,000 years ago during the late Pleistocene epoch, glaciers covered northern New Jersey and Long Island, but did not extend south to Sandy Hook. Sea levels rose as the glaciers melted and about 8,000 years ago, a south to north littoral drift began depositing sand and forming a spit between the Navesink River and Atlantic Ocean. The currents continued to shape an elongated landform with major deposits accumulating at the northern end of the peninsula creating a recurved or hook-shaped formation (Figure 2.1).[1]

Based on archeological data, the earliest Native Americans arrived in New Jersey from 12,000 to 10,000 years ago. Settlements were located along major rivers and competing theories assert that either these base camps were occupied for long periods throughout the year or seasonally, when food resources were available. Archeological surveys at Sandy Hook have identified Native American artifacts and possible sites on the southern portion of the peninsula away from recent littoral deposits at the northern end of the peninsula and inland from the dynamically changing shoreline.[2]

The first European encounters with the Sandy Hook landscape occurred in the sixteenth century as countries vied for western trade routes to Asia. Italian explorer Giovanni da Verrazano sailed past Sandy Hook in 1524 and was followed the next year by Estevan Gomez. Although born in Portugal, Gomez sailed for Spain and by 1529 a Spanish map recorded the peninsula as "Cabo de Arenas" or Cape of Sands.[3]

Sailing on behalf of the Dutch United East India Company, English explorer Henry Hudson sailed along the Atlantic coast and anchored in the Sandy Hook Bay in 1609. Given its proximity to the shipping channel, the Dutch and English disputed claims over Sandy Hook through the mid-seventeenth century until Dutch governor Peter Stuyvesant surrendered all Dutch New World lands to the English in 1663.[4]

In the early 1600s, the Unami branch of the Lenni Lenape occupied central New Jersey. The Lenape were part of the Algonquian language group and were dispersed throughout New Jersey in autonomous bands. European contact brought warfare, disease, and alcoholism that decimated the Lenape population

By 1759, estimates placed the Lenape population at 300 for all of New Jersey with few remaining in the state by the start of the nineteenth century.[5]

EARLY DEVELOPMENTS AND FORTIFICATIONS

From the colonial era to the mid-nineteenth century, Sandy Hook lacked permanent coastal defenses. Early developments on the peninsula focused on maritime safety, transportation, and temporary fortifications. One of the first permanent structures on Sandy Hook provided navigational assistance to ships in the narrow channel to New York Harbor. After several shipwrecks in 1761, merchants pressured the New York Assembly to purchase a four-acre site on Sandy Hook in order to construct a lighthouse. For the next three years, Isaac Contro led the building effort to erect an octagonal, masonry structure that rose to 105 feet in height. The beacon was lit on June 11, 1764 and became the fifth operational lighthouse in the thirteen original colonies (Figure 2.2).[6]

During the Revolutionary War, the lighthouse aided friend and foe alike including British troops navigating the waters off of Sandy Hook. Recognizing the importance of the lighthouse, the British occupied the peninsula during the war and constructed a stockade around the structure to deter an attack. In addition, the British Army used Sandy Hook as a secure staging ground to disembark from after the Battle of Monmouth in 1778.[7]

During the War of 1812, American troops were stationed on the peninsula to prevent British reoccupation and to secure naval access to New York City. A half mile north of the lighthouse, a wooden stockade called Fort Gates was constructed and armed with cannon (Figure 2.3). After the war, American troops were withdrawn from Sandy Hook and the stockade and other temporary structures deteriorated. Playing a role in the young nation's first wars, the strategic importance of Sandy Hook was well established and the United States purchased two large parcels of land comprising most of the peninsula in 1817.[8]

After the War of 1812, the government continued development on Sandy Hook in support of maritime activities. Although the lighthouse aided navigation, violent storms punished mariners along Sandy Hook and the New Jersey coast prompting Congress to pass a bill in 1848 for a series of lifeboat stations between Sandy Hook and Little Egg Harbor. By May 1849, the U. S. Treasury Department's Revenue Marine Board completed eight stations, set at ten-mile intervals, from Spermaceti Cove on Sandy Hook south to Long Beach Island near Little Egg Harbor.[9] The Spermaceti Cove station was located three miles south of the Sandy Hook Lighthouse (Figure 2.4).

In 1855, the Revenue Marine Board constructed a second station on Sandy Hook northeast of the lighthouse.[10] New stations were constructed in 1872 at both

Sandy Hook locations and the northern station was designated Station No. 1 while the Spermaceti Cove station was designated Station No. 2. In subsequent decades, conflicts arose between the Sandy Hook Proving Ground and the location of both stations. In 1891, a new station was completed northwest of the Sandy Hook Lighthouse along the bay and in 1894, a new station was completed 232 yards west of the 1872 station at Spermaceti Cove.[11]

As early as 1759, commercial ferry service operated between New York City and Sandy Hook.[12] The Raritan and Delaware Bay Railroad Company, a predecessor of the New Jersey Southern Railroad, created a ferry and railroad service between New York City and Long Branch, New Jersey in 1860. New York passengers first traveled on a ferry to Port Monmouth, New Jersey and then transferred to a train for the remainder of the trip to Long Branch. Five years later, the company established a shorter route from Sandy Hook to Long Branch. Ferries arrived at a wharf on Spermaceti Cove and proceeded south along the coast making stops at towns growing with recreational amenities.[13] The wharf was relocated to Horseshoe Cove in 1870 and rail service did not extend north of the cove until the Army Ordnance Department established a line in 1889 (Figure 2.5).[14]

THE FORT AT SANDY HOOK 1859–1895

By the early 1800s, permanent stone fortifications such as Fort Wadsworth on Staten Island and Castle Clinton at the southern end of Manhattan guarded upper New York Harbor and the city (Figure 2.6). Mindful of Sandy Hook's role in the Revolutionary War and War of 1812, the Army Corps of Engineers prepared plans in 1857 for a fort to protect the lower harbor shipping channel and prevent an enemy force from anchoring and staging an attack from the peninsula. Work began the same year with the construction of a dock near the northwest tip of Sandy Hook. With a facility established to receive material and laborers, construction began on a large, five-bastioned granite fort in 1859 (Figure 2.7).

Known as the Fort at Sandy Hook, the pentagonal structure stood at the north end of the peninsula and enclosed approximately eighteen and a half acres. The north and east facade of the fort paralleled the shipping channel along Sandy Hook's Atlantic coastline where it northwest into the lower harbor (Figure 2.8). Construction accelerated with the start of the Civil War in 1861 but halted in 1868 before the entire fort was completed (Figure 2.9).[15] The defenses offered by the fort, and other stone and masonry fortifications, were surpassed by Civil War-era artillery improvements. With construction stopped on the fort, a cycle began at Sandy Hook that would last throughout the Cold War of new defensive structures and technologies being implemented just as offensive capabilities advanced that rendered the prior generation of defenses obsolete.

CIVIL WAR-ERA ARTILLERY ADVANCEMENTS

The Civil War allowed emerging artillery technologies to be battle tested and conclusions about the effectiveness of rifled bores and pointed projectiles changed the design of coastal defense batteries at Sandy Hook and across the country. Prior to the Civil War, major artillery on land, at sea, and at coastal fortifications consisted of cast iron, smooth bore guns with spherical projectiles. Coastal fortifications, like the Fort at Sandy Hook, were not immune to damage from this type of artillery. However, the projectiles were being fired from a ship, moving under sail power, making it difficult to obtain repeated direct hits necessary to destroy a stone and masonry wall.

The first Civil War-era innovation in artillery was the successful implementation of pointed projectiles. Spherical projectiles, or cannonballs, could do more damage if they were increased in size and had a corresponding larger barreled gun. A pointed projectile could be designed with the same diameter as a sphere, but with more mass and less drag as it traveled through the air. Fired from the same caliber gun, pointed projectiles were heavier and faster moving, resulting in more damage upon impact.

The superior pointed projectiles were coupled with an innovation in producing rifled bores. Rifling is a term describing the spiral grooves on the inside of a gun's bore that spin the projectile. As the projectile travels, the spin stabilizes its trajectory and results in faster speeds, longer range, and improved accuracy. Artillery with rifled bores and pointed projectiles could have more destructive power at a greater distance than earlier ordnance. A single direct hit from this new weaponry could obliterate a rigid stone and masonry wall (Figure 2.10). Coastal defense batteries were also made more vulnerable by steam-powered ships that had better maneuverability and could be equipped with defensive metal plating.

In response to the powerful impacts of this new artillery, Civil War troops discovered that earthen embankments, often reinforced by wood pilings, provided better protection and the promise of easier repairs compared to stone and masonry construction. Unlike shattering stone, the earth could absorb the projectile's force and the resulting crater could be readily filled with nearby earth and sand.[16] Observation and experience with defensive earthen structures in the Civil War would influence the design of coastal defense batteries during the second half of the nineteenth century.

SANDY HOOK PROVING GROUND

Civil War artillery advancements harkened the beginning of a new generation of armaments, but did not address what the United States should do with over a thousand existing smooth bore guns. Congress concurred with the need to test the conversion of smooth bore to rifled artillery and appropriations were signed into law in 1872 to facilitate the tests.[17] Various locations along the eastern seaboard of the United States were considered for establishing a new proving ground with a seven to eight mile uninhabited range. While potential locations and their acquisition were debated, the military reservation at Sandy Hook was selected as a temporary facility in 1874. The Army hastily constructed wood platforms and carriages and the first test fire of a converted smooth bore gun occurred in October 1874.[18] The temporary facility became more permanent in 1881 with the construction of a Proof Battery and concrete platforms for mounting and testing guns.[19] The Sandy Hook Proving Ground, with a proof battery and supporting, auxiliary structures, was the first development on the peninsula that responded to artillery advancements from the Civil War era.[20] A new generation of coastal defenses would join the granite fort and Proving Ground within the next decade.

THE ENDICOTT BOARD

As experts debated the location for a permanent proving ground site, an economic crisis started with the Panic of 1873 and lasted until 1878. As a result, Congress reduced coastal defense spending and ultimately stopped its funding in 1875.[21] Pressure for a new generation of coastal defenses came from the public, officers in the Army and Navy, and members of Congress who were concerned about the advancement of foreign navies and the lack of maintenance on existing defenses.

During President Grover Cleveland's first term, in 1885 to1889, Secretary of War William C. Endicott convened a board comprised of Army and Navy personnel and knowledgeable civilians to study locations, fortification types, armament, and protective materials for coastal defenses. The Endicott Board met in 1885 and early the following year released findings that called for defensive structures at twenty-six coastal locations, including Sandy Hook, and three additional sites along the Great Lakes.[22]

Prior to the Endicott Board, coastal defenses placed canons within parapet openings and on top of stone and masonry forts (Figure 2.11). In contrast to this approach and to address the threat posed by improved artillery, the Endicott Board recommended that new coastal defenses utilize rifled artillery emplaced in concrete platforms. The platforms would be shielded by a concrete wall and from the top of the wall, additional concrete would slope away and then be covered with earth for impact absorption and concealment into the surrounding landscape (Figure 2.12). As a result of the Endicott Board's recommendations, the first steam-powered, gun-lift battery and the first concrete mortar battery in the nation would be constructed at Sandy Hook.

BATTERY POTTER (GUN LIFT BATTERY #1)

In advance of constructing two new batteries, the Army upgraded transportation and housing facilities. The wharf near the northwest point of the peninsula, primarily used by the Ordnance Department to receive artillery for the Proving Ground, was extended in 1891 to receive cement, broken stone, and lumber for the battery projects. Narrow gauge railroad lines were installed on the wharf and laid out to the proposed battery sites for delivering materials. The Army also constructed temporary buildings to house a civilian workforce needed on Sandy Hook for the new battery projects.[23]

Excavations began for the Mortar Battery in November 1890 and were followed three months later by the groundbreaking for Battery Potter. Construction on both batteries occurred simultaneously throughout the early 1890s. Battery Potter has the distinction of being the first completed, partially armed, and tested battery following the Endicott Board's recommendations and therefore, the discussion will now focus on Battery Potter and be followed by the Mortar Battery.

Prior to its designation as Battery Potter, Sandy Hook's first coastal defense battery utilizing concrete construction and rifled guns was referred to as the Gun Lift Battery #1. In addition to incorporating new materials and artillery, the battery's innovative design featured a steam-powered hydraulic lift that raised the guns up into firing position after they had been loaded within a protective structure. Viewed from above, the Gun Lift Battery was D-shaped with the straight segment of the "D" facing west and a curving facade facing the Atlantic to the east. The terreplein stood approximately forty feet above surrounding grades and contained two openings for raising and lowering the 12-inch caliber guns. East of the guns, a concrete superior slope gently descended to a sentry route known as a *chemin de ronde* that was fronted by a parapet wall. A concrete slope angled away from the parapet and met an engineered earthwork that continued to slope down to surrounding grades and blended the massive concrete structure with the surrounding dune landforms (Figure 2.13).

Before excavating for the Gun Lift Battery, the Army constructed temporary storage facilities and installed mixing equipment to the west of the battery site for concrete production. Rail cars transported cement and broken stone from the wharf to the construction site, which were mixed with water and sand to produce concrete in close proximity to the building site. Sand was excavated and brought to the production site from nearby pits (Figure 2.14).

In April 1891, two months after excavation work began, workers started placing concrete for the Gun Lift Battery.[24] Construction continued until winter weather slowed concrete production. By June 1892, a majority of the battery's northern section was complete and the boiler, gun lift mechanism, and carriage were installed at the north emplacement. Two months later, the first 12-inch gun was raised to the terreplein and mounted at the north emplacement. Two rounds were test fired in September 1892 inaugurating a new era of coastal defense for metropolitan New York (Figure 2.15).[25]

As winter approached, colder weather again slowed concrete production and work crews focused on creating the engineered earthwork around the exterior walls of the battery. From December until June 1893, over 5,000 cubic yards of sand were added around the structure to a height of twenty feet above the surrounding grades.[26] The Army placed sand at a 2:3 slope resulting in a steep finished surface that was susceptible to erosion. In order to limit erosion and camouflage the earthwork with the surrounding dunes, the north, south, and east facing slopes were planted with cedar trees and small shrubs. The plant material was likely obtained from other locations on the peninsula and transplanted to the engineered earthwork.[27]

The west facing slope was also planted, however, this earthwork was part of a defensible entrance for the Gun Lift Battery and received low growing sod instead of small cedars and shrubs. Concerned about a land-based assault on the battery, the Army Corps of Engineers designed a castellated entry that extended west from the main concrete structure. The entry was constructed with granite blocks salvaged from the Fort at Sandy Hook. Two octagonal towers flanked either side of a main door. The door and first and second stories of the towers contained gun loop slots so machine guns could fire on potential attackers (Figure 2.16). As part of the defensive scheme, vegetation on the west slope needed to be low growing in order to permit an unobstructed field of fire (Figure 2.17).

By the end of 1893, the Gun Lift Battery was essentially complete with masonry construction finished, the engineered earthwork installed, and plant material added to the steep, sandy slopes. However at this time, the battery only had one 12-inch gun emplaced. The gun lift mechanism for the south emplacement was installed in February 1894 and then delays in manufacturing the gun carriage hindered the full operational start of the battery.[28] Over a year later, the carriage was delivered and installed and the second 12-inch gun emplaced. After successfully test firing ten alternating shots from the two guns, the Gun Lift Battery was cleared for service in August 1895.[29]

MORTAR BATTERY

Complementing the capabilities of the artillery at the Gun Lift Battery was a battery of sixteen mortars, recessed in a massive earthen landform, just south of the Sandy Hook lighthouse. Compared to the long-barreled guns at the Gun Lift Battery, mortars were stubby and set at steep angles to fire their projectiles in a high, arcing trajectory. A group of eight or sixteen mortars was planned to fire together and their respective 700-pound projectiles would collectively descend on the decks of ships like oversized pellets from a shotgun blast (Figure 2.18). To achieve high arcing trajectories that struck ships in the channel, Sandy Hook's Mortar Battery had to be located further away from the shoreline than the Gun Lift Battery (Figure 2.19).[10]

Construction began in 1890 on the Mortar Battery. The battery contained four concrete platforms that were recessed in a protective mound of earth and sand that rose to almost thirty-five feet. A rectangular concrete wall bounded the earthen mound, the longer legs of which were oriented in a southeast to northwest direction. At the wall's southwest and northeast corners, the Army constructed counterscarp galleries to defend against a land-based attack. If enemy forces ever penetrated the Mortar Battery's perimeter wall, machine gunners stationed in the counterscarp galleries had unobstructed lines of fire along the face of the wall (Figure 2.20).

Given the orientation of the battery, recessed platforms were located in the southwest, southeast, northwest, and northeast portions of the structure. Vertical retaining walls rose up from each platform and met a concrete blast slope that tapered to a wider opening and held back the mounded earth (Figure 2.21). The southwest and northwest platforms were entered through a concrete gallery featuring high, concrete retaining walls. Passageways to access the southeast and northeast platforms, as well as ammunition magazines, were located under the protective cover of the built up earthwork.

The first step in constructing Mortar Battery was excavating a stable base for each mortar platform, then pouring a concrete slab for the base. Similar to the work undertaken at the Gun Lift Battery, concrete was produced on site with dedicated storage space for broken stone and cement. Ships transported both products to Sandy Hook and then rail cars brought stone and cement to a site southwest of the Mortar Battery (Figure 2.22). The Army excavated sand from nearby pits and mixed with the other two components in close proximity to where the final concrete was placed.

In addition to the concrete facility, rail lines were installed to three sand pits near the Mortar Battery in order to transport sand for the battery's mounded, protective covering (Figure 2.23). When temperatures were too cold to mix and place concrete, laborers began filling rail cars by hand with sand. When the cars arrived at Mortar Battery, derricks hoisted a removable container and dumped the sand around the finished concrete work. The sand filling progressed slowly and during the winter months of 1892 and 1893, steam-powered shovels were brought to the site to improve the quantity and speed of the excavation and placing work.[11]

Over 150,000 cubic yards of sand were placed at Mortar Battery and settling and high winds displaced some of the material.[12] To better secure the fill material and protect their tremendous construction expenditures, site engineer Lt. James G. Warren directed the planting of sod, cut from a marsh south of the battery, on the slopes rising form the concrete blast slopes to the top of the mound. The remainder of the mound was covered in native heather and cedar boughs that were tolerant of dry and sunny conditions. Additionally, records show that oats were sown on the slopes to help deter erosion.[13]

Masonry construction was completed at Mortar Battery in 1893 and a year later, each of the four platforms was armed with four 12-inch guns. The guns were test fired in June 1894 and Sandy Hook's Mortar Battery became the first completed and operational concrete mortar battery in United States.

THE ESTABLISHMENT OF FORT HANCOCK

The creation of the Sandy Hook Proving Ground and the construction of new coastal defense batteries brought personnel from the Army Ordnance Department and the Army Corps of Engineers respectively to the peninsula. In addition to Battery Potter and the Mortar Battery, the Army constructed an experimental Dynamite Gun Battery in 1893. Located at the northern end of the peninsula, the battery utilized compressed air to fire projectiles instead of gunpowder.[14] With three batteries completed, additional personnel from the Army Corps of Artillery were needed for fulltime operation and maintenance of the new structures.

In order to provide housing and support facilities for the Army Corps of Artillery, the Secretary of War issued a general order establishing Fort Hancock on October 30, 1895. The Army designated the fort in honor of Major General Winfield Scott Hancock, a veteran of the Mexican and Civil Wars, who rose to national recognition for his heroics during the Civil War.[15] The Army Corps of Engineers, based out of New York City, would be on Sandy Hook as needed for battery construction and shoreline stabilization projects. The Ordnance Department and Corps of Artillery would have permanent facilities but each would retain separate and distinct identities under the supervision of their own commanding officers.[16]

At the time Fort Hancock was established, the Army Ordnance Department, Army Corps of Engineers, and Army Corps of Artillery shared the peninsula with federal personnel for the U. S. Lighthouse Service, the U. S. Lifesaving Service, and Western Union Telegraph Company.[17] All of these organizations shaped and modified the landscape in performing their duties.

LANDSCAPE SUMMARY - 1895

The general arrangement of developed versus non-developed areas at Sandy Hook appeared by 1895. Development was concentrated at the northern end of the peninsula with the former granite fort, wharf, lifesaving station, lighthouse, Proving Ground, and coastal defense batteries all north of Horseshoe Cove (Drawing 2.2). The railroad bisected the middle section of the peninsula which was primarily undeveloped except for a wharf and ice houses near Horseshoe Cove (Drawing 2.2). The southern portion of the peninsula contained limited development but was marked by the Spermaceti Cove lifesaving station and a dike south of the cove that sheltered it from the currents of the Navesink River (Drawing 2.1).

An 1889 map prepared by the Army Corps of Engineers shows the overall composition of vegetation and natural features several years prior to Fort Hancock's establishment. Large woody vegetation covered the undeveloped, middle section of the peninsula. Sand dune and beach areas were wider on the Atlantic side and narrower along Sandy Hook Bay. A relatively large marsh extended north of Horseshoe Cove and a tidal marsh bordered the edges of Spermaceti Cove. A string of long, narrow ponds punctuated the middle of the peninsula east of a primary north-south circulation route. Vegetation cover was sparse and clearing occurred around the Ordnance Department quarters and the Sandy Hook Lighthouse. Additional cleared areas appeared in association with the newly constructed batteries and the railroad lines (Drawings 2.1-2.2).

At the northern end of Sandy Hook, the pentagonal outline of the Fort at Sandy Hook dominated the landscape. Never completed, the Army removed portions of the Fort's exterior walls by the 1890s and reused the massive granite blocks for shoreline stabilization and new projects such as Battery Potter's defensible west facade. The southwest bastion of the Fort served as a control and observation facility for underwater mines. A storage building for the mines stood immediately south of the bastion. West of the Fort, the Dynamite Gun Battery stood isolated near the extreme northwest tip of the peninsula. The battery was oriented to engage enemy ships as they headed west in the main channel across the northern tip of the peninsula (Drawing 2.2).

East of the Fort, the Sandy Hook Proving Ground consisted of concrete platforms, a Machine Shop, and smaller supporting structures to store and observe ordnance tests. North of the Proving Ground, Western Union established a telegraph station. The Ordnance Department housed personnel south of the Fort and west of the Proving Ground. South of this housing, the Army constructed Battery Potter and the Mortar Battery, emplaced their guns, and prepared the batteries to defend the southern approach to New York. Construction was ongoing at Battery Granger and would be finalized in 1896 (Drawing 2.2).

Immediately north of the Mortar Battery, the 1764 lighthouse continued to warn mariners of the shallow waters around the peninsula. A keeper's house was located west of the lighthouse and secondary beacons were positioned north of the Fort and along Sandy Hook Bay. To further aid sea travel, lifesaving stations were established northwest of the Sandy Hook Lighthouse and at Spermaceti Cove (Drawings 2.1-2.2).

Access to and from the peninsula was by ships arriving at one of two wharves or via the railroad that stretched down the coastline to Long Branch, New Jersey. A wharf near the northern end of the peninsula featured separate docks for the Ordnance Department and Army Corps of Engineers. Another wharf, originally constructed for New Jersey Southern Railroad, was located at Horseshoe Cove.

Three railroad lines originated from the northern wharf and branched off to separate destinations. The northern line covered the shortest distance and terminated at a storage building for underwater mines near the southwest bastion of the Fort. The central line carried ordnance east to the Proving Ground and a branch off this line continued south across the entire length of the peninsula. The southern line from the wharf divided into three separate branches that served construction efforts and later munitions delivery to Battery Potter, the Mortar Battery, and Battery Granger (Drawing 2.2).

An east-west roadway paralleled the rail line from the northern wharf to the Proving Ground and secondary branches off of this road provided access to the Officers' Quarters. Also branching off of this east-west road was a north-south road that began east of the Ordnance Department Wharf and extended south to Spermaceti Cove. In addition to the roadways, the Ordnance Department constructed a wood plank walk from the Proving Ground south along the Atlantic coastline to the 3,000 yard target. The walk allowed ordnance officers to easily make their way across the dunes and evaluate shell impacts (Drawing 2.2).

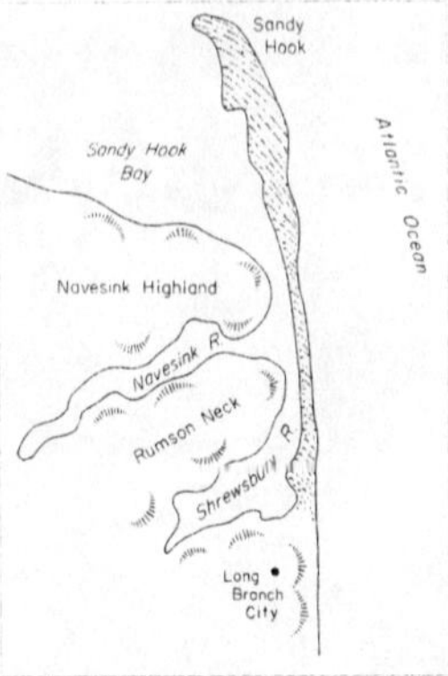

Figure 2.1. Formation of Sandy Hook. A south to north littoral drift deposited sand and formed a spit between the Navesink River and Atlantic Ocean. Waves and winds moving westward continued to shape the landform with major deposits accumulating at the northern end creating a recurved or hook-shaped formation (Charles B. Hunt, *Natural Regions of the United States and Canada*, San Francisco: W. H. Freeman and Company, 1974).

Figure 2.2. Sandy Hook Lighthouse. At the conclusion of three years of construction, the beacon was lit at the Sandy Hook Lighthouse on June 11, 1764 and became the fifth operational lighthouse in the thirteen original colonies (Gateway National Recreation Area Museum Collection, hereafter GATE, 28836).

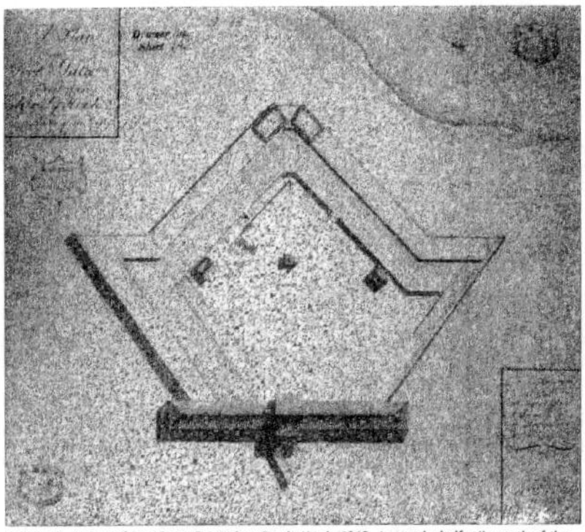

Figure 2.3. A Plan of Fort Gates Erected on Sandy Hook, 1813. Located a half-mile north of the lighthouse, a wooden stockade called Fort Gates was constructed to prevent British occupation and to secure naval access to New York City during the War of 1812 (James J. Lee III and Lauren Laham, *Historic Structure Report: Battery Potter, Mortar Battery and Battery Gunnison*, United States Department of the Interior, National Park Service, 2007).

Figure 2.4. Spermaceti Cove Lifeboat Station, circa 1930. In 1849, the U. S. Treasury Department's Revenue Marine Board established a lifesaving station at Spermaceti Cove to protect mariners along the southern portion of Sandy Hook (U. S. Coast Guard, "Station Spermaceti Cove, New Jersey," http://www.uscg.mil/history/stations/SPERMACETICOVE.pdf).

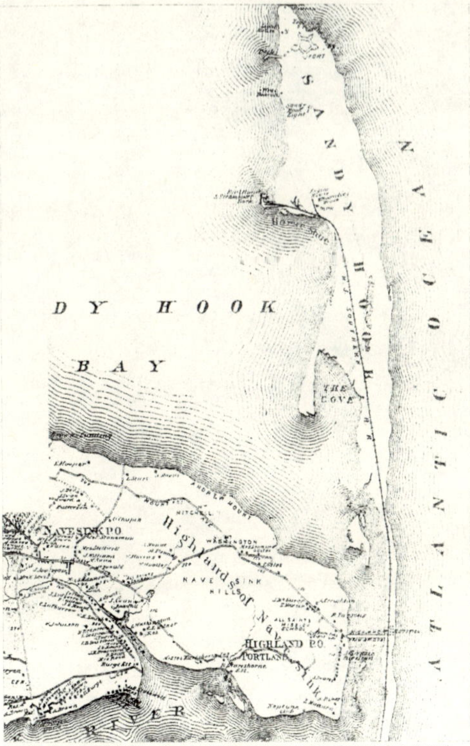

Figure 2.5. Detail of Sandy Hook from "Portions of Middletown and Ocean Townships," in the Beers, Comstock and Cline *Atlas of Monmouth County, New Jersey*, 1873. In 1865, ferry service was established from Manhattan to Sandy Hook where passengers transferred to a train headed to Long Branch. The railroad line, as seen on this 1873 map, did not extend north of Horseshoe Cove until the U. S. Army Ordnance Department established a line in 1889 (GATE 2255).

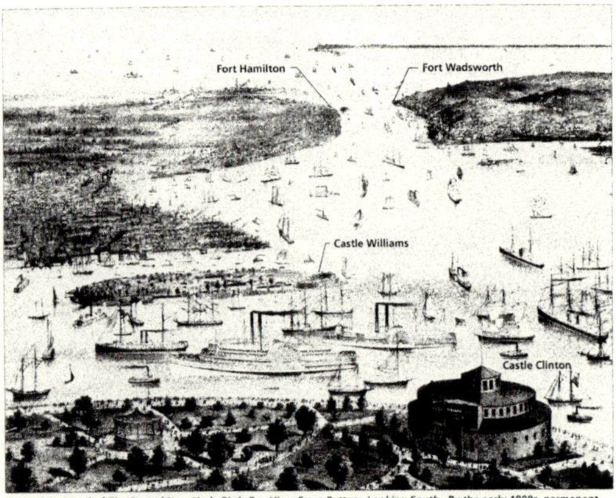

Figure 2.6. Detail of *The Port of New York: Birds Eye View From Battery, Looking South.* By the early 1800s, permanent stone fortifications such as Castle Clinton and Fort Wadsworth on Staten Island guarded Upper New York Harbor and the city (Library of Congress, annotated by Olmsted Center).

Figure 2.7. The Ordnance Department dock or wharf, circa 1900–10. In 1857, work began on construction of a dock near the northwest tip of the peninsula to facilitate construction on a five-bastioned granite fort (GATE 7319).

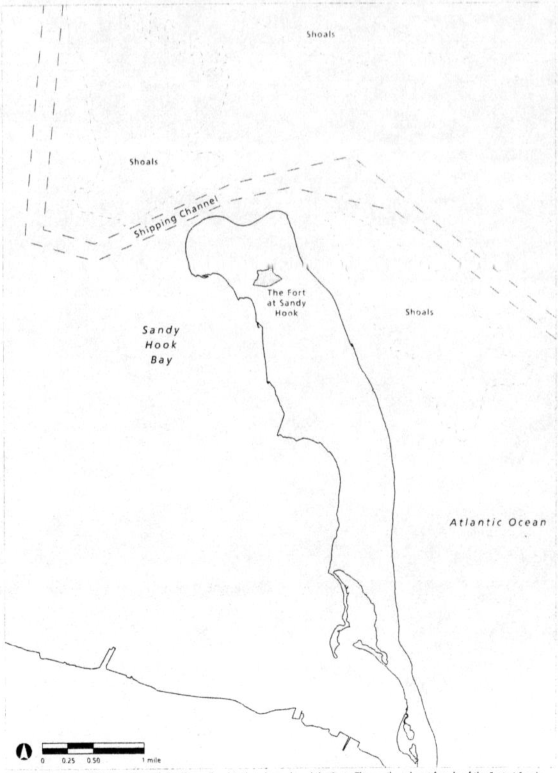

Figure 2.8. Diagram of the Sandy Hook landform, the shipping channel, and the Fort. The north and east facade of the Fort at Sandy Hook paralleled the natural shipping channel that avoided shallow waters near the peninsula. The channel followed Sandy Hook's Atlantic coastline and turned northwest into Lower New York Harbor (Olmsted Center, 2010).

Figure 2.9. View looking west at the Fort at Sandy Hook, circa 1880–85. With the start of the Civil War in 1861, construction accelerated on the Fort but was halted in 1868 before the entire structure was completed. The Proving Ground machine shop can be seen in the foreground (GATE 7298 and 7299).

Figure 2.10. Fort Sumter, South Carolina, September 8, 1863. Similar to Fort Sumter, coastal defense batteries using stone and masonry construction were made obsolete by artillery with rifled bores and pointed projectiles (Library of Congress).

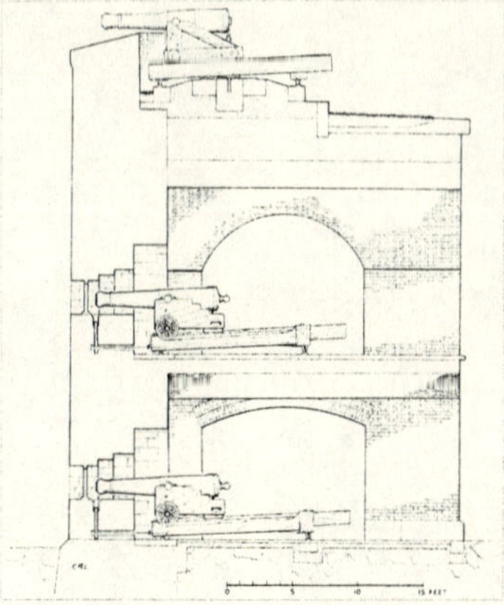

Figure 2.11. Section of masonry fort and smooth-bore cannons. Early coastal defenses placed canons within parapet openings and on top of stone and masonry forts (Emanuel Raymond Lewis, *Seacoast Fortifications of the United States: An Introductory History*, Annapolis, MD: Naval Institute Press, 1993).

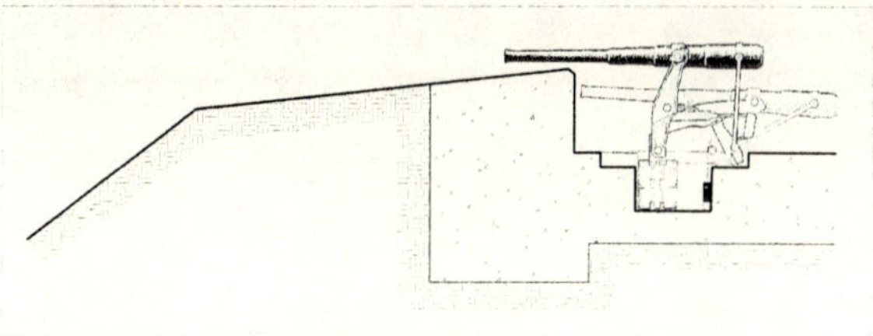

Figure 2.12. Section of disappearing gun in concrete and earth-shielded battery. Following the Endicott Board's recommendations, new coastal defenses utilized rifled artillery emplaced in concrete platforms that were shielded by concrete and earth for impact absorption and concealment into the surrounding landscape (Hugh Brown, Harpers Ferry Center Commissioned Art Collection, Exhibit 12/Graphic # 12-7 and Olmsted Center).

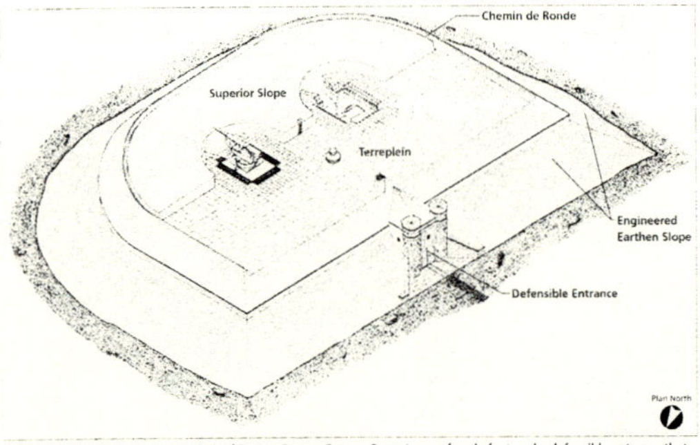

Figure 2.13. Annotated isometric view of Battery Potter. Battery Potter's west facade featured a defensible entrance that resembled a castle. At the top of the battery, two openings were constructed in the terreplein for raising and lowering the guns. East of the guns, a concrete superior slope gently descended to a sentry route known as a *chemin de ronde* that was fronted by a parapet wall. A concrete slope angled away from the parapet and met an engineered earthen slope that blended the massive concrete structure in with the surrounding land (GATE 10312 and Olmsted Center).

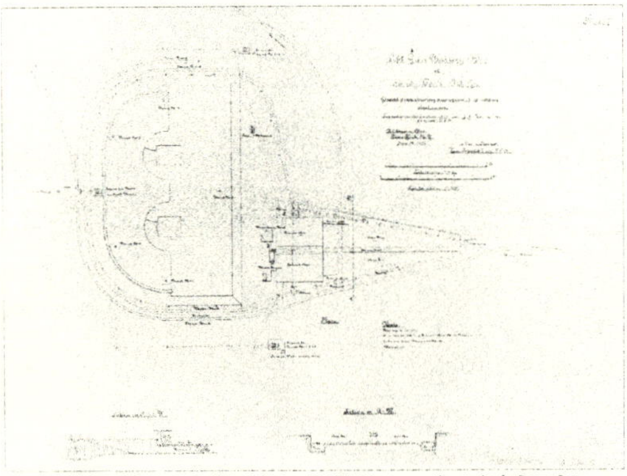

Figure 2.14. Lift Gun Battery No. 1 at Sandy Hook, N.J., June 30, 1892. Prior to excavation starting for Battery Potter, temporary storage facilities were constructed and mixing equipment installed for concrete production. Cement and broken stone were transported by railroad to the production site west of the battery (Lee and Laham, *Historic Structure Report*).

Figure 2.15. Battery Potter's north emplacement, September 12, 1892. The first of Battery Potter's two 12-inch guns was mounted at the north emplacement in August 1892. A month later, two rounds were test fired inaugurating a new era of coastal defense for metropolitan New York (GATE 7804).

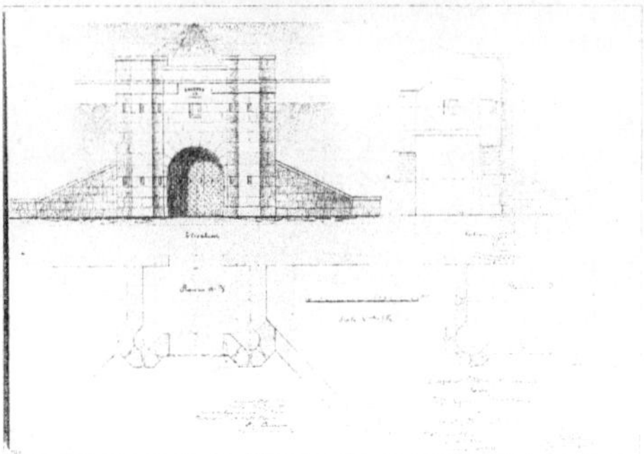

Figure 2.16. Proposed Main Entrance to the Lift Gun Battery at Sandy Hook, N.J., January 14, 1892. Concerned about a land-based assault, the Army Corps of Engineers designed a castellated entry for Battery Potter. The entry was constructed with granite blocks salvaged from the Fort at Sandy Hook and the two towers contained gun loop slots so machine guns could fire on potential attackers (Lee and Laham, *Historic Structure Report*).

Figure 2.17. West elevation of Battery Potter, circa 1893. As part of the defensive scheme for Battery Potter's west facade, vegetation on the west slope was low growing in order to permit an unobstructed field of fire from the granite towers (GATE 7813).

Figure 2.18. Four mortars mounted in a mortar pit, the Mortar Battery, June 30, 1894. Compared to the long-barreled guns at Battery Potter, mortars were stubby and set at steep angles to fire their projectiles in a high, arcing trajectory (GATE 7864).

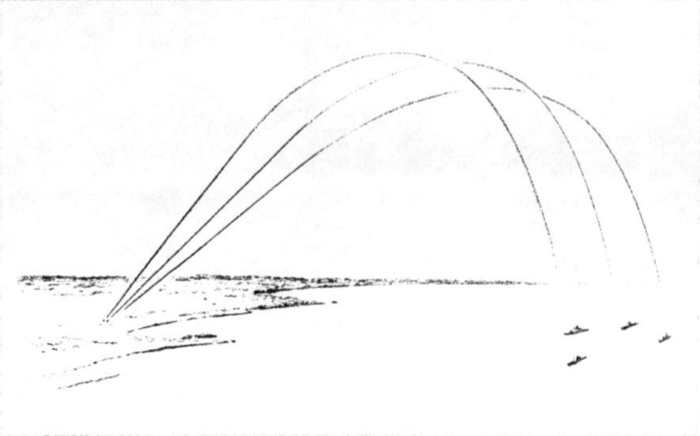

Figure 2.19. Illustration of projectile trajectory from the Mortar Battery. In order to achieve high arcing trajectories that would strike ships in the channel, Sandy Hook's Mortar Battery had to be located further west from the Atlantic shoreline than Battery Potter (Hugh Brown, Harpers Ferry Center Commissioned Art Collection, Exhibit 15/Graphic # 15-7).

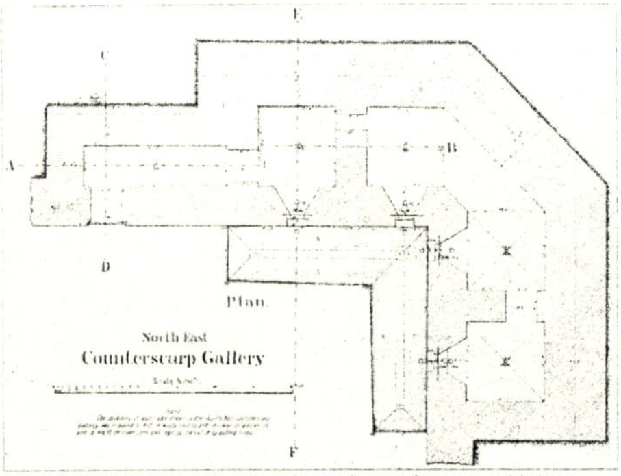

Figure 2.20. Plan for counterscarp gallery, 1895. In the event that enemy forces penetrated the Mortar Battery's perimeter wall, machine gunners were stationed in counterscarp galleries that had unobstructed lines of fire along the face of the wall (GATE 10669).

Figure 2.21. Placing sand around the northwest mortar pit, the Mortar Battery, 1893. Vertical concrete walls rose up from each mortar platform and met a concrete blast slope that tapered to a wider opening. The vertical walls and blast slope held back the Mortar Battery's engineered earthwork (Lee and Laham, *Historic Structure Report*).

Figure 2.22. Plan for concrete plant at the Mortar Battery, 1892. Similar to the work undertaken at Battery Potter, concrete for the Mortar Battery was produced at a dedicated, constructed facility that stored and mixed broken stone, cement, sand, and water. Broken stone and cement arrived at the site by a railroad that originating at the government wharf (GATE 10676).

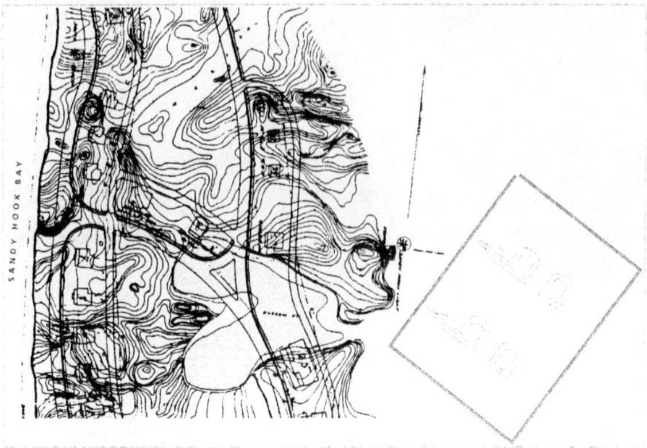

Figure 2.23. Plan of sand borrow pit and relationship to the Mortar Battery. Sand for concrete production and to create the Mortar Battery's engineered earthwork was excavated from nearby deposits known as borrow pits (highlighted by gray tone) and brought to the site by rail lines (Olmsted Center, 2009).

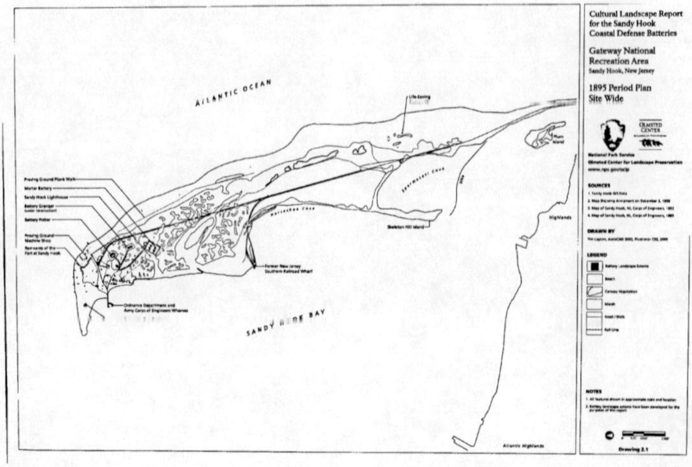

ATLANTIC OCEAN
SANDY HOOK BAY
Proving Ground Plank Walk
Mortar Battery
Sandy Hook Lighthouse
Battery Granger
Battery Potter
Proving Ground Machine Shop
Remnants of the Fort at Sandy Hook
Ordnance Department and Army Corps of Engineers Wharves
Former New Jersey Southern Railroad Wharf
Skeleton Hill Island
Horseshoe Cove
Spermaceti Cove
Plum Island
Highlands
Atlantic Highlands
Cultural Landscape Report for the Sandy Hook Coastal Defense Batteries
Gateway National Recreation Area
Sandy Hook, New Jersey
1895 Period Plan
Site Wide
National Park Service
Olmsted Center for Landscape Preservation
SOURCES
DRAWN BY
LEGEND
NOTES
Drawing 2.1

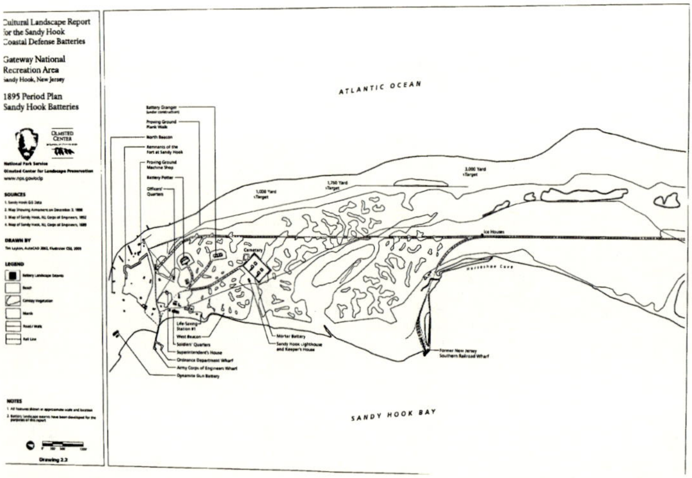
Cultural Landscape Report
for the Sandy Hook
Coastal Defense Batteries
Gateway National
Recreation Area
Sandy Hook, New Jersey
1895 Period Plan
Sandy Hook Batteries
Olmsted Center
National Park Service
Olmsted Center for Landscape Preservation
www.nps.gov/oclp
SOURCES
DRAWN BY
LEGEND
NOTES
Drawing 2.2
ATLANTIC OCEAN
Battery Granger
Proving Ground
Plank Walk
North Beacon
Remnants of the
Fort at Sandy Hook
Proving Ground
Machine Shop
Battery Potter
Officers' Quarters
1,000 Yard
Target
1,750 Yard
Target
3,000 Yard
Target
Cemetery
Ice Houses
Horseshoe Cove
Life-Saving
Station #1
West Beacon
Soldiers' Quarters
Superintendent's House
Ordnance Department Wharf
Army Corps of Engineers Wharf
Dynamite Gun Battery
Mortar Battery
Sandy Hook Lighthouse
and Keeper's House
Former New Jersey
Southern Railroad Wharf
SANDY HOOK BAY

EXPANSION OF COASTAL DEFENSES 1895–1919

Following the establishment of Fort Hancock in1895, the Army constructed additional coastal defense batteries recommended by the Endicott Board at Sandy Hook during the early twentieth century. When the United States entered World War I on April 6, 1917, seven coastal defense structures had been completed in addition to Battery Potter and the Mortar Battery and two more were under construction.

The Endicott Board outlined an ambitious coastal defense program that if fully implemented, required funding amounting to roughly half the entire federal budget.[14] The pace of construction at Sandy Hook and throughout the country fluctuated with varying appropriations but finally peaked with the start of the Spanish-American War in 1898. Public fears rose about an inadequately defended coastline and in response, robust military budgets were approved and construction accelerated on coastal defense batteries.

The defensive system recommended by the Endicott Board consisted of three categories—large caliber gun batteries, rapid fire gun batteries, underwater control mines. The battery types and mines were designed to engage specific threats and to work together as part of a defensive system. For example, strategically placed control mines would force an enemy battleship to travel slowly through a shipping channel allowing large caliber gun batteries more time to fire and disable or eliminate the ship. Rapid fire gun batteries would defend against minesweepers and shallow-draft boats that could travel outside the shipping channel. Lacking a component of this system made a coastal site vulnerable to a specific attack. Given the commercial and military importance of New York City, Sandy Hook required both battery categories and control mine facilities to defend the southern approach to the harbor.

Although an important component in the history of Sandy Hook's coastal defenses, the Mine Casemate is presently on U. S. Coast Guard property and is outside the study area for this Cultural Landscape Report. The review of the coastal defense batteries is divided according to category and first covers the large caliber gun batteries and then the rapid fire gun batteries. Within each category the batteries are presented chronologically according to the dates of artillery emplacement.

NAVAL ARMS RACE AND THE TAFT BOARD

At the start of the twentieth century, naval artillery consisted of a mixture of caliber sizes with none approaching the size and range of the 12-inch guns emplaced at Sandy Hook's coastal defense batteries. Engineers in Italy, Japan, and Great Britain all proposed battleships with large caliber armament schemes and the British completed the first such vessel with the successful launching of the HMS *Dreadnought* in 1906. The *Dreadnought*'s launch and early trials were closely observed as the ship combined large caliber armament, electronic range finding system, and faster steam-powered propulsion (Figure 2.24). The ship's design was groundbreaking and nations raced to build comparable battleships of their own that were generally categorized as dreadnoughts while all earlier ships were disparagingly referred to as pre-dreadnoughts.[39]

For the battleship's armament, the *Dreadnought* replaced a mixture of caliber sizes with ten 12-inch guns arranged as pairs on five separate turrets. When a pre-dreadnought ship fired mixed-caliber artillery at a target and missed, it was difficult to identify the different projectiles and make adjustments to the corresponding guns. *Dreadnought's* uniform-sized artillery simplified adjustments and resulted in volleys of projectiles with increased precision.[40]

Following *Dreadnought*'s launch, the United States and other world powers strategically shifted from naval defense to offensive capabilities at sea. In an effort to display United States naval power, President Theodore Roosevelt ordered four squadrons of battleships and escorts on a tour around the world in December 1907. The touring squadrons were popularly called the Great White Fleet due to their brightly painted hulls.

As the Navy's role changed to engaging an enemy force hundreds of miles away from the United States, coastal defense systems required reevaluation yet again. In similar fashion to the Endicott Board, Roosevelt convened military and civilian experts headed by Secretary of War William Howard Taft to review the nation's coastal defenses in 1905. In addition to reviewing Endicott Board recommendations, the Taft Board sought to incorporate technological changes made during the twenty-year period.[41]

The Taft Board did not alter the armament and defensive recommendations made by the Endicott Board. Instead, the Taft Board reinforced and accelerated the implementation of new technology including searchlights to illuminate channels and harbors at nighttime and the general electrification of coastal defenses.[42] In 1913, an approved project called for thirteen 60-inch searchlights and two 36-inch searchlights at several locations guarding the southern entrance to New York Harbor. Five of the 60-inch searchlights were designated to go to Sandy Hook, and by November 1916, the peninsula's first searchlight was operational at a location 1,000 feet south of Battery Gunnison.[43] By March 1918, the Army installed the remaining four searchlights with one located at the northwest point of the peninsula, one directly east of the Mine Casemate, and two approximately a mile south of Battery Gunnison.[44] The Taft Board also addressed coastal defenses for American territories acquired from Spain at the conclusion of the Spanish-American War. Except for six batteries at Fort

MacArthur near Los Angeles, new coastal defenses built after the Taft Board report were outside the continental United States in Hawaii, the Philippines, and at the Panama Canal.[45]

Part of the Taft Board's recommendations addressed improving fire control—the process of acquiring and firing on enemy ships. Available land to construct multiple observation points as well as advances in optical instruments and electronic communications among the observation points, plotting rooms, and batteries resulted in the continued superiority of land artillery over naval artillery through the early part of the twentieth century. Target systems were established that used both single and two observation points equipped with precise optical instruments. With two observations points, called base end stations, a ship and its distance from each station would be identified simultaneously. The readings would be communicated to a plotting room and triangulated to find the ship's position and projected course. After calculating this information, instructions would be relayed for aiming and firing the artillery. The communications between observation, plotting, and firing were increasingly handled by telephone (Figure 2.25). In addition to using two observation points, single observation points were installed in elevated structures and towers. Using this system, the distance to a ship was calculated based on the known height of an optical instrument and the angle it was depressed to sight the target. The Army used both systems for the coastal defense batteries at Sandy Hook and the systems, "...represented the most significant advance to be made in harbor defense fire control until the introduction of radar during World War II."[46]

The accuracy of triangulation improved with greater distance between two observation points. The Army's ability to locate stations at greater distances on land than between ships at sea gave coastal defense artillery an advantage over naval artillery. The coastal defense batteries at Sandy Hook were one component of a system that guarded the southern approach to New York Harbor. Batteries were also constructed at Fort Tilden on the Rockaway peninsula and at Fort Wadsworth and Fort Hamilton guarding the Narrows between the lower and upper harbor. In order to improve triangulation accuracy, the Army constructed an observation tower for Fort Tilden at Sandy Hook (Figure 2.26).[47] For the high-angle gun carriage batteries built on Sandy Hook's western coast, a pair of observation stations stood a mile north of the batteries and another pair stood south of the peninsula in the Navesink Highlands. Electronic communication among the stations, batteries, and forts permitted targeting and firing information to be shared across greater distances.

Controlling new territories, specifically Hawaii and the Philippines, allowed American military personnel to observe former coastal defense batteries constructed and maintained by the British and Japanese. An April 1910 memorandum notes a difference in the design of earthworks and the use of vegetation and camouflage to conceal these batteries. Specifically, the author cites:

> ...the great care that had evidently been taken by each of these governments to conceal the gun batteries and positions finder stations by means of screens of trees and shrubbery, and also, in case of English barbette batteries, by painting both guns and carriages in splotched or splashed colors of the varied hues of the surrounding landscape. In contrast with this I was equally impressed with the lack of concealment of our own coast defenses on the Pacific Coast and the way the batteries and position finder stations on that coast are exposed. The smooth geometrical slopes or our batteries, differing entirely from the rough natural slopes of the English and Japanese batteries, showed their locations at once, – making them stand out in bold relief against the natural background.[48]

Planting efforts to conceal or obscure coastal defense batteries at Sandy Hook and other American locations were not an innovation of the Taft Board. Before the Taft Board convened, the Army completed Battery Potter and the Mortar Battery and added vegetation in order to limit erosion and blend the batteries into the adjacent landscape. Following the increase in naval power around the world and the Taft Board report, the Army was more formal in articulating the need for vegetation to conceal coastal defense batteries from detection at sea. Three weeks after highlighting the differences between American and foreign coastal defense batteries, the Army's Office of the Chief of Coast Artillery issued a memorandum instructing that new batteries should be constructed while minimizing the number of existing trees removed and with engineered slopes that "conform in appearance" to the surrounding landscape and avoid "geometric contours."[49] The instructions also call for a general planting scheme composed of, "tall trees as a rule, should be planted in rear or and between adjacent batteries and in rear and on the sides of stations; low trees at the foot of batteries, bushes and shrubs on the superior slopes of batteries and low shrubs in irregular splotches between guns." The memorandum acknowledges that effective concealment cannot be achieved in a single planting effort and that one week every spring and fall should be devoted to planting on and around the batteries. The instructions also cite the need for future replacement plantings and routine watering.[50] Using vegetation to conceal batteries from ships was deemed so important that in 1914, the Army assigned a forester to examine batteries and recommend tree planting.[51]

LARGE CALIBER GUN BATTERIES

Sandy Hook's coastal defense batteries were constructed, armed, and modified in response to the needs identified by the Endicott and Taft boards. As part of the strategy articulated by the boards, coastal defenses were comprised of large caliber gun batteries, rapid fire gun batteries, and underwater mines. Sandy Hook's first batteries, Battery Potter and the Mortar Battery, were both large caliber gun batteries. From their initial construction to the World War I armistice, these two would be joined by other large caliber gun batteries designed to engage enemy ships in the narrow channel north and east of the peninsula.

The additional large caliber batteries at Sandy Hook were developed in response to technological improvements in artillery design, particularly the gun carriages, but also to provide a more effective defensive system. Test firing of Battery Potter's two guns in 1895 demonstrated an average firing rate of three and a half minutes per shot.[52] Improvements in steam-powered propulsion meant enemy ships would spend less time in a battery's field of fire. The Army countered increased ship speed by placing control mines along the channel and also by constructing successive large caliber batteries. Located from south to north along Sandy Hook, the successive batteries provided a greater field of fire against faster ships.

Improvements in artillery design also resulted in a cycle of construction and disarmament for Sandy Hook's large caliber gun batteries during the first two decades of the twentieth century. In addition to the main shipping channel, defenses at Sandy Hook could fire on a ship on the western or bay side of the peninsula beginning with Battery Potter's 360-degree field of fire. When new artillery made Battery Potter's steam-powered gun lifts obsolete and the guns were disarmed, the Army constructed Battery Arrowsmith was constructed on the western shoreline. The cycle repeated when longer-range guns at Batteries Kingman and Mills lead to the disarmament of Battery Arrowsmith.

Battery Potter

In 1896, one year after emplacing the second gun at Battery Potter, the Army successfully tested the Buffington-Croizer counterweight gun carriage at the Sandy Hook Proving Ground. After loading a gun mounted on this new carriage, a counterweight raised the gun barrel into firing position above a concrete structure. The recoil from firing the gun brought the barrel back down below the structure to conceal it and provided cover to the artillerymen reloading the gun. A trained crew could fire two rounds per minute with a counterweight carriage gun compared to a single round every three a half minutes with the steam-powered gun lift at Battery Potter.[53] Just as advances in artillery during the Civil War eclipsed the defensive capabilities of the Fort at Sandy Hook, the new carriage produced in the closing years of the nineteenth century made Battery Potter's steam-powered gun lifts obsolete.

Although its gun lift mechanism was inferior, Battery Potter's contribution to coastal defenses at Sandy Hook continued for another fifty years. Early modifications at Battery Potter focused on improved target identification and new utilities for the entire fort. In 1899, the Army built a sixty foot tall range-finder tower west of Battery Potter. The steel tower supported a wood observation shelter sheathed with galvanized iron.[54]

Between 1901 and 1902, the Army constructed a central powerhouse for Fort Hancock's lighting system near the northwest corner of Battery Potter. The one-story brick building with a slate roof housed the lighting system's boilers and transformers. In addition, the Army constructed a coal shed to store fuel for the boilers north of the powerhouse in 1903.[55]

The powerhouse stood several feet west of Battery Potter's defensible, west facade. Given its proximity to the facade, the Army removed a portion of the grass-planted earthen slope to accommodate the building (Figure 2.27). The engineered slope had been a defensive feature specifically planted with low growing species instead of the shrubs and cedars used on the battery's other facades. The low growing vegetation permitted an unobstructed field of fire for machine guns stationed in Battery Potter's castellated entry.

The construction of the powerhouse and coal shed would appear contradictory to Battery Potter's defensive scheme, however, it represented a shift in the Army's coastal defense philosophy. Instead of defending against a land-based assault at Battery Potter, the Army decided to counter an invading force before they reached land with rapid fire guns and electronically controlled mines. Sacrificing the slope was arguably an easy decision with rapid fire guns emplaced and controlled mines laid. Future large caliber gun batteries in a system of coastal defenses emphasized firepower toward the shipping channel and a lack of defensive features on the rear approach of the batteries.

Although new large caliber batteries were constructed and operational in the early years of the twentieth century, Battery Potter remained active during this time because it offered a 360-degree field of fire and could also engage a ship on the west side of the peninsula. In 1906, with construction planned for Battery Arrowsmith to guard the western shoreline, the Army disarmed Battery Potter and sold the steam-powered gun-lift mechanism for salvage.[56]

Although disarmed, Battery Potter was not abandoned. To improve the targeting of enemy ships, the Army retrofitted Battery Potter with fire control buildings to assist nearby batteries. Potter's expansive viewshed and high terreplein made it a logical choice for siting equipment that relied on a clear view of approaching ships (Figure 2.28).

The Army submitted final plans for a small building containing two fire control stations in March 1905. Construction started that spring in the southwest corner of Battery Potter's terreplein and was completed in September. The Army designed the building to serve the Mortar Battery and divided each station into an observation room and a plotting room.[57] Two years later, the Army constructed two more buildings north of the first fire control building. One building was configured as a grouping of five distinct, interconnected structures and the other building was designed as a grouping of two (Figure 2.29). The buildings served the large caliber guns at Nine Gun Battery and Battery Granger as well as the rapid fire guns at Battery Peck and Battery Gunnison.[58]

In order to support the communications between the fire control buildings and various batteries, the Army built two switchboard rooms at the southwest corner of Battery Potter in 1907.[59] Similar to the powerhouse constructed five years earlier, the two buildings stood close to Potter's west facade and required further removal of the grass-planted earthen slope. Having been interrupted by two sets of buildings, the slope now started from either side of the castellated entrance and quickly wrapped back into the concrete wall (Figure 2.30).

West of Battery Potter, the Army constructed two dormitory buildings were constructed in 1908 for the expanded personnel needed to operate the fire control systems. The larger of the two buildings housed officers and the smaller housed enlisted men. The final modification related to improving identification and targeting was the addition of an exterior stairway in 1915.[60] Located at the southwest corner of the battery, the stairs provided easy access for personnel manning the nine fire control stations on the terreplein.

Mortar Battery

Test firings at the Mortar Battery during 1894 impacted the protective earth and sand slopes. The steep grade above each pit's concrete blast slope proved difficult to stabilize. In 1900, post commander Major Burbank recorded the "dislodgement of a quantity of turf revetment of the slope in front of the mortar used."[61] In order to improve the slope's stability, the Army re-graded these slopes at a 2:1 ratio.

The sand slopes also presented problems in maintaining the artillery. Having been promoted to colonel, post commander Burbank wrote of drifting sand in the gun emplacements causing maintenance problems. To address this problem, three to four inches of wet cinders were placed on Mortar Battery's slopes.[62]

In 1901, the Army constructed a steel tower inside Mortar Battery's western perimeter wall. At the top, the structure supported a wood-frame building approximately fifteen feet square with a surrounding three foot wide catwalk. The tower served as a battery commander's station that identified targets for crews in the four pits.[63] To facilitate better communication between the acquisition of targets and aiming of artillery, construction began on telephone data booths in 1905. The Army installed the booths above the southwest corner of each pit and supported each by arched, concrete spans.[64]

In 1903, a decade after completion, the Army designated the Mortar Battery Battery Reynolds in honor of Major-General John F. Reynolds who died during the first day of fighting at Gettysburg. The first decade of the twentieth century also witnessed new structures added at the Mortar Battery to improve the process of identifying, targeting, and firing on enemy ships.

Following the construction of the data booths, the designation of the Mortar Battery was split to identify separate batteries for the north and south firing pits. A 1906 general order designated the north pits in honor of Major-General Alexander McCook, another Civil War veteran. The south pits retained the earlier Battery Reynolds name.[65] Between 1906 and 1907, the Army added two battery commander's stations on top of the earth and sand cover to correspond with the separate batteries. From these concrete commander's stations, aiming and firing instructions were relayed to the telephone data booths and then down to the firing pits. With the commander's stations and data booths completed, the Army converted the steel tower to a weather station to provide information on atmospheric conditions affecting the trajectory of projectiles.[66]

Although measures were enacted to deal with displaced sand from the artillery fire, difficulties continued with Mortar Battery's engineered earthwork. A 1910 plan for upgraded drainage and electrical systems provided instructions to inspect the earth slopes after each rain storm to look for gullying. Personnel were not permitted to walk on the slopes except for inspection or repair.[67]

To improve coastal defenses during World War I, the Army established a battery in the high bluffs of Navesink that overlooked Sandy Hook and the Atlantic Ocean. Fort Hancock operated the battery and transferred one mortar from each of Mortar Battery's pits to adequately arm the new site.[68] The new Navesink battery, located further south than any of the batteries on Sandy Hook, expanded the range at which enemy targets could be engaged and improved the defensive system. Ships approaching New York City from the south would first encounter mortar fire from the Navesink battery. Whether unscathed or crippled, ships proceeding north would then face fire from the Mortar Battery and the other large caliber gun batteries at Sandy Hook. If a ship made it past the northern tip of Sandy Hook, large caliber gun batteries positioned at Fort Hamilton and Fort Wadsworth, on the east and west side of the Narrows respectively, were prepared to fire as the ship approach the entry to Upper New York Harbor. The new battery at Navesink, along with those at Sandy Hook, Fort Hamilton, and Fort Wadsworth, combined to form a redundant defense system that provided continued resistance against an enemy advancing north toward New York City (Figure 2.31).[69]

The World War I efforts to mobilize troops and expand coastal defenses abruptly ended following the armistice on November 11, 1918. At Sandy Hook and across the country, personnel were drastically reduced during the early months of 1919. Coupled with the reduction in personnel and spending, advances in naval artillery during the war eclipsed the range of the Mortar Battery's guns. The mortars were subsequently disarmed and sold to civilians between the winter of 1919 and spring of 1920.[70]

Battery Granger

In the mid-1890s, as trials were underway at the Proving Ground to test the new counterweight gun carriage for service, construction began on a new concrete battery that would incorporate this new system. Completed in 1896, the Ten-inch Battery #1 was the first large caliber gun battery at Sandy Hook to use the new counterweight carriage. Located between Battery Potter to the north and Mortar Battery to the south, each of the battery's two platforms was armed with a 10-inch gun in 1897. The Army installed concrete platforms fourteen feet above the surrounding grade to meet a parapet wall that rose an additional ten feet higher. From the platforms, a series of concentric steps proceeded down three feet to the wells where the carriages and guns were mounted. One hundred twenty-four feet separated the center lines of the two guns with the south emplacement labeled #1 and the north emplacement #2.[71] From the top of the parapet wall, a concrete superior slope continued away from the structure for twenty feet followed by an additional thirty feet of earth and sand. The concrete and engineered earthwork descended away from the wall at a ten percent slope. The slope of the earthwork then increased to a 2:3 ratio and met the surrounding, unaltered grades (Figure 2.32).

Prior to receiving an official designation, typically in honor of a military hero, new coastal defense batteries were named according to their projectile diameter followed by a sequential number for the order in which they were constructed. Plans for defending the southern approach to New York City called for other batteries on Sandy Hook and an 1898 map identifies the Ten-inch Battery #1 and several other batteries with this descriptive naming convention (Figure 2.33). Replacing the descriptive name, the army designated the Ten-inch Battery #1 as Battery Granger in 1900 in honor of Civil War veteran Major General Gordon Granger.[72]

A decade after the guns were emplaced, the Army updated Battery Granger to reflect the current practices on the efficient operation of a counterweight carriage gun.[73] They extended the platforms behind the guns in order to allow for more convenient loading of munitions. In addition, they added an enclosed, concrete battery commander's station between the two gun emplacements providing a central location and greater protection for the commanding officer (Figure 2.34).

Adjacent batteries and existing structures, such as the Sandy Hook lighthouse, imposed limits on a battery's field of fire. At Battery Granger and at other batteries on Sandy Hook, the *Report of Completed Works* recorded information on interference and obstacles in the field of fire. Based on current research, the report for Battery Granger records the only instance of trees creating an obstacle. For emplacement #1, trees are listed as an obstacle between 298 degrees 17 minutes and 332 degrees 3 minutes (Figure 2.35). After listing the angle measurements, the report notes in parentheses that "trees can be cut away." The report does not provide additional information on where the trees were located in relation to Battery Granger or confirm if the trees were removed to improve the field of fire.[74]

Nine Gun Battery

Having successfully tested the counterweight carriage at the Proving Ground and installed it at Battery Granger, the Army built additional batteries for the faster firing carriage with a greater range. To compliment the two 10-inch guns at Battery Granger, construction began on a three-gun emplacement—the Ten-inch Battery #2—in 1897. The battery was located north of batteries Granger and Potter and was built over the east facade of the former granite fort (Figure 2.36). This location paralleled the main shipping channel along Sandy Hook's eastern shoreline. The Army completed construction and emplaced the three guns in 1898. That same year, the United States declared war on Spain following the explosion of the USS *Maine* in Havana Harbor and a public outcry for military action. Funding increased for additional coastal defenses, including two batteries to the north and south of the Ten-inch Battery #2.[75]

To supplement the first set of 12-inch guns at Battery Potter, the Army equipped the two new batteries with 12-inch guns on counterweight carriages. They constructed a Twelve-inch Battery #2 north of the Ten-inch Battery #2, which followed the angle between the east and north facades of the former granite fort. The new 12-inch guns provided fire on the shipping channel as it turned northwest and headed around the tip of Sandy Hook toward lower New York Harbor. South of the Ten-inch Battery #2, the Twelve-inch Battery #3 was designed to emplace two more guns along the peninsula's eastern shoreline. The new batteries were completed in 1899 and armed in 1900. With seven guns emplaced, the structure was commonly referred to as the Seven Gun Battery. The Army dedicated the battery in honor of Civil War veteran Major-General Henry W. Halleck in 1900.[76]

Following the Spanish-American War, the Filipinos fought U. S. annexation and the military budget remained robust. At the southern end of Battery Halleck, the Army completed an additional battery in 1902 and armed in 1904 with two 12-inch guns. The combined nine guns mounted across a continuous concrete structure was the largest grouping of artillery built following the Endicott and Taft recommendations. The scale of this coastal defense demonstrates the strategic importance of the channel approach to New York City.[77]

With nine guns emplaced, the Army determined that one battery commander could not efficiently coordinate firing all of the guns. To address this problem, they designated the Nine Gun Battery as four separate batteries (Figure 2.37). The original three 10-inch guns remained Battery Halleck. The northern most guns, built in the second phase, were designated Battery Alexander in honor of Revolutionary War General William Alexander. The other second phase guns south of Halleck were designated Battery Bloomfield in honor of New Jersey governor and Revolutionary War General Joseph Bloomfield. The southern-most guns were designated Battery Richardson in honor of Major General Israel B. Richardson who was killed during the Civil War at the Battle of Antietam.

Battery Arrowsmith

Battery Arrowsmith represented a unique and first-of-its-kind coastal defense construction at Sandy Hook. When Battery Potter's guns were removed in 1906, the peninsula no longer had large caliber artillery with a 360-degree field of fire. Fearing that Fort Hancock was susceptible to an attack from Sandy Hook Bay and its western shore, planning began for a battery at Horseshoe Cove Point. Crews completed masonry construction in 1908 and that same year, the battery was named in honor of Lieutenant Colonel George W. Arrowsmith who was killed at Gettysburg during the Civil War. A year later, the Army emplaced three 8-inch guns at Battery Arrowsmith to defend against any attack on Sandy Hook's western shore.

The guns were spaced 128-feet apart and a separate magazine was located east of each gun platform. The magazines were concealed with earth and sand cover that rose slightly over twenty feet above the surrounding grades (Figure 2.38). Just as Battery Potter's steam gun lifts were quickly eclipsed by the counterweight carriage, Battery Arrowsmith's protection of the bay side was not needed after the installation of new coastal artillery in 1919.[78] The new artillery, mounted on a different carriage design, provided a 360-degree field of fire that could defend Sandy Hook Bay.

Batteries Kingman and Mills

The British introduced improved artillery on the *Dreadnought* and as World War I approached, foreign navies developed similar artillery that threatened the relatively small counterweight carriage guns at Sandy Hook. Battleships were equipped with new turrets that positioned and fired artillery at higher angles. With this modification that utilized the same guns and projectiles, ships could now be positioned further offshore and out of the range of coastal defense batteries. In addition, the counterweight carriages that lowered a battery's guns behind protective concrete and earth for loading were now susceptible to incoming fire from a ship's higher trajectory projectiles.

In response to this new threat, construction began on two large caliber gun batteries utilizing a high-angle gun carriage with a greater range. In comparison to the seven to eight mile range of counterweight carriage guns, the new artillery had a range of over twenty miles.[79] The Army mounted the high-angle carriages on rotating platforms that resulted in a 360-degree field of fire. Instead of relying on concrete and mounds of earth and sand to protect the artillery, the new batteries were located on the bay side of the peninsula to be as far away as possible from potential enemy fire and sight lines.

The Army completed masonry construction of both batteries in late 1917.[80] Each battery included two open, circular platforms that were 100 feet in diameter. Mounted in the center of the circle, the emplaced guns were 420 feet apart with the south gun identified as #1 and the north as #2. In the area between the platforms, earth covered concrete structures that housed artillery shells, gunpowder, plotting rooms, a storeroom, a latrine, and quarters for the soldiers stationed at either battery. Located approximately two miles from the quarters at Fort Hancock, the engineered earthwork also served to protect the neighboring platform from a misfire and rose approximately twenty-eight feet above the surrounding grades (Figures 2.39 and 2.40).

The storeroom, latrine, and quarters were located in the western quarter of the underground structures and were separated from the shell, powder, and plotting rooms to the east by a covered passageway. The passageway was eighteen feet wide, paved with concrete, and featured standard-gauge railroad tracks embedded into the paving to accommodate rail deliveries of shells and gunpowder to the batteries (Figure 2.41). When needed, soldiers retrieved shells and gunpowder from the casemated storage areas and transported them on hand carts to either circular platform (Figure 2.42). To improve the conditions for soldiers at both batteries, steam heat was added to the plotting rooms, quarters, and latrines in September 1919.

That same year, the Army emplaced both batteries with twelve-inch guns that had no concealment or protection from above (Figure 2.43). The northern battery was designated in honor of Brigadier General Dan C. Kingman who served as Chief of Engineers for the Army Corps between 1913 and 1916. The southern battery, 750-feet from Kingman's #1 emplacement, was designated in honor of Brigadier General Albert L. Mills, a Medal of Honor recipient from the Spanish-American War.[81]

RAPID FIRE GUN BATTERIES

As a complement to the large caliber gun batteries that guarded the approach to New York Harbor, rapid-fire gun batteries protected areas outside the main shipping channel that were susceptible to attack by swift, shallow-draft boats like landing craft and torpedo boats. In addition, the rapid-fire gun batteries protected the minefields laid outside the channel from enemy minesweepers. At Sandy Hook, the Army located the majority of rapid fire gun batteries at the northern tip of the peninsula. This position allowed the batteries to protect control mines laid adjacent to the shipping channel north of the peninsula (Figure 2.44).

Battery Engle

Construction started on Sandy Hook's first rapid fire gun battery in 1897. The battery was located near the northern end of the peninsula and designed to mount a single 5-inch gun. As tension grew between the United States and Spain over control of the Caribbean and the approach to the Panama Canal, construction on the battery was completed and it was armed on April 21, 1898. Four days later, Congress declared war on Spain and public pressure and funding increased for coastal defenses.[82]

The Army constructed the battery was constructed with a twenty-one foot diameter concrete platform set approximately eight feet above surrounding grades (Figure 2.45). The platform contained a deep, cylindrical opening to hold a balanced pillar mounted gun (Figure 2.46). To the east of the platform, a magazine included six feet of concrete cover.

In 1903, the 5-inch rapid fire battery was designated in honor of Captain Archibald H. Engle who was killed in the Civil War Battle of Resaca. Battery Engle and the single 5-inch gun did not have a long service life. At the close of the nineteenth century, rapid-fire guns were manufactured with 3-, 4-, 4.7-, 5-, and 6-inch caliber sizes. During World War I, caliber sizes were simplified to either 3-inch or 6-inch. As a result, Battery Engle's 5-inch gun was declared obsolete and disarmed in 1918.[83]

Battery Urmston

Beginning in 1899, the Army constructed a six gun, rapid-fire battery west of Battery Engle along Sandy Hook's northern shoreline. Construction occurred in three phases and spanned five years beginning with building gun emplacements #1 and #2 at the eastern end of the battery. Following this first phase, construction started on the western end for gun emplacements #5 and #6. These emplacements were completed in November 1900 and all four were armed with balanced pillar mounted guns (Figure 2.47). When not in use, the pillar mounted guns could be mechanically lowered below the concrete parapet. As they were lowered, the gun barrels rotated ninety degrees and were placed in a notch in the parapet.

Battery Urmston's initial four emplacements shared a similar design with steps leading to a rear platform approximately five feet above surrounding grade. From the rear platform, another set of steps led to the gun platforms approximately four feet higher in elevation. A separate magazine stood to the east of each platform, and like Battery Engle, included six feet of concrete cover. The top of the magazine protruded approximately three and a half feet above the gun platform.

In June 1904, the final phase of construction at Battery Urmston included gun emplacements #3 and #4 between the two previous sections. Unlike the earlier rapid-fire guns, the artillery at emplacements #3 and #4 were set on fixed pedestal mounts that could not be lowered. With all six emplacements completed, the battery was named in honor of Lieutenant Thomas D. Urmston who was killed during the Civil War (Figure 2.48).

In order to identify targets and direct the firing of the guns, the commanding officer at Battery Urmston stood on top of the concrete magazine located between two emplacements (Figure 2.49). As a component of the Taft Board's recommendations to improve the targeting of enemy ships, a dedicated observation station with an optical instrument known as a coincidence range finder (CRF) was completed at Battery Urmston in February 1919. The observation station was an open concrete structure that measured ten feet wide by thirteen feet long. Located between emplacements #4 and #5, the station was also fitted with a pipe frame and covered with canvas to provide some protection against the weather (Figure 2.50).

Battery Morris

To provide a complete field of fire along Sandy Hook's northern tip, the Army constructed a third rapid fire gun battery between Battery Engle and Battery Urmston. Masonry construction was completed in 1903 on the four platform battery and it was designated in 1904 in honor of Colonel Lewis Morris who was killed during the Civil War Battle of Cold Harbor. The guns at Battery Morris were intended to be mounted on pedestal carriages. Due to development and production delays of the carriages, the guns were not emplaced until 1909.[84]

The four platforms were constructed approximately nine feet above surrounding grades and were accessed by steps that led to two intermediate levels. Between the four emplacements were three magazines that featured a combination of concrete and earth cover. The top of the earth cover on the magazines rose seven feet above the gun platforms (Figure 2.51).

Battery Peck

A final rapid fire battery joined Urmston, Morris, and Engle on the northern end of Sandy Hook. Located immediately east of Battery Engle, construction began in 1901 on a battery that supported two 6-inch rapid fire guns. This new battery had a greater range and worked in conjunction with the remotely-detonated minefields to stop a shallow-draft boat that ventured out of the main shipping channel.

The Army emplaced the 6-inch guns in 1903 on barbette mounts that did not lower the guns behind a protective parapet. A semi-circular, armor plate that wrapped around either side of the gun barrel provided minimal protection. That same year, the Army designated the battery in honor of Lieutenant Freemont P. Peck who was accidentally killed at the Sandy Hook Proving Ground in 1895.

Battery Peck's two emplacements were spaced 112 feet apart with gun #1 and #2 located on the east and west halves respectively. Soldiers accessed the gun platforms by steps on the west and east sides and in the middle of the structure. The steps led to a rear platform approximately nine feet above surrounding grades. From the rear platform, steps proceeded up five and a half feet to the gun platforms. The magazines were located below this built-up structure and accessed from the ground level through one of three doors (Figure 2.52).

Battery Gunnison

In 1898, the Army planned to build a rapid fire battery southeast of Nine Gun Battery's southern end.[85] However, this proposed location conflicted with the ongoing operation of the Sandy Hook Proving Ground and construction was delayed. In 1903, the Army selected an alternative location further south on the peninsula than any battery previously built. Initial work included an extension of the rail lines and clearing for the new battery.[86] Construction was completed a year later and the battery was designated in honor of Captain John W. Gunnison who was killed in the Utah Territory in 1853. In 1905, two six-inch guns were mounted on disappearing counterweight carriages. These six-inch rapid-fire guns worked in the same manner as their larger caliber siblings. A counterweight raised the gun barrel into position and the recoil from firing the gun lowered the barrel below a concrete parapet wall.

Two gun emplacements, aligned on a north-south line, faced the Atlantic Ocean to the east and were spaced 125 feet apart on center. The platforms were constructed approximately five and a half feet above surrounding grades. On each platform, steps led down two feet to gun wells where the carriages and guns were mounted. A parapet wall rose eight feet above each platform and transitioned to a concrete superior slope that pitched away from the structure. In between the two platforms, numerous interior rooms for communications, offices, and equipment storage were shielded with concrete and earth cover that rose three and a half feet higher than the top of the parapet wall (Figure 2.53). The earth and sand slope on the east side of the battery helped to blend the structure into the surrounding landscape and camouflage it from ships at sea. Grasses and low-growing shrubs on the engineered earthwork contributed to the concealment. The west facade was not camouflaged and the concrete and metal framework of the structure was clearly visible when approaching from the west (Figure 2.54).

The importance of the engineered earthwork in protecting the concrete structure from artillery fire and providing camouflage can be seen in a plan prepared in October 1905 (Figure 2.55). The plan includes notes for the artillery garrison stationed at Battery Gunnison and instructs that:

> Immediately after each rain the earth slopes shall be carefully inspected; any slight tendency to gully or slough shall be at once remedied. Any serious gullying shall be at once reported in writing to the Engineer Officer in charge of the district. No person shall be allowed to walk up or down the earth slopes at any time, except when necessary to inspect or repair them.

The earth and sand cover was susceptible to erosion from heavy storms and unnecessary foot traffic. Regular inspection and maintenance were required to ensure the earthwork remained an intact component of the battery's defenses.

The October 1905 plan for drainage and electrical systems highlights the issues of water infiltration and moisture buildup that resulted from covering a concrete structure with earth. The plan shows the layout of pipes to remove water from the recessed gun wells and also floor drains and associated drain lines on the interior of the battery. In addition to the drainage structures that remove accumulated water on the interior, notes at the bottom of the plan instruct that, "All doors should be opened from daylight until 2 P.M. on clear days, when there is a good breeze and temperature is above 60°." At Battery Gunnison, moisture inside the structure was limited by drainage infrastructure and by routinely opening doors for improved air movement.

CLOSURE OF THE SANDY HOOK PROVING GROUND

In order to support the expanded coastal defenses at Sandy Hook, Fort Hancock grew to provide housing, administration, and facilities to cover all facets of military life. With the United States entering World War I in April 1917, personnel at the fort swelled to over 4,000 and the Army constructed temporary wooden structures for officers, enlisted men, and mess halls in groups called cantonments.[57]

The expansion created a danger to personnel and property as testing continued at the Proving Ground. Additionally, the Proving Ground needed greater distances to test longer-range artillery being developed to counter improved naval armament. Given the conflict between the Proving Ground and coastal defenses, Sandy Hook seemed less than ideal for testing new artillery. The Proving Ground's commanding officer in 1917, Lieutenant Colonel Ruggles, cited other shortcomings for Sandy Hook. In a February letter to Army Chief of Ordnance William Crozier, Ruggles highlighted the shortcomings including tests disrupted by frequent bad weather, conflicts with ships in the channel, and an inability to test if a naval war broke out. Ruggles suggested several sites on the Chesapeake Bay with adequate space for a new proving ground. In March 1918, the Army established the Aberdeen Proving Ground on the western shore of the Chesapeake Bay in Harford County, Maryland. As facilities became operational at Aberdeen, testing at Sandy Hook transitioned to the new site and the Sandy Hook Proving Ground was phased out by 1919.[58]

LANDSCAPE SUMMARY – 1919

For forty-five years, Sandy Hook housed both the Proving Ground and coastal defenses that represented the latest in military technology and armament. With the departure of the Proving Ground and end of World War I, personnel and activity at Sandy Hook diminished. The coastal defense batteries, Proving Ground, and development related to World War I can all be seen on the period plans for 1919 (Drawings 2.3-2.4).

Aerial photographs from 1920 greatly enhanced the information presented on the period plans of Sandy Hook (Figure 2.56). The Beach Erosion Board took the photographs along the New Jersey coast from Cape May to Sandy Hook. The board was a component of the Army Corps of Engineers that has since been incorporated into the Corps's Coastal and Hydraulics Laboratory. Some of the historic images contain a 1920 annotation and the date is further supported by photographs showing an open inlet near Cape May that naturally closed in 1921.[59]

The general arrangement of development concentrated at the northern end of the peninsula continued as coastal defenses expanded, Fort Hancock responded to World War I, and the Proving Ground relocated to Aberdeen, Maryland. Total developed area at the northern end increased with the construction of Fort

Hancock's barracks, mess halls, and supporting structures along the western shoreline (Drawing 2.4). Development in the southern section of the peninsula increased as well with the addition of Batteries Kingman and Mills and a series of long railroad spurs lined with sheds for ammunition storage (Drawing 2.4). With the additional personnel mobilized for World War I, the density of developed areas increased with cantonments and temporary facilities. Cantonments can be seen on the period plans west of Nine Gun Battery, south of the Ordnance Department Wharf, and north of Horseshoe Cove (Drawing 2.4).

In addition to increased development, the peninsula's landform grew in the early decades of the twentieth century. The littoral drift along Sandy Hook's Atlantic coastline resulted in deposits accumulating at the northeast end of the landform. The east facade of the Fort at Sandy Hook had once been approximately 600 feet from the Atlantic Ocean when Fort Hancock was established. In contrast, Nine Gun Battery—constructed over the east facade—was located over 1,200 feet from the shoreline by 1920 (Drawing 2.3).

As the northern end of the peninsula gained land area, it lost areas of large, woody vegetation with the construction of Fort Hancock, additional batteries, and World War I cantonments. Although not indicated on late 1890s plans, the semi-circular layout of Fort Hancock's Parade Ground and buildings was arguably influenced by low-lying, marshy ground to the south that would have been too troublesome to fill and build upon (Drawing 2.4).

Circulation routes traversed the middle of the peninsula, but the area remained primarily undeveloped. Except at a World War I cantonment, the middle section retained contiguous areas of large, woody vegetation. A series of railroad spurs interrupted several elongated ponds that punctuate the middle of peninsula. The ponds appeared smaller in area than indicated on earlier maps (Drawing 2.4).

The greatest concentration of structures for coastal defenses lay at the northern end of the peninsula, strategically positioned in relation to the major shipping channel. Near the northwest tip of the peninsula the Dynamite Gun Battery, completed in 1893, was disarmed in 1902 and converted into the Mine Casemate. As part of the coastal defense system, the casemate was used to electronically detonate control mines placed outside the major shipping channel.

East of the Mine Casemate, the rapid fire gun batteries Urmston, Morris, Engle, and Peck provided a field of fire against attack by swift, shallow-draft boats that could venture out of the major shipping channel. Southeast of Battery Peck, the Nine Gun Battery was constructed over the east facade of the former mid-nineteenth century granite fort and emplaced with a mixture of 10- and 12-inch large caliber guns on counterweight carriages. South of Nine Gun Battery, the

Proving Ground expanded its Proof Battery and the number of supporting buildings for testing ordnance (Drawing 2.4).

East of the Proof Battery, Battery Potter was disarmed in 1906 but continued to perform a role in the coastal defense mission. Fire control stations were added to Battery Potter's terreplein and immediately west of the structure, a powerhouse, coal shed, and switchboard rooms were constructed. South of Battery Potter, Battery Granger was completed in 1896 and was the first battery at Sandy Hook to use the Buffington-Croizer counterweight carriage. South of Battery Granger, Battery Gunnison was constructed as the only rapid fire battery on the peninsula's eastern shore. West of Battery Gunnison, the Mortar Battery included a battery commander's tower inside the structure's perimeter wall and telephone data booths above each firing pit to improve aiming and firing.

West of the Mortar Battery, the Army completed housing and support facilities for Fort Hancock and positioned around a triangular Athletic Field and semi-circular Parade Ground. Officers' Row, the most pronounced feature of Fort Hancock's design, was achieved by constructing a line of eighteen homes west of the Athletic Field and Parade Ground with front facades oriented to Sandy Hook Bay (Drawing 2.4).

South of the Parade Ground, the Army constructed Battery Arrowsmith on a point of land projecting into Horseshoe Cove. The battery protected against enemy ships entering Sandy Hook Bay after the 360-degree field of fire guns atop Battery Potter were disarmed (Drawing 2.4). Further south along the western shoreline, Batteries Kingman and Mills were constructed north of Spermaceti Cove. The two batteries featured high trajectory, longer-range guns that could engage enemy ships further out in the Atlantic while remaining out of the enemy's view and artillery range (Drawing 2.4).

The increased number of coastal defense batteries and structures for Fort Hancock necessitated an expansion of the road and railroad circulation systems in order to move people and supplies. Railroad access had been the only connection between Sandy Hook and the mainland to the south. Paralleling the railroad, Hartshorne Drive was established as the major north-south vehicular route across the peninsula. A secondary north-south route, Atlantic Drive, started at Battery Gunnison, proceeded south, and then turned west to form a perimeter loop with Hartshorne Drive. Between Battery Gunnison and Fort Hancock's barracks, a major east-west connector called Gunnison Road was established.

The Ordnance Department Wharf near the northern end of peninsula expanded and a small dock in Horseshoe Cove remained from the mid-nineteenth century wharf constructed by the Central Railroad of New Jersey. Railroad lines diverged from the Ordnance Wharf and provided access to points north, south, and east. North of the Mortar Battery, a railroad line terminated for Fort Hancock's coal storage area. Additionally, the number of railroad lines increased for the Proving Ground with five spurs constructed to align with the individual bays of the Proof Battery (Drawing 2.4).

Figure 2.24. HMS Dreadnought, circa 1906–07. The British completed the first battleship featuring 12-inch caliber guns with the successful launching of the HMS Dreadnought in 1906. Dreadnought's artillery matched the range of coastal defense artillery and lead to an international naval arms race ("British Navy Ships--HMS Dreadnought 1906-1922," U. S. Department of the Navy, Naval Historical Center, http://www.history.navy.mil/photos/sh-fornv/uk/uksh-d/drednt9.htm).

Figure 2.25. Interior of Battery Potter plotting room, circa 1907. Part of the Taft Board's recommendations to incorporate the latest technology resulted in improvements to fire control—the process of acquiring and firing on enemy ships. The communications between observation, calculating, and firing were increasingly handled by telephone, seen mounted on the wall in this image (GATE 7819).

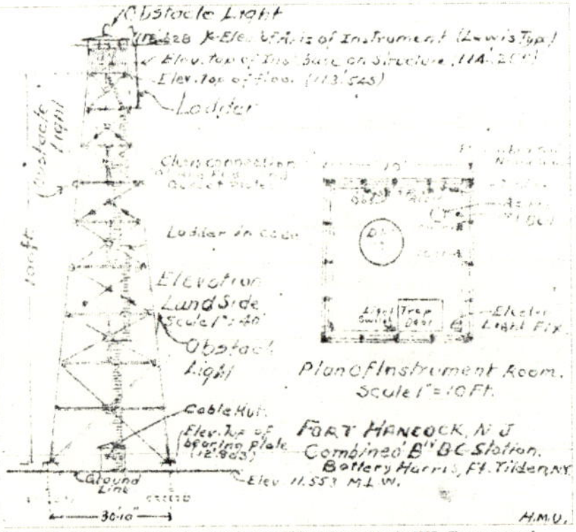

Figure 2.26. Battery commander's station for Fort Tilden's Battery Harris, 1927. The accuracy of triangulating an enemy ship's position improved with greater distance between two observation points. The Army erected a tower at Sandy Hook to support the aiming accuracy of the guns at Fort Tilden, located on the Rockaway peninsula in New York (Report of Completed Works, CDSG ePress).

Figure 2.27. View looking northeast at Battery Potter, circa 1906. Between 1901 and 1903, the Army constructed a central powerhouse and coal shed for Fort Hancock's lighting system near the northwest corner of Battery Potter. A portion of engineered earthwork on the battery's west facade was removed to accommodate the buildings, visible on the left (GATE 7818).

Figure 2.28. View looking southeast of Battery Potter, 1893. Battery Potter's expansive viewshed of the main shipping channel and high terreplein made it a logical choice for siting fire control stations. Note the relationship between the battery and a ship in the Atlantic seen in the distance (GATE 7811).

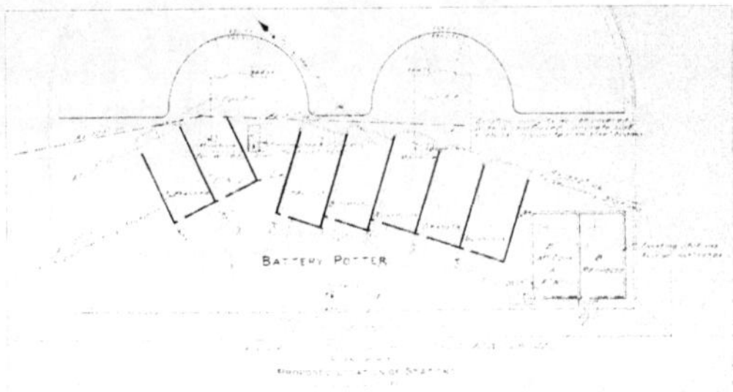

Figure 2.29. Plans for fire control stations at Battery Potter, 1905. By 1907, the Army constructed three fire control buildings on top of Battery Potter's terreplein. The buildings were divided into distinct, interconnected structures that served the Mortar Battery, Nine Gun Battery, Battery Granger, Battery Peck, and Battery Gunnison (GATE 10706).

Figure 2.30. West facade of Battery Potter showing switchboard rooms, circa 1907. In order to support the communications between the fire control buildings and various batteries, the Army built two switchboard rooms at the southwest corner of Battery Potter in 1907. The two buildings required further removal of the engineered earthwork along the battery's west facade (GATE 7814).

Figure 2.31. Southern entrance to New York Harbor, 1919. During World War I, four mortars from the Mortar Battery were transferred to a new battery at Navesink. This new battery, along with those at Sandy Hook, Fort Hamilton, and Fort Wadsworth, combined to form a defense-in-depth system against an enemy advancing north toward New York City (Report of Completed Works, CDSG ePress).

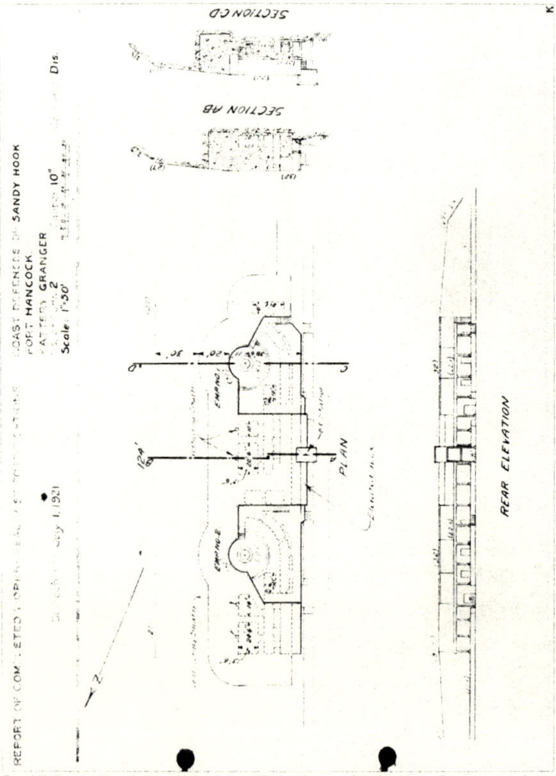

Figure 2.32. Plan, elevation, and sections of Battery Granger, 1921. From the two emplacements at Battery Granger, a concrete slope and engineered earthwork extended fifty feet to the east. The earthwork sloped at ten percent then increased to a 2:3 ratio and reunited with the surrounding, unaltered grades (Report of Completed Works, CDSG ePress).

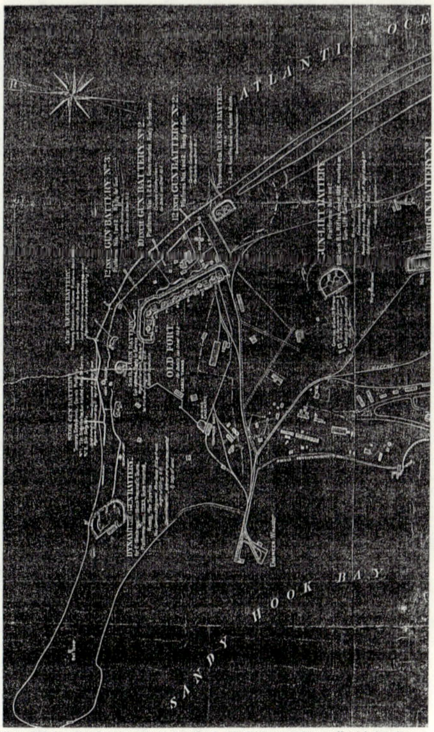

Figure 2.33. Map Showing Armament on December 3, 1898. Prior to receiving an official designation, typically in honor of a military hero, new coastal defense batteries were named according to their projectile diameter followed by a sequential number for the order in which they were constructed. Battery Granger is identified on this map as Ten-inch Battery #1 (GATE files, as cited in Norma E. Williams, *Cultural Landscape Report for Proving Ground and Wartime Expansion Areas, Sandy Hook Unit, Gateway National Recreation Area*, United States Department of the Interior, National Park Service, July 1999).

Figure 2.34. View looking southeast at Battery Granger, circa 1907. In 1907, Battery Granger was updated by extending platforms behind the guns for more convenient loading of ammunition. Additionally, an enclosed, concrete battery commander's station was added between the gun emplacements (Thomas Hoffman, *Fort Hancock*, Charleston, SC: Arcadia Publishing, 2007).

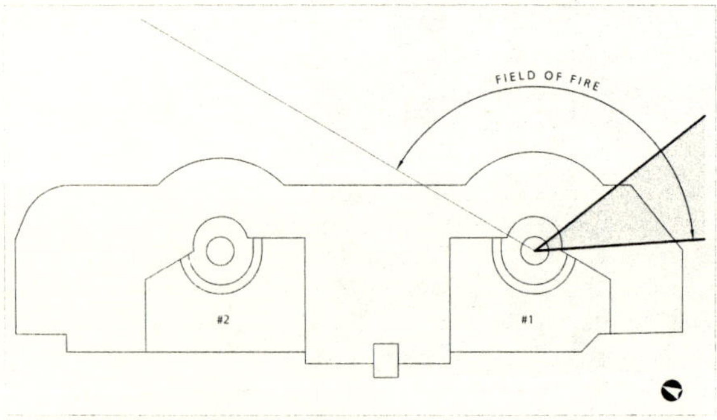

Figure 2.35. Diagram of obstacles affecting Battery Granger's emplacement #1. The Report of Completed Works recorded information on interference and obstacles in a battery's field of fire. At Battery Granger, trees are listed as an obstacle for emplacement #1 between 298 degrees 17 minutes and 332 degrees 3 minutes (shaded area). In parentheses the report notes that "trees can be cut away" but the report does not confirm if trees were removed (Olmsted Center, 2010).

Figure 2.36. View looking northwest at construction of Nine Gun Battery, 1897. Construction began on a three-gun emplacement (center) in 1897 that would become the first component of the Nine Gun Battery. The first phase was built over the east facade of the Civil War-era granite fort whose projecting bastions can be seen in the photograph. The east facade of the fort and the new concrete battery paralleled the main shipping channel along Sandy Hook's eastern shoreline (GATE 7880).

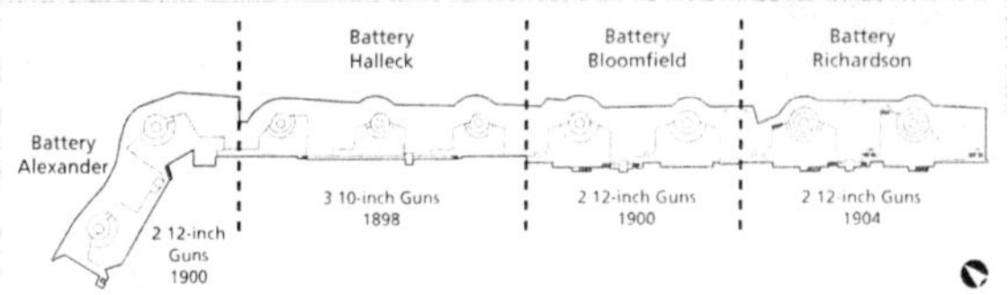

Figure 2.37. Diagram of Nine Gun Battery's individual names and construction dates. The emplacements at Nine Gun Battery were constructed in phases and divided into four separate batteries. The first three emplacements were designated Battery Halleck, south of Halleck was Battery Bloomfield and south of Bloomfield was Battery Richardson. The northernmost guns were designated Battery Alexander (Olmsted Center, 2009).

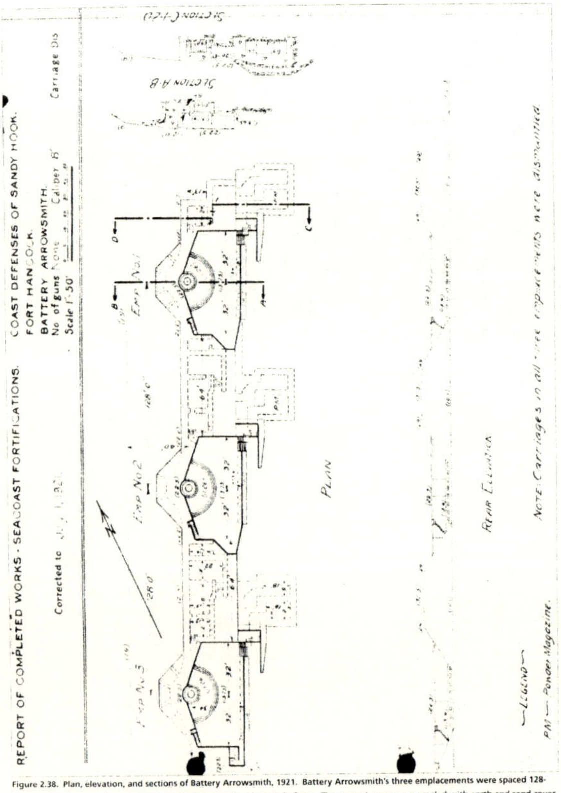

Figure 2.38. Plan, elevation, and sections of Battery Arrowsmith, 1921. Battery Arrowsmith's three emplacements were spaced 128-feet apart and a separate magazine was located east of each gun platform. The magazines were concealed with earth and sand cover that rose slightly over twenty feet above the surrounding grades (Report of Completed Works, CDSG ePress).

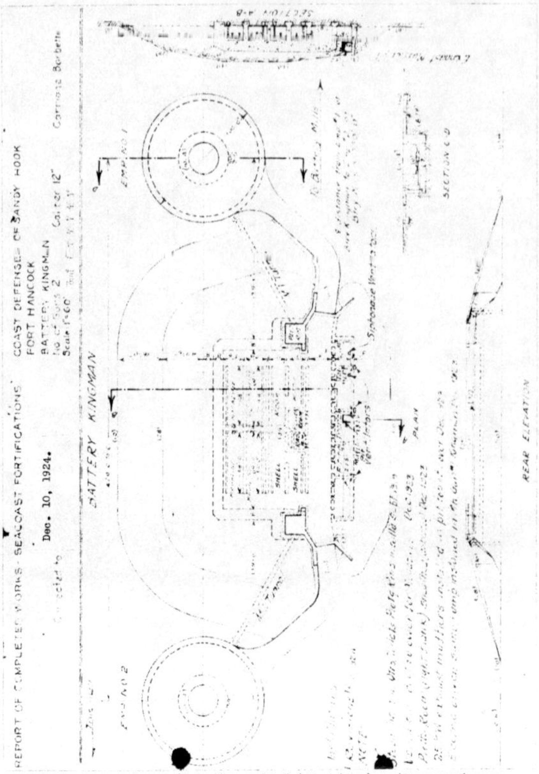

Figure 2.39. Plan, elevation, and sections of Battery Kingman, 1924. The battery's design featured two open emplacements separated by an engineered earthwork. The earthwork covered a concrete structure for storage and personnel and also served to protect the neighboring platform from a misfire (Report of Completed Works, CDSG ePress).

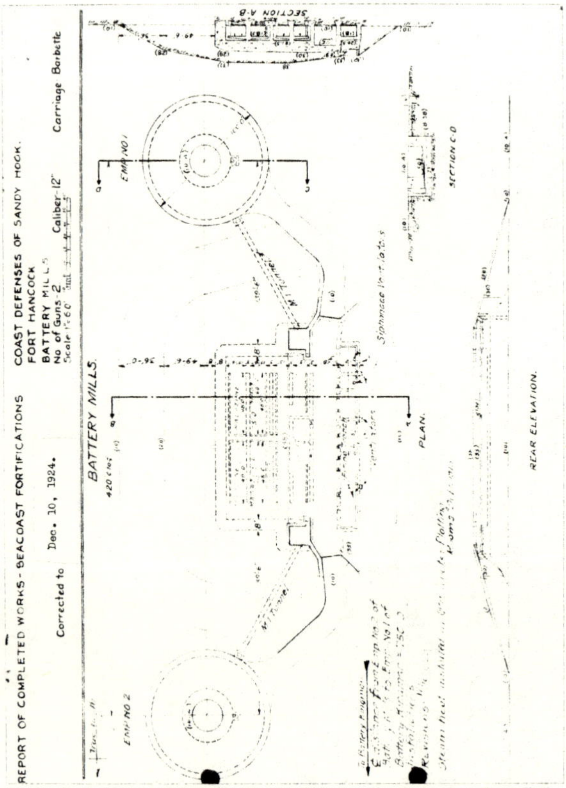

Figure 2.40. Plan, elevation, and sections of Battery Mills, 1924. Battery Mills featured an identical design to Battery Kingman. The 12-inch caliber guns emplaced at both batteries had a range of over twenty miles (Report of Completed Works, CDSG ePress).

Figure 2.41. View looking northeast at entrance to covered passageway, Battery Kingman, circa 1940. A covered passageway featured standard-gauge railroad tracks embedded into concrete paving to accommodate rail deliveries of shells and gunpowder to the battery (GATE 8092).

Figure 2.42. View of concrete route to emplacement #1, Battery Kingman, circa 1920s. Soldiers retrieved shells and gunpowder from the casemated storage areas (background) and transported them on hand carts to either circular gun platform (GATE 17820).

Figure 2.43. View looking south at emplacement #1, Battery Kingman, circa 1940–41. In 1919, both Batteries Kingman and Mills were armed with twelve-inch guns that had no concealment or protection from above. The guns were mounted on high-angle carriages set on rotating platforms that resulted in a 360-degree field of fire. Battery Mills' emplacement #2 and central earthwork can be seen in the background (GATE 938).

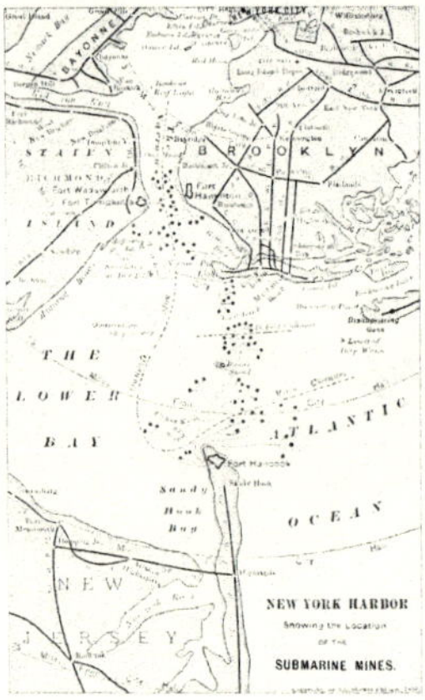

Figure 2.44. Plan of control mine placement, southern approach to New York Harbor, 1898. At Sandy Hook, the majority of rapid fire gun batteries were located at the northern tip of the peninsula in order to protect control mines from minesweepers and shallow-draft boats that ventured outside of the main shipping channel (GATE 21843).

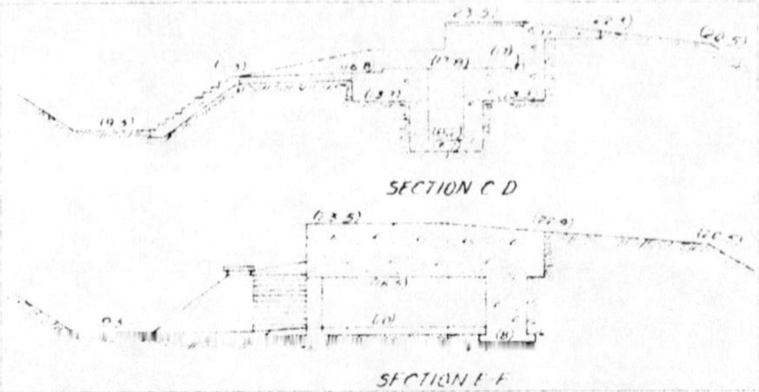

Figure 2.45. Sections through gun platform (top) and magazine (bottom) for Battery Engle, 1921. The Army constructed Battery Engle with a twenty-one foot diameter concrete platform set approximately eight feet above surrounding grades. East of the platform, the Army constructed a magazine with seven feet of concrete cover (Report of Completed Works, CDSG ePress).

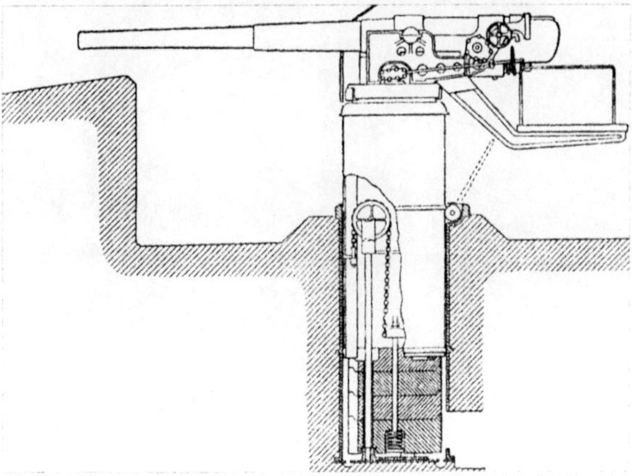

Figure 2.46. Section of balanced pillar-mounted rapid fire gun. The single emplacement at Battery Engle was designed to hold a 5-inch caliber, balanced pillar mounted gun. Counterweights raised or lowered the gun above or below a concrete parapet wall (Thomas Hoffman, *Fort Hancock*, Charleston, SC: Arcadia Publishing, 2007).

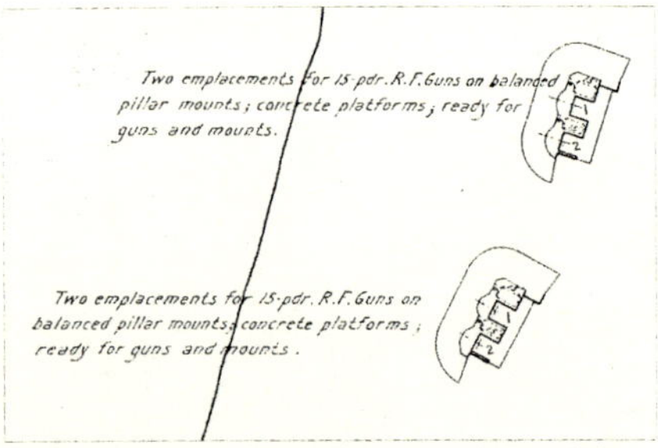

Figure 2.47. Detail of Armament Sketch, Fort Hancock, New Jersey, December 31, 1901. The first two phases of construction for Battery Urmston produced two separate structures containing two emplacements each. This map labels the artillery as "15-pdr." because the 3-inch caliber projectiles weighed fifteen pounds (GATE 4628).

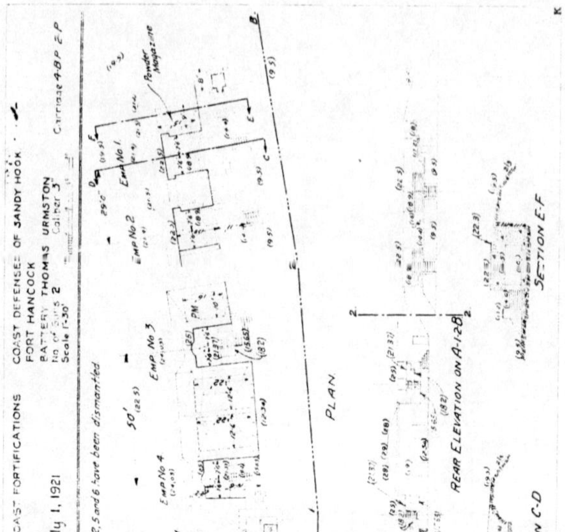

Figure 2.48. Plan, elevation, and sections of Battery Urmston, 1921. The final phase of construction at Battery Urmston, completed in June 1904, built two emplacements between the two previously finished sections (Report of Completed Works, CDSG ePress).

Figure 2.49. View looking northeast at Battery Urmston, circa 1904–08. The commanding officer at Battery Urmston stood on top of the concrete magazine located between two emplacements in order to identify targets and direct the firing of the guns (Thomas Hoffman, *Fort Hancock*, Charleston, SC: Arcadia Publishing, 2007).

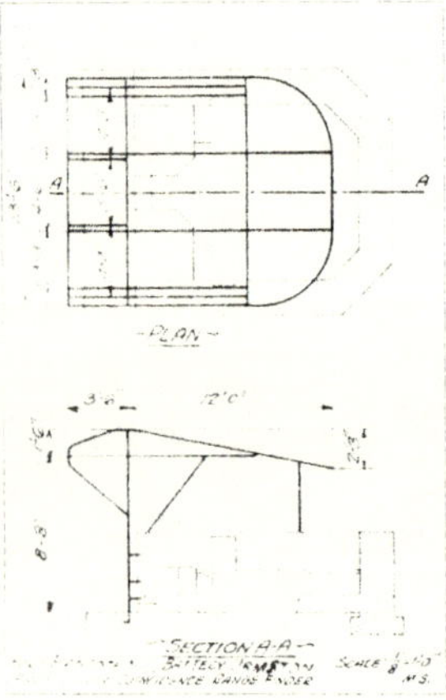

Figure 2.50. Plan and sections of cover over Battery Urmston's commander's station, 1921. In order to improve the targeting of enemy ships, a dedicated concrete structure was constructed between Battery Urmston's emplacements #4 and #5 for observation. The open station was fitted with a pipe frame and covered with canvas to provide some protection against the weather (Report of Completed Works, CDSG ePress).

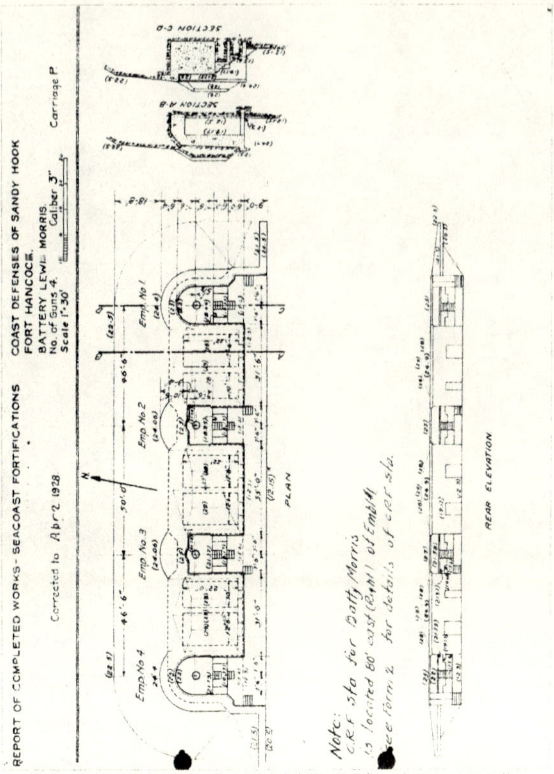

Figure 2.51. Plan, elevation, and sections of Battery Morris, 1928. Each of Battery Morris' four emplacements was separated by a magazine that featured a combination of concrete and earth cover. The top of the earth cover on the magazines rose seven feet above the gun platforms (Report of Completed Works, CDSG ePress).

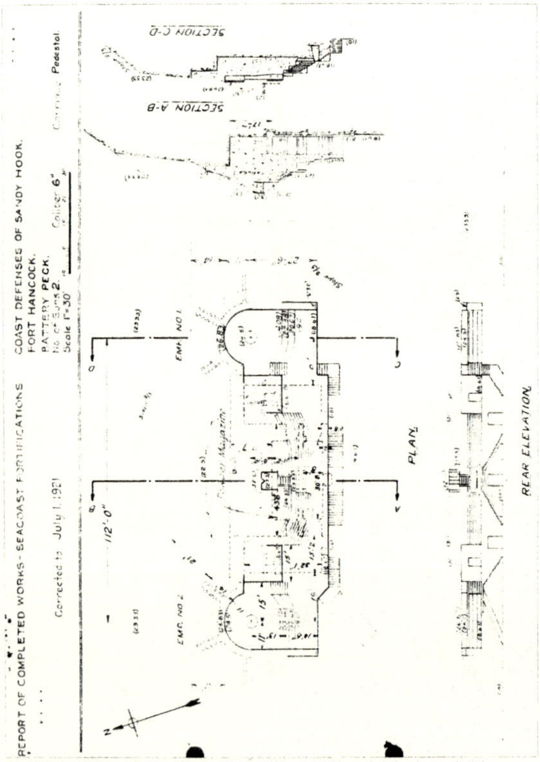

Figure 2.52. Plan, elevation, and sections of Battery Peck 1921. Soldiers accessed Battery Peck's guns by steps that led to an intermediate platform and then additional steps that proceeded up five and a half feet to the gun platforms. The battery's magazines were located below this built-up structure and accessed from the ground level through one of three doors (Report of Completed Works, CDSG ePress).

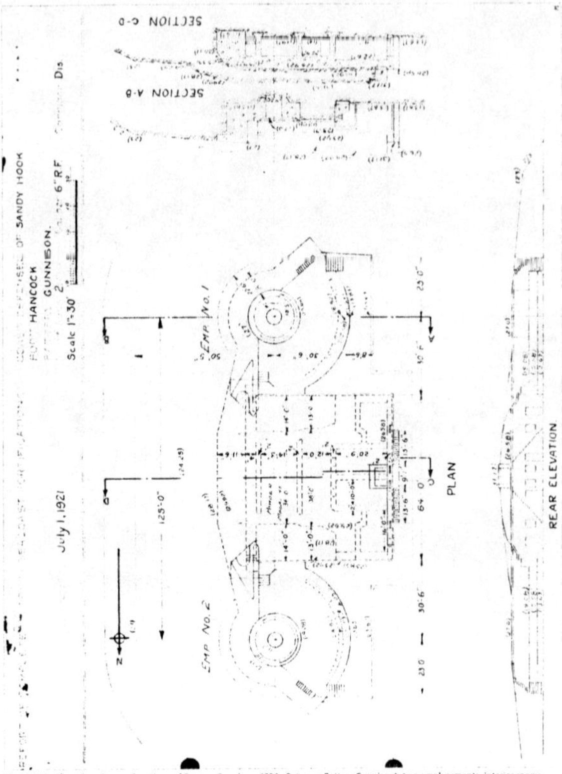

Figure 2.53. Plan, elevation, and sections of Battery Gunnison, 1921. Between Battery Gunnison's two emplacements, interior rooms used for communications, offices, and equipment storage were shielded with concrete and earth cover that rose three and a half feet higher than the top of the parapet wall (Report of Completed Works, CDSG ePress).

Figure 2.54. View looking northeast at Battery Gunnison, circa 1930–41. Although the east facade featured an engineered earthwork and planting compatible with the surrounding area, the west facade was not camouflaged or concealed. The concrete and metal framework of the structure was clearly visible when approaching from the west (Thomas Hoffman, *Fort Hancock*, Charleston, SC: Arcadia Publishing, 2007).

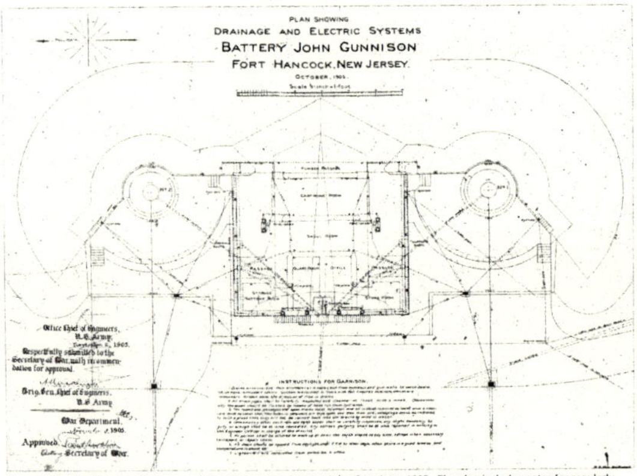

Figure 2.55. Plan Showing Drainage and Electric Systems, Battery John Gunnison, 1905. The plan includes notes for regularly inspecting and maintaining the engineered earthwork as component of Battery Gunnison's defenses. The engineered earthwork was susceptible to erosion from heavy storms and unnecessary foot traffic (Lee and Laham, *Historic Structure Report*).

Figure 2.56. Detail of aerial photograph, 1920. The information presented on the 1919 period plans was greatly enhanced by aerial photographs of Sandy Hook from 1920. The photographs were taken along the New Jersey coast from Cape May to Sandy Hook by the Beach Erosion Board, a component of the Army Corps of Engineers (Army Corps of Engineers Coastal and Hydraulics Laboratory).

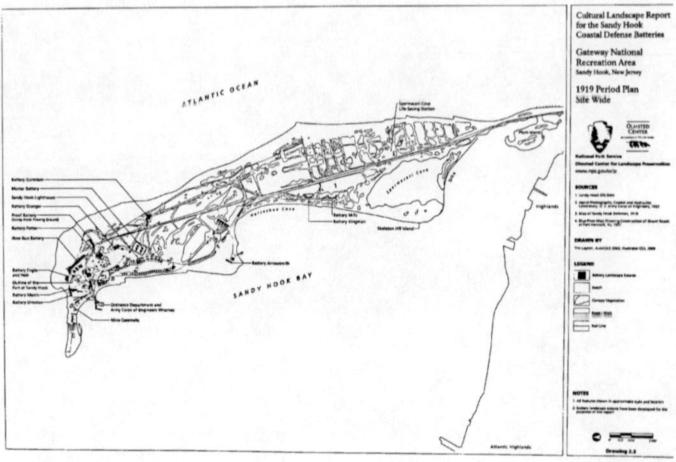
ATLANTIC OCEAN
SANDY HOOK BAY
Spermaceti Cove
Life-Saving Station
Battery Gunnison
Mortar Battery
Sandy Hook Lighthouse
Battery Granger
Proof Battery
(Sandy Hook Proving Ground)
Battery Potter
Nine Gun Battery
Battery Engle
and Peck
Outline of the
Fort at Sandy Hook
Battery Morris
Battery Urmston
Ordnance Department and
Army Corps of Engineers Wharves
Mine Casemate
Battery Arrowsmith
Horseshoe Cove
Battery Mills
Battery Kingman
Skeleton Hill Island
Spermaceti Cove
Plum Island
Highlands
Atlantic Highlands
Cultural Landscape Report
for the Sandy Hook
Coastal Defense Batteries
Gateway National
Recreation Area
Sandy Hook, New Jersey
1919 Period Plan
Site Wide
Olmsted Center
National Park Service
Olmsted Center for Landscape Preservation
www.nps.gov/oclp
SOURCES
DRAWN BY
LEGEND
Battery Landscape Extents
Beach
Canopy Vegetation
Road / Walk
Rail Line
NOTES
1. All features shown in approximate scale and location
Drawing 2.3

Cultural Landscape Report
for the Sandy Hook
Coastal Defense Batteries

Gateway National
Recreation Area
Sandy Hook, New Jersey

1919 Period Plan
Sandy Hook Batteries

OLMSTED
CENTER

National Park Service
Olmsted Center for Landscape Preservation
www.nps.gov/oclp

SOURCES

1. Sandy Hook GIS Data
2. Aerial Photographs, Coastal and Hydraulics Laboratory, U. S. Army Corps of Engineers, 1920
3. Map of Sandy Hook Defenses, 1910
4. Blue Print Map Showing Construction of Gravel Roads at Fort Hancock, NJ, 1907

DRAWN BY

Tom Layton, AutoCAD 2002, Illustrator CS3, 2009

LEGEND

- Battery Landscape Extents
- Beach
- Canopy Vegetation
- Road / Walk
- Rail Line

NOTES

1. All features shown in approximate scale and location
2. Battery landscape extents have been developed for the purposes of this report

Drawing 2.4

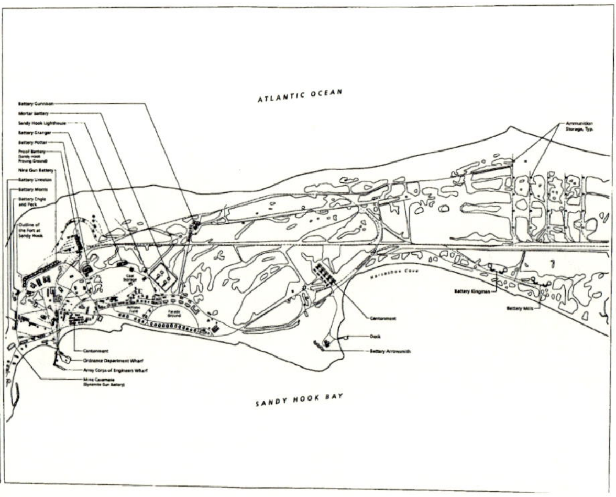

CARETAKER STATUS AND WORLD WAR II 1919–1945

The World War I efforts to mobilize troops and expand coastal defenses abruptly ended following the armistice on November 11, 1918. At Sandy Hook and across the country, personnel were drastically reduced and the coastal defense batteries were assigned to a minimal level of upkeep referred to as caretaker status. Between December 1918 and June 1919, Sandy Hook's batteries saw their personnel reduced from twenty-four officers and 1,535 enlisted men to fifteen officers and 386 enlisted men.[90]

From the armistice to the conclusion of World War II, personnel levels fluctuated at Sandy Hook due to caretaker status, the activation of National Guard units, and training and coastal defense functions during the war. The Army reduced the number of operational batteries at Sandy Hook and other sites defending New York Harbor because the range of large caliber 12- and 16-inch guns provided a greater field of fire. At Sandy Hook, Batteries Kingman and Mills were positioned on the western side of the entry to Lower New York Harbor. On Long Island, New York, the Rockaway peninsula marked the eastern side and in this location, 16-inch guns were emplaced at Fort Tilden's Battery Harris. These three batteries covered any possible approach of a major battleship and during World War II, were joined by Battery Lewis in the Navesink Highlands. Similar to Battery Harris, Battery Lewis had 16-inch guns that extended the field of fire further south and east into the Atlantic Ocean (Figure 2.57).

Advances in aviation technology during the inter-war period redefined coastal defense strategies. The potential to use airplanes in reconnaissance and bombing campaigns required the redesign of large caliber batteries, including Kingman and Mills. The expanded role of aviation also resulted in new detection technologies, which were tested and installed at Sandy Hook. In the mid-1930s, the Army Signal Corps Laboratories at nearby Fort Monmouth developed detection systems that transmitted radio waves and determined aircraft location, range, and azimuth based on the reflected waves. The system became known as radar—an acronym for Radio Detecting and Ranging.[91] Due to its secure location and the opportunity to test radio waves on passing ships and planes, the Army Signal Corps established radar facilities at Sandy Hook (Figure 2.58).[92] Working with Western Electric, the Signal Corps built a group of eight wooden warehouses approximately a half mile east of Batteries Kingman and Mills near the Atlantic coastline. Each warehouse contained a SCR-268 radar unit, the Army's first operational radar, and allowed tests on the systems in relative secrecy without exposure to weather.

By August 1943, the Army installed eleven radar sites in New Jersey, Staten Island, and the Rockaway peninsula to help guard the southern approach to New York Harbor (Figure 2.59). Two of the radar sites stood on the Sandy Hook peninsula to detect ships and low-flying planes and transmit range and azimuth data to specific batteries. The first site at Sandy Hook for a SCR-682 radar unit was the top of an existing fire control tower (Figure 2.60). The tower was constructed in the late 1920s for Battery Harris and was located approximately 700 feet west of Battery Gunnison. For the second site, the Army constructed a new tower approximately a quarter mile south of the Signal Corps' wooden radar shelters (Figure 2.61). This tower housed a SCR-296 radar unit that sent target information to the rapid fire guns at Battery Gunnison.

CARETAKER RESPONSIBILITIES

The primary goal for caretaker status personnel was to prevent the serious deterioration of the batteries' armament, fire control, and communication systems. The Army maintained these components so they could be immediately placed into active service when required.

In order to maintain the batteries, caretaker's duties involved monthly inspections and emphasized the cleaning and maintenance of the guns and carriages. In addition, caretakers were to inspect the emplacement, slopes, and interior rooms during their monthly inspections. If deemed by the inspection, gutters and drainage sumps had to be cleaned out and problems with vegetation addressed, including watering during hot summer months. Following instructions on battery construction drawings, such as the 1905 drainage plan for Battery Gunnison, damp interiors were improved by opening doors on warm, sunny days and promoting better ventilation. Performing all of these tasks and successfully maintaining a battery depended on the number of caretaker personnel assigned and whether they had to divide their time and energies among numerous duties.[93]

Personnel reductions immediately after World War I were followed by new national policy and an international treaty that kept the caretaker system active until the mid-1930s. With the defeat of Germany and the exhaustion of other European powers, future conflicts seemed unlikely at this time and public support for military spending waned. In this political environment, Congress passed the National Defense Act of 1920 that provided a new organizational model and regulations for the Army. The Act significantly cut active Army personnel and restructured the service to be comprised of the Regular Army, the National Guard, and the Organized Reserves. The National Guard and Reserves would provide the necessary manpower if conflict erupted and the focus of the Regular Army became training these non-permanent forces. Reduced active personnel were coupled with decreased funding and Sandy Hook's coastal defenses remained in caretaker status.[94]

In addition to a new national military policy, emphasis on coastal defenses was further diminished by the Washington Naval Treaty, ratified in 1922. Under the terms of the treaty, the United States, Great Britain, Italy, France, and Japan all agreed to limit new naval construction and armament. With the strength of international navies a known and fixed quantity, there was little support beyond rudimentary maintenance for coastal defenses.

By 1930, thirty-five coastal defense groups that were developed and active between 1890 and 1917 were reduced to only ten in active status. Sandy Hook, part of the Southern New York Harbor Defenses, and the Eastern New York Harbor Defenses at the confluence of the East River and Long Island Sound, joined an additional thirteen defense groups in caretaker status. Ten defense groups were abandoned and of the ten active groups, half were located in the foreign territories of Hawaii, Panama, and the Philippines. In the northeast United States, only the Long Island Sound Harbor Defenses that guarded the eastern entry to the Sound remained on active status.[95]

MOBILE ARTILLERY

Changes in the overall military strategy following World War I and the reduction in personnel and funding created an emphasis on mobile artillery. In the 1919 annual report to the Secretary of War, the Chief of Coast Artillery stated:

> In the past our seacoast guns were mounted on fixed carriages because we had no others on which guns of requisite power could be mounted. But now we have mobile mounts for long range, powerful guns, and economy of force would seem to demand that we take advantage of this strategical and tactical mobility to effect artillery concentration at threatened points and thus use to the fullest possible extent our available artillery resources.[96]

The flexibility afforded by tractor-drawn artillery had been proven during World War I. Additionally, a stock of large caliber guns manufactured for use in Europe had never been shipped and being available, could be readily converted into new mobile artillery.[97]

Mobile artillery was comprised of large caliber guns and mortars mounted on either tractor-drawn flatbeds or railway cars. At Sandy Hook, a railroad line branched off the main line and proceeded in a north-south direction closer to the Atlantic coast line. From this branch, the Army constructed three spurs were constructed to the west that extended into a dune area near the middle of the peninsula (Figures 2.62). On these spurs, the Army positioned two 8-inch railway guns and two 12-inch railway mortars between the dunes facing the shipping channel (Figure 2.63).[98] By July 1944, a map prepared by the Army Corps of Engineers indicates the original spurs were removed and reconstructed with an orientation to the east. The total number of spurs was also increased from three to five (Figure 2.64). To support the mobile artillery, the Army also mounted collapsible searchlights on railway cars to illuminate and identify enemy ships and appeared in service at Sandy Hook by March 1918 (Figure 2.65).[99]

THREATS FROM THE AIR AND CHANGES IN CONCEALMENT STRATEGIES

The focus of coastal defense batteries countering naval strength shifted following World War I. During the war, aircraft—including lighter than air blimps and balloons—were used primarily for reconnaissance but also engaged in strategic bombing and aerial combat. Less than a year after the armistice, defenses to counter an aerial attack were approved for Sandy Hook and 3-inch anti-aircraft guns were planned for installation at the former Dynamite Gun Battery, the Mortar Battery, Battery Arrowsmith, and Sandy Hook's Coast Guard station.[100]

Billy Mitchell, a brigadier general in the Army's Air Service during World War I, recognized the offensive capabilities of aircraft and their potential to revolutionize warfare. In 1921, the Navy conducted bombing test on seized German ships with Mitchell coordinating the Army's bombers. The ships were stationary targets lacking crews and sank after successive attacks with larger bombs. Navy officials argued that a maneuvering ship and responsive crew could have escaped the attack, however for Mitchell and the press covering the event, the test demonstrated the effectiveness of airpower over surface targets.[101]

In addition to bombing tests, the 1920s witnessed advances in aviation design. Pilots competed to finish longer-distance flights and in 1927, Charles Lindbergh completed the first transatlantic flight to continental Europe. Taking less than a day and a half, Lindbergh's journey demonstrated that the vast oceans that had kept America separated from European and Asian conflicts were increasingly easy to cross. As plane engines became more powerful, more sophisticated weaponry could be added and aerial bombing campaigns would become a standard component of warfare. Aerial bombing represented a major threat to coastal defenses. The existing concealment strategy relied on earth and sand cover to blend the battery into the surrounding dune landscape. This engineered earthwork was then planted with a combination of trees and shrubs at various heights to conceal the battery when viewed from a ship at sea. A 1910 memorandum from the Army's Office of the Chief of Coast Artillery outlined concealment procedures and clearly instructed that, "Before the actual planting begins the post and company commanders should observe the defenses carefully from the water to see where the screening effect is most needed and to decide as to how it can best be effected."[102] However, the efforts made to conceal a battery and its seaward-facing slope could not protect the concrete structure from overhead identification.

In order to protect coastal defense batteries when viewed from the air, the concealment strategy expanded to include increased plant cover, netting, and camouflage painting. In May 1943, the Chief of Coast Artillery at Fort Hancock provided a status on the batteries, reporting:

> Obscurement grading and netting installed at Kingman and Mills. Planting 90% complete at Kingman and 30% complete at Battery Mills. Obscurement planting and painting at Battery Gunnison completed. Obscurement planting and painting completed at Urmston, Morris, Peck, Alexander, Halleck, Bloomfield, and Richardson. Camouflage painting of Potter and Granger completed.[103]

With the exception of Battery Arrowsmith, disarmed after Kingman and Mills became operational in 1919, all of Sandy Hook's batteries are listed as having new concealment or "obscurement" strategies implemented. This is noteworthy because by July 1944, an Army Corps of Engineers map listed Battery Granger and the Nine Gun Battery comprised of Alexander, Halleck, Bloomfield, and Richardson as disarmed. Even as the structures were nearing the end of their service, the Army deemed it necessary to upgrade their protection from overhead identification. A more detailed discussion of the changes made to Battery Kingman and Mills, including planting efforts, is covered under a separate heading in this section.

PREPARATION FOR WORLD WAR II

Growing conflict in Europe and Asia during the 1930s forced an isolationist United States to prepare for war and to reevaluate the nation's coastal defense system. In 1936, Japan withdrew from the Washington Naval Treaty and two years later, Germany annexed Austria and continued with invasions into Czechoslovakia and Poland, beginning a second worldwide war.

In 1940 the U. S. War Department convened a board, similar to the Endicott and Taft boards, to prepare a new coastal defense plan. The board standardized new battery designs and artillery. Large-caliber artillery constructed during World War II was comprised of either 16- or 12-inch guns. Utilizing only two gun sizes and consistent battery design resulted in simplified tactics, training, maintenance, and ammunition manufacturing.[104]

Recognizing that more personnel would be needed to prepare for an imminent conflict, Congress amended the Selective Service Act in September 1940 and decreased the minimum age requirement to register from 21 to 18 years old. That same month, President Franklin Roosevelt federalized the 245th New York National Guard Regiment making them the 245th Coastal Artillery Regiment stationed at Fort Hancock. To accommodate the personnel increase, the Army established tent cities and built a new contingent of wooden barracks and mess halls known as Camp Low north of Horseshoe Cove (Figure 2.66).[105]

No longer constrained by a minimal workforce that defined caretaker status, Sandy Hook and the nation's other coastal defense sites returned to active status. The number of military and civilian personnel on Sandy Hook grew tremendously to between 7,000 and 12,000 from 1942 to 1943. The large number of personnel was partially due to training exercises conducted at Fort Hancock for troops before deployment overseas.[106] Congress authorized new coastal defense projects and renovation of two batteries at Sandy Hook with the latest defensive strategies.

To maintain consistency with the presentation in earlier sections, the coastal defense batteries will be divided into either large caliber gun batteries or rapid fire gun batteries. Within each category, the individual batteries will be presented chronologically according the dates that artillery was emplaced.

LARGE CALIBER GUN BATTERIES

Battery Potter

During World War II, the fire control stations on top of Battery Potter were no longer required due to longer-range guns, new range finding towers, and the disarming of older counterweight carriage artillery. The buildings and the sweeping views from the top of Potter were assigned new roles to support defensive efforts during the war. The Army converted the northernmost building on top of Potter's terreplein into a meteorological station to observe and track wind direction and weather phenomenon affecting artillery firing. To support the meteorological station, the Army installed a metal tether to the north of the building to attach weather balloons for recording wind speeds and direction.

During World War II, the central building, composed of five interconnected structures, served as a Command and Observation Post for the New York Harbor Defense Command Post (HDCP) stationed at Mortar Battery. Throughout the war, the HDCP coordinated coastal defense activities from the eastern end of Long Island to Atlantic City, New Jersey. With the war efforts becoming increasingly focused on combat in Europe, the Command and Observation Post was deactivated on March 1, 1944.[107]

On May 1, 1943, the Army established the Harbor Entrance Control Post (HECP) in the southernmost building on top of Potter's terreplein. From this vantage, personnel monitored the main shipping channel and controlled all ship traffic coming into and out of New York Harbor (Figure 2.67). Approximately six weeks after Germany's surrender to the Allies, the HECP was deactivated on June 18, 1945.[108]

Mortar Battery

Advances in naval artillery demonstrated during World War I that the 12-inch mortars at Mortar Battery would be ineffective in future conflicts. The Mortar Battery was disarmed in 1920, however, the engineered earthwork and protected interior spaces were utilized in the decades that followed until the deactivation of the New York Harbor Defense Program in 1950.

In addition to exhibiting the power of naval artillery, World War I introduced new threats posed by aircraft flying reconnaissance missions and bombing campaigns. Responding to this new offensive capability, the Army mounted two 3-inch anti-aircraft guns on top of Mortar Battery's engineered earthwork between 1922 and 1923. The top of the earthwork, about thirty-five feet higher than the surrounding grade, offered a strategic elevation for the guns and the battery's interior rooms were utilized for ammunition storage and defensive shelter.

In 1937, an additional anti-aircraft gun was added to the top of the engineered earthwork and the three guns were designated A. A. Gun Battery No. 2. The three gun positions were identified on a 1944 Army Corps of Engineers map of Sandy Hook (Figure 2.68). With the start of World War II, the 3-inch anti-aircraft guns were supplemented by a machine gun platform consisting of four .50-caliber machine guns. Although not designated on the 1944 map, the smaller machine guns can be seen in a World War II-era photograph (Figure 2.69).[109]

The magazines and connecting tunnels at the Mortar Battery, protected under the engineered earthwork, also played important roles after World War I and through World War II. In 1922, a switchboard room was installed in the longitudinal gallery that connected the northern mortar pits with the magazines in the center of the battery. The switchboards facilitated communications for all of Fort Hancock's fire control systems (Figure 2.70).[110] Communications personnel and equipment were afforded protection by the engineered earthwork but had to contend with potential water infiltration and an accumulation of moisture inside the concrete structure. The *Report of Completed Works*, updated a year prior to the installation of the switchboard, recorded that the interior spaces of the Mortar Battery were damp. The Army added more communication infrastructure to the interior of the Mortar Battery and installed dehumidifying systems.

Between 1940 and 1941, the Army converted the Mortar Battery's remaining interior spaces into the New York Harbor Defense Command Post (HDCP) (Figure 2.71).

Communications personnel staffed the post twenty-four hours a day and coordinated coastal defenses from the eastern end of Long Island to Atlantic City, New Jersey. The Mortar Battery's protected magazines and galleries became known as the "catacombs of Fort Hancock" and later, "The Bombproof." To further protect the personnel and vital role of electronic communications, air lock rooms, gas-proof doors, and ventilation systems were added to the interior spaces in case of a poison gas attack.[111] In addition to gas proofing, repairs and modifications for establishing the HDCP included soundproofing and dehumidifying. The most expensive task, over a third of the total amount, was spent on dehumidifying.[112]

The exterior of Mortar Battery was also modified to support the communication operations inside and provide additional defense against aerial detection. No longer needed as a defensive structure and anticipating an increase in personnel and facilities, the Army demolished the north, the east, and a portion of the south perimeter wall in 1938. At the same time, they cut an entry into the west perimeter wall just north of the gallery that led to the southwest mortar pit. The entry became the primary access point for communications personnel entering the structure.[113] The exterior also received an upgraded concealment treatment to better disguise the open, concrete mortar pits when viewed from above. A 1943 photograph from the Sandy Hook lighthouse shows netting with camouflage patterning over the gallery and southwest mortar pit (Figure 2.72).

Batteries Kingman and Mills

The 12-inch guns emplaced at Batteries Kingman and Mills in 1919 had significantly greater range than the counterweight guns at Nine Gun Battery and Battery Granger. Capable of firing at targets over twenty miles away, the guns at Kingman and Mills needed new range finding stations to identify targets at greater distances. In response, the Army built steel towers with range finding stations located in booths at the top.[114] In March 1922, two towers—one dedicated for the fire control of Kingman and the other for Mills—were completed about a half mile south of Battery Gunnison along Atlantic Drive. Both towers were approximately forty feet tall and each contained a depression-type range finder (Figure 2.73). Five years later, a one hundred-foot tall tower was installed approximately 700 feet west of Battery Gunnison to provide fire control for Battery Harris at Fort Tilden (Figures 2.74 and 2.75).

Although batteries Kingman and Mills were innovative coastal defenses when installed, their design provided no protection against aerial detection and bombing, a flaw which had to be addressed as the United States entered World War II. The War Department's 1940 coastal defense plan utilized only 16- or 12-inch large-caliber guns, such as those at Batteries Kingman and Mills. When viewed from above, the existing batteries' open concrete platforms read as bull's-eye targets (see Figure 2.43). A new casemated battery design, retrofitted to Kingman and Mills, protected guns, magazines, and operation centers with a complete covering of concrete and earth (Figures 2.76 and 2.77). The shell, gunpowder, and plotting rooms located between the two gun platforms were already covered with an engineered earthwork that rose to an elevation of thirty-eight feet. The Army increased this protective covering by four feet, covered each gun platform with over eight feet of concrete, and then capped each with an additional twelve feet or more of sand and earth. A concrete canopy, tapering from five to fourteen feet thick, overhung the platform so only the barrel of the gun was exposed (Figure 2.78). The new casemates for Batteries Kingman and Mills featured two feet minimum of earth and sand cover at the surface that covered a two-foot thick concrete "burster course." As aerial bombs became more powerful, the burster course was intended to detonate a bomb near the surface of the casemate before it could penetrate deeper into the earthwork and cause more damage to the battery and its soldiers.

Between 1941 and 1942, the Army casemated the open gun platforms at Batteries Kingman and Mills. Work extended into 1943, including improvements to electrical power, sanitary sewer, and the dehumidifying system, all of which were initially installed in 1937. Preparing both batteries for World War II also included gasproofing and adding a power room to the west of the quarters and store room (Figure 2.79). In order to deliver ammunition and gunpowder, the Army moved the railroad tracks that had previously traveled under a covered passageway to the west of casemated battery (see Figure 2.76). Heat was installed in the new power rooms in 1944 and that same year, each battery had three individual dehumidifying units added to the existing system to remove moisture from their main corridors.[115]

The engineered earthworks for Batteries Kingman and Mills rose up approximately forty feet above the surrounding land and contrasted with the flat, slightly undulating coastal topography. A greater concern than the size of the earthworks was their contrast to the surrounding vegetation and easy identification when viewed from above. In May 1943, the Chief of Coast Artillery at Fort Hancock reported that "obscurement" grading and netting had been installed at the batteries and that planting was ninety percent complete at Kingman and thirty percent complete at Mills.[116]

Six months after this report, correspondence indicated the initial planting at Kingman and Mills was not successful. Army Corps of Engineers Lieutenant Colonel Charles K. Panish reported that:

> 1) It is requested that the R. & U. Branch [Repairs and Utilities] accomplish the replacement of shrubs and trees at Batteries Kingman and Mills at subject location during the fall 1943 planting season as shown on Drawing CAM-4-53....

> 2) The basic planting at these installations comprised a large proportion of Groundsel Bush which failed to survive transplanting. It is recommended at this time to replace the missing shrubs with Rugosa Roses in small sizes using the soil in place for the planting operation. Some losses occurred in the tree planting also and it is recommended at this time that only a few of these are required for replacement in the obscurement program.... The plant quantities indicated are estimated to produce a continuous shrub cover when planted to supplement the existing plants.
> 3) The work is estimated to costs as follows:
> 11,900 shrubs @ $.75 $8,925.00
> 125 trees @ $4.00 $500.00
> Total $9,425.00[117]

Correspondence between the Army Corps of Engineers and the Office of the Chief of Coast Artillery continued after this request until May 1944 when Kingman and Mills were no longer actively manned. The debate on planting at Kingman and Mills focused on appropriate plant species, quantities, and whether additional vegetative cover was needed for erosion control or concealment. Based on the correspondence, Kingman and Mills were originally planted with trees and shrubs with the shrubs inconsistently spaced at three to ten feet on center.[118]

By 1944, planted or naturalized grass species and "weedy growth" were part of the cover on the engineered earthworks and confirmed by a report indicating "that no dust or soil erosion exists at Batteries Kingman and Mills, the existing grass and weedy growth giving adequate permanent erosion protection to the seacoast fortifications."[119]

In May 1944, as the focus of World War II concentrated on a major European campaign and with the naval forces of Nazi Germany incapacitated, the debate on planting at Kingman and Mills was concluded when the Eastern Defense Command determined that:

> ...in the event of the category of defense increasing it would be required to fully man these batteries and therefore the concealment afforded by Passive Protection measures would be absolutely necessary. Planting required under Passive Protection measures cannot be done effectively at the time of change of category of defense but should be cared for in a continuous maintenance proposition.[120]

Although the proposal for replacement planting was approved, it is unknown if the plan was funded or implemented in the final year of World War II. The protective casemates and concealment plantings at Batteries Kingman and Mills were obsolete by the time the war concluded. The introduction of long range, high-altitude bombers, the V1 and V2 rockets, and the atomic bomb demonstrated offensive capability that eclipsed Batteries Kingman and Mills, and both were disarmed in 1948.

RAPID FIRE GUN BATTERIES

Batteries Engle and Peck

Disarmed in 1918 as a result of simplifying rapid fire artillery, Battery Engle was not abandoned, but modified before major military reductions were implemented following World War I. Alterations to Battery Engle occurred in 1920 to improve the fire control of nearby Battery Peck. The Army converted Battery Engle's magazine, shielded by seven feet of concrete cover, into a plotting room and constructed a coincidence range finding station over the concrete gun well (Figure 2.80). The station was nineteen feet square and its floor was set approximately four and a half feet higher than the gun well. A fifteen foot-long coincidence range finder was installed inside the station at a height twenty-seven feet above mean low water.

In concert with the alterations made at Battery Engle, the Army also improved Battery Peck in 1920. Prior to the modifications, an officer for Battery Peck stood on an open, concrete platform centered between the two emplacements (Figure 2.81). The new construction created a fully-enclosed, concrete, battery commander's station (Figure 2.82). To improve the range of Battery Peck's 6-inch guns, concrete was cut out of the emplacements in August 1928. Removing some of the concrete permitted the guns to rise to a twenty degree elevation. Increasing the angle of the gun from a horizontal position—zero degrees—to twenty degrees allowed Battery Peck's guns to strike targets further from the coastline.[121]

The improvements to Battery Peck, including the fire control modifications made to Battery Engle, remained in service until 1943. At that time, the Army relocated Battery Peck's guns to Battery Gunnison. Peck's 6-inch guns could fire quicker than the 6-inch guns they replaced at Gunnison and as a result, Battery Gunnison was designated New Battery Peck. The Army did not mothball the former Battery Peck, but instead installed two 90mm anti-aircraft guns and designated the structure Battery Number 8 (Figure 2.83).[122]

Batteries Urmston and Morris

Although a new coincidence ranger finder station was completed at Battery Urmston in early 1919, a majority of the battery's artillery was removed a year later and during World War II, the remaining guns were transferred to a new location along the peninsula's eastern coastline. In March 1920, the Army approved removal of the guns at emplacements #1, #2, #5 and #6. These four guns used balanced pillar mounts, which proved to be inferior to the pedestal mounted system used for other rapid fire guns.[123] Battery Urmston's pedestal mounted guns at emplacements #3 and #4 remained active until the start of World War II. In 1942, the Army removed the two pedestal mounted guns and relocated them to the dunes north of Battery Gunnison (Figure 2.84). The dune emplacement was operational in July 1943 and designated Battery Number 6. The battery was also referred to as "New Battery Urmston" and worked with the Harbor Entrance Control Post at Battery Potter to observe and potentially engage ships approaching New York Harbor via the channel.[124] To protect New Battery Urmston from aerial detection the *Report of Completed Works*, updated in September 1943, records that the guns were "concealed with camouflage fabric on a sliding frame."[125]

Unlike Battery Urmston, the four pedestal mounted guns at Battery Morris remained in service throughout World War II. As part of the Army's efforts to improve fire control, a coincidence range finder station was added east of Battery Morris in 1920.[126] The concrete structure, thirteen feet by thirteen feet, was constructed approximately ten feet above the ground. A nine foot-long coincidence range finder was installed inside the station at a height approximately twenty-seven feet above mean low water (Figure 2.85). The instrument's height and the area north of the station free of large, woody vegetation combined to provide unimpeded views of the water and improved fire control for Battery Morris (Figure 2.86).

Battery Gunnison

Battery Gunnison, the last rapid fire gun battery completed, was also the only rapid fire emplacement along the eastern shore of Sandy Hook. In addition to protecting Gunnison's concrete structure, a sand embankment planted with native grasses and shrubs was constructed on the battery's east side to blend the gun battery in with the surrounding landscape.

Similar to engineered earthworks at other batteries, erosion was an ongoing issue to contend with at Gunnison. A January 1929 letter to the Army Corps Chief of Engineers indicated Gunnison's east embankment had eroded and additional sand would be required to repair the earthwork.[127]

In 1940, the War Department convened a board to prepare a new coastal defense plan. The conclusion of the board was that the rapid fire guns on counterweight carriages were deficient compared to the pedestal mounted versions. The counterweight carriage models were slower to load, had a shorter firing range, and had a limited field of fire. As a result of the board's findings, Battery Gunnison's guns and counterweight carriages were disarmed in 1942.[128]

Not wanting to leave the southern approach to New York Harbor without rapid fire guns, plans were approved in February 1943 to relocate the pedestal mounted guns from Battery Peck to Battery Gunnison. In order to mount Battery Peck's guns, a redesign of Gunnison's platform areas was needed to emplace the pedestal mounts. The current platforms, at the base of a parapet wall, had concrete added in order to create a level surface for mounting the guns (Figure 2.87). Once the new guns were installed, Battery Gunnison was designated New Battery Peck.

From 1943 to the end of World War II, Gunnison operated as directed by the Harbor Entrance Control Post stationed atop Battery Potter. Gunnison served as an examination battery that was intended to track targets and fire upon them when ordered. Orders for firing included "bring-to" shots designed to warn a commercial ship to stop until it received proper clearance and destructive fire on enemy vessels.[129]

DISARMED GUN BATTERIES

By 1919, three large caliber gun batteries were disarmed as new artillery, carriages, and improvements in battleship armaments made them obsolete. Guns were first removed at Battery Potter and then at Mortar Battery. Both of these structures were utilized during World War II as command posts for coastal defense coordination. The third large caliber gun battery, Battery Arrowsmith, was disarmed after Batteries Kigman and Mills became operational in 1919 with 360-degree fields of fire to protect the peninsula's west shoreline.

During World War II, two additional large caliber gun batteries were disarmed. The 10- and 12-inch artillery atop Nine Gun Battery and Battery Granger was removed because these guns did not have the range to strike better armed enemy battleships. Additionally, the batteries were suspectible to aerial bombing and not protected like the recently casemated Kingman and Mills. The "Report of Completed Works," a detailed account of equipment at each battery maintained by the Army Corps of Engineers, notes in a handwritten comment that the "salvage of armament" at Battery Granger was approved on January 22, 1943. Similar handwritten comments note that the artillery at Battery Halleck, the first three emplacemnts of Nine Gun Battery, were "listed for disposal" on November 4, 1942. A year later, the Army Service Forces directed the "salvage of armament and accessory equipment" at Batteries Richardson and Bloomfield.[130] Supporting the information in the Report of Completed Works, Nine Gun Battery, Battery Granger, and Battery Arrowsmith are all labeled "dismantled" on a July 1944 map of Sandy Hook prepared by the Army Corps of Engineers (Figure 2.88).

The geographic separation that afforded the United States a measure of protection against previous global conflicts proved inadequate against technological improvements during World War II. Entry into the war began with the long-range Japanese aerial attack on Pearl Harbor, and by the war's conclusion the introduction of long-range bombers, rockets, and atomic weapons far surpassed any defensive capability offered by large caliber, casemated guns like Batteries Kingman and Mills. In addition, long-range bombers could fly at a high altitude that positioned them substantially outside the range of rapid fire gun batteries. With both categories of batteries eclipsed by offensive weaponry, the remainder of Sandy Hook's coastal defense batteries were deactivated and disarmed by 1948. Although deactivated, the 6-inch rapid fire guns at Battery Gunnison remained emplaced and survived a thorough effort at Sandy Hook and across the country to collect coastal artillery for scrap metal.[131]

LANDSCAPE SUMMARY - 1945

In July 1944, perhaps sensing that the apex of World War II development had passed, the Army Corps of Engineers prepared maps recording structures, facilities, circulation, and the shoreline at Sandy Hook. The Army Corps of Engineers' plans are the primary source of information for the 1945 period plans (Drawings 2.5-2.6).

The quantity and density of development continued to be the greatest at the northern end of the peninsula with temporary structures, tent cities, and parking areas added in previously undeveloped areas. The middle and southern sections of Sandy Hook also witnessed increased development, however, the development was confined to relatively small pockets and did not occupy large sections of land. For example, in the middle portion of the peninsula temporary barracks, known as Camp Low, stood north of Horseshoe Cove. In the southern section, anti-aircraft emplacements and temporary radar shelters were established near the Atlantic coastline directly east of Batteries Kingman and Mills (Drawing 2.6).

Sandy Hook's coastline continued to change due to currents and the depositing of sand at the peninsula's northern end. When the Proving Ground closed in 1919, the narrowest part of the recurved spit was only 450 feet wide. As World War II was concluding, over 1,600 feet of new land was added through deposition north of this narrow portion (Drawing 2.5).

Unlike earlier historic maps, there is no indication of vegetation cover on the 1944 Army Corps of Engineers maps to inform the 1945 period plans. Comparing aerial photographs from 1933 and 1962 revealed that vegetation cover did not dramatically change except where cleared for World War II-era construction. New vegetation also appeared at recently formed inland areas as the coastline advanced north and provided an initial buffer for pioneer species.

Although development increased in the middle portion of the peninsula, the new facilities for radar, anti-aircraft emplacements, and storage were located in nodes and not widely distributed across the landscape. This development pattern resulted in larger areas of undisturbed woody vegetation (Drawing 2.6). New development also avoided a roughly circular-shaped pond shown east of Battery Mills and approximately in the center of the landform (Drawing 2.6).

The most dramatic change to Sandy Hook's coastal defense batteries during the World War II-era was the casemating of Batteries Kingman and Mills. The previously open gun platforms were covered with reinforced concrete and earthen mounds that rose approximately forty feet above the surrounding topography (Drawing 2.6). Less striking, but more widespread along the length of the peninsula, were the increased number of anti-aircraft artillery and searchlights to support the war effort. Searchlights punctuated the landscape from the northwest tip of the peninsula to its approximate center east of Horseshoe Cove. Similarly, anti-aircraft installations were located at the northern end in the former Battery Peck and as far south as the Spermaceti Cove Lifesaving Station. World War II personnel increases necessitated temporary structures and tent cities to accommodate Sandy Hook's swelling military population. Cantonments were constructed west of Nine Gun Battery, west of Battery Granger, and north of Horseshoe Cove. Two large tent city areas were established south of the Mortar Battery (Drawing 2.6).

Access to and from the peninsula was provided by ship, train, and automobile and once on Sandy Hook, railroad and vehicular infrastructure connected supply areas, barracks, and coastal defense batteries. At the northern end of the peninsula, the wharf expanded to a collection of four docks, each one providing separate service for the Army Corps of Engineers, Fort Hancock's Quartermaster, the Coast Guard, and mine delivery (Drawing 2.6).

Railroad and vehicular networks departed from the wharf to the north, east, and south. A narrow gauge rail line to the east provided transportation for control mines to storage facilities near the Mine Casemate (Drawing 2.6). The eastern rail line between the wharf and former Proving Ground remained operational and turning south past Nine Gun Battery, became the major north-south railroad route on the peninsula. A parallel line off this main north-south route headed further east toward the Atlantic coastline and with spurs projecting into the sandy dunes, provided a location for large caliber and mortar artillery mounted on rail cars. South of the rail car artillery spurs, another line branched off of the main north-south track and headed west to provide ammunition delivery for the 12-inch guns at Batteries Kingman and Mills (Drawing 2.6).

The major vehicular route, Hartshorne Drive, paralleled the north-south rail line in the southern half of the peninsula. At Horseshoe Cove, Hartshorne Drive curved to the west and followed the bay shoreline in front of Fort Hancock's Officer's Row. Vehicular access near the east coast of the peninsula was provided by Atlantic Drive and connected sites containing searchlights, observation towers, and power generation equipment. South of the Mortar Battery,

Gunnison Road served as an east-west connector between Hartshorne and Atlantic Drives (Drawings 2.5-2.6).

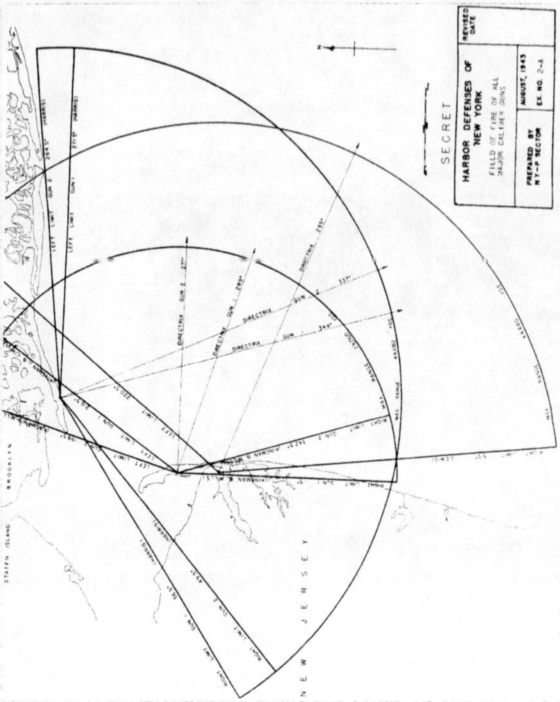

Figure 2.57. Harbor Defenses of New York, Field of Fire of all Major Caliber Guns, 1943. The number of operational batteries at Sandy Hook and other sites defending New York Harbor were reduced by World War II because the range of large caliber 12- and 16-inch guns provided a greater field of fire compared to earlier large caliber artillery. In addition to Sandy Hook, large caliber batteries were located at the Rockaway peninsula and Navesink Highlands (Engineers' Notebook, CDSG ePress).

Figure 2.58. Signal Corps Laboratories radar test facility at Sandy Hook, 1941. Due to its secure location and the ability to test radio waves on passing ships and planes, the Army Signal Corps established a radar test facility at Sandy Hook in the late 1930s (Thomas Hoffman, *Fort Hancock*, Charleston, SC: Arcadia Publishing, 2007).

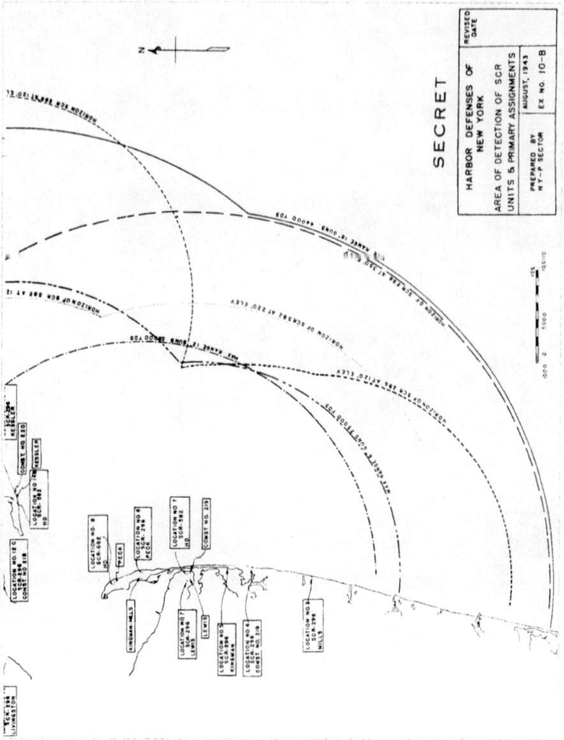

Figure 2.59. Harbor Defenses of New York, Area of Detection of SCR Units & Primary Assignments, 1943. By August 1943, eleven radar sites were installed in New Jersey, Staten Island, and the Rockaway peninsula to help guard the southern approach to New York Harbor. Two units were established on the Sandy Hook peninsula (Engineers' Notebook, CDSG ePress).

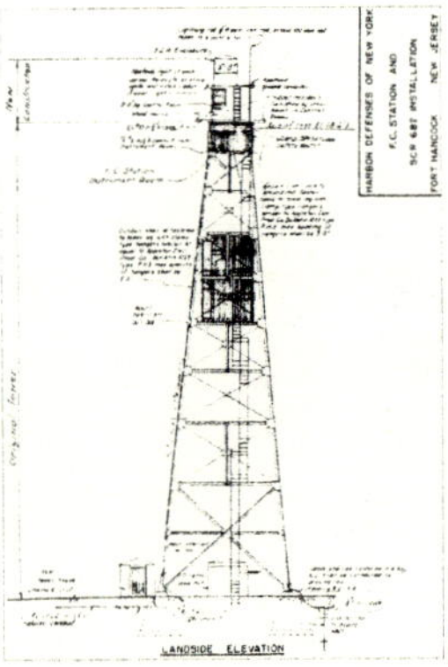

Figure 2.60. Elevation of SCR-682 radar installation, 1944. One of the radar installations at Sandy Hook added a SCR-682 radar unit to the top of an existing fire control tower originally constructed in the late 1920s for Battery Harris. (Report of Completed Works, CDSG ePress).

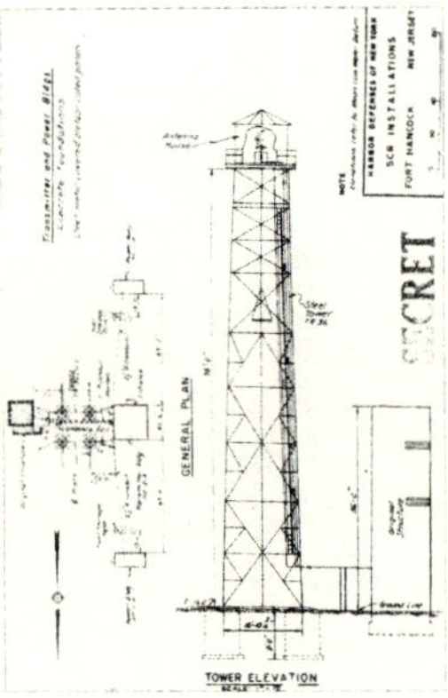

Figure 2.61. Elevation of SCR-296 radar installation, 1943. The Army constructed a new tower approximately a quarter mile south of the Signal Corps' test facility. This tower housed a SCR-296 radar unit that sent target information to the rapid fire guns at Battery Gunnison (Report of Completed Works, CDSG ePress).

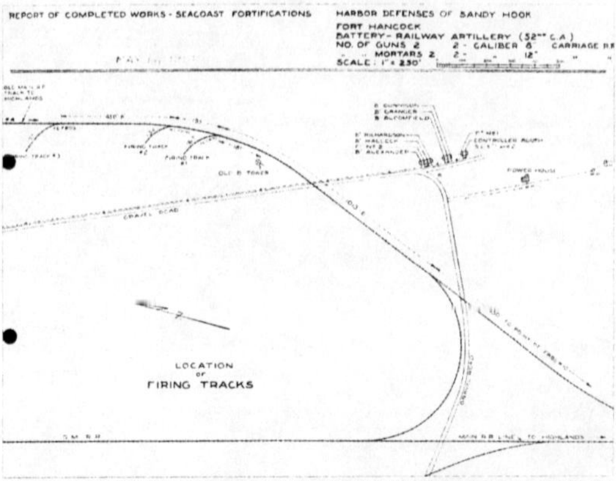

Figure 2.62. Location of Firing Tracks, 1931. Changes in the overall military strategy following World War I and the reduction in personnel and funding created an emphasis on mobile artillery. To support mobile artillery at Sandy Hook, a railroad line branched off the main line and proceeded in a north-south direction closer to the Atlantic coast line. From this branch, three spurs were constructed to the west for railcar mounted artillery (Report of Completed Works, CDSG ePress).

Figure 2.63. 8-inch caliber railway artillery, circa 1939. Mobile artillery was comprised of large caliber guns and mortars mounted on railway cars. The Army positioned two 8-inch caliber railway guns between the dunes facing the shipping channel (Thomas Hoffman, *Fort Hancock*, Charleston, SC: Arcadia Publishing, 2007)

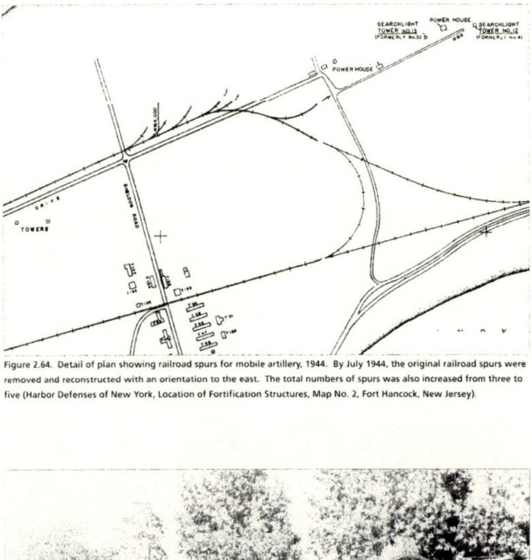

Figure 2.64. Detail of plan showing railroad spurs for mobile artillery, 1944. By July 1944, the original railroad spurs were removed and reconstructed with an orientation to the east. The total numbers of spurs was also increased from three to five (Harbor Defenses of New York, Location of Fortification Structures, Map No. 2, Fort Hancock, New Jersey).

Figure 2.65. Collapsible searchlight on railway car, no date. To support the mobile artillery, collapsible searchlights were also mounted on railway cars to illuminate and identify enemy ships. Collapsible searchlights appeared in service at Sandy Hook by March 1918 (Thomas Hoffman, *Fort Hancock*, Charleston, SC: Arcadia Publishing, 2007).

Figure 2.66. Construction of cantonments at Camp Low, circa 1940. To accommodate the personnel increase in preparation for World War II, tent cities were established and a new contingent of wooden barracks and mess halls known as Camp Low was built north of Horseshoe Cove (Thomas Hoffman, *Fort Hancock*. Charleston, SC: Arcadia Publishing, 2007).

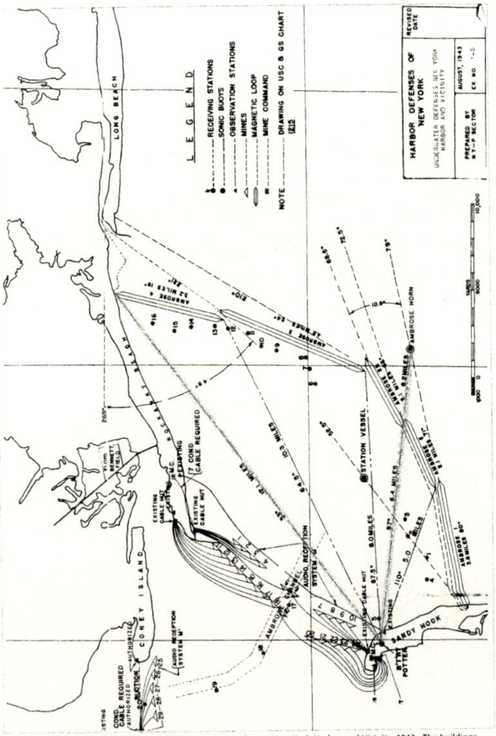

Figure 2.67. Harbor Defenses of New York, Underwater Defenses New York Harbor and Vicinity, 1943. The buildings and the sweeping views from the top of Potter were assigned new roles during World War II. The Army established the Harbor Entrance Control Post (HECP) on top of Potter's terreplein to monitor the main shipping channel and control all ship traffic coming into and out of New York Harbor. The HECP's coverage is highlighted in yellow. In addition, note the detection devices installed for submarines and control mines placed outside the shipping channel as part of a comprehensive defensive system (Engineers' Notebook, CDSG ePress).

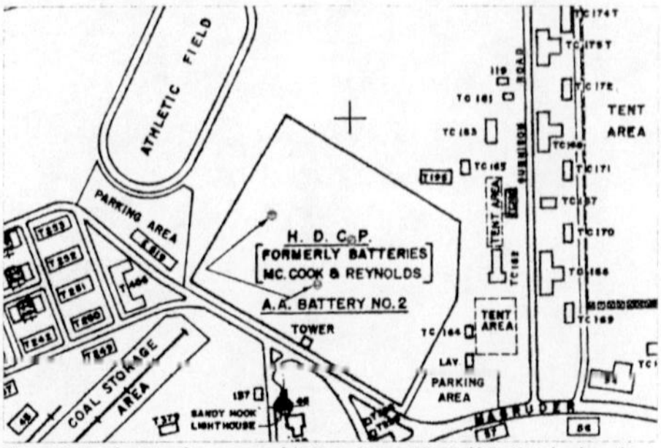

Figure 2.68. Plan of anti-aircraft guns on top of the Mortar Battery, 1944. World War I introduced new threats posed by aircraft flying reconnaissance missions and bombing campaigns. By 1937, three anti-aircraft guns, highlighted in yellow, were added to the top of the Mortar Battery's engineered earthwork (Harbor Defenses of New York, Location of Fortification Structures, Map No. 2, Fort Hancock, New Jersey).

Figure 2.69. View looking southwest at anti-aircraft gun on top of the Mortar Battery, circa 1941. With the start of World War II, the anti-aircraft guns were supplemented by a machine gun platform. A .50-caliber machine gun is visible in the background and the base of the Sandy Hook Lighthouse can be seen in the upper left (GATE 7588).

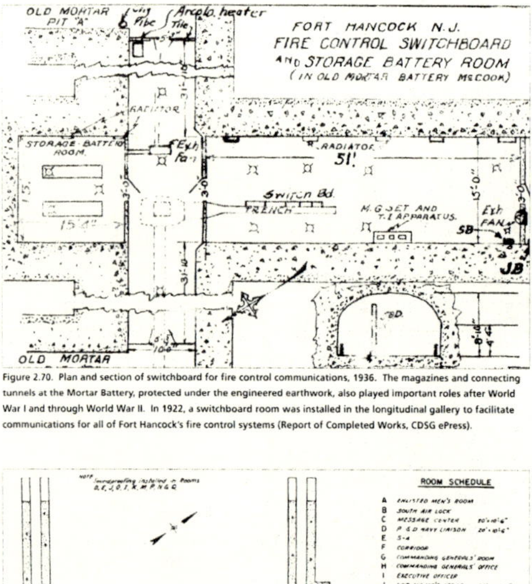

Figure 2.70. Plan and section of switchboard for fire control communications, 1936. The magazines and connecting tunnels at the Mortar Battery, protected under the engineered earthwork, also played important roles after World War I and through World War II. In 1922, a switchboard room was installed in the longitudinal gallery to facilitate communications for all of Fort Hancock's fire control systems (Report of Completed Works, CDSG ePress).

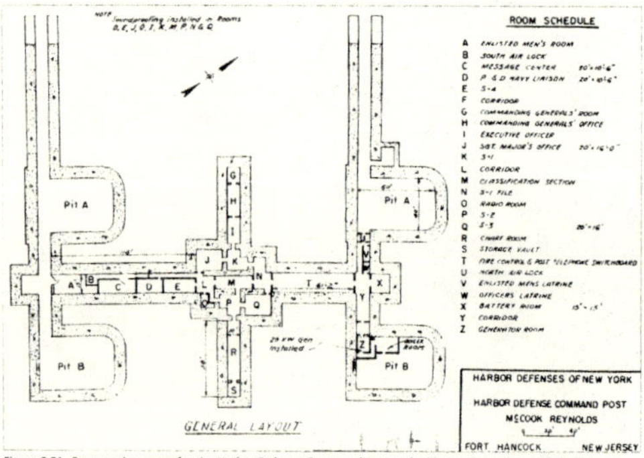

Figure 2.71. Room assignments for the Harbor Defense Command Post at the Mortar Battery, circa 1943. Between 1940 and 1941, the Mortar Battery's interior spaces were converted into the New York Harbor Defense Command Post (HDCP). The post was staffed twenty-four hours a day with communications personnel and coordinated coastal defenses from the eastern end of Long Island to Atlantic City, New Jersey (Report of Completed Works, CDSG ePress).

Figure 2.72. View looking southeast at the Mortar Battery, 1943. During World War II, the battery received an upgraded concealment treatment to better disguise the open, concrete mortar pits when viewed from above. Netting with camouflage patterning is visible over the gallery and the southwest mortar pit (GATE 1943-662).

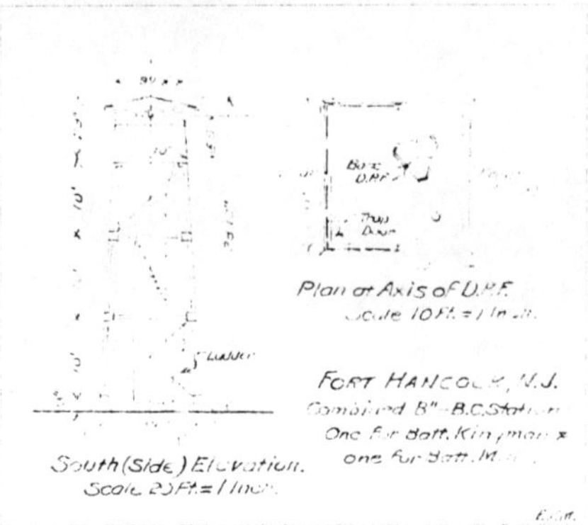

Figure 2.73. Elevation and plan for fire control station serving Batteries Kingman and Mills, 1922. Due to the range of their guns, the Army constructed two towers—one dedicated for the fire control of Kingman and the other for Mills—about a half mile south of Battery Gunnison along Atlantic Drive. Both towers were approximately forty feet tall and each contained a depression-type range finder (Report of Completed Works, CDSG ePress).

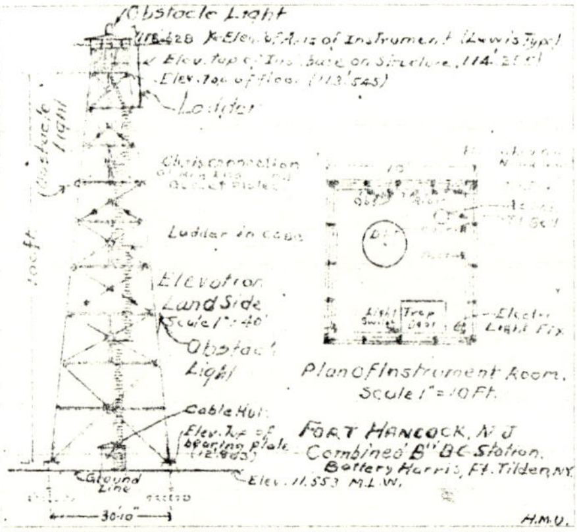

Figure 2.74. Elevation and plan for fire control station serving Battery Harris, 1927. A 100-foot tall tower was installed approximately 700 feet west of Battery Gunnison to provide fire control for Battery Harris at Fort Tilden (Report of Completed Works, CDSG ePress).

Figure 2.75. View of the fire control tower for Battery Harris, circa 1940. During World War II, the fire control stations on top of Battery Potter were no longer required due to longer-range guns, new fire control towers, and the disarming of older counterweight carriage artillery (Vic Bruzek Photos).

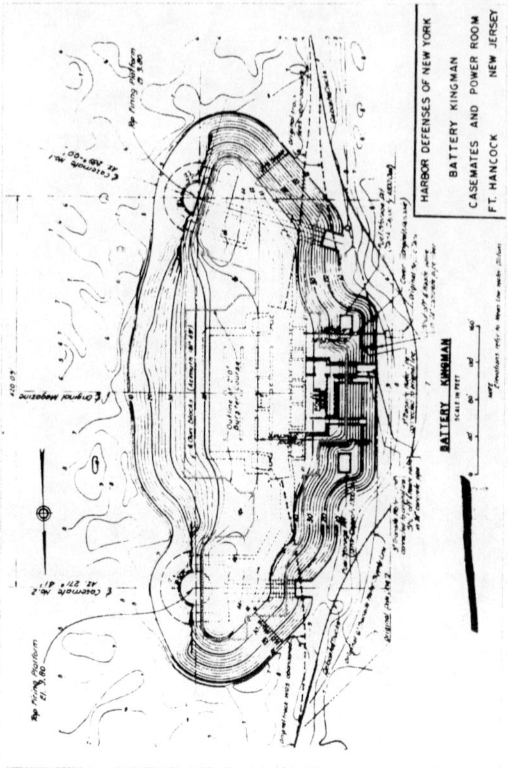

Figure 2.76. Plan of casemated guns at Battery Kingman, 1944. A new casemated battery design, retrofitted to Battery Kingman, protected guns, magazines, and the operations center with a complete covering of concrete and earth. The concrete burster course is highlighted in yellow (Report of Completed Works, CDSG ePress).

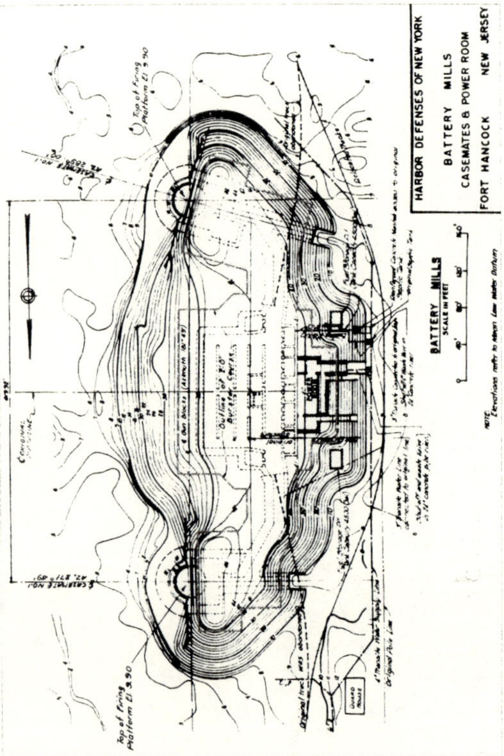

Figure 2.77. Plan of casemated guns at Battery Mills, 1944. Identical to Battery Kingman, a retrofitted design was constructed at Battery Mills. The two gun platforms and shell, gunpowder, and plotting rooms located between the platforms received a protective covering of concrete and earth. The concrete burster course is highlighted in yellow (Report of Completed Works, CDSG ePress).

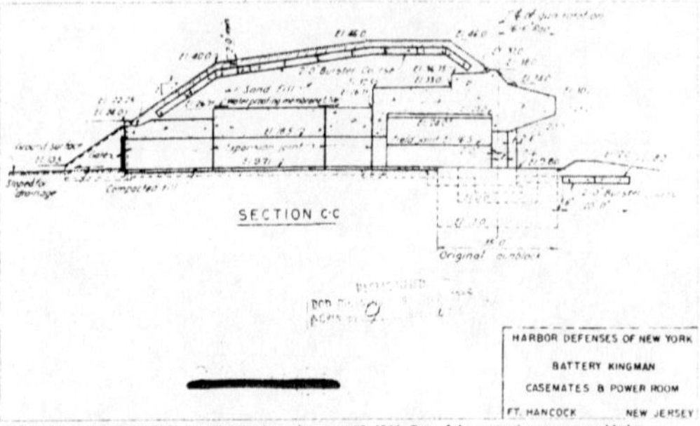

Figure 2.78. Section through Battery Kingman's emplacement #2, 1944. Two of the protective measures added to Batteries Kingman and Mills were concrete canopies that extended over the gun platforms and a concrete burster course intended to denote a bomb near the surface of the casemate before it could penetrate deeper into the earthwork and cause more damage (Report of Completed Works, CDSG ePress).

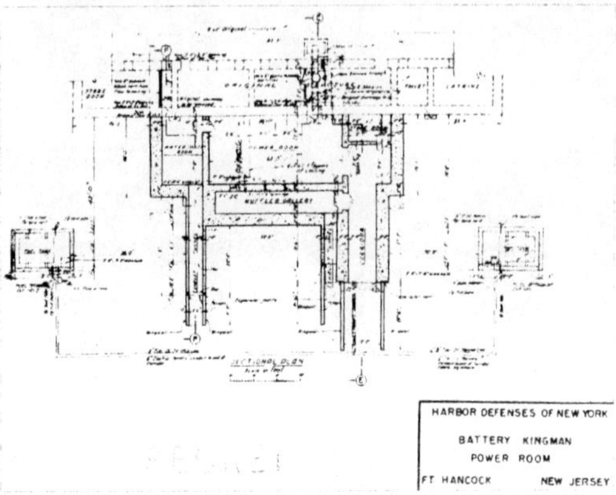

Figure 2.79. Plan of power room at Battery Kingman, 1944. Preparing Batteries Kingman and Mills for World War II also included adding a power room to the west of the quarters and store room. The existing railroad tracks that had traveled under a covered passageway were moved to the west of this addition (Report of Completed Works, CDSG ePress).

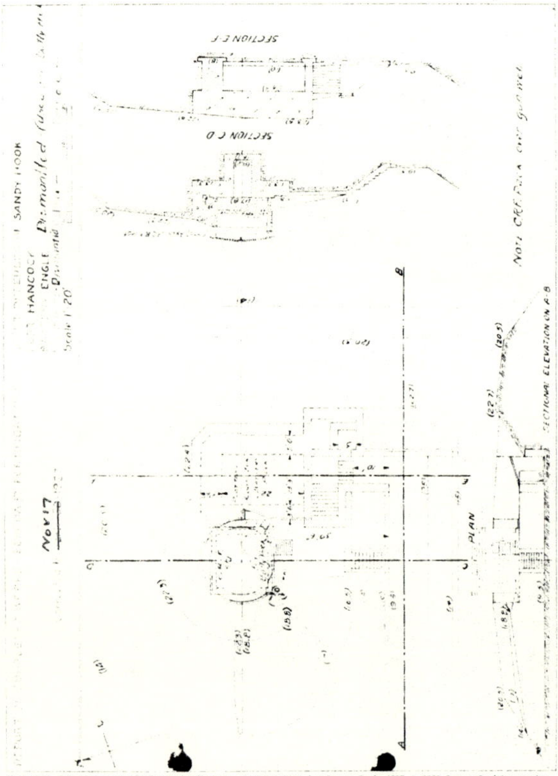

Figure 2.80. Coincidence range finding station for Battery Peck constructed on Battery Engle, 1927. In 1920, Battery Engle's magazine, shielded by seven feet of concrete cover, was converted into a plotting room and a coincidence range finding station was constructed over the concrete gun well to improve the fire control of nearby Battery Peck (Report of Completed Works, CDSG ePress).

Figure 2.81. Open battery commander's station at Battery Peck, circa 1905–10. Prior to the modifications in 1920, the battery commander for Battery Peck stood on an open, concrete platform centered between the two emplacements (Thomas Hoffman, *Fort Hancock*, Charleston, SC: Arcadia Publishing, 2007).

Figure 2.82. Covered battery commander's station at Battery Peck, 1921. In concert with the alterations made at Battery Engle, a fully-enclosed, concrete, battery commander's station, center, was added at Battery Peck. The coincidence range finding station constructed on top of Battery Engle can be seen on the right (Thomas Hoffman, *Fort Hancock*, Charleston, SC: Arcadia Publishing, 2007).

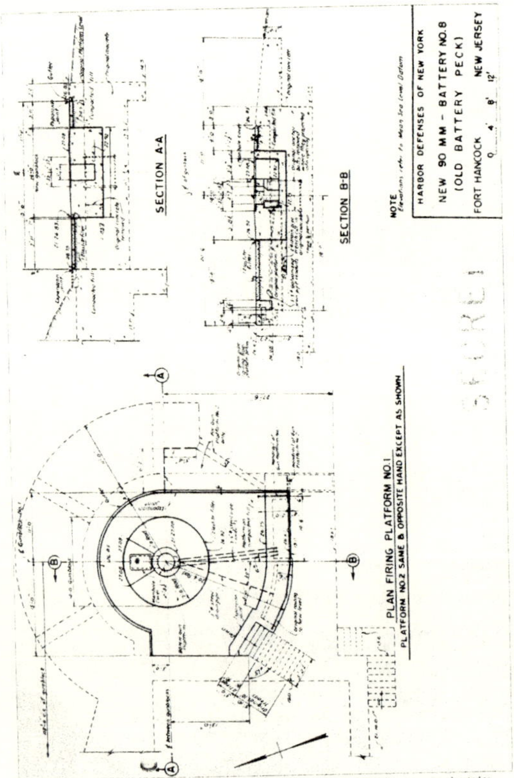

Figure 2.83. New 90 mm - Battery No. 8 (Old Battery Peck), circa 1943. In 1943, Battery Peck's guns were relocated to Battery Gunnison and Peck was outfitted with two 90mm anti-aircraft guns. With new artillery emplaced, the battery was designated Battery Number 8 (Report of Completed Works, CDSG ePress).

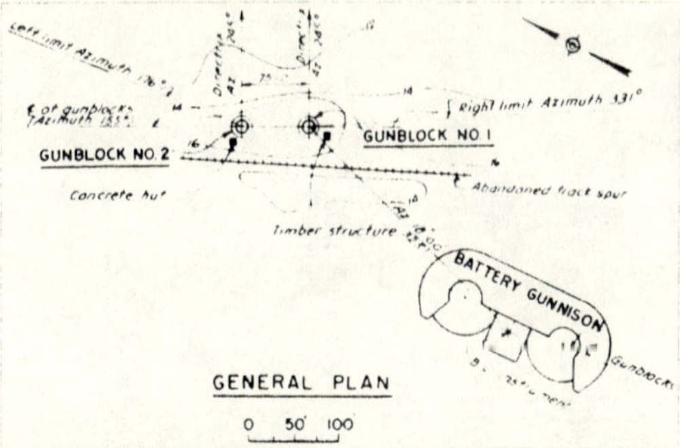

Figure 2.84. Plan for relocating Battery Urmston's guns, circa 1942. In 1942, the Army removed the two remaining guns at Battery Urmston and relocated them to the dunes north of Battery Gunnison. The dune emplacement was operational in July 1943 and designated Battery Number 6. The battery was also referred to as "New Battery Urmston" (Report of Completed Works, CDSG ePress).

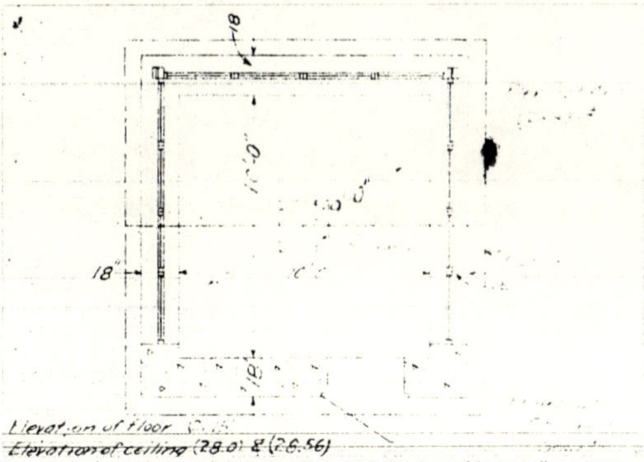

Figure 2.85. Plan for coincidence range finding station at Battery Morris, 1921. As part of the Army's efforts to improve fire control, a coincidence range finder station was added east of Battery Morris in 1920 (Report of Completed Works, CDSG ePress).

Figure 2.86. View looking northwest at coincidence range finder station east of Battery Morris, circa 1921. The instrument height of the range finder and the area north of the station free of large, woody vegetation combined to provide unimpeded views of the water and improved fire control for Battery Morris (GATE 7893).

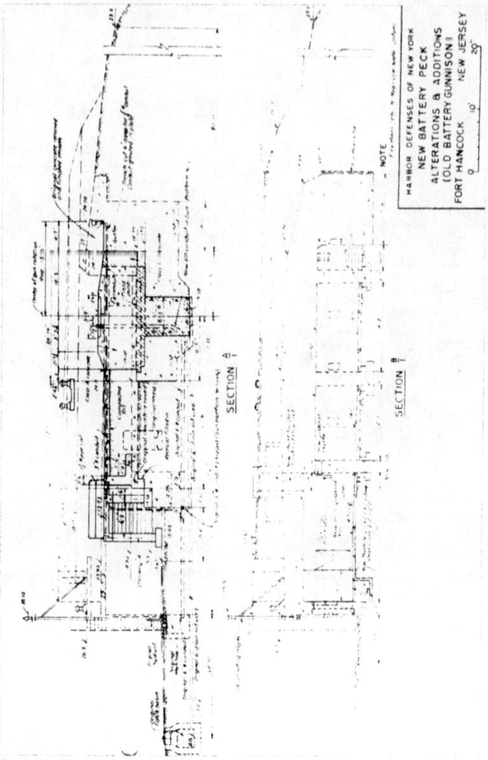

Figure 2.87. New Battery Peck, Alterations & Additions (Old Battery Gunnison), 1943. In order to mount Battery Peck's guns at Battery Gunnison, a redesign of the platform area was required. At the base of the parapet wall, the platforms had concrete added in order to create a level surface for mounting the guns. Once the new guns were installed, Battery Gunnison was designated New Battery Peck (Report of Completed Works, CDSG ePress).

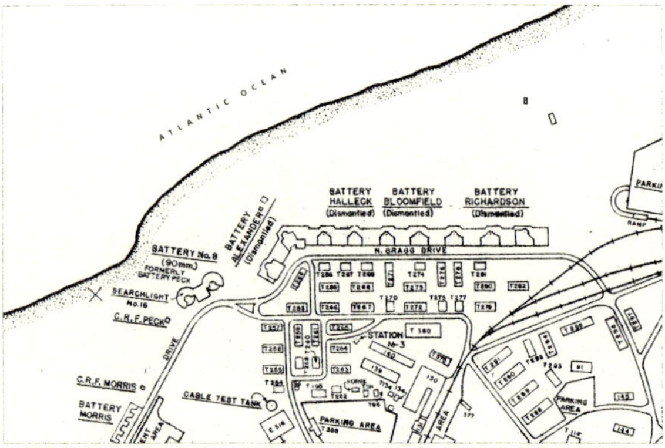

Figure 2.88. Detail of Fort Hancock Map, 1944. During World War II, the 10- and 12-inch artillery atop Nine Gun Battery and Battery Granger was removed because these guns did not have the range to strike better armed enemy battleships. Prepared in 1944, the map labels the four batteries that comprise Nine Gun Battery as "dismantled" (Harbor Defenses of New York, Location of Fortification Structures, Map No. 2, Fort Hancock, New Jersey).

;ultural Landscape Report
or the Sandy Hook
;oastal Defense Batteries

;ateway National
Recreation Area
andy Hook, New Jersey

945 Period Plan
Sandy Hook Batteries

ational Park Service
lmsted Center for Landscape Preservation
www.nps.gov/oclp

OURCES

Sandy Hook GIS Data

Location of Fortification Structures, Fort Hancock, NJ, July 29, 1944

RAWN BY

m Layton, AutoCAD 2002, Illustrator CS3, 2009

EGEND

Battery Landscape Extents

Beach

Canopy Vegetation

Marsh

Road / Walk

Rail Line

Bulkhead

NOTES

All features shown in approximate scale and location

Battery landscape extents have been developed for the purposes of this report

0' 300' 600' 1200'

Drawing 2.6

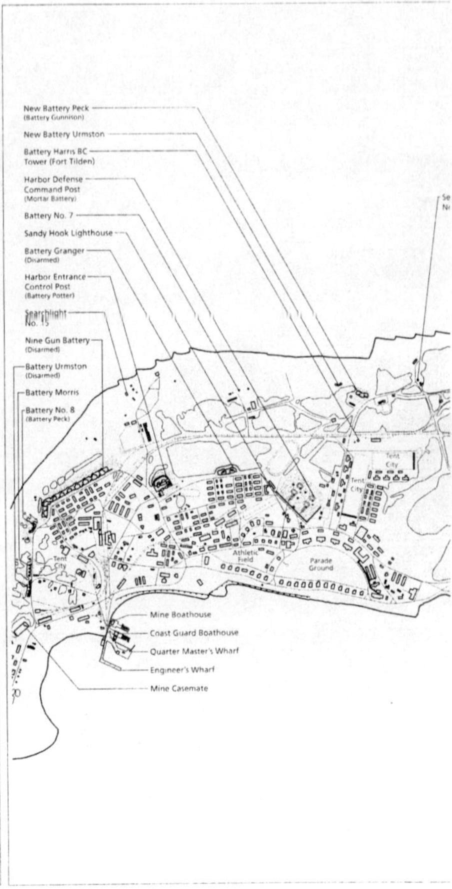

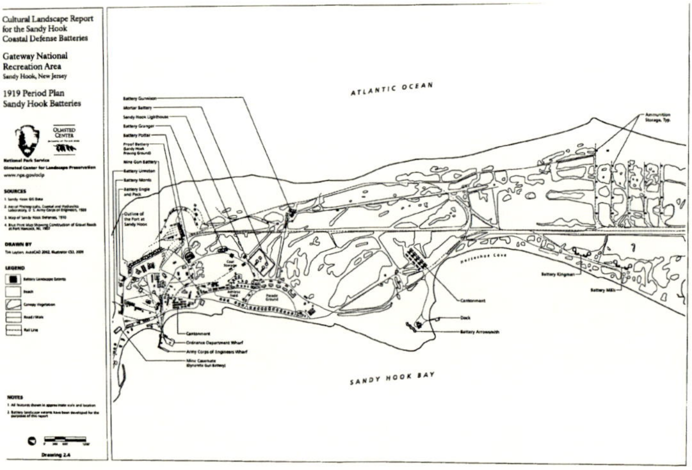
Cultural Landscape Report
for the Sandy Hook
Coastal Defense Batteries
Gateway National
Recreation Area
Sandy Hook, New Jersey
1919 Period Plan
Sandy Hook Batteries
Olmsted Center
National Park Service
Olmsted Center for Landscape Preservation
www.nps.gov/oclp
SOURCES
DRAWN BY
LEGEND
Battery Landscape Extents
Beach
Canopy Vegetation
Road / Walk
Rail Line
NOTES
1. All features shown in approximate scale and location
2. Battery landscape extents have been developed for the purposes of this report
Drawing 2.4
ATLANTIC OCEAN
Battery Gunnison
Mortar Battery
Sandy Hook Lighthouse
Battery Granger
Battery Potter
Proof Battery (Sandy Hook Proving Ground)
Nine Gun Battery
Battery Urmston
Battery Morris
Battery Engle and Peck
Outline of the Fort at Sandy Hook
Coal Storage
Parade Ground
Cantonment
Ordnance Department Wharf
Army Corps of Engineers Wharf
Mine Casemate (Dynamite Gun Battery)
Ammunition Storage, Typ.
Horseshoe Cove
Battery Kingman
Battery Mills
Cantonment
Dock
Battery Arrowsmith
SANDY HOOK BAY

NIKE MISSILE SYSTEMS AND THE COLD WAR 1945–1974

During World War II, advances in aviation made it possible to fly beyond the range of 3-inch anti-aircraft guns, similar to those emplaced at the top of Mortar Battery. Providing a greater range, the 90mm anti-aircraft gun became the new Army standard during the war and could strike a target flying at 30,000 feet.[132] This improved anti-aircraft artillery was installed at Sandy Hook on Battery Peck in 1943.

In the closing years of the war the Army realized that the 90mm guns, even with the assistance of radar technology, lacked the range, accuracy, and destructive power to defend against an aerial attack. On August 17, 1944, Army Ordnance officer Jacob W. Schaefer submitted a memorandum proposing the design of an anti-aircraft rocket which could be radar-guided from the ground.[133]

Six months later, the Army's Chief of Ordnance issued a contract to Western Electric and Bell Telephone Laboratories to determine the feasibility of a defensive missile system. The project was given the code name NIKE after the Greek goddess of victory and on November 27, 1951, a NIKE missile successfully destroyed a drone plane during tests at the White Sands Proving Ground in New Mexico.[134]

MILITARY REORGANIZATION AND THE ORIGINS OF THE COLD WAR

Similar to responses following World War I, the years immediately after World War II witnessed reductions in military personnel and spending. A logistical support unit, the 1225th Army Service Unit, remained stationed at Fort Hancock until the end of 1949. The reduction of combat and support personnel along with new offensive weaponry that surpassed Sandy Hook's existing coastal defense batteries resulted in Fort Hancock's deactivation on June 25, 1950.[135] The Army's departure from Sandy Hook did not last long as armed conflict erupted on the Korean peninsula. On April 10, 1951, Fort Hancock was reactivated for defense of the metropolitan New York area. Anti-aircraft gun batteries deployed during World War II were reestablished and the fort served as a staging center for training and equipping other anti-aircraft units.[136]

Instead of a civil war struggle between opposed domestic forces, the Korean War became an indirect contest between the United States and the Soviet Union. Fighting a common foe during World War II, the two nations emerged from the war as the unrivaled economic and military powers in the world. America's security was briefly bolstered as the only nation with atomic weaponry and atomic bombs were considered the ultimate deterrent to future conflict. Vast ideological differences between the two nations generated mutual distrust and competition to shape the post-war governments in Europe and Asia. Between

1945 and 1947, elections brought Communists to power in Yugoslavia, Albania, Romania, Bulgaria, Poland, and Hungary and the Soviet's sphere of influence extended over the majority of Eastern Europe.[137]

The United States began to address post-war strategies and defensive preparations with passage of the National Defense Act of 1947. The legislation created the consolidated Department of Defense and established an independent Air Force which had previously been organized as a component of the Army. In an address to Congress the following year, President Truman summarized the nation's new preparatory strategy stating:

> I believe that we have learned the importance of maintaining military strength as a means of preventing war. We have found that a sound military system is necessary in time of peace if we are to remain at peace.[138]

Four months later, on July 24, 1948, the Soviets blockaded access to the American, British, and French sections of Berlin. The Berlin Crisis persisted until September 1949 and ended any opportunity for cordial relations between the United States and Soviets. In testimony before the U. S. Senate, financier Bernard Baruch described the tensions between the two nations as a "cold war" and the term continued as an apt description of uneasy international relations for the next four decades.[139]

SOVIET ADVANCES IN WEAPONRY

The impetus to fully develop and implement the NIKE system came from increased international tensions coupled with improvements in Soviet weaponry. In October 1947, the Soviets introduced the Tu-4 "Bull" longer range bomber that had been developed by copying the American B-29 bomber.[140] The B-29 carried the atomic payloads for the attacks on Hiroshima and Nagasaki. Two years later, the Soviets successfully tested an atomic bomb and changed prior American military assumptions. First, the United States could no longer deter future conflict as the sole wielder of atomic power. Second, the test shattered perceptions that the Soviets were technologically inferior and greatly lagged behind American innovations. In 1953, the Soviets successfully tested a hydrogen bomb ten months after an American test and confirmed their capability and commitment to an arms race.[141] With bombers and nuclear bombs, the Soviets could launch a squadron from Siberia, fly over the North Pole, and attack targets in the United States. Land-based defenses were necessary to engage this type of attack, especially if the newly formed Air Force could not eliminate it in the air.

NIKE AJAX

Although conceived during World War II, development of the NIKE system was delayed due to reduced funding immediately after the war. Renewed attention to the NIKE program corresponded with increased tensions between the United States and Soviets, advances in Soviet weaponry, and finally, the start of the Korean Conflict in June 1950. Hostilities between North and South Korea threatened to draw the United States and the allied Chinese and Soviets into another world war. Even though a global conflict did not spread from the Korean peninsula, United States military policy began to focus on defensive preparations.[142]

In 1950, the Army reorganized defensive artillery units into the Army Anti-Aircraft Command (ARAACOM). That same year, improvements were made in the booster rocket and guidance systems leading to the successful test firing in November 1951. The first generation of NIKE missiles, known as Ajax, were twelve inches in diameter, twenty-one feet long, weighed over 2,455 pounds, and operated remarkably similar to the system outlined by Jacob Schaefer's 1944 memorandum.[143]

Ajax missiles were guided by a series of three radars. Incoming enemy aircraft were identified by long-range radar known as LOPAR for Low-Power Acquisition Radar. The LOPAR identification was transferred to a Target Tracking Radar (TTR) to determine the aircraft's azimuth, elevation, and range. Tracking information was then electronically sent to a computer which relayed guidance information to Missile Tracking Radar (MTR) to control the missile's flight. When launched, Ajax could travel at 2.3 times the speed of sound and obtain altitudes up to 70,000 feet. Upon arriving at the predicted intercept point, computers transmitted a burst signal that detonated three TNT warheads located in the nose, middle, and tail of the missile (Figures 2.89 and 2.90). Between 1954 and 1958, the Army deployed nearly 200 NIKE Ajax batteries around the nation's key urban, military, and industrial locations.[144] In the metropolitan New York area, nineteen batteries were established including a dual firing battery at Sandy Hook.

NIKE HERCULES

Four months after the successful test of NIKE Ajax at White Sands Proving Ground, the Bureau of Ordnance recommended studying the feasibility of equipping the missile with a nuclear warhead. In their study of Army and Air Force missile defense programs, John C. Lonnquest and David F. Winkler cite that a major limitation of the Ajax system was, "...the inability to discern individual bombers within a densely-packed flying formation."[145] For example, if two planes were flying close together, the radar would detect them as one object and guide the missile to hit the center of that object. At best, the missile would not score a direct hit and at worst, miss both targets completely. One way to correct this potential shortcoming would be to arm the missile with a nuclear warhead. Upon detonation, the nuclear warhead would create a larger and more powerful explosion that could destroy planes without a direct hit.

Ajax designers recommended two options for adding a nuclear warhead to the missile. First, a smaller warhead could be reconfigured and adapted for use on the Ajax. The second option involved using a larger warhead with more destructive power and incorporating it into a newly designed, larger missile. The Army selected the second option on condition that the new missile system would use the same facilities already being designed and constructed for the Ajax. In July 1953, the Army authorized the development of the second generation NIKE missile called Hercules. In addition to the larger warhead capacity, Hercules would feature a longer range and more stable fuel mixture than its predecessor.[146]

Three years after authorization, a Hercules missile successfully destroyed a drone aircraft at White Sands Proving Ground. Tests continued into 1957 using a solid fuel mixture that would replace the volatile liquid mixture of jet fuel and nitric acid used in Ajax.[147] Forty-one feet long and thirty one and half inches in diameter, Hercules' increased size accommodated not only a larger warhead, but four booster rockets compared to a single rocket on Ajax. The added thrust increased the range of Hercules up to three times greater than Ajax and obtained altitudes up to 150,000 feet.[148]

The new flight parameters of Hercules made it theoretically possible to engage bombers at higher altitudes and at greater distance but only if improvements were made to the NIKE radar system. In order to identify targets at a greater distance, Hercules sites added High-Powered Acquisition Radar or HIPAR. In June 1958, Hercules missiles began to be deployed at converted NIKE Ajax sites near New York City, Philadelphia, and Chicago. Over the next six years, 110 Ajax sites were converted and 35 sites were newly constructed for Hercules. The longer range of Hercules resulted in fewer sites than had been implemented for Ajax.[149]

THE NIKE SITES AT SANDY HOOK

The NIKE installation at Sandy Hook was one of nineteen missile sites that comprised the New York Defense Area. The defense area included the five boroughs of New York City and two counties to the north, the western half of Long Island, and the northeastern section of New Jersey. Regardless of a New York or New Jersey location, all of the NIKE sites were designated "NY" followed by a number to indicate their association with the defense area.[150]

The Department of Defense announced plans to construct the NIKE site at Sandy Hook, designated NY-56, in December 1953. With coastal defenses redirected away from naval threats to instead intercepting aircraft, proximity and range-finding views to important waterways were no longer important factors in selecting locations for NIKE sites. The selecting factor changed to adequate distance and a lack of obstructions between proposed NIKE radar and missile locations so radar and launch equipment could properly operate in tandem.

At Sandy Hook and across the country, NIKE installations were comprised of an Integrated Fire Control (IFC) or radar site and a launch site. The IFC contained the acquisition and tracking radar and was separated from the launch site by a minimum of 3,000 feet. More commonly, sites were separated by over a mile as was the case at Sandy Hook. Regardless of the exact distance, the two locations had to be within visual sight of each other so radar could lock onto a firing missile.[151] Buildings, tall vegetation, and utility poles are examples of objects that could interfere with radar transmissions (Figures 2.91 and 2.92).

The IFC and launch sites at Sandy Hook were located south of Fort Hancock and the temporary, World War II-expansion needed to accommodate increased personnel. The IFC was located roughly in the middle of the peninsula, in the largely undeveloped area southeast of the Camp Low barracks built during World War II. The launch site was located east of Batteries Kingman and Mills, across Hartshorne Drive, and immediately north of a small, existing pond. A 1944 Army Corps of Engineers map of Sandy Hook recorded a group of eight warehouses, labeled T-10 through T-17, that were in the general vicinity of the proposed launch site. The warehouses were constructed by Western Electric to shelter radar antenna during tests by the Army Signal Corps (Figure 2.93).

Sandy Hook's NIKE launch site represents one of the few dual battery installations constructed during the Cold War era. The Sandy Hook launch site contained four underground magazines that delivered missiles by an elevator to a row of launchers on the surface. The two magazines on the east side of the launch area formed one firing battery and the two on the west side formed the other. The IFC site to the north contained two control areas with separate radar systems for each firing battery. The eastern control area, designated #1, provided radar for the eastern firing battery while the western control area, designated #2, was assigned to the western firing battery.[152]

Integrated Fire Control (IFC) or Radar Site

During the previous generations of coastal defenses at Sandy Hook, the NIKE IFC site remained largely undeveloped. The Army's central railroad line bisected the future IFC location and during World War II, several temporary structures associated with Camp Low bordered either side of the tracks. A site plan for the

IFC, issued March 22, 1954, recorded six concrete foundations in the northern portion of the proposed site. None of the foundations were labeled with building designations and the majority appear small enough to be outbuildings or auxiliary structures. In addition, the site plan showed vegetation cover occupying more than half of the proposed area and contained the labels "brush and trees up to 35' high" (Figure 2.94).

The proposed IFC site was roughly triangular in shape with its longest perimeter running from west to east. The western point, accessible from Hartshorne Drive, contained Control Area #2. The eastern point contained Control Area #1 and was accessible from Atlantic Drive. The boundaries of the site converged at a northern point that contained the Ready Barracks and were accessible from Sheldon Road.[153]

For both control areas, the three types of radar shared the same relative position with the Acquisition Radar in the center flanked by the MTR to the west and TTR to the east. Each area also featured a long, rectangular, concrete pad located north of the Acquisition Radar. The pad was constructed for three trailers, stacked front to back, that held equipment and personnel for battery control, radar control, and spare computer and electronics parts. The wheels and undercarriage of each trailer were removed and the trailers set on wooden blocks on top of the concrete pad.[154]

The battery control trailer was immediately north of the Acquisition Radar and contained controls for the radar as well as a missile guidance computer. Furthest north on the pad was the radar control trailer that held computers and equipment for the TTR and MTR. In between the two was a maintenance and spare parts trailer (Figure 2.95).[155]

The TTR and MTR had to work in concert to predict an intercept point and direct the missile to that point. To calibrate both radars, a sixty-foot tall bore sighting mast, or collimation test mast, was erected at the northern end of the site near the Ready Barracks. A separate mast was installed for each control area and the site plan called out a ten degree unobstructed cone from the center of the TTR and MTR to the bore mast. The plan further explained that the site's contractor would be responsible for clearing the unobstructed visual cone, much of which passed through existing vegetation up to thirty-five feet high (Figure 2.96).

A four foot-wide concrete walk was proposed from each control area to its respective mast, however, on the site plan, the walk was labeled N.I.C.--an abbreviation for "not-in-contract." Another drawing showing the IFC site plan displayed a final revision date of January 22, 1960, and was annotated as "record work as built." Although the drawing recorded other changes to the site, for example, dry wells near both sets of trailers, the concrete walks to the masts were labeled "proposed walk" indicating they had yet to be installed (Figure 2.97).

Additional changes to the site between the beginning of construction in 1954 and the "record work as built" designation in 1960 include perimeter fencing, walks, and construction of a basketball court. Eight months after the site plan was issued, a revision was made that "clarified the fence and firebreak." The revised annotations listed the fence as type FE-6—a designation for chain link fence with a single extension arm supporting continuous strands of barbed wire. Top of fence elevations were added near the radar installations and accompanied by a section illustrating that the existing ground should be excavated prior to setting the fence posts. The excavation was necessary to maintain a consistent fence elevation and to not interfere with the transmission of the radar (Figure 2.98). The final notes added for the fence installation specify a thirty foot wide firebreak inside the perimeter fence. The combination of the firebreak and clearing for the boring masts resulted in a triangular area in the center of the site where existing, native vegetation remained undisturbed (Figure 2.99).

Although the walks to the boring masts were not installed, a concrete walk was constructed from each control area to the Ready Barracks between October 1955 and January 1960. Electrical conduit was buried alongside the walks and extended around the walkways at the barracks. A total of twelve light fixtures were added with five being located around the barracks, four located along the walk from Control Area #1, and three located along the walk from Control Area #2 (Figure 2.100).

During this same time period, a basketball court was added south of the Ready Barracks. Since the IFC was physically distant from the major facilities and recreation opportunities at Fort Hancock, the court served as a small recreation amenity when personnel staffed the site and was a common feature at NIKE installations across the country (Figures 2.101 and 2.102).[156]

Sandy Hook's NIKE site received the upgrade from the Ajax to the larger Hercules missile and necessary modifications were made at both the IFC and launch areas. Additionally, the IFC was part of a program called "Improved Hercules" that added more sophisticated radar designed to counter electronic interference from enemy aircraft.[157]

Site plans dated September 4, 1962, show the installation of a High-Powered Acquisition Radar or HIPAR system designed to detect incoming aircraft at a greater distance. A HIPAR Tower to mount the radar and a HIPAR Building for equipment and controls are shown north of Control Area #2 (Figure 2.103). West of the HIPAR Building, new Target Tracking and Target Ranging radars both components of the "Improved Hercules" system—are shown. A new Target

Tracking Radar is also shown at Control Area #1. Battery control and radar control trailers are still shown on the 1962 plan, however, at both control areas the maintenance and spare parts trailer has been removed and replaced with a building that served the same function labeled "Interconnecting Corridor" (Figure 2.104).

Launch Site

The Army originally intended for NIKE missiles to be stored above ground and estimated 119 acres were needed for a combined IFC and launch site. Since NIKE sites were going to defend populated urban, military, and industrial areas, available space was a constraining factor. To reduce the footprint of the launch site, designs for underground magazines were prepared that resulted in an approximate forty acre-requirement for the IFC and launch sites. On October 28, 1953, ARAACOM directed that the underground magazine design would be used in most instances.[158]

The launch site at Sandy Hook was roughly T-shaped in plan. The long leg of the "T" began at Hartshorne Drive and proceeded east toward the Atlantic Ocean where it divided into shorter northern and southern sections. The western portion of the "T" contained the Ready Barracks and the southern section contained the Missile Maintenance Area. The northern section contained the underground missile magazines and launching racks and all three areas were surrounding by a perimeter fence (Figure 2.105).

Due to groundwater very close to the surface throughout the peninsula, the magazines and launching racks were located in an area with existing grades between elevations of sixteen and twenty feet. Generally higher than other areas on the peninsula, this location, with the addition of fill material, would permit the underground magazine design. The proposed elevation for the launchers was twenty-feet and they were contained within a 460 by 490-foot engineered plateau at a similar elevation (Figure 2.106).

As mentioned previously, a group of eight existing structures used for radar testing during the late 1930s were located near the proposed launch site. On a site plan issued March 22, 1954, buildings T-14 through T-17 were shown and labeled as "two story frame warehouse" with additional annotations indicating they are unoccupied. T-16 and T-17 were located within the proposed construction area and are labeled to be removed and salvaged. The same site plan includes future provisions for two more magazines beyond the four planned for construction. Although never constructed, planning for the future magazines positioned the northern location of the perimeter fence away from any conflict and created secured, undeveloped space at the northern end of the launch site. Included with the layout of the perimeter fence were annotations labeling firebreaks near the missile magazines and Missile Maintenance Area. North of the missile magazines, labels identify a twenty foot firebreak outside of the fence. South of the Missile Maintenance Area, labels identify a fifty foot firebreak with twenty feet occurring outside the fence and thirty feet inside. It is unclear if the thirty-foot interior firebreak continued around the entire fence or was only intended for the Missile Maintenance Area (Figure 2.107).

A week after the site plan was issued, revisions were made south of the magazines and launchers for the area that included an acid storage shed, acid fueling station, J.P. (a type of jet fuel) fueling station, concrete walkway, earth mounds, and appurtenant gravel pavements and grading. These facilities were needed for the missile's liquid fuel mixture of jet fuel and nitric acid. In addition, to protect the site from an accidental detonation after a missile was armed with its three warheads, a crescent-shaped earth mound was shown near the south perimeter of the site wrapping around the east, south, and west sides of the Warhead Building and acid fueling station. North of the Warhead Building, another earth mound paralleled the building's north facade and almost connected to the curved ends of the southern mound. The southern mound was labeled "earth mound, seeded slopes, top elevation of mound = 21.00, slopes 3 in 1." The northern mound had the same information listed in two separate annotations (Figure 2.108).

Construction was completed on the launch site in the spring of 1955, however, building activities would resume three years later to convert the site from the Ajax to the larger Hercules missile.[150] The storage racks, launcher rails, and elevators required modifications to accommodate Hercules. In addition, security improvements were imperative before nuclear warheads would be stored at the launch site. Revision dates on historic drawings for the Hercules conversion indicate changes were made through 1960. On February 23, 1961, a site plan drawing was labeled "record work as built" indicating construction had finished and final revisions were made to the original drawing to show completed conditions (Figure 2.109).

To accommodate the larger missiles, a concrete walk in the Missile Maintenance Area was widened from six to twelve feet. In both the 1954 and 1958 drawings, the walk is labeled for use by a dolly that would transport missiles from the Testing and Assembly Building to the Warhead Building (Figure 2.110). Security improvements for the launch site included additional fencing, new floodlight fixtures, and construction of a kennel for guard dogs. The perimeter fence remained from the 1954 plan and a new "inner security fence" was added around the magazine section of the launch site.

A 1958 electrical plan for the launch site showed a new wiring diagram for a "protective lighting system" around the magazine area. Eight light fixtures were shown in plan and an accompanying detail indicates they were twelve foot-tall wood poles mounted with 1,500 watt wide-beam floodlights (Figure 2.111). The floodlights would create a beam of light in the direction that the fixture was mounted. In order to communicate the desired mounting direction, the plan shows a cone, representing the beam, emanating from a circle that represents the pole. Each of the eight fixtures are shown with their beams paralleling the path of the inner security fence and not faced towards the launchers. Based on this plan, the lights were not intended to facilitate night operation but to illuminate the inner security fence and facilitate better security surveillance (Figure 2.112).

In addition to the inner fence and floodlights, a kennel was added to the Sandy Hook site to house guard dogs patrolling the area between the inner and outer fences (Figure 2.113). The kennels, along with the dual fences, were identifiable features of converted and newly installed NIKE Hercules sites throughout the country (Figure 2.114).[160] At Sandy Hook, the kennel was originally designed to be constructed south of the Missile Maintenance Area. In a revision dated August 1958, the kennel was relocated to the northwest corner of magazine area, arguably for closer proximity to the inner fence and to utilize space intended for future magazine expansion that was never developed (Figure 2.115).

ICBMS, NIKE ZEUS, AND A NEW DEFENSE PHILOSOPHY

During the 1950s, the United States and Soviet Union escalated their arms race and began developing missiles that would travel beyond the Earth's atmosphere and be able to strike targets half-way around the world. Known as intercontinental ballistic missiles or ICBMs, this new offensive technology shifted the threat away from the long range bombers that the NIKE system was intended to stop. The Soviet Union announced they had an operational ICBM in 1957 and following the launch of Sputnik that same year, the United States accelerated their program and had the Atlas ICBM operational in 1959.[161]

In response to this new offensive weaponry, the Secretary of Defense assigned the Army with development of an anti-missile, missile system called Zeus that utilized existing NIKE infrastructure in 1958.[162] For the next three years funds were allocated for research and development, but not for implementation at existing NIKE sites. Opposition mounted against the Zeus system as the scientific community argued existing radar systems lacked the sophistication to discern between an ICBM and debris jettisoned from its booster rockets. Furthermore, arguments against the concept of an anti-missile, missile system contended it could be defeated by overwhelming the system with a massive convoy of decoy missiles with only one missile being armed with a nuclear warhead. Funding for Zeus was cancelled in 1963, however, debate, research, and development on an anti-ballistic missile system continued throughout the 1960s.[163]

Personnel cuts began at NIKE sites in 1967 as a result of the Zeus system's cancellation and Hercules being tactically ineffective against ICBMs. The cuts were hastened by escalating war efforts in Vietnam and in 1968, the first NIKE sites were deactivated.[164] The perpetuating contest of new offensive weaponry followed by improved defensive capabilities that resulted in over a century of coastal defense innovations at Sandy Hook, ended with the doctrine of mutually assured destruction. Defense philosophy shifted from costly artillery and infrastructure to guaranteeing that the United States and the Soviet Union had the same apocalyptic nuclear capabilities. This mutual assurance prevailed as the only way to prevent nuclear war. On February 4, 1974, Secretary of Defense James Schlesinger announced plans to close forty-eight NIKE installations across the country including the Sandy Hook site. In the following months, the Army removed missiles and equipment from Sandy Hook and formally deactivated the site in a ceremony held on August 15, 1974.[165]

BASE CONSOLIDATION AND TRANSFER TO THE NATIONAL PARK SERVICE

With the NIKE system's defenses eclipsed by the threat of ICBMs and an expanding war in Vietnam, priorities were adjusted for federal defense spending. In January 1967, the Department of Defense announced plans for thirty-three military base closings and consolidations including Fort Hancock.[166] Prior to this announcement, new stakeholders emerged on the Sandy Hook peninsula and began the transformation of a strategic military installation into a premier recreation destination.

Beginning in 1962, New Jersey State Parks purchased twelve acres at the southern end of the peninsula for developing beach access and fishing. Between the highway bridge that entered Sandy Hook and Spermaceti Cove, the State established a parking area and a comfort station for recreational fishing. North of this narrow strip, the State leased 460 acres from the Department of Defense that extended to the southern boundary of the NIKE launch site. In this area, New Jersey State Parks developed two beach sites with bathhouses and parking facilities. The two beach sites and fishing areas to the south combined to provide parking for approximately 3,500 vehicles (Figures 2.116 and 2.117). Two years later, the State leased an additional 285 acres that extended west from Hartshorne Drive—the main north-south vehicular route—to include land along Horseshoe Cove and Skeleton Hill Island (Figure 2.118).[167]

Already established as a popular recreation site, the Fort Hancock closure announcement brought together Monmouth County and New Jersey state officials and representatives from the Departments of Defense and the Interior to develop and analyze alternatives for Sandy Hook. Chief among their concerns was maintaining the peninsula for public recreation, however, other competing proposals included a new Coast Guard airbase, Army and Coast Guard housing, and recreational facilities for military personnel.[168]

One of the main alternatives generated by this group was to designate Sandy Hook as a National Seashore under the management of the National Park Service. Beginning in 1961, a lack of public access to undeveloped seashore areas led to the creation of parks at Cape Cod, Fire Island, and Assateague Island. In proposing a National Seashore at Sandy Hook, the group proposed that "the peninsula could provide a significant and much needed recreational unit within the heart of the nation's most densely populated region."[169]

With Fort Hancock slated to close, the alternatives studied for Sandy Hook did not lead to an individual park unit, but incorporated Sandy Hook with sections of Brooklyn, Queens, and Staten Island into a new park. On October 27, 1972, President Richard Nixon signed legislation enabling the creation of the Gateway National Recreation Area recognizing the cultural and natural resources and recreation opportunities along lower New York Harbor. On August 15, 1974, the Army held a ceremony to deactivate Fort Hancock's NIKE site and recognize the service of the Army Air Defense personnel. The ceremony dedicated Guardian Park located south of the Fort Hancock Parade Ground. The park's design featured a cruciform concrete walkway oriented in a north-south and east-west direction. Four commemorative items were placed at the end of each walkway and the intersection was marked by the second stage of a NIKE Hercules missile. A flagpole was erected at the north and a NIKE Ajax missile at the south walkway. A granite monument commemorating soldiers killed during a NIKE explosion in Middletown, New Jersey was placed on the west. Opposite the monument, a 75mm park howitzer was sited to commemorate traditional coastal artillery. Four months later, on December 31, 1974, Fort Hancock was officially deactivated and the next day, transferred to the National Park Service.[170]

LANDSCAPE SUMMARY - 1974

Upon transfer to the National Park Service, development at Sandy Hook was concentrated at the northern and southern ends with a largely undeveloped middle section. The greatest density of development was focused around the historic structures lining Fort Hancock's Parade Ground and Athletic Field. The temporary structures and cantonment areas constructed during World War II were removed and resulted in open areas that had formerly been dense arrangements of wooden buildings and tents. The U. S. Coast Guard established a more formal presence on the northern end of the peninsula and constructed several new buildings. The Coast Guard also assumed operation of the wharf on Sandy Hook Bay.

In the middle section of the peninsula, the Army had constructed and abandoned the NIKE IFC site with radar systems to detect enemy planes and guide surface-to-air missiles. Approximately one mile south, the NIKE launch site was constructed with underground magazines and launchers for the missiles. South of the NIKE launch site, New Jersey State Parks leased 745 acres that comprised a majority of the peninsula's southern half. The State Parks' lease extended to a twelve-acre parcel they owned at the bridge between Sandy Hook and the Town of Highlands. In the two areas, the State Parks developed several parking lots, bathhouses, and dedicated fishing access (Drawing 2.7).

Currents and tides continued to alter the Sandy Hook shoreline and resulted in the formation of the North Pond northeast of Nine Gun Battery. The pond formed in a low-lying area as new sand deposits advanced the shoreline further north and east from the historic battery. On the west side of the peninsula, the northern shoreline of the point at Horseshoe Cove retreated and Sandy Hook Bay crept closer to Battery Arrowsmith's concrete walls (Drawing 2.7).

The largest area of undisturbed, woody vegetation was located south of Battery Gunnison and the Mortar Battery and north of the NIKE IFC site. Between the NIKE ICF and launch sites, the Army had maintained vegetation at a low height to allow unobstructed radar signals between the Missile Tracking Radar, control vans, and individual missiles. With the NIKE facility deactivated in 1971 and regular maintenance discontinued, the quantity and density of vegetation between the two NIKE locations increased (Drawing 2.8).

All of the large caliber and rapid fire gun batteries were disarmed after World War II, and in the roughly thirty years from between the conclusion of the war and the transfer of Sandy Hook to the National Park Service, none of the structures were demolished. The batteries remained unattended with little or no maintenance attention. As a result, large woody vegetation encroached on the concrete structures and engineered earthworks. New vegetation growth can be seen at batteries Urmston, Morris, Engle, Peck, Potter, Granger, Nine Gun Battery, and the Mortar Battery (Drawing 2.8). In contrast, batteries Gunnison, Kingman, and Mills, retained earthworks primarily free of large, woody vegetation (Drawing 2.8).

Vegetation around the perimeters and within the two NIKE sites was highly managed for radar operation and security. Firebreaks were maintained along the fences at both sites and as a result, a clear separation can be seen between vegetation masses and fence lines. At the NIKE IFC site, a roughly triangular mass of vegetation existed within the site between the radar and ready barrack locations. Since this area did not interfere with radar operation or security, it was left unaltered during the initial construction and subsequent use of the site (Drawing 2.8).

During previous eras, Sandy Hook was accessible by ship, train, and automobile with trains and automobiles having independent circulation networks across the peninsula. When transferred to the National Park Service in 1975, automobile circulation dominated the landscape. After World War II, the majority of railroad ties and tracks were removed and the former rail beds converted to unpaved roads or trails. Two large parking lots were installed on the State Park's leased land to accommodate visitors traveling by car to the beaches. In addition to these two lots, smaller lots were constructed to the south near the bridge to Highlands. All of the State Park lots combined to provide approximately 3,500 spaces (Drawing 2.7).

Similar to the condition of former railroad beds, circulation features from World War II-era cantonments remained as unpaved roads or trails. Although the wooden structures and tents were removed, networks of unpaved roads and trails can be seen west of Battery Granger and south of the Mortar Battery where temporary facilities were constructed. The roads and open area for the tent city south of the Mortar Battery was converted into trailer park for the Coast Guard. The former cantonment west of Nine Gun Battery was designated a camping area for vacationing military personnel (Drawing 2.8).

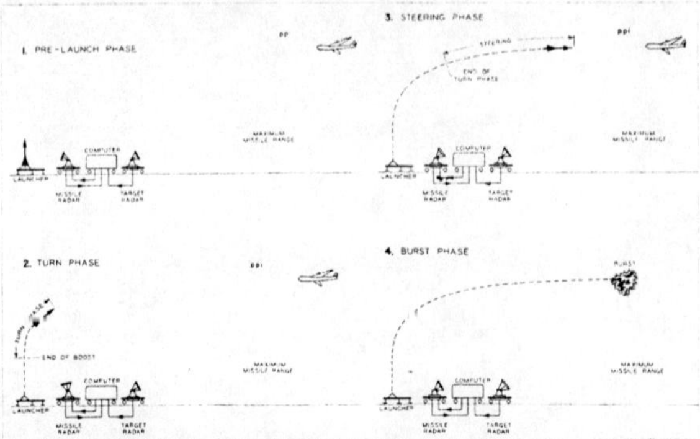

Figure 2.89. NIKE Ajax missile flight diagram. Ajax missiles were guided by a series of three radars. Incoming enemy aircraft were identified by acquisition radar and then transferred to Target Tracking Radar (TTR) to determine the aircraft's elevation and range. Based on tracking information, missile guidance was calculated and sent to Missile Tracking Radar (MTR) to control the missile's flight. Upon arriving at the predicted intercept point, computers transmitted a burst signal to detonate the missile (Mary T. Cagle, *Historical Monograph: Development, Production, and Deployment of the NIKE Ajax Guided Missile System 1945–1959*, United States Department of Defense, Army Ordnance Missile Command, June 1959).

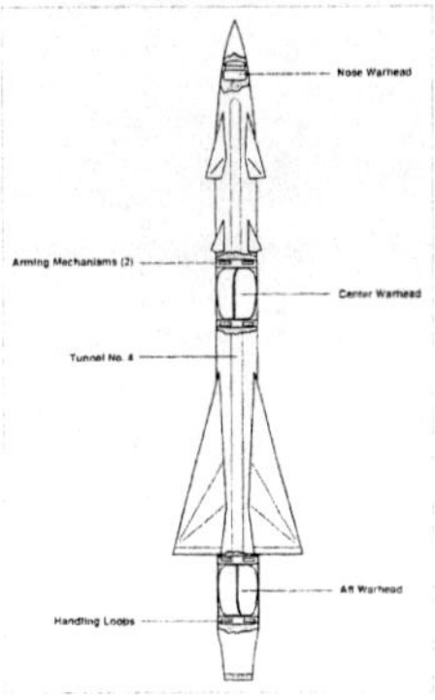

Figure 2.90. Warhead location in NIKE Ajax missile. Three TNT warheads were located in the nose, middle, and tail of an Ajax missile and were detonated by a radio-transmitted signal (John C. Lonnquest and David F. Winkler, *To Defend and Deter: The Legacy of the United States Cold War Missile Program*, United States Department of Defense, Army Construction Engineering Research Laboratories, November 1996).

Figure 2.91. "NIKE" Project, Topographical Plan Between Control and Launching Areas, 1954. At Sandy Hook, the NIKE radar and launch sites were separated by over a mile but needed unobstructed radar signals to transmit between the Missile Tracking Radar, control vans, and individual missiles. This plan indicates vegetation clearing in two wedge-shaped areas to the missile launchers and two linear corridors to the control vans (highlighted in red) originating from the radar site, located off the plan to the north (GATE 11040d and Olmsted Center).

Figure 2.92. "NIKE" Project, Profile Between Control and Launch Area, 1954. Buildings, tall vegetation, and utility poles are examples of objects that could interfere with radar transmissions in a vertical, as well as a horizontal plane. The Army Corps prepared these profiles to show the unobstructed vertical area needed between Sandy Hook's radar and launch sites. The "additive item" annotation indicates that removing interfering vegetation and objects may have been part of a contractor's bid and proposed work or completed by Army personnel (GATE 11040e).

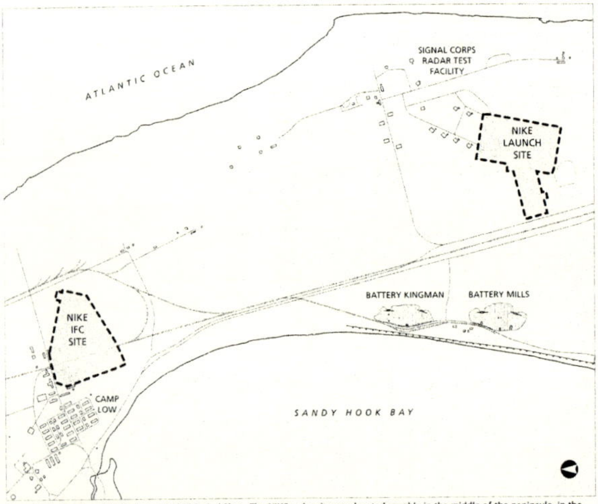

Figure 2.93. Overlay of NIKE sites and 1945 Period Plan. The NIKE radar site was located roughly in the middle of the peninsula, in the largely undeveloped area southeast of the Camp Low barracks built during World War II. The launch site was located east of Batteries Kingman and Mills, across Hartshorne Drive, and in the vicinity of eight warehouses constructed for radar tests by the Army Signal Corps (Olmsted Center, 2010).

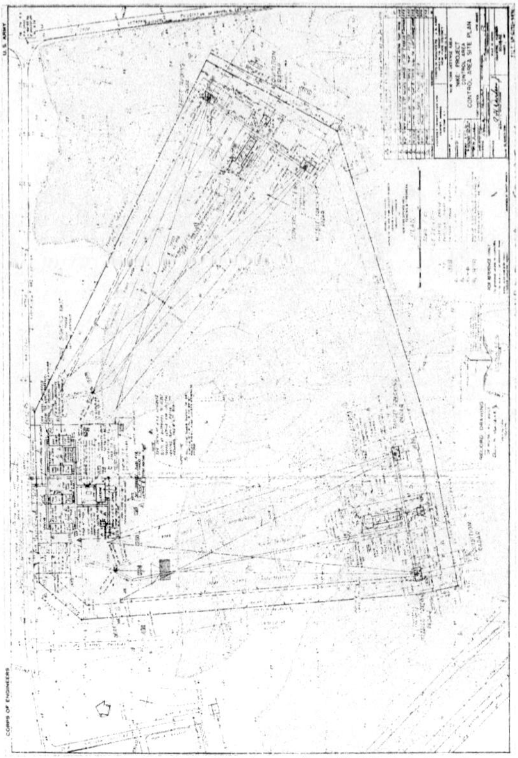

Figure 2.94. "NIKE" Project, Control Area Site Plan, 1954. In the proposed layout of the NIKE radar site, six concrete foundations (shaded gray) lack building descriptions and appear small enough to be outbuildings or auxiliary structures. The plan also shows vegetation cover (shaded green) occupying more than half of the proposed area and labeled "brush and trees up to 35' high" (GATE 11052 and Olmsted Center).

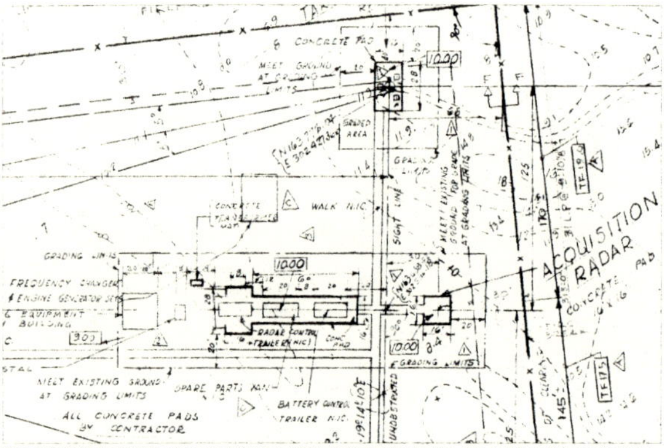

Figure 2.95. Detail of acquisition radar and control trailers, NIKE Project, Control Area Site Plan, 1954. At both control areas, two trailers located north of the acquisition radar contained computers and equipment for radar and missile guidance. In between the two trailers was a third used for maintenance and storing spare parts (GATE 11052).

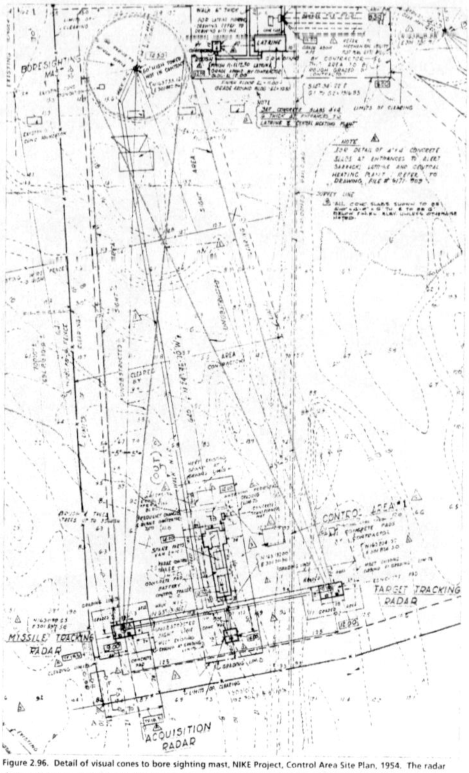

Figure 2.96. Detail of visual cones to bore sighting mast, NIKE Project, Control Area Site Plan, 1954. The radar site's contractor was responsible for clearing an unobstructed visual cone (highlighted in red) to the bore sighting mast in order to calibrate the TTR and MTR radars. The cone passes through an area of existing vegetation up to thirty-five feet high that was removed (GATE 11052 and Olmsted Center).

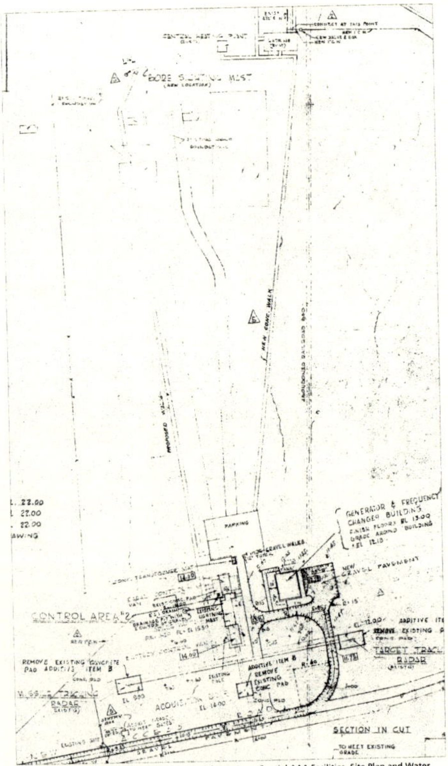

Figure 2.97. Detail of proposed walk to bore sighting mast, Special AAA Facilities, Site Plan and Water Line, 1955. Although this drawing was updated to record "as built" conditions in 1960, the concrete walks to the bore sighting masts are still labeled "proposed walk" and lack an indication that they were completed (GATE 11053).

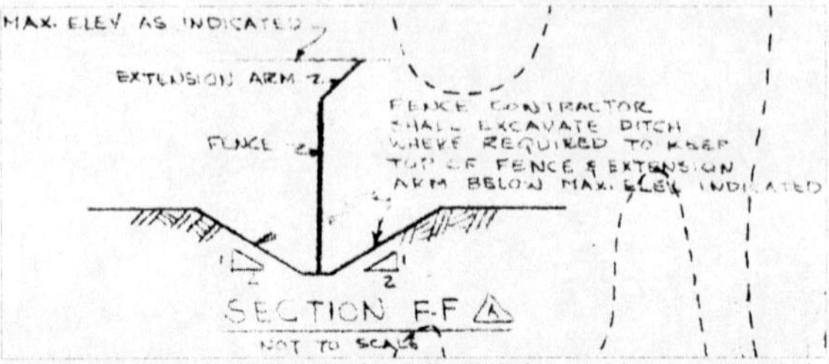

Figure 2.98. Section of perimeter fence, NIKE Project, Control Area Site Plan, 1954. The fence section indicates that the existing ground should be excavated in order to maintain a consistent top of fence elevation and to avoid interference with the transmission of the radar (GATE 11052).

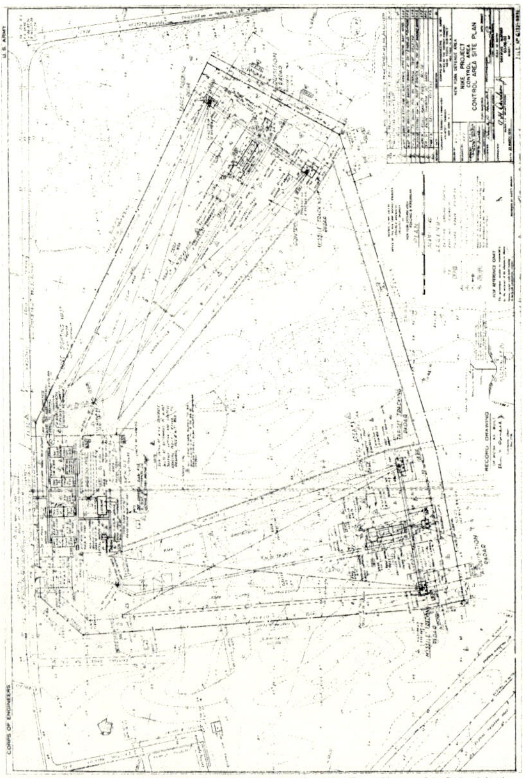

Figure 2.99. Limit of vegetation clearing, NIKE Project, Control Area Site Plan, 1954. The combination of the firebreak for the perimeter fence and clearing for the boring masts results in a triangular area (highlighted in red) in the center of the site where existing, native vegetation remained undisturbed (GATE 11052 and Olmsted Center).

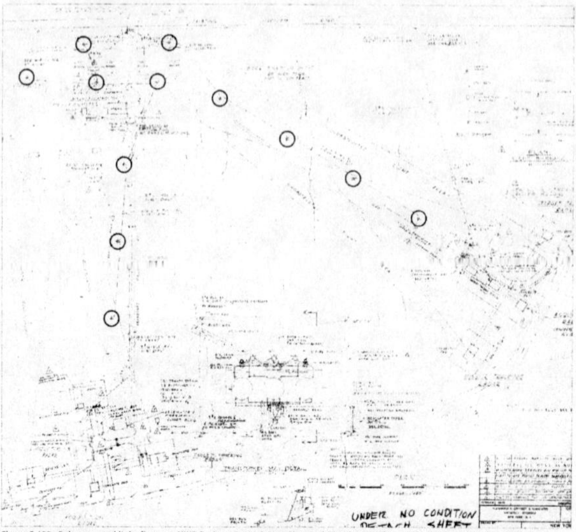

Figure 2.100. Pole-mounted light fixtures, NIKE Project, Control Area Electrical Distribution Plan, 1954. Between October 1955 and January 1960, electrical conduit was buried alongside pedestrian walkways in the radar site and a total of twelve light fixtures (circled) were added (GATE 11046 and Olmsted Center).

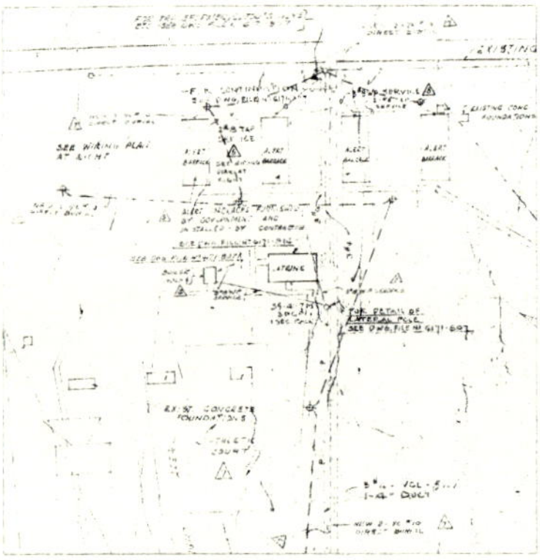

Figure 2.101. Detail of basketball court, NIKE Project, Control Area Electrical Distribution Plan, 1954. South of the Ready Barracks, a basketball court was added between October 1955 and January 1960 (GATE 11046).

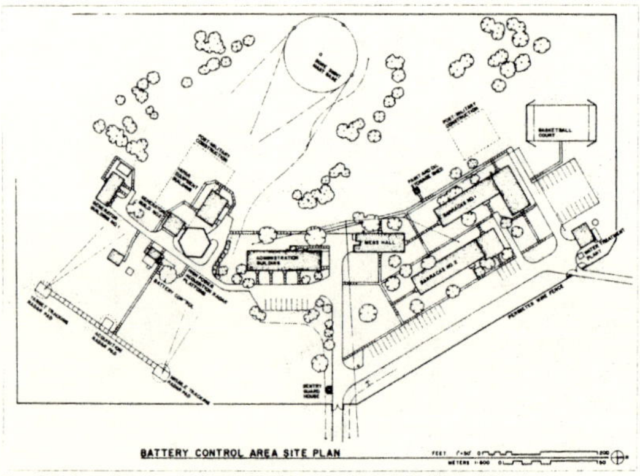

Figure 2.102. Battery Control Area Site Plan, NIKE Missile Base SL-40, Monroe County, Illinois. NIKE installations across the country frequently contained basketball courts as a recreational amenity for activated personnel (Historic American Engineering Record, IL - 117).

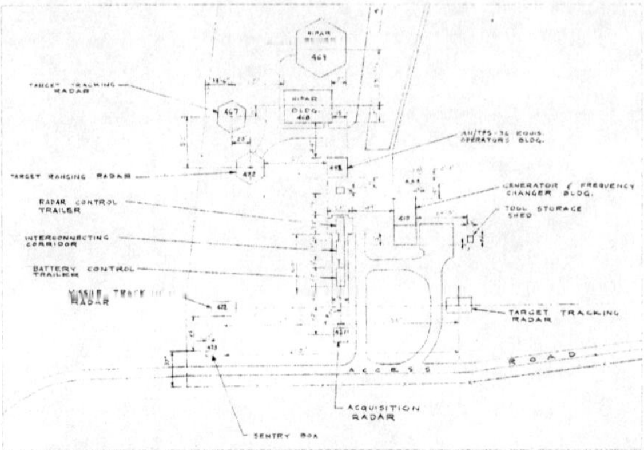

Figure 2.103. Detail of HIPAR radar installations, Site Plan, Control Area, Fort Hancock, 1962. North of Control Area #2, a High-Powered Acquisition Radar or HIPAR tower and a HIPAR Building for equipment and controls were installed to detect incoming aircraft at a greater distance and support the longer-range Hercules missile. As part of the "Improved Hercules" system, new Target Tracking and Target Ranging radars were also added to counter electronic interference from enemy aircraft (GATE 11057).

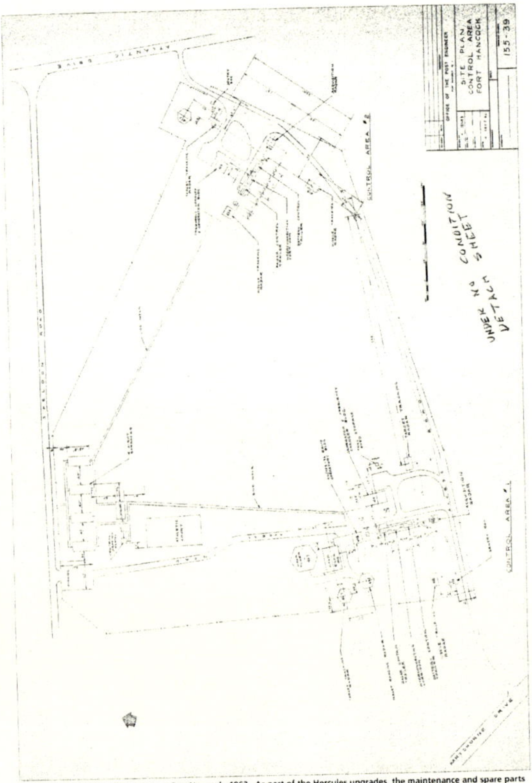

Figure 2.104. Site Plan, Control Area, Fort Hancock, 1962. As part of the Hercules upgrades, the maintenance and spare parts trailer was removed and replaced with a building that served the same function labeled "Interconnecting Corridor" (GATE 11057).

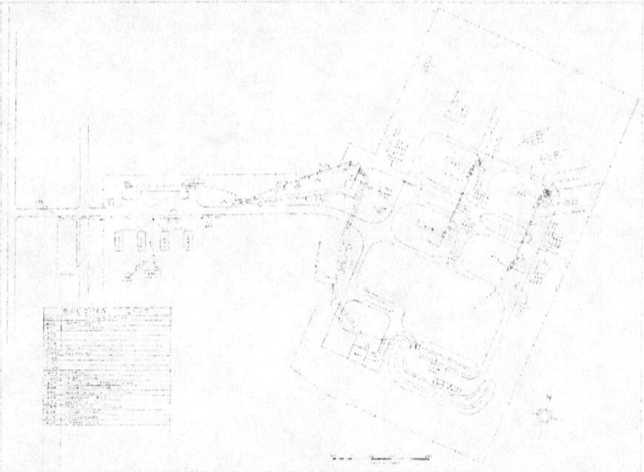

Figure 2.105. Overall site configuration of NIKE launch site, 1962. The launch site at Sandy Hook was roughly T-shaped in plan. The western portion of the "T" contained the alert barracks and the southern section contained the missile maintenance area. The northern section contained the underground missile magazines and launching racks and all three areas were surrounding by a perimeter fence (GATE 11061).

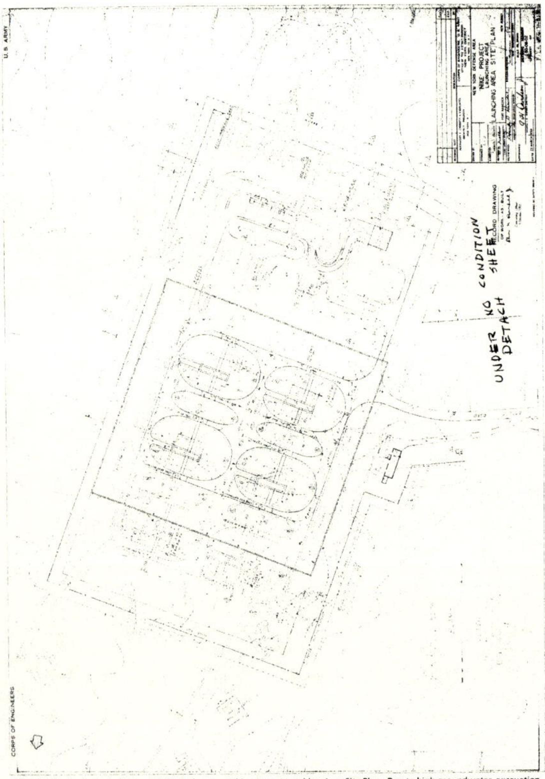

Figure 2.106. Engineered plateau, "NIKE" Project, Launching Area, Launching Area Site Plan. Due to high groundwater, excavation for the missile magazines was minimized by a proposed engineered plateau (highlighted in red) that was built above and around the reinforced concrete structure (GATE 11048 and Olmsted Center).

Figure 2.107. Detail of perimeter fence and firebreak, "NIKE" Project, Launching Area, Launching Area Site Plan. The layout of the perimeter fence was shifted north to accommodate plans for two future magazines north of the intended four magazines. Included with the fence layout are annotations labeling a twenty foot firebreak outside of the fence line (GATE 11048).

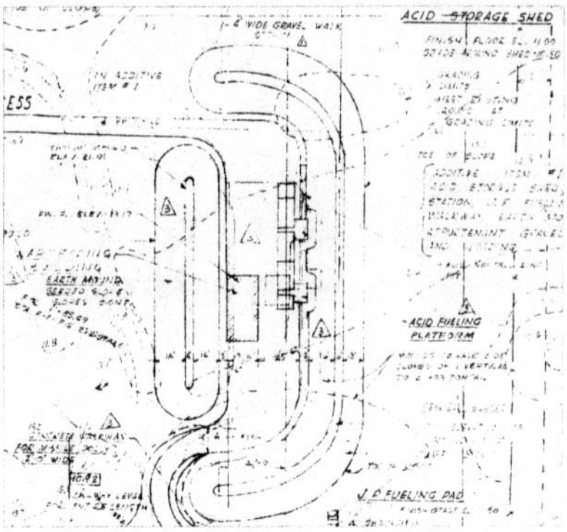

Figure 2.108. Detail of earth mounds in Missile Maintenance Area, "NIKE" Project, Launching Area, Launching Area Site Plan. To protect the site from an accidental detonation after a missile was armed with its three warheads, two engineered earthworks were constructed on the north and south sides of the Warheading Building. The plans labels both "earth mound, seeded slopes, top elevation of mound = 21.00, slopes 3 in 1" (GATE 11048).

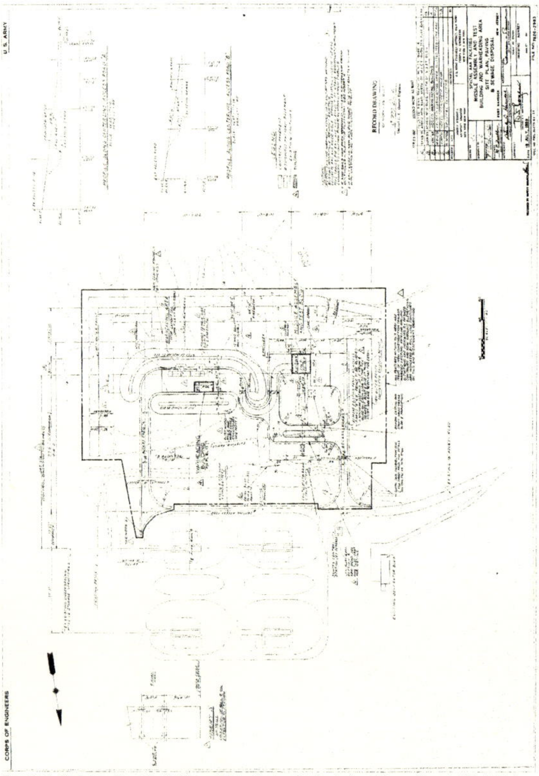

Figure 2.109. Missile Assembly and Test Building and Warheading Area, Site Plan; Paving and Sewage Disposal, 1958. Updated with "as built" information dated February 23, 1961, this plan shows alterations made to the Missile Maintenance Area for the larger Hercules missile (GATE 7620-2983).

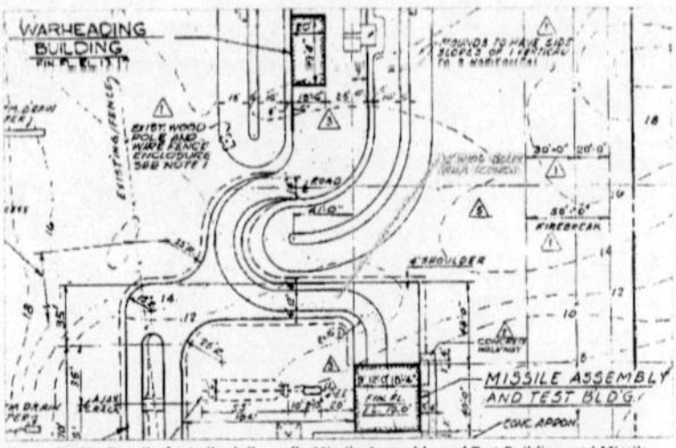

Figure 2.110. Detail of missile dolly walk. Missile Assembly and Test Building and Missile Maintenance Area, Site Plan; Paving and Sewage Disposal, 1958. To accommodate the larger Hercules missiles, a concrete walk was widened from six to twelve feet (highlighted in yellow). The walk was designed for use by a dolly that would transport missiles from the Testing and Assembly Building to the Warheading Building (GATE 7620-2983).

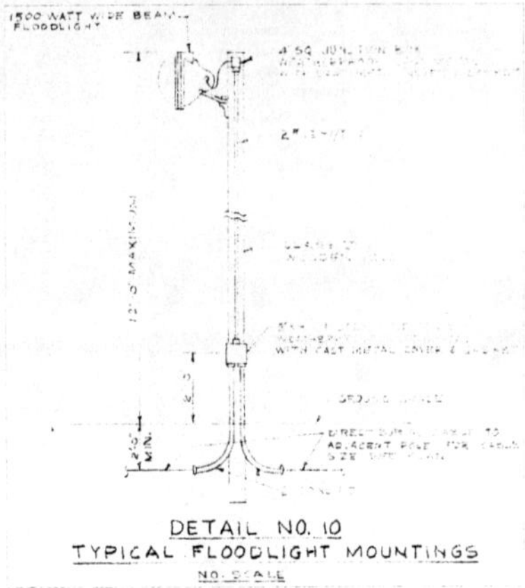

Figure 2.111. Detail of floodlight, Launching Area Plan, Electrical, 1958. Designed to be armed with a nuclear warhead, the Hercules missiles necessitated security improvements at the launch site. A component of the improvements added new 1,500 watt floodlight fixtures mounted on twelve foot-tall wood poles (GATE 11056).

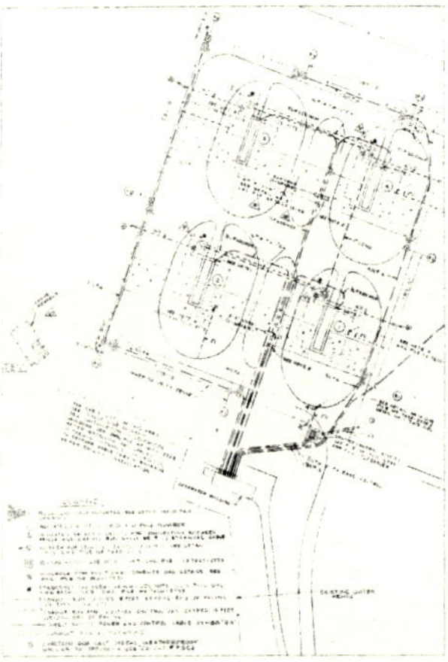

Figure 2.112. Detail of floodlights along inner perimeter fence, Launching Area Plan, Electrical, 1958. Each of the eight floodlights (highlighted in yellow) are shown with their beams paralleling the path of the inner security fence and not faced towards the launchers. Based on this plan, the lights were not intended to facilitate night operation but to illuminate the inner security fence and facilitate better security surveillance (GATE 11056).

Figure 2.113. NIKE sentry dog. In addition to the inner fence and floodlights, a kennel was added to the Sandy Hook launch site to house guard dogs that patrolled the area between the inner and outer fences ("Missile Age Minutemen: A Salute Honoring the Army National Guard Air Defense Units, 1954-1974," Indiantown Gap Military Reservation, Annville, PA, September 14, 1974).

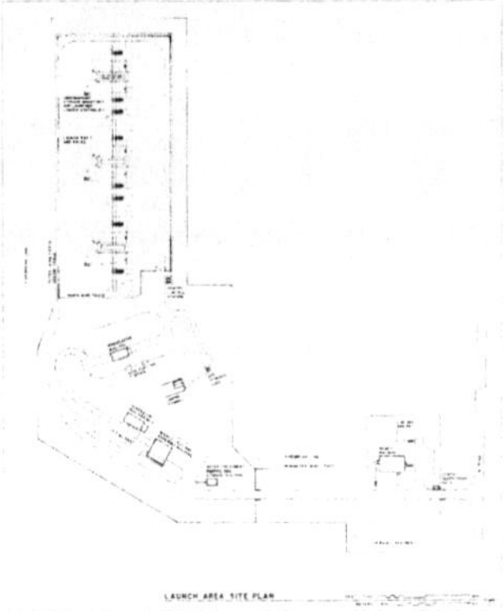

Figure 2.114. Launch Area Site Plan, NIKE Missile Base SL-40, Monroe County, Illinois. As part of increased security necessitated by the nuclear warheads added for the Hercules missile, launch sites across the country added kennels to house trained attack dogs. The dogs and their handlers patrolled the area between the outer perimeter fence and the inner fence that surrounded the missile launchers (Historic American Engineering Record, IL - 117).

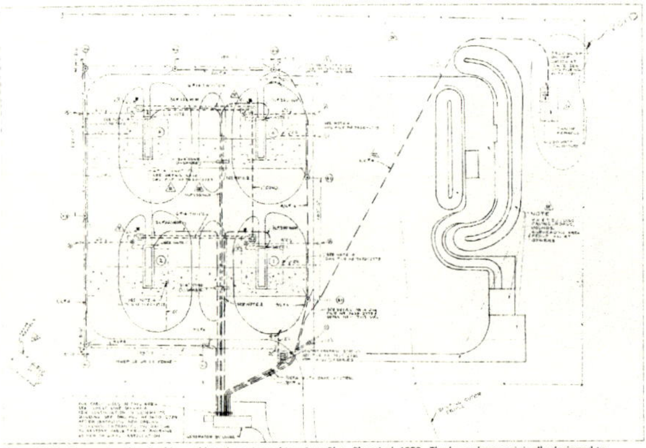

Figure 2.115. Proposed and revised kennel locations, Launching Area Plan, Electrical, 1958. The kennel was originally designed to be constructed south of the Missile Maintenance Area but was relocated to the northwest corner of magazines, arguably for closer proximity to the inner fence and to utilize space intended for future magazine expansion that was never developed (GATE 11056).

Figure 2.116. View looking north at New Jersey State Park entrance, 1967. Beginning in 1962, New Jersey State Parks purchased and leased land at the southern end of the peninsula to offer beach access and recreational fishing opportunities. In conjunction with acquiring the land, the state developed parking facilities for approximately 3,500 vehicles (*Sandy Hook: A Study of Alternatives*, United States Department of the Interior, National Park Service, 1967).

Figure 2.117. View looking northwest at beach usage, 1967. On leased property, New Jersey State Parks developed two beach sites with bathhouses. In addition, State Parks converted the Spermaceti Cove Lifesaving Station (background) into a nature center (*Sandy Hook: A Study of Alternatives*, United States Department of the Interior, National Park Service, 1967).

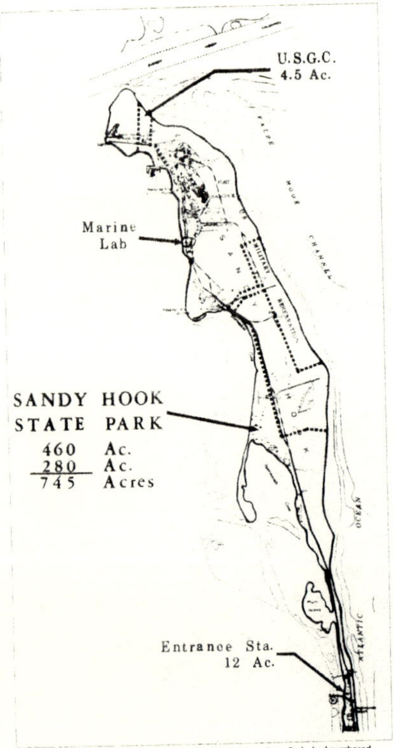

Figure 2.118. Map of leased land, 1967. By 1964, New Jersey State Parks had purchased twelve acres at the southern end of the peninsula and leased another 745 acres from the Department of Defense that extended from the Route 36 bridge to the southern boundary of the NIKE launch site (*Sandy Hook: A Study of Alternatives*, United States Department of the Interior, National Park Service, 1967).

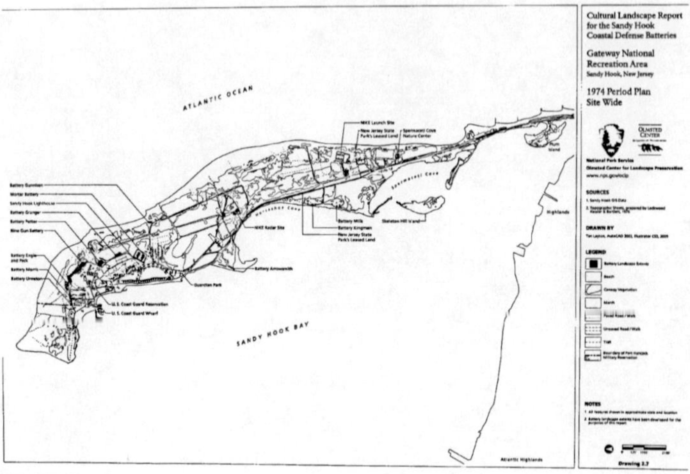
ATLANTIC OCEAN
SANDY HOOK BAY
Battery Gunnison
Mortar Battery
Sandy Hook Lighthouse
Battery Granger
Battery Potter
Nine Gun Battery
Battery Engle and Peck
Battery Morris
Battery Urmston
U. S. Coast Guard Reservation
U. S. Coast Guard Wharf
Guardian Park
Battery Arrowsmith
NIKE Radar Site
NIKE Launch Site
New Jersey State Park's Leased Land
Spermaceti Cove Nature Center
Spermaceti Cove
Battery Mills
Battery Kingman
New Jersey State Park's Leased Land
Skeleton Hill Island
Plum Island
Highlands
Atlantic Highlands
Cultural Landscape Report for the Sandy Hook Coastal Defense Batteries
Gateway National Recreation Area
Sandy Hook, New Jersey
1974 Period Plan Site Wide
Olmsted Center
National Park Service
Olmsted Center for Landscape Preservation
www.nps.gov/oclp
SOURCES
DRAWN BY
LEGEND
Beach
Marsh
Trail
NOTES
Drawing 3.7

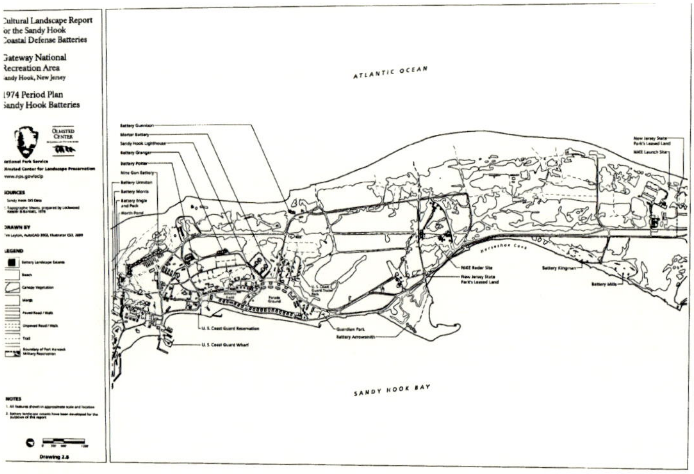
ultural Landscape Report
or the Sandy Hook
oastal Defense Batteries
ateway National
ecreation Area
andy Hook, New Jersey
1974 Period Plan
andy Hook Batteries
OLMSTED
CENTER
ational Park Service
lmsted Center for Landscape Preservation
www.nps.gov/ocip
OURCES
RAWN BY
EGEND
NOTES
Drawing 2.6
ATLANTIC OCEAN
Battery Gunnison
Mortar Battery
Sandy Hook Lighthouse
Battery Granger
Battery Potter
Nine Gun Battery
Battery Urmston
Battery Morris
Battery Engle
and Peck
North Pond
U. S. Coast Guard Reservation
U. S. Coast Guard Wharf
Parade
Ground
Guardian Park
Battery Arrowsmith
Horseshoe Cove
NIKE Radar Site
New Jersey State
Park's Leased Land
Battery Kingman
Battery Mills
New Jersey State
Park's Leased Land
NIKE Launch Site
SANDY HOOK BAY

NATIONAL PARK SERVICE ADMINISTRATION 1975–PRESENT

Following the transfer from the Army to the National Park Service, planning efforts began for Sandy Hook and the entire Gateway National Recreation Area culminating in the publication of Gateway's General Management Plan in 1979. The General Management Plan was prepared to identify pertinent issues and guide decision-making processes for the next two decades.

At Sandy Hook, strategic coastal defense locations and supporting military infrastructure had shaped development on the peninsula since the Revolutionary War. With the completion of the General Management Plan, priorities shifted to balancing recreational opportunities with natural and cultural resource protection. Specifically, with development focused around historic Fort Hancock at the northern end and the former New Jersey State Park facilities at the southern end of the peninsula, the interior section was recognized for its "spacious coastal landscapes and natural features [that] are an important part of the Sandy Hook resource and are deserving of protective management and uses that will allow their perpetuation."[171]

Located within the largest metropolitan area in the nation, Sandy Hook and its miles of undeveloped oceanfront stood apart in stark contrast, offering unique recreational opportunities for residents in the immediately surrounding urban and suburban areas. Access for up to two million visitors annually was almost exclusively by automobile and accordingly, planning efforts focused on road configurations, parking, and alternative transportation development.

The National Park Service sought to distribute parking and visitor concentrations more evenly by decreasing parking on the southern portion of the peninsula and creating new parking and beach facilities near Battery Gunnison and Nine Gun Battery. The General Management Plan proposed a 350-car parking area at the former NIKE launch site for visitation and access to a proposed, small beach center located off the site's northeast corner (Figure 2.119).[172] In the years following the General Management Plan, neither the beach center nor the parking area was developed in this area.

Alternative transportation planning has addressed increasing ferry service, using shuttle buses to connect the northern and southern sections of the peninsula, and dedicated bicycle routes. Recently, the park has installed a Multi-Use Path that starts at the south entrance and continues north to the ferry landing. The path was designed to accommodate bicycle, roller blade, and pedestrian traffic and routing visitors past the perimeters of the NIKE IFC and launch sites (Figure 2.120). Presently, plans are being developed to create secondary paths branching off the main Multi-Use Path that will bring visitors to other coastal defenses and facilitate new interpretive opportunities at these cultural sites.

The U. S. Coast Guard, which has maintained a presence on Sandy Hook since the establishment of a lifesaving station in 1848, continues to operate a facility at the northern end of Sandy Hook. In addition to the Coast Guard, several other institutions have partnered with the park, leasing buildings in the Fort Hancock Historic District. The National Oceanic and Atmospheric Administration's (NOAA) Marine Fisheries Service constructed a new research facility in 1985 following a fire that destroyed previous laboratories staffed by the Department of the Interior's Bureau of Sport Fisheries and Wildlife Service.[173] NOAA's research efforts were joined by the New Jersey Audubon Society that established the Sandy Hook Observatory in 2001 to provide educational programs and events that address the peninsula as a resource for migratory birds.[174]

Complementing these research and educational endeavors, Monmouth County established two educational facilities in the Fort Hancock Historic District. Brookdale Community College created a field classroom for environmental and marine studies in Fort Hancock's Building 53, the Post Exchange Building. South of the Mortar Battery along Gunnison Road, the Marine Academy of Science and Technology (MAST) was founded in 1981 to provide high school instruction in marine science and engineering (Figure 2.121).[175] These organizations may be joined by others as the park contemplates lease options involving future partners in rehabilitating thirty-three historic buildings in the Fort Hancock Historic District.

SAFETY, STABILIZATION, AND RESEARCH

Although the General Management Plan called for greater interpretation of the coastal defense batteries and improving access for the public, efforts in the last three decades have focused on safety issues, stabilization, and research. In order to warn visitors of potentially hazardous conditions at Battery Peck, Battery Granger, and Nine Gun Battery, the park erected chain-link fencing and signage between pedestrian routes and the structures. At Battery Gunnison, the park demolished a concrete bridge in 2001 to eliminate hazards created by the deteriorating concrete. The bridge spanned between the south gun platform and the shell hoist (Figure 2.122).[176]

Visitor access had once been permitted to the top of the Mortar Battery and the park installed post and cable fencing in the late 1970s to keep visitors away from the hazardous, open mortar pits.[177] Due to increased erosion and the creation of social trails across the historic earthwork, the park closed access to the top around 1990.[178] More successful efforts at providing visitor access have been made at Battery Potter. In 2003, the park rehabilitated an exterior metal stairway on the south side of the battery. As part of the same project, new pipe railing was added along the top of the west facade and also the top of the gun parapet walls.

The same year, new metal pipe railing was added to the stairs and around perimeter of gun platforms at Battery Gunnison.[179]

The physical condition of the coastal defense structures and visitor access have not been the park's only concerns. The tides and currents that began shaping Sandy Hook over 8,000 years ago continue to affect the peninsula and at times, seriously threaten historic resources. A violent winter storm in December 1974 removed several vertical pilings from the bayside bulkhead west of Batteries Kingman and Mills. With a portion of the structure breached, subsequent storms in the 1970s destroyed the majority of the bulkhead and began eroding the shoreline.[180]

An especially destructive storm affecting Sandy Hook and the northeastern United States struck in February 1978. In addition to erosion near Batteries Kingman and Mills, hurricane-force wind gusts and storm surges washed away the natural dune formations east of the NIKE launch site and carved away at the narrow, southern portion of the peninsula where beach parking and bathhouses had been established.[181] In the early 1980s, the park pumped sand to reinforce the depleted recreational beaches. As part of this process, sand was initially added in between Batteries Kingman and Mills to set up a construction staging area for remainder of project.[182] To better respond to future beach erosion, the park recently installed and tested a sand-slurry pipeline system that can more efficiently replenish eroded areas.

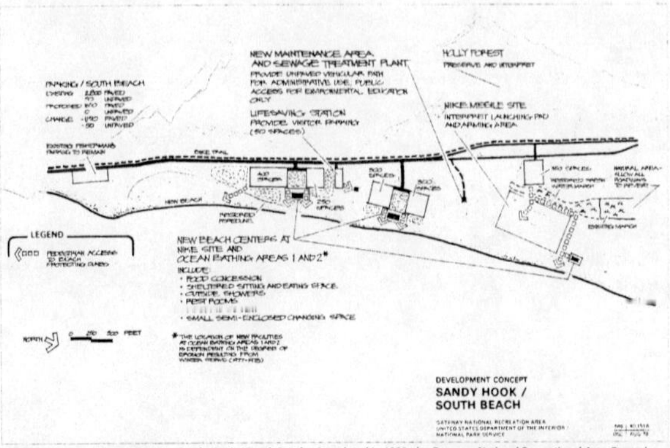

Figure 2.119. Development Concept Sandy Hook / South Beach. Completed in 1979, the Gateway National Recreational Area General Management Plan proposed a 350-car parking area at the former NIKE launch site for visitation and access to a proposed, small beach center located off the site's northeast corner. In the years following the General Management Plan, neither the beach center nor the parking area was developed in this area (*General Management Plan: Gateway National Recreation Area–New York/New Jersey*, United States Department of the Interior, National Park Service, 1979).

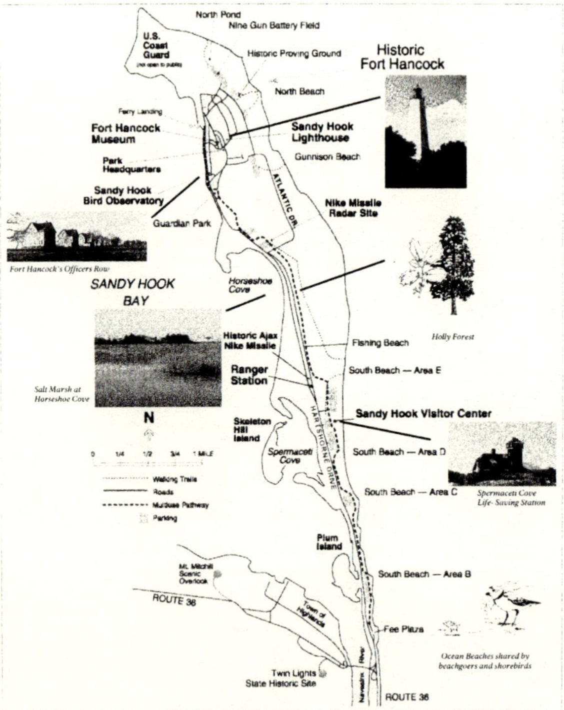

Figure 2.120. Multi-use path map. Recently, the park installed a Multi-Use Path that starts at the south entrance and continues north to the ferry landing. The path was designed to accommodate bicycle, roller blade, and pedestrian traffic and routes visitors past the perimeters of the NIKE radar and launch sites (http://www.nps.gov/gate/planyourvisit/upload/mup%20map.pdf).

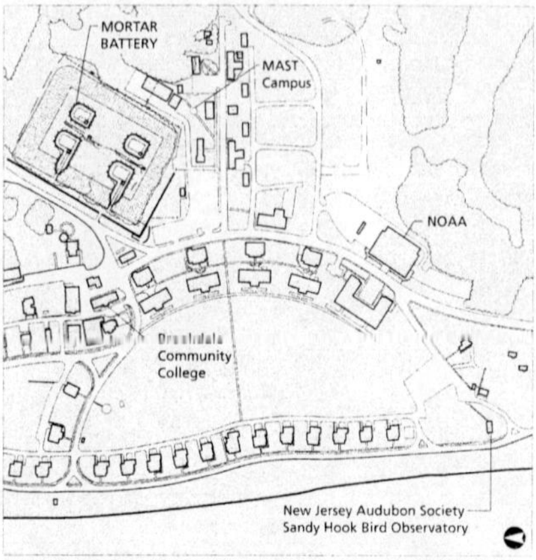

Figure 2.121. Map of partner facilities. Several institutions have partnered with the Sandy Hook Unit leasing buildings in the Fort Hancock Historic District including the National Oceanic and Atmospheric Administration (NOAA), the New Jersey Audubon Society, Brookdale Community College, and the Marine Academy of Science and Technology (MAST) vocational high school (Olmsted Center, 2010).

Figure 2.122. Detail of Harbor Defenses of New York, Battery Gunnison, Alterations and Additions, Fort Hancock, New Jersey, 1943. In 2001, the park demolished a concrete bridge (highlighted in yellow) at Battery Gunnison in order to eliminate hazards created by the deteriorating concrete. The bridge spanned between the south gun platform and the shell hoist (GATE 10689).

ENDNOTES

[1] U. S. Geological Survey, "NYC Regional Geology - Atlantic Coastal Plain," http://3dparks.wr.usgs.gov/nyc/coastalplain/coastalplain.htm; U. S. Geological Survey, "Volumetric Change Analysis along Gateway National Recreation Area - Sandy Hook and Fire Island National Seashore," http://ngom.usgs.gov/dsp/mapping/volumetric_change.html.

[2] The Louis Berger Group, Inc., *Archeological Investigations of the Magruder Road Demolition and Repaving and Gunnison Road Realignment Project Sandy Hook, New Jersey* (United States Department of the Interior, National Park Service, Denver Service Center, January 2004), 6-8.

[3] *Sandy Hook: A Study of Alternatives* (United States Department of the Interior, National Park Service, 1967), 18.

[4] James J. Lee III and Lauren Laham, *Historic Structure Report: Battery Potter, Mortar Battery and Battery Gunnison. Fort Hancock, New Jersey, Sandy Hook Unit, Gateway National Recreation Area* (United States Department of the Interior, National Park Service, 2007), 17-18.

[5] Berger Group, *Archeological Investigations of the Magruder Road*, 9.

[6] *Sandy Hook: A Study of Alternatives*, 19; Maritime Heritage Program, "Sandy Hook Light National Historic Landmark Study," National Park Service, http://www.nps.gov/history/maritime/nhl/sandy.htm.

[7] Lee and Laham, *Historic Structure Report*, 21-22.

[8] Ibid., 22.

[9] Edwin C. Bearss, *Historic Resource Study and Historic Structure Report Historical Data Section Spermaceti Cove Life-Saving Station, Sandy Hook Unit, Gateway National Recreation Area, New York/New Jersey* (United States Department of the Interior, National Park Service, January 1983), 7-8.

[10] Ibid., 17-18.

[11] James J. Lee III, *Spermaceti Cove Life-Saving Station Historic Structure Report* (United States Department of the Interior, National Park Service, 2008), 14-18. In 1878, the Revenue Marine Bureau transferred control of stations to the newly formed U. S. Life-Saving Service. In 1915, the Life-Saving Service merged into the U. S. Coast Guard.

[12] *Sandy Hook: A Study of Alternatives*, 19.

[13] Joel Rosenbaum and Tom Gallo, *Iron Horses Across the Garden State* (Piscataway, NJ: Railplace Company, Inc., 1985), 9; *Sandy Hook: A Study of Alternatives*, 19.

[14] Rosenbaum and Gallo, *Iron Horses Across the Garden State*, 9; Norma E. Williams, *Cultural Landscape Report for Proving Ground and Wartime Expansion Areas, Sandy Hook Unit, Gateway National Recreation Area* (United States Department of the Interior, National Park Service, July 1999), 14. Prior to the 1889 Ordnance Department line between their wharf and the Sandy Hook Proving Ground, mule teams and wagons hauled material over wood plank roads. For further information, please see Williams, 9-14. In 1893, the government purchased the New Jersey Southern Railroad line on Sandy Hook to provide an overland route for the Ordnance Department. For further information, please see Edwin C. Bearss, *Historic Resource Study The Sandy Hook Proving Ground 1874-1919*, 148-149.

[15] Lee and Laham, *Historic Structure Report*, 25; Williams, *Proving Ground and Wartime Expansion Areas*, 8.

[16] Emanuel Raymond Lewis, *Seacoast Fortifications of the United States: An Introductory History* (Annapolis, MD: Naval Institute Press, 1993), 66-68.

[17] Edwin C. Bearss, *Historic Resource Study The Sandy Hook Proving Ground 1874-1919* (United States Department of the Interior, National Park Service, September 1983), 6.

[18] Bearss, *Sandy Hook Proving Ground*, 13-14; Lee and Laham, *Historic Structure Report*, 26.

[19] Bearss, *Sandy Hook Proving Ground*, 52-53.

[20] For detailed information on the Sandy Hook Proving Ground, please see Bearss, *Sandy Hook Proving Ground*.

[21] Lewis, *Seacoast Fortifications*, 77.

[22] Ibid.

[23] Lee and Laham, *Historic Structure Report*, 58.

[24] Ibid., 63.

[25] Ibid., 64-66 and 76.

[26] Ibid., 68-69. Five thousand cubic yards is roughly equivalent to the amount held by 2,500 standard pickup truck beds. Lined up end to end, 2,500 pickup trucks would cover eight miles— greater than the distance from Battery Potter to the Route 36 bridge to Highlands.

[27] Ibid., 70.

[28] Ibid., 78.

[29] Ibid., 79.

[30] Lewis, *Seacoast Fortifications*, 79; Terrance McGovern and Bolling Smith, *American Coastal Defenses 1885-1950* (New York: Osprey Publishing Limited, 2006), 24.

[31] Lee and Laham, *Historic Structure Report*, 201-2.

[32] Ibid., 202. A six story building the size of a football field is roughly equivalent to the volume of earth and sand placed at the Mortar Battery.

[33] Ibid., 202.

[34] Thomas Hoffman, "Fort Hancock Gun Batteries: Revised Draft Text" (working paper, Sandy Hook Unit, 1999).

[35] Lee and Laham, *Historic Structure Report*, 32.

[36] Ibid., 33.

[37] Ibid., 19.

[38] McGovern and Smith, *American Coastal Defenses 1885-1950*, 12.

[39] JR Potts, "HMS Dreadnought," Military Factory, http://www.militaryfactory.com/ships/detail.asp?ship_id=HMS-Dreadnought; "British Navy Ships—HMS Dreadnought 1906-1922," U. S. Department of the Navy, Naval Historical Center, http://www.history.navy.mil/photos/sh-fornv/uk/uksh-d/drednt9.htm.

[40] Potts, "HMS Dreadnought"; "British Navy Ships—HMS Dreadnought 1906-1922".

[41] Lewis, *Seacoast Fortifications*, 89.

[42] Ibid., 89-90.

[43] Engineer's Ledger–Harbor Defenses of New York, CDSG ePress, Harbor Defenses of New York #1.

[44] Ibid.

[45] Lewis, *Seacoast Fortifications*, 130.

[46] Lewis, *Seacoast Fortifications*, 93; McGovern and Smith, *American Coastal Defenses 1885-1950*, 51-52.

[47] Reports of Completed Works, CDSG ePress, Harbor Defenses of New York #4.

[48] NARA, RG 177 Records of the Chiefs of Arms, Office of the Chief of Coast Artillery, 1901-1917, folder, box 69.

[49] NARA, RG 177 Records of the Chiefs of Arms, Office of the Chief of Coast Artillery, box 49, folder 5352.

[50] Ibid.

[51] Ibid.

[52] Lee and Laham, *Historic Structure Report*, 79.

[53] Thomas Hoffman, *Fort Hancock* (Charleston, SC: Arcadia Publishing, 2007), 59; Lee and Laham, *Historic Structure Report*, 79.

[54] Lee and Laham, *Historic Structure Report*, 146.

[55] Ibid., 144.

[56] Ibid., 120-121.

[57] Ibid., 134.

[58] Ibid., 138.

[59] Ibid., 145.

[60] Ibid., 124.

[61] Major B. Burbank, Office of the Post Commander, Fort Hancock, N.J., to Adjunct General, Department of the East, N.Y.C., March 28, 1900, as cited in Lee and Laham, *Historic Structure Report*, 233.

[62] Lee and Laham, *Historic Structure Report*, 234.

[63] Ibid., 237.

[64] Ibid., 235.

[65] Lee and Laham, *Historic Structure Report*, 234; Hoffman, "Fort Hancock Gun Batteries: Revised Draft Text".

[66] Lee and Laham, *Historic Structure Report*, 237.

[67] Plan Showing Drainage and Electrical Systems, Battery Reynolds, Fort Hancock, N.J., September 1910. Approved by Roessler, Sept. 9, 1910; Chief of Engineers Wm. H. Bixby, Sept 14, 1910; and Acting Secretary of War Robert Shaw Oliver, Sept 17, 1910; Sheet 88-20, Drawer 45, RG77, NACP., as cited in Lee and Laham, *Historic Structure Report*, 240.

[68] Lee and Laham, *Historic Structure Report*, 242.

[69] A similar system existed to defend against enemy ships entering Long Island Sound, the East River, and attacking New York City from the east. A series of batteries were located at the eastern entry to Long Island Sound and further west where the Sound and East River meet near the present-day Throngs Neck Bridge.

[70] Lee and Laham, *Historic Structure Report*, 242.

[71] Plan drawings of batteries position the structure with the top of the page facing the target. With this orientation established, the numbering convention always starts from right to left.

[72] Hoffman, "Fort Hancock Gun Batteries: Revised Draft Text"; James Tobias, "Frequently Asked Questions - Naming Army Installations," U. S. Army Center of Military History, http://www.history.army.mil/html/faq/base_name.html. Less commonly, designations could be for geographic location, Native American tribes, or non-military individuals.

[73] Hoffman, *Fort Hancock*, 56.

[74] Reports of Completed Works, CDSG ePress, Harbor Defenses of New York #4.

[75] Hoffman, telephone conversation with the author, February 23, 2009.

[76] Hoffman, "Fort Hancock Gun Batteries: Revised Draft Text".

77 Another large grouping is at Fort Mott in southern New Jersey that features a six gun battery to guard the approach on the Delaware River to Philadelphia.

78 Hoffman, "Fort Hancock Gun Batteries: Revised Draft Text".

79 Hoffman, *Fort Hancock*, 100.

80 Hoffman, "Fort Hancock Gun Batteries: Revised Draft Text".

81 Ibid.

82 Hoffman, *Fort Hancock*, 65. The Spanish-American War was not a prolonged military struggle that sustained increased spending on coastal defenses. The war formally ended less than a year after it started with the Treaty of Paris on December 10, 1898. The treaty required Spain to completely withdraw from Cuba and cede Puerto Rico, the Philippines, and Guam to the United States.

83 Lewis, *Seacoast Fortifications*, 87; Thomas Hoffman, telephone conversation with the author, February 23, 2009.

84 Hoffman, "Fort Hancock Gun Batteries: Revised Draft Text".

85 Hoffman, *Fort Hancock*, 71.

86 Lee and Laham, *Historic Structure Report*, 301.

87 Williams, *Proving Ground and Wartime Expansion Areas*, 29; Lee and Laham, *Historic Structure Report*, 35.

88 Bearss, *Sandy Hook Proving Ground*, 256-59; Lee and Laham, *Historic Structure Report*, 29.

89 Andrew Morang, "Historical Aerial Photographs Made Available by the ERDC Coastal and Hydraulics Laboratory," U. S. Army Corps of Engineers Coastal and Hydraulics Laboratory, http://chl.wes.army.mil/shore/newjersey/shore1920/.

90 Lee and Laham, *Historic Structure Report*, 242.

91 David F. Winkler, *Searching the Skies: The Legacy of the United States Cold War Defense Radar Program* (United States Department of Defense, Air Force Air Combat Command, June 1997), 9.

92 Hoffman, *Fort Hancock*, 111.

93 Mark A. Berhow, "Caretaker Status in the Coast Artillery, 1912-1948," *The Coast Defense Study Group Journal* 14, no. 4 (2000): 49-51.

94 Berhow, "Caretaker Status," 48-50; "Chapter 2: American Military History, Volume II," U. S. Army Center of Military History, http://www.history.army.mil/books/AMH-V2/AMH%20V2/chapter2.htm.

95 Berhow, "Caretaker Status," 50.

96 Annual Report of the Chief of Coast Artillery, 1919, CDSG ePress, 4044.

97 Lewis, *Seacoast Fortifications*, 102.

98 Reports of Completed Works, CDSG ePress, Harbor Defenses of New York #4; Hoffman, *Fort Hancock*, 108-109.

99 Letter from the District Engineer, 2nd District, New York, March 14, 1918, CDSG ePress, Harbor Defenses of New York #1. The letter records six 60-inch lights at Sandy Hook including one mounted on a standard gauge rail car.

100 Journal of the District Engineer, September 27, 1920, CDSG ePress, Harbor Defenses of New York #1.

101 "Billy Mitchell," Air and Space Power Journal, http://www.airpower.maxwell.af.mil/airchronicles/cc/mitch.html.

102 NARA RG 177 Records of the Office of the Chief of Coast Artillery, Box 49, Folder 5352.

103 Ibid.

[104] Lewis, *Seacoast Fortifications*, 116.

[105] Hoffman, *Fort Hancock*, 121.

[106] Lee and Laham, *Historic Structure Report*, 36.

[107] Ibid., 143.

[108] Ibid.

[109] Ibid., 247.

[110] Ibid., 242-243.

[111] Ibid., 243-245.

[112] Report of Completed Works, CDSG ePress, Harbor Defenses of New York #4.

[113] Lee and Laham, *Historic Structure Report*, 244.

[114] Hoffman, *Fort Hancock*, 102.

[115] Report of Completed Works, CDSG ePress, Harbor Defenses of New York #4.

[116] NARA RG 177 Records of the Office of the Chief of Coast Artillery, Box 49, Folder 5352.

[117] Lt. Col. Charles K. Panish to the Commanding General, 2nd Service Command, Army Service Forces, Nov 5 1943, NARA RG 177 Records of the Office of the Chief of Coast Artillery, Box 49, Folder 5352.

[118] Jan 20, 1944, NARA RG 177 Records of the Office of the Chief of Coast Artillery, Box 49, Folder 5352.

[119] NARA RG 177 Records of the Office of the Chief of Coast Artillery, Box 49, Folder 5352.

[120] Headquarters Eastern Defense Command, Governors Island to Chief of Engineers, Army Service Forces, May 12 1944, NARA RG 177 Records of the Office of the Chief of Coast Artillery, Box 49, Folder 5352.

[121] Report of Completed Works, CDSG ePress, Harbor Defenses of New York #4.

[122] Hoffman, "Fort Hancock Gun Batteries: Revised Draft Text".

[123] Hoffman, *Fort Hancock*, 70.

[124] Hoffman, "Fort Hancock Gun Batteries: Revised Draft Text"; Hoffman, e-mail message to the author, February 23, 2009; Lee and Laham, *Historic Structure Report*, 325.

[125] Report of Completed Works, CDSG ePress, Harbor Defenses of New York #4.

[126] Hoffman, *Fort Hancock*, 69.

[127] Capt. R. Wilkenson to Chief of Engineers, Jan 1, 1929, Preservation and Repair, Miscellaneous, folder 16 Box 35, correspondence Relating to Fortification Projects 1907-1930, Entry 802, NARA RG 77, Northeast Region, as cited in Lee and Laham, *Historic Structure Report*, 323.

[128] Lewis, *Seacoast Fortifications*, 116; Lee and Laham, *Historic Structure Report*, 324.

[129] Lee and Laham, *Historic Structure Report*, 325.

[130] Report of Completed Works, CDSG ePress, Harbor Defenses of New York #4. Salvage and disposal comments are not listed for Battery Alexander at the Nine Gun Battery. Handwritten notes indicate the artillery and carriages were removed from Battery Alexander and stored or turned over to the Chief of Ordnance.

[131] Lewis, *Seacoast Fortifications*, 132. The 6-inch guns at Battery Gunnison were replaced with similar guns from Fort Hamilton's Battery Livingston in 1948. These guns were removed in the mid-1960s and then brought back to Battery

Gunnison for interpretive purposes in 1975. For additional information, please see Lee and Laham, *Historic Structure Report*, 328-329.

[132] Roy S. Barnard, *The History of ARADCOM Volume 1: The Gun Era 1950-1955* (United States Department of Defense, Headquarters ARADCOM, [1973?]) 12-13.

[133] Ibid., 14-15.

[134] John C. Lonnquest and David F. Winkler, *To Defend and Deter: The Legacy of the United States Cold War Missile Program* (United States Department of Defense, Army Construction Engineering Research Laboratories, November 1996), 170-171.

[135] Judith Q. Sullivan, *Building 32 Quartermaster's Storehouse, Fort Hancock, Historic Structure Report, Sandy Hook Unit, Gateway National Recreation Area* (United States Department of the Interior, National Park Service, 2004), 28.

[136] Ibid.

[137] Barnard, *The History of ARADCOM*, 28.

[138] Ibid.

[139] Thomas Hoffman, "Cold War Defender: Draft Text" (working paper, Sandy Hook Unit, 2005), 1.

[140] Mark Berhow, *U. S. Strategic and Defensive Missile Systems 1950-2004* (Osprey Publishing, 2005), 7.

[141] John A. Martini and Stephen A. Haller, *What We Have We Shall Defend: An Interim History and Preservation Plan for Nike Site SF-88L, Fort Barry, California* (United States Department of the Interior, National Park Service, Golden Gate National Recreation Area, 1998), 3.

[142] Hoffman, "Cold War Defender: Draft Text", 2.

[143] Lonnquest and Winkler, *To Defend and Deter*, 165.

[144] Ibid., 165-168.

[145] Ibid., 57 and 179.

[146] Ibid., 180.

[147] On September 30, 1955, the liquid fuel mixture exploded during tests at White Sands Proving Ground killing one and injuring five others. The accident convinced the design team that a solid fuel was necessary. For additional information on Hercules development, please see Lonnquest and Winkler, *To Defend and Deter*, 179-180.

[148] Lonnquest and Winkler, *To Defend and Deter*, 177-180.

[149] Ibid., 177 and 182.

[150] Hoffman, "Cold War Defender: Draft Text", 4.

[151] Lonnquest and Winkler, *To Defend and Deter*, 172.

[152] Hoffman, "Cold War Defender: Draft Text", 4-5. Control Area designations are not consistent based on historic plans for the IFC site. Plans from the 1950s follow the convention detailed above and for consistency with previous park publications, this designation will be used. All plans obtained in this research that date to 1962 reverse the designation and label the western area Control Area #1 and the eastern area #2. One site plan from 1954 labels both areas #1.

[153] In addition to access from already established vehicular routes, a wetland in between IFC and Launch may have impacted site selection, i.e., only relatively low-growing plant material present in the wetland versus the holly forest.

[154] NIKE was originally discussed as a semi-mobile defense system that would be dispatched from a central location to one of many preconfigured launch sites. Greatly influenced by the tragic losses at Pearl Harbor, this concept was dismissed because it could not immediately respond to a surprise attack. For further information please see Lonnquest and Winkler, *To Defend and Deter*, 171.

[155] Lonnquest and Winkler, *To Defend and Deter*, 173.

[156] Martini and Haller, *What We Have We Shall Defend*, 45.

[157] Lonnquest and Winkler, *To Defend and Deter*, 180.

[158] Ibid., 171-172. The combined NIKE IFC and launch sites at Sandy Hook are approximately thirty-three acres.

[159] Hoffman, "Cold War Defender: Draft Text", 4.

[160] Lonnquest and Winkler, *To Defend and Deter*, 182.

[161] Berhow, *U. S. Strategic and Defensive Missile Systems*, 12.

[162] Throughout the 1950s, the Army and Air Force extensively argued over which service branch had responsibility to defend against aircraft and missile attacks. For additional information, please see Barnard, *The History of ARADCOM*, 27-28 and 31-39 and Lonnquest and Winkler, *To Defend and Deter*, 60-63.

[163] Lonnquest and Winkler, *To Defend and Deter*, 110.

[164] Hoffman, "Cold War Defender: Draft Text", 10.

[165] Edwin C. Bearss, *Historic Resource Study Fort Hancock: 1948-1974, Sandy Hook Unit, Gateway National Recreation Area, Monmouth County, New Jersey* (United States Department of the Interior, National Park Service, November 1982), 162-164.

[166] *Sandy Hook: A Study of Alternatives*, 5.

[167] Ibid., 27. At the time the report was published, the 285 acres leased in 1964 were not developed or available to the public due to security concerns and a lack of fencing. Batteries Kingman and Mills, disarmed in 1948, were located within this newly leased area.

[168] Ibid., 5.

[169] Ibid., 33.

[170] Lee and Laham, *Historic Structure Report*, 37.

[171] *General Management Plan, Gateway National Recreation Area, New York/New Jersey* (United States Department of the Interior, National Park Service, August 1979), 12.

[172] Ibid., 88.

[173] Northeast Fisheries Science Center, "James J. Howard Marine Sciences Laboratory," National Oceanic and Atmospheric Administration, http://sh.nefsc.noaa.gov/.

[174] "Sandy Hook Bird Observatory," New Jersey Audubon Society, http://www.njaudubon.org/Centers/SHBO/.

[175] "Marine Academy of Science and Technology," Monmouth County Vocational School District, http://www.mast.mcvsd.org/.

[176] Lee and Laham, *Historic Structure Report*, 329.

[177] Ibid., 248.

[178] Ibid.

[179] Ibid., 127 and 329.

[180] Hoffman, telephone conversation with the author, February 23, 2009.

[181] *General Management Plan*, 14.

[182] Hoffman, telephone conversation with the author, February 23, 2009.

EXISTING CONDITIONS

The following chapter describes the physical setting for the Sandy Hook Unit of the Gateway National Recreation Area and current landscape characteristics for the coastal defense batteries. The setting of the Sandy Hook peninsula serves as the context for the coastal defense battery sites and is followed by a narrative description of the landscape associated with eleven extant batteries and two separate sites that comprise the NIKE missile battery. Landscape characteristics documented for the batteries include spatial organization, topography, circulation, buildings and structures, vegetation, tactical views, and small-scale features.

The existing conditions for the eleven extant batteries is presented in geographical order from north to south starting with Battery Urmston and ending with Batteries Kingman and Mills. The section concludes with the NIKE radar site and the NIKE launch site. Although an important component in the history of Sandy Hook's coastal defenses, the Mine Casemate is presently on U. S. Coast Guard property and is outside the study area for this cultural landscape report. In addition Battery Arrowsmith, located on a sandbar protruding into Sandy Hook Bay, is not documented. The waters of the bay have compromised the structural integrity of Battery Arrowsmith and the next major storm may break apart the concrete structure and underlying sandbar.

Narrative descriptions of the batteries' landscape characteristics are supplemented with photographs and existing conditions maps. The project team inspected the battery sites in April 2008 and January 2009. Map sources included GIS information from the park, an AutoCAD digital survey drawing from the National Park Service Denver Service Center, and a 1990 hand-drafted survey by Carrera and Associates.[1] A 2006 color aerial orthophoto provided information on canopy outlines for masses of vegetation, the configuration of the existing shoreline, and confirmed the location of existing buildings, roads, and other landscape features. The extents of each battery landscape have been identified and drawn on existing conditions mapping to serve the purposes of this report. While these arbitrary battery landscape boundaries did not historically exist, this report has developed these minimal boundaries to differentiate historic structures, engineered landforms, and battery service-related areas that are part of Gateway National Recreation Area's cultural resources from the adjacent naturalized landscape.

Within the set of existing conditions maps prepared for this report, the first map shows the overall landform, major circulation features, and concentrations of buildings at a scale of 1"=2100'. This map does not show the peninsula south of Plum Island where the land continues to taper and a bridge spans the Navesink River to connect Sandy Hook and the town of Highlands. The second map shows more detail among the batteries, buildings, circulation features, and masses of vegetation at a scale of 1"=1200' beginning with batteries Urmston and Morris to the north and ending with the NIKE launch site to the south. The final series of twelve maps show the individual batteries and their specific landscape features at a larger scale varying from 1"=30' to 1"=150' depending on the overall area of the site.

Plan drawings of batteries position the structure with the top of the page facing the target. With this orientation established, the numbering convention for gun emplacements always starts from right to left. The exception to this convention is the Mortar Battery, oriented parallel to the west perimeter wall, and the NIKE battery sites. Since the engineered earthworks and topography are such an important component of the landscape, a reference elevation will be given for each battery. The reference elevation is derived from the existing conditions mapping and represents an average of the surrounding grades that were not modified in the construction of the coastal defense batteries. The height of structures and engineered earthworks will be described based on the established reference elevation.

PHYSICAL SETTING

Located in the northeast corner of Monmouth County, New Jersey, Sandy Hook extends six and a half miles from the town of Highlands into lower New York Harbor. The landform parallels the primary deep water channel into New York Harbor and is nineteen miles south of the southern tip of Manhattan. The Sandy Hook peninsula is bounded by the mouth of the Navesink River that opens into Sandy Hook Bay on the west and the Atlantic Ocean on the north and east. The landform is a recurved sand spit that formed over thousands of years by a south to north littoral drift in the Atlantic Ocean. The currents continue to shape the elongated landform by removing material from the southern, narrower end and depositing new material at the wider, northern end of the peninsula.

Coastal forces such as tides, storm surges, salt spray, and strong winds influence and affect the landscape characteristics on the peninsula. The topography of Sandy Hook is relatively flat with undulating dunes shaped by waves and wind. Typical elevations range from zero to twenty feet and the highest points on the peninsula are engineered earthworks that were constructed as part of the coastal defense batteries. Protected from wind and salt spray, the central portion of the peninsula features over 200 acres of a maritime holly forest with American holly (*Ilex opaca*) as the dominant plant species. In contrast to this undisturbed central area, developed areas are primarily concentrated at either the north or south end of the peninsula. The southern end features recreational facilities for visitors to enjoy the undeveloped beaches and natural areas associated with the ocean and bay. The northern end contains the Fort Hancock Historic District and an active U. S. Coast Guard base. The majority of buildings in the Fort Hancock Historic District were constructed between the late 1800s and early 1900s with the establishment of the Proving Ground and coastal defense batteries to guard the southern approach to New York City.

BATTERY URMSTON

Located at the northern end of the Sandy Hook peninsula, Battery Urmston faces north toward the ocean and the shallow waters outside the main shipping channel. The battery consists of six emplacements, three to the west and three to the east, separated by an earth-covered, central storeroom. Battery Urmston is bounded by a perimeter fence marking U. S. Coast Guard property to the west and south and by an engineered earthen mound separating it from Battery Morris to the east (Drawing 3.3).

The reference elevation for Battery Urmston is ten feet and south of the battery, the topography is relatively flat. North of the emplacements, the top of the engineered earthwork rises to more than twenty feet and slopes away from the battery for approximately seventy feet. Two high points punctuate the topography around Battery Urmston. The first, over twenty-five feet in elevation, is formed from earth covering the central storeroom. The second rises to slightly higher than twenty-three feet and separates Battery Urmston from Battery Morris.

Pedestrian access to Battery Urmston is not clearly defined and there is currently no vehicular access to the structure. East of Battery Urmston, a remnant of North Bragg Drive that passes to the south of Battery Morris and terminates at a chain-link fence marking Coast Guard property. From the end of this deteriorating road, the fence serves as a guide for pedestrian access to Battery Urmston. There is no path or trail between the fence and the battery and the density of vegetation impedes easy access. Due to the difficulty in accessing Battery Urmston, no social trails were observed around the battery or on the engineered earthwork during the project team's inspection.

The gun platforms for emplacements #1, #2, #5, and #6 are T-shaped with full-width steps that lead up the long leg of the "T" to where rapid fire guns would have been mounted. At the north end of the platforms, narrow notches form the short legs of the "T" and served as a recessed space to rest pillar mounted guns when not in use (Figure 3.1). The centers of platforms #1 and #2 and platforms #5 and #6 are separated by approximately thirty feet. Gun platforms #3 and #4 are rectangular with a narrow set of steps heading up the center. At the north end of each platform, a semi-circular notch is located that held a pedestal mounted gun. Approximately forty-five feet separate platform #2 and #3 and platform #4 and #5. The earth-covered storeroom separates platform #3 and #4. Concrete magazines are located between the other platforms and an open battery commander's station is immediately west of platform #4.

Efflorescence can be seen on many of the vertical concrete surfaces indicating water has penetrated the concrete and is drawing out salts and other impurities to the surface (see Figure 3.1). Spalling surfaces are present in the gun platforms and the tops of the magazines have substantial cracks. Guardrails are located at stairwells leading to the magazines and a handrail is installed along an external set of stairs leading to the battery commander's station. Both types of railings show a heavy degree of corrosion and are staining the concrete below them. Access to existing doors is blocked by vegetation that has grown up in the stairwells (Figure 3.2).

In a triangular area between the Coast Guard perimeter fence and battery, ailanthus (*Ailanthus altissima*), Virginia creeper (*Parthenocissus quinquefolia*), poison ivy (*Toxicodendron radicans*), and honey locust saplings (*Gleditsia triacanthos*) overrun the space and result in limited pedestrian access. On the north-facing engineered slope of Battery Urmston, large woody vegetation primarily consists of eastern red cedar (*Juniperus virginiana*), beach plum (*Prunus maritima*), hackberry (*Celtis occidentalis*), and ailanthus (*Ailanthus altissima*). These species have also found suitable locations to grow in the low-lying areas, flat surfaces, and cracks of the battery (Figure 3.3).

The views from the gun platforms and battery commander's station to the water are primarily impeded by woody vegetation growing at the interface of the engineered slope and concrete battery structure (Figure 3.4). It is difficult to evaluate the impact on views beyond these immediate vegetative obstructions. In general, there appears to be minimal tall vegetation beyond the engineered slope and no additional buildings or structures. At the eastern end of the Battery Urmston, there is an engineered earthwork that rises up between the battery and Battery Morris. The earthwork ends abruptly at a concrete retaining wall that extends from Urmston. Immediately east of the retaining wall, a four-foot high, wood-slat fence meanders up the earthwork and wraps around toward the gun platform. The fence is painted maroon red and is in fair condition.

BATTERY MORRIS

Battery Morris shares the northern ended of the peninsula with Battery Urmston and is located approximately sixty-five feet east of Urmston's emplacement #1. Morris is oriented to the north and consists of four emplacements separated by three earth-covered magazines. The battery is bounded on the south by a U. S. Coast Guard perimeter fence and a complex of Coast Guard housing immediately beyond the fence. Battery Morris includes a separate coincidence range finder (CRF) station located approximately seventy-five feet from the battery's gun platform #1 (Drawing 3.4).

The reference elevation for Battery Morris is ten feet and south of the battery, the topography is relatively flat. North of the emplacements, the top of the engineered earthwork rises to more than twenty feet and slopes away from the battery for approximately thirty feet. The toe or northern end of the engineered earthwork forms one side of a swale at an elevation of fifteen feet. The swale then rises up to the north to an elevation of twenty feet. Surface water gathered by the swale would flow from west to east. The three magazines that separate the gun platforms are covered with earth that rises to an elevation of approximately twenty-four feet.

There is currently no vehicular access to Battery Morris and visitors wishing to see the structure have to walk west from Nine Gun Battery and Battery Peck to access a trail that leads to the structure. The trail has a variable width and is a remnant of North Bragg Drive. The trail surface is comprised of broken asphalt and accumulated leaf litter and debris. Emerging woody vegetation obscures a clear definition of the trail and makes pedestrian access difficult (Figure 3.5).

The four gun platforms at Battery Morris are centered approximately 50 feet apart. Each platform is divided into three levels with the highest level on the north side. Narrow concrete steps lead from the ground level on the south to the first level at platforms #1, #2, and #3. From the first level, central concrete stairs lead to the gun platforms. Woody vegetation is growing in and around the stairs to the point where they are difficult to ascend (Figure 3.6). Gun platforms #1 and #4 are semi-circular while platforms #2 and #3 are rectangular with a semi-circular notch at their north end. The CRF station is a thirteen foot by thirteen foot square concrete structure supported by concrete legs at each corner. A metal step ladder attaches to the structure on the south side and provides access to a floor with an elevation of approximately nineteen feet. The step ladder is severely corroded and in poor condition. Efflorescence can be seen on many of the vertical surfaces, however, no major spalling concrete surfaces are present at the battery. The concrete at the CRF has deteriorated to the extent that metal reinforcing members are exposed and corroding. Doors on the south side of Battery Morris appeared to be in good to fair condition, however, thickets of woody vegetation block access to them.

Ailanthus (*Ailanthus altissima*), Virginia creeper (*Parthenocissus quinquefolia*), poison ivy (*Toxicodendron radicans*), and honey locust saplings (*Gleditsia triacanthos*) dominate the trail to Battery Morris and the narrow corridor along the Coast Guard perimeter fence. Vegetation on the engineered earthwork and growing on the battery structure includes eastern red cedar (*Juniperus virginiana*), black locust (*Robinia pseudoacacia*), beach plum (*Prunus maritima*), hackberry (*Celtis occidentalis*), and ailanthus (*Ailanthus altissima*). A large hackberry, approximately eighteen-inches diameter at breast height, is growing on the battery to the west of gun platform #4 (Figure 3.7). In addition to the large woody species, there appears to be greater quantities of Japanese honeysuckle (*Lonicera japonica*) and Asiatic bittersweet (*Celastrus orbiculatus*) growing on the engineered earthwork of Battery Morris then at nearby Battery Urmston. Vegetation completely surrounds the CRF and the plant material is dense enough that identifying the elevated structure from the access trail is difficult.

The downrange views from Battery Morris to the water are primarily impacted by vegetation growing at the interface of the engineered earthwork and concrete battery structure. North of the engineered earthwork, vegetation growing on the north slope of a swale may obstruct views as well. Vegetation immediately north of the CRF blocks any views to the water. At gun platforms #1 and #2, wood two-by-four guard panels are installed and are in poor condition (see Figure 3.6). Similar to the wood guard panels, a wood picket fence is located to the north and east of gun platform #1 (Figure 3.8). The fence is painted maroon red and is also in poor condition.

BATTERIES ENGLE AND PECK

Batteries Engle and Peck are two separate structures that emplaced rapid fire guns until 1920 when artillery was removed from Battery Engle and the concrete gun platform converted to a coincidence range finder (CRF) station for Battery Peck. Given their geographic proximity and historic association of battery and range-finding station, the existing conditions for Batteries Engle and Peck will be described in a combined section. The two batteries are located at the northern end of the peninsula approximately 150 feet west of Nine Gun Battery and 350 feet east Battery Morris. Battery Engle is oriented north and Battery Peck is oriented northeast toward the point where the Atlantic Ocean wraps around Sandy Hook. For description purposes, the targeting direction of the guns and front of both batteries will be assigned north. Batteries Engle and Peck are bounded by an unpaved road to the west, North Bragg Drive to the south, and a trail between Battery Peck and Nine Gun Battery to the east (Drawing 3.5).

The reference elevation for Batteries Engle and Peck is six feet and similar to Battery Urmston and Battery Morris, the topography is relatively flat south of the structures. In contrast to other batteries that have a clear toe of slope, Batteries Engle and Peck appear to be built into the side of a plateau. Immediately north of the batteries, the earth and sand rise to an elevation of twenty-two feet and continue at that elevation for over 100 feet to the north. The landform then gradually descends down and merges with the undulating coastal dunes.

Vehicular access west of Nine Gun Battery is restricted by a gate across North Bragg Drive. West of the gate, the road turns and parallels the south elevations of Batteries Engle and Peck before merging with an unpaved road that turns north and proceeds into the dunes. A spur off the unpaved road heads east and terminates in an open area around an observation platform built over a one story, wood-frame structure. Several social trails proceed south from the observation platform to Batteries Engle and Peck indicating most pedestrians arrive at the observation platform first and then wander between the two batteries.

Battery Peck consists of two circular gun platforms, a covered concrete commander's station, and magazines accessed from the ground level on the south side of the structure. From the ground level, a three sets of concrete steps lead up to an intermediate level. A set of steps is located at the west end, the east end, and in the center of the structure. Additional steps, one set for each platform, lead from the intermediate level to the former gun emplacements. Each platform is roughly forty feet in diameter, however, it is difficult to discern the full extent of the concrete structure due to accumulated sand and vegetation. Approximately 110 feet separate the two gun platforms. The battery commander's station is centered between two platforms and a tall metal pole is attached with metal brackets to the east side of the structure. Efflorescence can be seen on many of the vertical surfaces and spalling is present on both horizontal and vertical surfaces (Figure 3.9). Handrails and guardrails are located along steps and intermediate level leading to the gun platforms. The railings are in fair to poor condition with corrosion covering most pieces. Some assemblies lack any solid material where the vertical members fasten the railing to a solid support (Figure 3.10).

The concrete coincidence range finder station constructed on top of Battery Engle is nineteen feet square and covered with a low-pitched concrete roof. The structure appears in fair condition with some minor efflorescence visible on the roof (Figure 3.11). Northeast of Battery Engle, a communications trailer sits abandoned. The trailer is a frequent target for graffiti (Figure 3.12). North of both batteries, an observation platform stands on top of a one story, wood-frame structure (Figure 3.13). The platform permits panoramic views across Lower New York Harbor and is regularly used for bird watching.

The vegetation on Battery Peck's engineered earthwork is primarily deciduous and comprised of beach plum (*Prunus maritima*) and hackberry (*Celtis occidentalis*). Eastern red cedars (*Juniperus virginiana*) are also present but not in the density seen at other batteries at Sandy Hook. South of Battery Peck, the vegetation is very dense and the area is nearly impassable (Figure 3.14). Battery Engle is surrounded by dense woody vegetation on its south, west, and north sides that curtails access and limits views of this relatively small concrete structure.

Views from Battery Peck's commander's station to the water are blocked by woody vegetation. In addition, views from gun platform #2 are obstructed by the observation platform and wood-frame structure to the north. Vegetation to the north of Battery Engle obstructs a view to the water used for target range finding. Small-scale features associated with Batteries Engle and Peck primarily consist of different types of fences. Approximately ten feet north of North Bragg Drive, a chain-link fence and signage have been installed to warn visitors of potentially hazardous conditions and block access to Battery Peck's south elevation. East of Battery Engle, a wooden split-rail fence is installed to limit social trails and erosion on the engineered earthwork. West of the communications trailer, about twenty feet of chain-link fence is located in dense vegetation. The fence is twelve-feet high and topped with barbed wire, however, it is overrun with Japanese honeysuckle and other vines and is in poor condition. West of the vehicular access gate on North Bragg Drive, an interpretive wayside is located in the shoulder of the road.

NINE GUN BATTERY

Nine Gun Battery is a massive concrete structure comprised of nine emplacements that supported a mixture of 10- and 12-inch caliber guns. The battery parallels the main shipping channel with seven of the emplacements facing east and the remaining two angled to the north following the channel around the northern end of the peninsula. The alignment of Nine Gun Battery follows the east and north facades of the Civil War-era Fort at Sandy Hook.

Nine Gun Battery was constructed in phases between 1898 and 1904 and designated as four batteries. From north to south, the four batteries are Battery Alexander, Battery Halleck, Battery Bloomfield, and Battery Richardson (Figure 3.15). In order to show a similar level of detail for Nine Gun Battery and the other coastal defense batteries, Nine Gun Battery is shown on two drawings that divide the structure into a northern and southern half (Drawing 3.6).

Nine Gun Battery is located 150 feet east of Batteries Engle and Peck and 600 feet northeast of Battery Potter. The reference elevation for Nine Gun Battery is ten feet and the engineered earthwork, north and east of the concrete structure, starts at an approximate elevation of twenty-eight feet. The earthwork slopes away from the battery for approximately seventy feet and arrives at an elevation of ten feet. From the toe of the engineered earthwork the topography continues to gradually fall and forms a depression at an elevation of six feet before rising up to form a dune that parallels the coastline. A coastal pond, North Pond, and an associated estuarine wetland are located northeast of the battery and on the Atlantic Ocean side of this dune.

The major circulation route to Nine Gun Battery is along North Bragg Drive which parallels the west facade of the structure and wraps around the battery's northern end to provide a route to Batteries Engle and Peck. Parking is available south of the battery at Parking Lot J, a short walking distance to the structure. A social trail is present that leads from emplacement #8 down the engineered earthwork and connects to a trail in a valley between Nine Gun Battery and Batteries Engle and Peck.

The gun platforms at Nine Gun Battery feature recessed, circular gun wells that held large caliber artillery mounted on counterweight carriages. The centers of the platforms are spaced approximately 125 feet apart for the three platforms associated with Battery Halleck. The remaining six platforms are spaced approximately 140 feet apart. Covered, concrete battery commander's stations are centered between the two platforms for Batteries Alexander, Bloomfield, and Richardson. At Battery Halleck, the covered commander's station is located south of emplacement #6. Northeast of emplacement #8, large granite blocks are visible immediately beyond the concrete terreplein (Figure 3.16). These blocks are remnants of the northeast bastion of the Civil War-era Fort at Sandy Hook.

Several dozen doors and windows are missing or not properly mounted at the magazines, commander's stations, and other auxiliary rooms at Nine Gun Battery (Figure 3.17). A cantilevered structure between emplacements #5 and #7, intended to provide access to the battery commander's station, is in poor condition (Figure 3.18). Both handrails and guardrails are present at Nine Gun Battery and are generally in good to fair condition (Figure 3.19). At transitions between the ground level and gun platforms and also the gun platforms and terreplein, there are stairs and ramps that lack any kind of railing (Figure 3.20).

North of emplacement #8 and the toe of the engineered earthwork are ruins of a red brick fog horn building, likely built circa 1890-1910. The ruins stand on the ridge of the dune that parallels the coastline and are surrounded by a grove of trees. The trail between Nine Gun Battery and Batteries Engle and Peck provides access to the ruins, however, the trail is obscured by dense vegetation.

Eastern red cedar (*Juniperus virginiana*), beach plum (*Prunus maritima*), and hackberry (*Celtis occidentalis*) comprise the majority of woody vegetation species growing around and on Nine Gun Battery. In addition to growing on the engineered earthwork, eastern red cedars have emerged in the cracks and cold joints of the horizontal concrete surfaces (Figure 3.21). Phragmites (*Phragmites* sp.), also called common reed, is growing in the wells at emplacements #6, #7, and #9 (Figure 3.22). The views from the gun platforms and battery commander's station to the water are primarily obstructed by woody vegetation growing at the transition between the concrete structure and engineered earthwork. A dense stand of eastern red cedars are present in an area between emplacements #5 through #9.

Small-scale features at Nine Gun Battery include a fence to discourage visitor access and an interpretive wayside. Paralleling the west and south facades of the battery, a chain-link fence and signage have been erected to warn visitors of potentially hazardous conditions. Southwest of emplacement #8 outside the fence, an interpretive wayside is installed.

BATTERY POTTER

Battery Potter has the distinction of being the first completed, partially armed, and tested coastal defense battery in the United States following the Endicott Board's recommendations in 1885. The battery is located 600 feet south west of Nine Gun Battery and 700 feet north of Battery Granger. Battery Potter is D-shaped in plan with its curved portion facing east and main entry on the west. The main entry is through an arched opening flanked by defensive stone towers. Constructed from granite blocks salvaged from the Civil War-era fort, the main entry resembles a castle (Figure 3.23 and Drawing 3.7).

The reference elevation for Battery Potter is ten feet and the top of the concrete structure rises up to an elevation over forty-five feet. On the north, south, and east sides of Battery Potter, a large engineered earthwork wraps around the facades and rises up to an elevation of approximately twenty-three feet. At the southwest corner of the battery, the engineered earthwork juts away from the structure and rises to a high point of approximately twenty-seven feet. Along the west facade of the battery granite cheek walls extend from each stone tower and retain a relatively small, triangular-shaped portion of engineered earthwork on either side of the entry. Northeast of the battery, the topography gradually descends from the toe of the engineered slope and forms a depression between the battery and Atlantic Drive.

The northwest corner of Battery Potter's site is defined by the intersection of North Bragg Drive and Hudson Drive. Vehicular access to the battery is along either of these two roads. Southwest of the main entry, a small parking area departs from Hudson Drive, loops around a small building, and joins back up with Hudson Drive (Figure 3.24). From the parking area visitors follow a sidewalk past two switchboard buildings to a landing at the main entry. The landing is paved with bluestone laid in a random rectangular pattern. South of the switchboard buildings, a social trail leads up the battery's engineered earthwork, arrives near a high point, and disappears on the downhill side.

The top surface of Battery Potter, known as the terreplein, contains two openings that were used to raise and lower 12-inch caliber guns. East of the former gun emplacements, a concrete superior slope gently descends to a sentry route known as a *chemin de ronde* that is fronted by a parapet wall (Figures 3.25 and 3.26). A concrete slope angles away from the parapet and meets the engineered earthwork. On the terreplein, two groups of deteriorating concrete structures are located west of the former gun emplacements (Figure 3.27). The structures served as fire control stations after Battery Potter's artillery was removed and feature large openings in their east elevations to provide views to the Atlantic Ocean. South of the concrete structures, two concrete pillars remain from another structure that served as fire control station (Figure 3.28). To increase visitor safety, the National Park Service has recently added guardrails between the superior slope and the terreplein where the guns were emplaced. Guardrails are also installed on the western portion of the roof to prevent access to the sloped portion of the concrete structure. Both groups of railings are in good condition (Figures 3.29 and 3.30). A T-shaped metal pole is located north of the fire control stations and was used in observing and recording weather phenomenon as a means of adjusting and improving artillery firing (Figure 3.31). In addition to the railings and pole, an exterior, metal stairway leads from the southwest corner of the terreplein to the ground level.

On the ground level, several auxiliary structures and the foundation of a battery commander's tower are located west of Battery Potter. A one story coal shed and powerhouse are located near the northwest corner of the battery. Two switchboard rooms, also one story high, are located near the southwest corner of Battery Potter. A concrete cable hut separates two points of vehicular access between Hudson Drive and the unpaved parking area. Across from the parking area and west of Hudson Drive, a concrete foundation occupies a small opening in a dense stand of woody vegetation (Figure 3.32). The foundation supported a metal tower used to identify targets and improve fire control.

Large woody vegetation on Battery Potter's engineered earthwork is predominantly eastern red cedar (*Juniperus virginiana*) and hackberry (*Celtis occidentalis*). Some of the individual trees are greater than twenty-feet in height.

Woody vegetation is not only limited to the engineered earthwork. The sloped portion of the concrete battery, rising approximately ten-feet above the engineered earthwork, has eastern red cedars growing in cracks and in large spalling areas (Figure 3.33). The *chemin de ronde* has become a collection area for leaf litter and debris and hosts woody vegetation (Figure 3.34). On the battery's west facade, Virginia creeper (*Parthenocissus quinquefolia*) is growing on the vertical walls and sloped portion of the concrete structure. Northwest of the battery, two deciduous trees are located in a lawn area near the intersection of North Bragg Drive and Hudson Drive.

The superior slope of Battery Potter offers an opportunity to view the Atlantic approach to New York Harbor and understand the configuration of coastal defense batteries at Sandy Hook. Vegetation growing on the engineered earthwork interferes with views to the water, however, the battery's height above the surrounding area provides relatively open views (see Figures 3.24 and 3.28). Small-scale features at Battery Potter consist of an interpretive wayside and wheelstops installed to limit parking to the existing unpaved area. The wayside is situated west of the battery's entry and south of the powerhouse building. Sections of wooden telephone poles are laid just east of Hudson Drive and north of the parking area to prevent vehicles from parking in the open area in front of Battery Potter.

BATTERY GRANGER

Battery Granger's two emplacements face east and the structure is located approximately 700 feet south of Battery Potter and 650 feet northeast of the Mortar Battery along Hudson Drive (Drawing 3.8). The reference elevation for Granger is seven feet and the engineered earthwork, north of the concrete structure, starts at an approximate elevation of twenty-eight feet. The earthwork slopes away from the battery for over sixty feet, arriving at an elevation of ten feet, and unites with the gradually undulating coastal topography. The engineered earthwork wraps around the north end of the battery slopes against the concrete wall on the west elevation. On the south end, a concrete wall extends from the battery and retains the raised earthwork to the east. Vehicular access to Battery Granger is provided along Hudson Drive. East of the northbound travel lane, a portion of Hudson Drive widens to allow limited parallel parking beside the battery's west elevation. There are no sidewalks or pedestrian routes along Hudson Drive and there is no evidence of social trails around the battery or on the engineered earthwork.

Battery Granger consists of two gun platforms with recessed, circular gun wells that held large caliber artillery mounted on counterweight carriages. The centers of the platforms are spaced approximately 125 feet apart. A covered concrete battery commander's station is centered between the two platforms and cantilevers beyond the structure's west facade. The south end of each gun platform is accessed by concrete steps that lead up from the ground level. Concrete steps from the south end of platform #2 and north end of platform #1 lead to an elevated walkway that connects the platforms to the battery commander's station. Above the gun platforms, the concrete terreplein shows evidence of an asphalt-based product either used to fill joints or remaining in the joints after use as part of a larger concrete surface treatment (Figure 3.35). Efflorescence can be seen on some vertical concrete surfaces and small spalling areas are present on both horizontal and vertical surfaces. Guardrails are located along the gun platform on either side of the battery commander's station. The railings are in good to fair condition showing limited corrosion.

The vegetation on Battery Granger's engineered earthwork is primarily hackberry (*Celtis occidentalis*) and eastern red cedar (*Juniperus virginiana*). The eastern red cedars appear more heavily concentrated at the interface of the engineered slope and concrete terreplein. A large hackberry, approximately thirty-inches diameter at breast height, is located near the southwest corner of the battery at the toe of the engineered slope. Phragmites (*Phragmites* sp.), also called common reed, is growing in the gun wells at both platforms. The views from the battery commander's station to the water are blocked woody vegetation first encountered at the edge of the terreplein. Vegetation beyond the engineered earthwork may also impact views, however, that cannot be completely ascertained until the obstructions closest to the commander's station are removed. East of the vehicular pull-off along Hudson Drive, an interpretive wayside is installed. Between the wayside and battery, a chain-link fence and signage have been erected to warn visitors of potentially hazardous conditions (Figure 3.36).

MORTAR BATTERY

Sandy Hook's Mortar Battery has the distinction of being the first completed and operational concrete mortar battery in the United States. Unlike other large caliber gun batteries, the Mortar Battery utilized sixteen short-barreled guns called mortars. The mortars were grouped into four sets of four each and emplaced in platforms recessed into a massive earth and concrete structure. The mortars were set to fire projectiles at high arcing trajectories, and given the distance the projectiles could travel, the structure was set further west from the Atlantic coastline than other coastal defenses.

The Mortar Battery is located east of Hudson Road and opposite the Sandy Hook Lighthouse. The battery is 650 feet southwest of Battery Granger and approximately a quarter mile northwest of Battery Gunnison. In addition to Hudson Road on the west, the Mortar Battery is bounded by a parking lot off of Magruder Road to the south and the Marine Academy of Science and Technology (MAST) campus to the east. The Mortar Battery is a rectangular structure with its narrower side and guns oriented northeast toward the main shipping channel. Historically, the battery's gun direction has been described as north and for consistency, the existing conditions description will use this orientation. The four pits that held the mortars will be described directionally as the northwest, northeast, southwest, and southeast emplacements (Drawing 3.9).

The reference elevation for the Mortar Battery is eight feet and this elevation is consistent with a relatively flat, surrounding area that includes Fort Hancock's Parade Ground to the west. The rectangular, engineered earthwork rises up to an elevation of forty-five feet in the center and slopes down to thirty-five feet above the D-shaped openings for each emplacement. The platform for each emplacement has an elevation of approximately seven feet.

Pedestrians enter the Mortar Battery through one of two wide paths on the west side of the structure. One path is north of the end of a perimeter wall and the other passes through an opening in the wall. A gravel and wood-chip surfaced trail connects the two paths and offers access to the southwest and northwest emplacements. Long concrete galleries lead from the trail to the emplacements. Access to the northeast and southeast emplacements is through interior routes that are not open to the general public. South of the southwest gallery, a trail leads up the engineered earthwork and continues across the top before terminating in an area between the northwest and northeast emplacements. The head of the trail is blocked by fencing, but dilapidated cribbing and signs of erosion testify that the route was once well used. North of the Mortar Battery's engineered earthwork, a poorly defined trail leads to an open field east of the structure. The density of vegetation along the trail makes it difficult to discern the route.

The major constructed feature of the Mortar Battery is the engineered earthwork. On the west and a portion of the south sides, a concrete perimeter wall wraps around the battery. In the southwest corner, an L-shaped concrete structure extends from the wall. This enclosed structure served as the counterscarp gallery and housed machine gunners in the event that the perimeter wall was breached. Two concrete battery commander's stations are located at the top of the engineered earthwork. One station is south of the two north emplacements and the other is south of the two south emplacements. Both are surrounded by vegetation and have been defaced with graffiti. In addition to the commander's stations, four concrete telephone data booth are located above the southwest corner of each emplacement and supported by arched, concrete spans. Efflorescence can be seen on some of the vertical concrete surfaces and spalling is present on both horizontal and vertical concrete surfaces (Figure 3.37).

The vegetation on the Mortar Battery's engineered earthwork is primarily eastern red cedar (*Juniperus virginiana*) with smaller quantities of beach plum (*Prunus maritima*) and ailanthus (*Ailanthus altissima*). The understory is primarily Japanese honeysuckle (*Lonicera japonica*) that has grown dense enough to ensnare anyone walking on the structure. In addition to the engineered earthwork, large woody vegetation has established between the perimeter wall and the trail to the northwest and southwest emplacements. The main species along the perimeter wall is hackberry (*Celtis occidentalis*) (Figure 3.38).

During its operation, the Mortar Battery's artillery crews did not directly sight their targets on the water. Present-day vegetation beyond the engineered earthwork does block views, however, these views were not necessary for the battery's function.

Small-scale features associated with the Mortar Battery include various types of fencing, remnants of a structure, a wayside, and signage. On the east side of the battery, a chain-link fence separates the engineered earthwork from MAST campus. The fence also wraps around a portion of the south side of the battery. East of the trail to the northwest and southwest emplacements, woven-wire mesh fencing is installed to discourage visitors from climbing up the engineered earthwork (Figure 3.39). The fencing is in good to fair condition with some indications that people have climbed over it and embarked up the earthwork. At the top of the Mortar Battery, several wood post and wire cable fences are installed along a path to discourage anyone from getting too close to the mortars and a potentially fatal fall. The fencing is being overtaken by vegetation and is in fair to poor condition (Figure 3.40). East of the west perimeter wall and centered between the southwest and northwest emplacements are a concrete footing and metal ring that appear to be remnants of an early twentieth century steel tower used as a battery commander's station and later, a weather station. Signage and a wayside provide visitors with information on the Mortar Battery. Two signs are located outside the perimeter wall on either side of the entry near the southwest emplacement. Inside the wall, a wayside is located just south of the gallery to the southwest mortar pit (Figure 3.41).

BATTERY GUNNISON

Battery Gunnison is the only rapid fire gun battery oriented to the east and is located about a quarter mile southeast of the Mortar Battery. Of all the coastal defense batteries at Sandy Hook, Battery Gunnison most readily conveys its military role in protecting the southern approach to New York because the concrete structure is emplaced with two 6-inch caliber guns (Figure 3.42).[3] Battery Gunnison is bounded by the Gunnison Beach facility to the north and west, Atlantic Drive to the west, and a waste water treatment plant to the south (Drawing 3.10).

The reference elevation for Battery Gunnison is ten feet and west of the battery, the topography is relatively flat. The top of the engineered earthwork rises to twenty-two feet immediately north of the gun platforms and slopes away from the battery for approximately fifty feet. The engineered earthwork wraps around both emplacements at the north and south of the battery. The high point of the engineered earthwork is located between the two emplacements covering a central, concrete structure. The earth and sand above the structure rises to twenty-six feet in elevation.

Due to its location near the Gunnison Beach facility, there are clearly defined and maintained routes for vehicular and pedestrian circulation at Battery Gunnison. Vehicles traveling on Atlantic Drive can enter a large surface parking area, Parking Lot G, located west of the battery. A pedestrian walkway leads from the parking lot east to the beach facility. A concrete walk parallels the unpaved route to the beach and gently winds toward gun platform #2 at the battery. In addition to formal routes, there are social trails associated with Battery Gunnison. A trail is present southeast of gun platform #1 and proceeds down the engineered earthwork. There is no continuation of the trail or connection to another circulation feature at the toe of the engineered slope. Another trail is visible between the two gun platforms and a circular route connects to this trail demonstrating a path of travel around the top of the central, concrete structure.

Battery Gunnison's two gun platforms are circular and the centers are spaced approximately 125 feet apart. Each platform is roughly fifty feet in diameter and has a raised surfaced to receive the pedestal mounted guns (see Figure 3.42). Two sets of concrete steps provide access to each gun platform. Steps are located to the west and north for platform #1 and to the west and south for platform #2.

Between the two platforms is a nearly square concrete structure that houses the battery's magazines, plotting room, and storage rooms. The top of this structure is covered with earth and sand and on the north and south sides, concrete vaults protrude through the earthwork so projectiles could be hoisted up to each platform. In addition to the hoists, a concrete battery commander's station is located on top of the magazine near the west edge. The battery commander's station is U-shaped in plan and lacks a roof or other covering. Efflorescence can be seen on some of the vertical surfaces and spalling is present on both horizontal and vertical surfaces (Figure 3.43). Handrails are installed along the stairs leading up to the guns platforms and guardrails are located around platforms themselves. The railings are in good condition and have an intermediate horizontal rail between ground level and the top rail.

The vegetation on Battery Gunnison's engineered slopes is primarily eastern red cedar (*Juniperus virginiana*) and beach plum (*Prunus maritima*) (Figure 3.44). As the toe of the engineered slope transitions to the wind-swept dunes, more beachgrass and scrub vegetation is encountered. Recent vegetation removal has been conducted near the top of the engineered earthwork as evidenced by newly cut stumps (see Figure 3.43). West of the battery, eight deciduous tree are randomly placed in an open lawn area that extends from the battery to the beach facility and Atlantic Drive.

Views from the gun positions to the water are relatively open with some obstructions caused by eastern red cedars growing near the top of the engineered earthwork (see Figure 3.42). Small-scale features at Battery Gunnison include bollards and an interpretive wayside. Along Atlantic Drive, wood posts support sections of rope and form a decorative vehicular barrier that parallels road. West of platform #2, a wayside is installed along the concrete walk that connects the beach facility to the battery.

BATTERIES KINGMAN AND MILLS

Batteries Kingman and Mills represent the last generation of large caliber guns installed at Sandy Hook to counter early twentieth century improvements in naval artillery. The two batteries are located on the western side of the peninsula along Sandy Hook Bay. The batteries are immediately south of Horseshoe Cove and are oriented to the east with two emplacements per battery. Seven hundred fifty feet separate Battery Kingman's southern emplacement from Battery Mills' northern emplacement. Since the initial construction, emplaced guns, and later modifications for both batteries were nearly identical, existing conditions will be described pertaining to the both structures with separate highlights for specific landscape features.

A maritime forest, composed primarily of American holly (*Ilex opaca*), is located east of Batteries Kingman and Mills. West of the batteries, forty feet or more separate Sandy Hook Bay from the structures. Except for the casemated batteries, the surrounding topography is flat with changes of five feet or less in elevation. The reference elevation for Batteries Kingman and Mills is five feet. The engineered earthworks, roughly oval in shape, rise to an elevation of forty feet in the middle. Two high points are present on each earthwork over the battery's gun emplacements that rise to forty-five feet (Drawings 3.11 and 3.12).

Vehicular circulation to Batteries Kingman and Mills is along a non-descript road that intersects Hartshorne Drive and proceeds west to the batteries. This access road is closed to the general public and locked by a vehicular gate. As the road approaches the bay, it splits into a northern route to Battery Kingman and a southern route to Battery Mills. The branch heading north to Battery Kingman is paved with asphalt and continues along the bay until terminating at the casemated entry to the battery. North of the entry and around the remainder of the battery, the road is a combination of gravel and compacted earth. The branch leading to and encircling Battery Mills is also unpaved. On the west side of Battery Mills a portion of this road, approximately 200-feet, has been washed away by the bay (Figure 3.45). There are no dedicated pedestrian routes around Batteries Kingman and Mills. For Battery Kingman, some historic maps indicate trails ascending and on top of the engineered earthwork, however, no clear trails were observed. On top of Battery Mills, a segment of a trail is visible but there is no connection from the base of the earthwork to the trail.

The major constructed feature of Batteries Kingman and Mills is the engineered earthwork that rises in stark contrast to the surrounding land (Figure 3.46). For both batteries, three entries are located on the west side of the engineered earthwork that provided access to the guns and covered magazines and storage areas. All three have a concrete frame that supports an open metal gate. Concrete cheek walls extend perpendicular from either side of the frame to retain the engineered slopes. The main entry is in the center of the structure and the other two are aligned on center with each gun emplacement. At Battery Mills, the main entry and entry for emplacement #1 are inaccessible due to the density of vegetation (Figure 3.47). Above the emplacements, concrete canopies extend over the gun platforms to shield the artillery from overhead fire. The canopies and concrete facades around the emplacement openings show efflorescence and at Battery Mills emplacement #2, large spalling areas (Figures 3.48 and 3.49).

Several structures emerge from the top of the two batteries' earthworks. At Battery Kingman, a concrete box is located south of emplacement #2 and a concrete pipe protrudes southwest of the same emplacement (Figures 3.50 and 3.51). At Battery Mills, a tapered concrete box and metal pipe is located near the center top of the earthwork and a concrete pipe is visible southwest of emplacement #1 (Figures 3.52 and 3.53). These structures are most likely associated with ventilation or served as flues for furnaces. On the west side of Battery Kingman, a strip of concrete is exposed near the top of the earthwork and is possibly a piece of the reinforced concrete buster course, installed two feet below the surface, to protect the battery from aerial bombing (Figure 3.54). Although not a direct part of either battery, components of another structure are located west of Battery Kingman. Approximately fifty feet west from the shoreline, a line of wood pilings, remnants of a bulkhead, stand in Sandy Hook Bay.

The engineered earthworks are mostly populated with mature eastern red cedar (*Juniperus virginiana*), hackberry (*Celtis occidentalis*), and ailanthus (*Ailanthus altissima*). In addition to these major species, a few scrub pine (*Pinus virginiana*) were observed (Figure 3.55). At Battery Mills, three planetrees (*Platanus × acerifolia*) are located near the western toe of the slope. The understory is primarily a vine mixture of Japanese honeysuckle (*Lonicera japonica*), greenbrier (*Smilax* sp.), and poison ivy (*Toxicodendron radicans*) so dense that walking to the top of the battery would be undesirable and extremely difficult with the vegetation fully leafed out.

Unlike other large caliber gun batteries at Sandy Hook, a direct view of the water and potential targets was never a designed feature of Batteries Kingman and Mills. The batteries relied on observations from other vantage points and electronic communication to aim their guns. Not surprisingly, the existing vegetation east of the batteries blocks any view to the water from the emplacements. Although the engineered earthworks provide an elevated position, the density of vegetation on top of the structures blocks views in almost all directions.

Small-scale features associated with Batteries Kingman and Mills are located on top of the engineered earthworks and on the ground level to the east of the batteries. On top of the earthworks and above each emplacement, a six-foot high chain-link fence is installed. The fences appear to be in good to fair condition with vines twining their way through the chain-link mesh (see Figure 3.49). Near the high point above Battery Kingman's emplacement #2, a post and wire fence is installed in a U-shaped configuration with an open end facing south (Figure 3.56). The fence is overrun by vines and other vegetation. East of the batteries, two series of wood guardrails are installed along the eastern edge of the unpaved roads. The guardrails are in fair to poor condition and located across from the gun emplacements (Figures 3.57 and 3.58).

NIKE RADAR SITE

The NIKE radar and launch sites are approximately a mile apart and located off of Hartshorne Drive, Sandy Hook's major north-south thoroughfare. The radar site is roughly triangular in shape and enclosed by a perimeter security fence. The site contains three areas set around an undisturbed area in the middle. Separate groups of structures comprise Control Area #1, Control Area #2, and the Ready Barracks (Drawing 3.13). The longest perimeter of the sites runs from west to east. The western point of the site, accessible from Hartshorne Drive, contains Control Area #2. The eastern point contains Control Area #1 and is accessible from Atlantic Drive. The boundaries of the site converge at a northern point that contain the Ready Barracks and are accessible from Sheldon Road.

Unlike earlier coastal defense batteries, the topography at the NIKE radar site shows no major engineered or constructed earthworks. The topography is consistent with the slight variations seen in other interior locations on the Sandy Hook peninsula. Areas have been modified to create level surfaces for buildings, radar towers, and circulation features. Other than those modifications, there are no conspicuous features of the radar site's topography.

Vehicular circulation to the NIKE radar site is along the major north-south route, Hartshorne Drive. An access drive off of Hartshorne Drive leads east to Parking Lot L and the parking lot continues east towards the perimeter fence surrounding Control Area #2. The park's Multi-use Path (MUP) skirts the eastern edge of the lot and proceeds north toward the Fort Hancock Historic

District. Pedestrian access from either the parking lot or the MUP is controlled by a locked gate that is part of the perimeter fence. Inside the radar site, a paved vehicular road connects Control Areas #1 and #2. From each control area, a vehicular route leads to the Ready Barracks (Figure 3.59). From Control Area #1, the route is paved and ends in a hammerhead turnaround. From Control Area #2, the route is unpaved and terminates west of the barracks in an irregularly-shaped parking area. The parking area contains loose stockpiles of bricks and other construction materials. A concrete sidewalk between each control area and the Ready Barracks provides pedestrian access between the locations (Figure 3.60).

The three distinct areas at the NIKE radar site contain two separate radar facilities corresponding to the two firing batteries at the launch site and barracks with integrated mess halls to house and feed personnel when on active duty at the site. The buildings and structures at Control Area #1 include three radar towers with rectangular platforms (417–419) and one radar tower with a hexagonal platform (473). The metal towers are in good to fair condition with evidence of corrosion and have guardrails around the perimeter of their elevated platforms. Four concrete block buildings, each one-story high, are also located in Control Area #1 and are designated Equipment Building (454), Generator Building (414), Connecting Corridor (411), and Sentry Box (413). An abandoned Army generator stands northwest of the Equipment Building (454), parallel to the building's facade. A five-foot high concrete structure is also present that served as a pedestal for a type of acquisition radar known as ABAR (453). The concrete block buildings are in fair to poor condition with deteriorating paint, failing mortar joints, and unsecured windows and doors.

Similar to Control Area #1, the buildings and structures present at Control Area #2 include three radar towers with rectangular platforms (420–422) and two towers with hexagonal platforms (467 and 472). Control Area #2 also features a hexagonal concrete foundation that held the HIPAR radar unit (469). The metal towers are in good to fair condition with evidence of corrosion and have guardrails around the perimeter of their elevated platforms. In addition to the towers and foundation, Control Area #2 contains four concrete block buildings, each one story high, that are designated Generator Building (410), HIPAR Building (468), Connecting Corridor (409), and Sentry Box (423). These structures are in fair condition with better exterior paint than their counterparts in Control Area #1.

The final area at the NIKE radar site contains the buildings and structures for the Ready Barracks. Two barrack buildings (402 and 403) are located in the northern portion of the site. The buildings are rectangular and constructed with corrugated metal siding and roofing set on concrete foundations. The barracks are in good to fair condition with some evidence of corrosion. Adjacent to the barracks are two rectangular concrete foundations (404 and 405) that mark the footprint of barracks that are no longer extant. Two additional buildings complete the ensemble for the Ready Barracks. The Boiler Room (107) is a one story, corrugated metal shed located south of the barracks. East of the shed is the Latrine (406) that is constructed from concrete block and stands one story high. Both buildings are in good to fair condition with some damage observed in the soffits of the Latrine.

At the NIKE radar site, vegetation primarily consists of eastern red cedars (*Juniperus virginiana*), shrub species such as bayberry (*Myrica* sp.) and sumac (*Rhus* sp.), and grass species. The vegetation encroaches on buildings, vehicular and pedestrian circulation features, and the perimeter fence. In many cases, vegetation is immediately adjacent to a building or feature (Figures 3.61 and 3.62). During the radar site's operation, a view was maintained to allow unobstructed radar signals between the each Missile Tracking Radar and the control vans and individual missiles at the launch site. It is difficult to determine if those views are presently opened or blocked because the vertical components at the launch site are not extant.

Small-scale features at the NIKE radar site include the perimeter security fence, a basketball court, and pedestrian lights. The perimeter fence is comprised of chain-link sections secured to H-shaped posts. The top of each post holds a single extension arm that supports strands of barbed wire. The perimeter fence is in fair to poor condition. An asphalt basketball court is located approximately forty feet south of the Ready Barracks. The long axis of the court is oriented north to south and sections of chain-link fence enclose the north and south ends. Pedestrian-scale lights line both walks from the control areas to the Ready Barracks. The lights are also located along walks to the north and south of the barrack buildings. The lights are in good to fair condition with the exception of one light pole, near the east end of the Ready Barracks, which is knocked over (Figure 3.63).

NIKE LAUNCH SITE

Located south of the radar site and east of Batteries Kingman and Mills, the NIKE launch site is roughly T-shaped in plan and bounded by a perimeter fence. The long leg of the "T" begins at Hartshorne Drive and proceeds east toward the Atlantic Ocean where it divides into shorter northern and southern sections. The western portion of the "T" contains the Ready Barracks and the southern section contains the Missile Maintenance Area. The northern section contains the underground missile magazines and concrete pads that supported the launching racks. The concrete pads are oriented north to south for firing missiles to the east (Figure 3.64 and Drawing 3.14).

The base elevation for the NIKE launch site is eight feet. Surrounding elevations vary from six to sixteen feet excluding a dune crest and beach along the Atlantic coastline. The Ready Barracks area matches the base elevation and then proceeding east, the topography rises along the central access road to the missile magazines (Figure 3.65). At the missile magazines, a plateau with an approximate elevation of twenty feet provides a level surface for the concrete pads that supported the launching racks and adequate cover for the underground missile storage. South of the magazines, the plateau slopes down to an elevation of twelve feet at the Missile Maintenance Area. In the Missile Maintenance Area, two engineered earthworks emerge on either side of the Warhead Building. North of the building, a narrow, elliptical earthwork rises to an elevation of twenty feet. South of the building, a crescent-shaped earthwork also rises to an elevation of twenty feet. The tips of the crescent wrap around the Warhead Building to the north and almost form a continuous landform with the northern earthwork. Recycling storage bins and a debris pile from a New Jersey state beach cleaning program presently stand against the eastern portion of the crescent earthwork (Figure 3.66). In addition, the northeast tip of the earthwork has been removed. The two engineered earthworks provided protection when missiles were fitted with warheads and fueled with a volatile mixture of jet fuel and oxidizers. North of the Warhead Building, park law enforcement has set up a firearms range in a low lying area. The depressed land form allows a range to be established with the land rising around the depression acting as a backstop (Figure 3.67).

The northbound lanes of Hartshorne Drive border the west edge of the launch site and provide vehicular access. An approximate 50-foot by 180-foot asphalt parking area is located west of Hartshorne Drive and across from the gated entry to the site. The southern end of the parking area features a NIKE Hercules missile and communications trailer display secured in a rectangular area by a chain-link fence. The park's Multi-use Path (MUP) heads in a north to south direction between Hartshorne Drive and the launch site's outer fence. Both vehicles and pedestrians enter the launch site along a paved route that departs from Hartshorne Drive and continues through the site as the central access road. Access to the site is limited by a regularly locked gate that crosses the paved entry.

The central access road is paved with asphalt and heading east from the entry, the road continues past the Ready Barracks and terminates at a "T" intersection with perpendicular routes leading to the Missile Magazines and Missile Maintenance Area. Two asphalt-paved spurs branch off from the central access road prior to the "T" intersection. East of the entry gate, the first spur departs from the access road and heads south between the Ready Barracks and the outer security fence. The road turns to the east and continues behind the Ready Barracks' Latrine (434). East of the Ready Barracks, the second spur proceeds northeast from the central access road and provides a route to the Generator Building (429). At the "T" intersection, an asphalt road continues south from the central road and provides access to the Missile Assembly and Test Building (449) and Warhead Building (450) in the Missile Maintenance Area. North of the "T" intersection, an unpaved route wraps around the Missile Magazines on the outside of the inner security fence. Located north of the Warhead Building (450) and south of the unpaved route around the Missile Magazines, an unpaved area has been carved out to store and clean New Jersey state beach cleaning vehicles. The beach cleaning vehicles also travel on this unpaved route for convenient access to the beach immediately east of the launch site.

Pedestrian circulation at the launch site includes a network of walkways in the Ready Barracks and a path to access the Canine Kennel (458). The individual barracks and support buildings that comprise the Ready Barracks area are connected by a series of three-foot wide concrete walkways. The walkways are oriented parallel and perpendicular to the buildings and are presently in good condition. At the northwest corner of the Missile Magazines, a path departs from the unpaved road outside the inner fence, winds through dense vegetation, and arrives at the Canine Kennel (458). There is no continuation of the path or a connection to other circulation features at the Canine Kennel.

The three distinct areas at the NIKE launch site contain buildings and structures for missile storage, maintenance, security, and barracks to house personnel. The Missile Magazine area contains the four underground magazines that stored Ajax and later Hercules missiles. The southwest magazine (428) is denoted Section A, the northwest magazine (427) is denoted Section B, the southeast magazine (426) is denoted Section C, and the northeast magazine (425) is denoted Section D. Two concrete block buildings, each one-story high, are located west of the underground magazines and are designated Generator Building (429) and Paint and Oil Storage (447). Both of the concrete block buildings are in fair condition, however, existing vegetation is encroaching on the structures. Northwest of the magazines, two buildings that supported the site's sentry dogs stand surrounded by dense vegetation. The Canine Kennel (458) is a one story structure with corrugated metal siding and roofing set on a concrete foundation. Immediately east of the Canine Kennel is a one story, concrete block building designated Kennel Storage (457). The density of vegetation around the buildings makes an assessment difficult, but both appear to be in fair condition. The final structure in the Missile Magazine area is a concrete foundation for a Sentry Hut (448) that is located west of the underground magazines.

South of the Missile Magazines are five buildings in the Missile Maintenance Area. Two concrete block buildings, each one-story high, are the largest structures in the area and are designated Missile Assembly and Test Building (449) and Warhead Building (450). Both of the concrete block buildings display signs of water damage on their exterior and are in fair condition. Three small, contemporary, wood-frame sheds are located east of the Missile Assembly and Test Building and a trailer is parked north of the same building.

West of the Missile Magazines and Missile Maintenance Area are nine buildings that comprise the Ready Barracks. Four barrack buildings (T-430–T-433) are located south of the central access road. The "T" prefix to the building number designates a building or structure the Army categorized as temporary rather than permanent. The barracks are rectangular in shape with corrugated metal siding and roofing set on concrete foundations. Located south of the barracks, the Bolier House (T-435) is also constructed from corrugated metal siding and roofing. All of the corrugated metal buildings are in good to fair condition with some evidence of corrosion. The Ready Barracks include three concrete block buildings, each one-story high, that are designated Latrine (434), Ready Building (437), and Sentry Hut (439). The Latrine and Ready Building are located south of the barracks and the Sentry Hut is located northwest of the barracks and immediately inside the entry gate to the launch site. All of the concrete block buildings are in fair condition. The final structure in the Ready Barracks is a concrete foundation for a Sentry Hut (456) that is located northeast of the barracks along the central access road.

At the NIKE launch site, vegetation primarily consists of eastern red cedars (*Juniperus virginiana*), shrub species such as bayberry (*Myrica* sp.) and sumac (*Rhus* sp.), and grass species. Eastern red cedars cover the majority of the engineered earthworks in the Missile Maintenance Area (Figure 3.68). A mixture of vegetation encroaches on buildings, vehicular and pedestrian circulation features, and the perimeter fence. In many cases, vegetation is immediately adjacent to a building or feature.

Small-scale features at the NIKE launch site include an inner and outer security fence, floodlights along the inner security fence, floodlights at the Missile Maintenance Area, spotlights in the Missile Magazine area, two antenna, and a missile display erected on the road in the Ready Barracks. Similar to the radar site, the launch site features a perimeter fence along its outside boundary and then adds an inner fence that encloses the missile magazines. Both fences are comprised of chain-link sections secured to H-shaped posts. The top of each post holds a single extension arm that supports strands of barbed wire. The inner and outer fences are in fair to poor condition and beach erosion has undermined portions of the outer fence near the northeast corner of the site (Figures 3.69 and 3.70).

At the Missile Magazine area, eight floodlights are positioned along the inner fence. Each light features a parabolic fixture mounted with a metal bracket to a round, wood pole (Figure 3.71). The fixtures are aimed parallel to the direction of the inner fence. Six similar lights are located at the Missile Maintenance Area with half located on the northern engineered earthwork and the other half on the southern engineered earthwork. The six lights are mounted at the top of round, metal poles. Vegetation encroaches on many of the floodlights, however, they are in good to fair condition. In the Missile Magazine area a single, round, wood pole stands near the Section B magazine (427). From ground level, the first eight to ten feet of the pole are painted yellow and a red "B" is featured on the yellow field. Two spotlights with parabolic metal hoods are mounted at the top of the pole (Figure 3.72).

East of the Missile Maintenance Area and approaching the outer fence, an antenna and monitoring equipment have been set up for collecting weather and tide information (Figure 3.73). A second antenna assists with collecting weather and tide information and is located south of the Missile Maintenance Area near the outer fence (Figure 3.74). In the southwest corner of the Ready Barracks, a missile display has been installed on the road connecting the central access road to the barracks' Latrine (434). The display informs visitors about the weaponry used at Sandy Hook's last generation of coastal defenses.

ENDNOTES

[1] The 1990 survey covers the entire peninsula and is recorded on twenty-seven sheets. Hard copies were found in the park's Engineering Office and as a component of this Cultural Landscape Report, the surveys were scanned. A copy of the scanned files has been sent to the park's GIS specialist.

[2] This naming convention is consistent with the *Historic Structure Report: Battery Potter, Mortar Battery and Battery Gunnison* completed in 2007. For additional information on different names historically assigned to the mortars, please see James J. Lee III and Lauren Laham, *Historic Structure Report: Battery Potter, Mortar Battery and Battery Gunnison. Fort Hancock, New Jersey, Sandy Hook Unit, Gateway National Recreation Area* (United States Department of the Interior, National Park Service, 2007), 191-192.

[3] The guns are not original to Battery Gunnison but acquired from a similar battery and installed for interpretive purposes.

Figure 3.1. View looking west at gun platform #5, Battery Urmston. The gun platforms for emplacements #1, #2, #5, and #6 are T-shaped with full-width steps that lead up the long leg of the "T." At the north end of the platforms, narrow notches served as a recessed space to rest pillar mounted guns when not in use (Olmsted Center, January 2009).

Figure 3.2. View looking northeast at stairwells to magazines, Battery Urmston. Both handrails and guardrails show a heavy degree of corrosion and are staining the concrete below them. Access to existing doors is blocked by vegetation that has grown up in the stairwells (Olmsted Center, January 2009).

Figure 3.3. View looking northwest at gun platform #3, Battery Urmston. Large woody vegetation primarily consists of eastern red cedar (*Juniperus virginiana*), beach plum (*Prunus maritima*), hackberry (*Celtis occidentalis*), and ailanthus (*Ailanthus altissima*). These species have also found suitable locations to grow in the low-lying areas, flat surfaces, and cracks of the battery (Olmsted Center, January 2009).

Figure 3.4. View looking northeast from gun platform #4, Battery Urmston. The views from the gun platforms and battery commander's station to the water are primarily impeded by woody vegetation growing at the interface of the engineered slope and concrete battery structure (Olmsted Center, January 2009).

Figure 3.5. View looking west at U.S. Coast Guard perimeter fence and Battery Morris. There is currently no vehicular access to Battery Morris and staff and visitors wishing to see the structure walk on a trail surface comprised of broken asphalt and accumulated leaf litter and debris. Emerging woody vegetation obscures a clear definition of the trail and makes access difficult (Olmsted Center, January 2009).

Figure 3.6. View looking north at emplacement #2, Battery Morris. Woody vegetation is growing in and around the stairs to the point where they are difficult to ascend and reach the gun platforms (Olmsted Center, January 2009).

Figure 3.7. View looking southeast, Battery Morris. A large hackberry, approximately eighteen-inches diameter at breast height, is growing on the battery to the west of gun platform #4 (Olmsted Center, January 2009).

Figure 3.8. View looking northeast at gun platform #1, Battery Morris. A wood picket fence is located to the north and east of the gun platform that is painted maroon red and is in poor condition (Olmsted Center, January 2009).

Figure 3.9. View looking northeast at corner of structure, Battery Peck. Efflorescence can be seen on many of the vertical surfaces and spalling is present on both horizontal and vertical surfaces indicating water has penetrated the concrete and is damaging the material (Olmsted Center, January 2009).

Figure 3.10. View of guardrail south of emplacement #1, Battery Peck. The railings are in fair to poor condition with corrosion covering most pieces. Some assemblies lack any solid material where the vertical members fasten the railing to a solid support (Olmsted Center, January 2009).

Figure 3.11. View looking northwest at Battery Engle (CRF Station Peck). The concrete coincidence range finder station (CRF) constructed on top of Battery Engle is located west of Battery Peck and features a low-pitched concrete roof. The structure appears in fair condition with some minor efflorescence visible on the roof (Olmsted Center, January 2009).

Figure 3.12. View looking north at a post World War II trailer, Batteries Engle and Peck. Northeast of Battery Engle, a communications trailer sits abandoned. The trailer is a frequent target for graffiti (Olmsted Center, January 2009).

Figure 3.13. View looking northeast at observation platform. North of Batteries Engle and Peck, an observation platform stands on top of a one story, wood-frame structure. The platform permits panoramic views across Lower New York Harbor and is regularly used for bird watching (Olmsted Center, January 2009).

Figure 3.14. View looking northwest at Battery Peck. Presently, the area south of Battery Peck is filled with dense vegetation and is nearly impassable (Olmsted Center, January 2009).

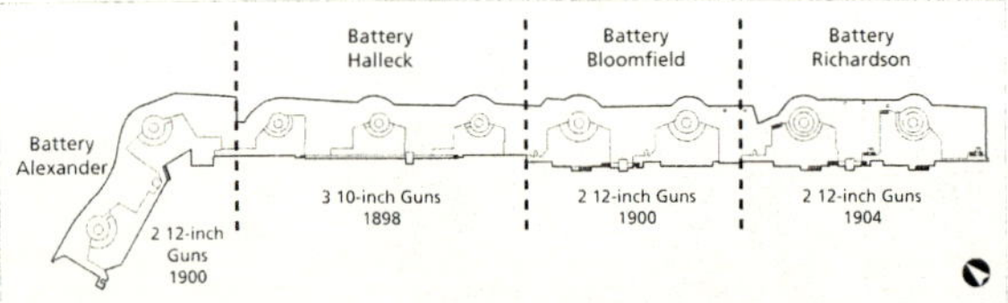

Figure 3.15. Diagram of Nine Gun Battery's individual names and construction dates. The emplacements at Nine Gun Battery were constructed in phases and divided into four separate batteries. The first three emplacements were designated Battery Halleck, south of Halleck was Battery Bloomfield and south of Bloomfield was Battery Richardson. The northernmost guns were designated Battery Alexander (Olmsted Center, 2009).

Figure 3.16. Granite blocks northeast of emplacement #8, Nine Gun Battery. Large granite blocks are visible immediately beyond the concrete terreplein. These blocks are remnants of the Civil War-era Fort at Sandy Hook (Olmsted Center, January 2009).

Figure 3.17. View of failing metal door, Nine Gun Battery. Several dozen doors and windows are missing or not properly mounted at the magazines, commander's stations, and other auxiliary rooms at Nine Gun Battery (Olmsted Center, January 2009).

Figure 3.18. View looking west at battery commander's station Halleck, Nine Gun Battery. A cantilevered structure between emplacements #5 and #7, intended to provide access to the commander's station, is in poor condition (Olmsted Center, January 2009).

Figure 3.19. View looking south at existing guardrail, Nine Gun Battery. Both handrails and guardrails are present at Nine Gun Battery and are generally in good to fair condition (Olmsted Center, January 2009).

Figure 3.20. View looking northwest at the concrete ramp to gun platform #1, Nine Gun Battery. At transitions between the ground level and gun platforms and also the gun platforms and terreplein, there are stairs and ramps that lack any kind of railing. This ramp has escutcheon plates but lacks a guardrail (Olmsted Center, January 2009).

Figure 3.21. View looking west toward battery commander's station Bloomfield, Nine Gun Battery. In addition to growing on the engineered earthwork, eastern red cedars (*Juniperus virginiana*) have emerged in the cracks and cold joints of the battery's horizontal concrete surfaces (Olmsted Center, January 2009).

Figure 3.22. View looking west at emplacement #7, Nine Gun Battery. Phragmites (*Phragmites* sp.), also called common reed, is growing in the gun wells at emplacements #6, #7, and #9 (Olmsted Center, January 2009).

Figure 3.23. View looking north at main entry, Battery Potter. The main entry is through an arched opening flanked by defensive stone towers. Constructed from granite blocks salvaged from the Civil War-era fort, the main entry resembles a castle (Olmsted Center, January 2009).

Figure 3.24. View looking west at entry to parking area, Battery Potter. Southwest of the main entry, a small parking area departs from Hudson Drive, loops around a small building, and joins back up with Hudson Drive (Olmsted Center, January 2009).

Figure 3.25. View looking northeast across superior slope, Battery Potter. On top of Battery Potter, the superior slope proceeds east from the terreplein that contained two openings for raising and lowering the 12-inch caliber guns (Olmsted Center, April 2008).

Figure 3.26. View looking north across *chemin de ronde*, Battery Potter. The superior slope gently descends to a sentry route known as a *chemin de ronde* that is fronted by a parapet wall (Olmsted Center, April 2008).

Figure 3.27. Fire control stations, Battery Potter. On the terreplein, two groups of deteriorating concrete structures are located west of the former gun emplacements. The structures served as fire control stations and feature large openings in their east elevations to provide views to the Atlantic Ocean (Olmsted Center, January 2009).

Figure 3.28. View looking northwest at concrete pillars, Battery Potter. South of the two groups of fire control stations, two concrete pillars remain from another structure that served as an additional fire control station (Olmsted Center, January 2009).

Figure 3.29. View looking south at guardrails, Battery Potter. To increase visitor safety, the National Park Service has recently added guardrails between the superior slope and the terreplein where the guns were emplaced (Olmsted Center, January 2009).

Figure 3.30. View looking north across terreplein, Battery Potter. As an additional safety measure, guardrails are installed on the western portion of the terreplein to prevent access to the sloped portion of the concrete structure (Olmsted Center, January 2009).

Figure 3.31. View looking northwest at metal pole, Battery Potter. A T-shaped metal pole is located north of the fire control stations and was used in observing and recording weather phenomenon (Olmsted Center, April 2008).

Figure 3.32. View looking northeast at foundation, Hudson Drive, and Battery Potter. Across from the parking area and west of Hudson Drive, a concrete foundation occupies a small opening in a dense stand of woody vegetation. The foundation supported a metal tower used to identify targets and improve fire control (Olmsted Center, January 2009).

Figure 3.33. View looking east from access stairs, Battery Potter. The sloped portion of the concrete battery, rising approximately ten-feet above the engineered earthwork, has eastern red cedars (*Juniperus virginiana*) growing in cracks and in large spalling areas (Olmsted Center, April 2008).

Figure 3.34. View looking east at the *chemin de ronde*, Battery Potter. The *chemin de ronde* is presently a collection area for leaf litter and debris that supports the growth of woody vegetation (Olmsted Center, January 2009).

Figure 3.35. Close-up view of concrete terreplein, Battery Granger. The concrete terreplein shows evidence of an asphalt-based product either used to fill joints or remaining in the joints after use as part of a larger concrete surface treatment (Olmsted Center, January 2009).

Figure 3.36. View looking northwest at engineered slope to rear of Battery Granger. Between Hudson Drive and the battery, a chain-link fence (left) and signage have been erected to warn visitors of potentially hazardous conditions (Olmsted Center, January 2009).

Figure 3.37. View looking west across southwest mortar pit, the Mortar Battery. Efflorescence and spalling are present on the concrete blast slope above the mortar pit. These symptoms of water infiltrating concrete can be seen on additional horizontal and vertical concrete surfaces at the Mortar Battery (Olmsted Center, January 2009).

Figure 3.38. View looking north along perimeter wall, the Mortar Battery. Large woody vegetation is growing between the perimeter wall and the trail to the northwest and southwest emplacements. The main species along the perimeter wall is hackberry (*Celtis occidentalis*) (Olmsted Center, January 2009).

Figure 3.39. View looking northeast at toe of engineered earthwork, the Mortar Battery. East of the trail to the northwest and southwest emplacements, woven-wire mesh fencing is installed to discourage visitors from climbing up the engineered earthwork (Olmsted Center, January 2009).

Figure 3.40. View near top of southwest mortar pit, the Mortar Battery. At the top of the Mortar Battery, several wood post and wire cable fences are installed that are in fair to poor condition (Olmsted Center, January 2009).

Figure 3.41. View looking east at wayside, the Mortar Battery. Inside the perimeter wall, a wayside is located just south of the gallery to the southwest mortar pit (Olmsted Center, January 2009).

Figure 3.42. View looking northeast at emplacement #2, Battery Gunnison. Of all the coastal defense batteries at Sandy Hook, Battery Gunnison most readily conveys its military role in protecting the southern approach to New York because the concrete structure is emplaced with two 6-inch caliber guns (Olmsted Center, January 2009).

Figure 3.43. View looking north from emplacement #1 to emplacement #2, Battery Gunnison. Spalling is present on a concrete feature due to infiltration of water and freeze-thaw cycles (Olmsted Center, January 2009).

Figure 3.44. View looking southeast at emplacement #2, Battery Gunnison. The vegetation on Battery Gunnison's engineered slopes is primarily eastern red cedar (*Juniperus virginiana*) and beach plum (*Prunus maritima*) (Olmsted Center, January 2009).

Figure 3.45. View looking south at eroded vehicular route, Battery Mills. On the west side of Battery Mills a portion of the road encircling the battery, approximately 200-feet, has been washed away by Sandy Hook Bay (Olmsted Center, January 2009).

Figure 3.46. View looking northeast at Battery Kingman. The major constructed feature of Batteries Kingman and Mills is the engineered earthwork that rises in stark contrast to the surrounding land (Olmsted Center, January 2009).

Figure 3.47. View looking east at entry to emplacement #1, Battery Mills. The main entry and entry for emplacement #1 are inaccessible due to the density of woody vegetation (Olmsted Center, January 2009).

Figure 3.48. View looking southwest at emplacement #2, Battery Kingman. Designed to shield the gun platform from overhead fire, the concrete canopy exhibits efflorescence indicating water is infiltrating the concrete and drawing out impurities to the surface (Olmsted Center, January 2009).

Figure 3.49. View looking west at emplacement #2, Battery Mills. Above the emplacement, large spalling areas on the concrete canopy result from infiltration of water and seasonal freezing and thawing (Olmsted Center, January 2009).

Figure 3.50. View looking north from the top of Battery Kingman. A concrete box, engulfed by Japanese honeysuckle (*Lonicera japonica*), is located south of emplacement #2 on the top of the engineered earthwork (Olmsted Center, January 2009).

Figure 3.51. Concrete pipe, Battery Kingman. A concrete pipe protrudes through the engineered earthwork northwest of emplacement #2 (Olmsted Center, January 2009).

Figure 3.52. View looking northwest from the top of Battery Mills. A tapered concrete box and metal pipe are located near the center top of the engineered earthwork. These structures are most likely associated with ventilation or served as flues for furnaces (Olmsted Center, January 2009).

Figure 3.53. Concrete pipe, Battery Mills. Southwest of emplacement #1, a concrete pipe emerges from the engineered earthwork (Olmsted Center, January 2009).

Figure 3.54. View looking south from the top of Battery Kingman. On the west side of Battery Kingman, a strip of concrete is exposed near the top of the earthwork and is possibly a piece of the reinforced concrete buster course installed to protect the battery from aerial bombing (Olmsted Center, January 2009).

Figure 3.55. Scrub pine south of emplacement #1, Battery Mills. A few scrub pine (*Pinus virginiana*) were observed on the engineered earthwork that primarily contained mature eastern red cedar (*Juniperus virginiana*), hackberry (*Celtis occidentalis*), and ailanthus (*Ailanthus altissima*) (Olmsted Center, January 2009).

Figure 3.56. Post and wire fence, Battery Kingman. Near the high point above Battery Kingman's emplacement #2, a post and wire fence is installed that is overrun by vines and other vegetation (Olmsted Center, January 2009).

Figure 3.57. View looking east at collapsed wood guardrail, Battery Kingman. Across from both gun emplacements, a series of wood guardrails are installed along the eastern edge of the unpaved road. The guardrails are in fair to poor condition (Olmsted Center, January 2009).

Figure 3.58. View looking east at wood guardrail, Battery Mills. Two series of wood guardrails are installed along the eastern edge of the unpaved road. The guardrails are in fair to poor condition and located across from the gun emplacements (Olmsted Center, January 2009).

Figure 3.59. View looking southeast from vehicular route to Control Area #1, NIKE radar site. From each control area, a vehicular route leads to the Ready Barracks. From Control Area #1, the route is paved and ends in a hammerhead turnaround south of the Ready Barracks (Olmsted Center, January 2009).

Figure 3.60. View looking north at walkway, Control Area #2, NIKE radar site. A concrete sidewalk between each control area and the Ready Barracks provides pedestrian access between the locations (Olmsted Center, January 2009).

Figure 3.61. View looking north at HIPAR foundation, NIKE radar site. The foundation is obscured by shrub species such as bayberry (*Myrica* sp.) seen in the foreground (Olmsted Center, January 2009).

Figure 3.62. View looking north along walkway to Ready Barracks, NIKE radar site. The eastern red cedars (*Juniperus virginiana*) are immediately adjacent to and encroaching on the walkway (Olmsted Center, January 2009).

Figure 3.63. View looking northwest at the Ready Barracks, NIKE radar site. Pedestrian-scale lights line both walks from the control areas to the Ready Barracks. The lights are in good to fair condition with the exception of one light pole which is knocked over (Olmsted Center, January 2009).

Figure 3.64. View looking west at elevator to missile magazine (425), NIKE launch site. The northern section of the launch site contains the underground missile magazines and concrete pads for launching racks. The concrete pads are oriented north to south for firing missiles to the east (Olmsted Center, April 2008).

Figure 3.65. View looking west along central access road, NIKE launch site. Heading east from the Ready Barracks, the topography rises along the central access road to the missile magazines (Olmsted Center, April 2008).

Figure 3.66. View looking south at engineered earthwork, NIKE launch site. South of the Warhead Building, a crescent-shaped earthwork rises to an elevation of twenty feet. The tips of the crescent wrap around the Warhead Building to the north and almost form a continuous landform with a northern earthwork (Olmsted Center, January 2009).

Figure 3.67. View looking north at firearms range, NIKE launch site. North of the Warhead Building, park law enforcement has set up a firearms range in a low lying area. The land rising around the depression acts as a backstop for the range (Olmsted Center, January 2009).

Figure 3.68. View looking southeast at engineered earthwork, NIKE launch site. Eastern red cedars (*Juniperus virginiana*) cover the majority of the engineered earthworks in the Missile Maintenance Area (Olmsted Center, January 2009).

Figure 3.69. Outer fence, NIKE launch site. The launch site features a perimeter fence along its outside boundary and then adds an inner fence that encloses the missile magazines. This section of fence is in fair condition (Olmsted Center, April 2008).

Figure 3.70. Outer fence, NIKE launch site. The inner and outer fences are comprised of chain-link sections secured to H-shaped posts. The top of each post holds a single extension arm that supports strands of barbed wire. This section of fence is in poor condition (Olmsted Center, January 2009).

Figure 3.71. Floodlight, NIKE launch site. At the Missile Magazine area, eight floodlights are positioned along the inner fence. Each light features a parabolic fixture mounted with a metal bracket to a wood pole. Six similar lights are located at the Missile Maintenance Area on the engineered earthworks (Olmsted Center, April 2008).

Figure 3.72. Spotlights, NIKE launch site. In the Missile Magazine area a single, round, wood pole stands near the Section B magazine (427). The first eight to ten feet of the pole are painted yellow and two spotlights with parabolic metal hoods are mounted at the top of the pole (Olmsted Center, April 2008).

Figure 3.73. View looking east at antenna, NIKE launch site. East of the Missile Maintenance Area and approaching the outer fence, an antenna and monitoring equipment have been set up for collecting weather and tide information (Olmsted Center, January 2009).

Figure 3.74. View looking northeast at antenna, NIKE launch site. A second antenna assists with collecting weather and tide information and is located south of the Missile Maintenance Area near the outer fence (Olmsted Center, January 2009).

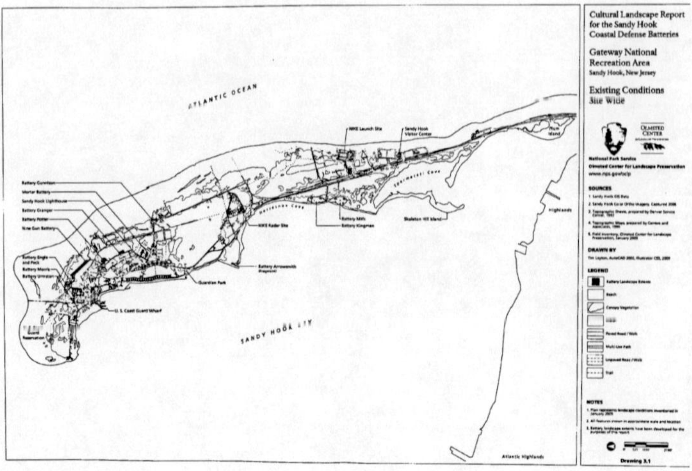

ATLANTIC OCEAN
NIKE Launch Site
Sandy Hook Visitor Center
Plum Island
Battery Gunnison
Mortar Battery
Sandy Hook Lighthouse
Battery Granger
Battery Potter
Nine Gun Battery
Battery Engle and Peck
Battery Mason
Battery Urmston
Battery Mills
Battery Kingman
NIKE Radar Site
Skeleton Hill Island
Highlands
Battery Arrowsmith
Guardian Park
U. S. Coast Guard Wharf
SANDY HOOK BAY
Atlantic Highlands
Cultural Landscape Report for the Sandy Hook Coastal Defense Batteries
Gateway National Recreation Area
Sandy Hook, New Jersey
Existing Conditions
Site Wide
National Park Service
Olmsted Center for Landscape Preservation
www.nps.gov/oclp
SOURCES
DRAWN BY
LEGEND
NOTES
Drawing 3.1

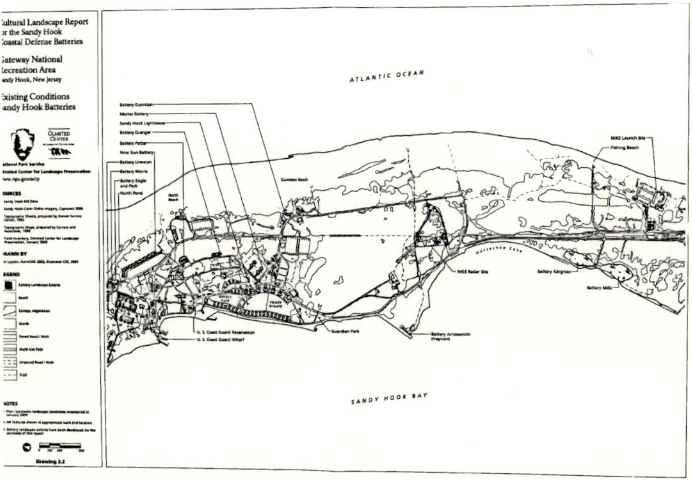

ultural Landscape Report
or the Sandy Hook
oastal Defense Batteries
ateway National
ecreation Area
andy Hook, New Jersey
xisting Conditions
andy Hook Batteries
Olmsted Center
Drawing 3.2
ATLANTIC OCEAN
Battery Gunnison
Mortar Battery
Sandy Hook Lighthouse
Battery Granger
Battery Potter
Nine Gun Battery
Battery Urmston
Battery Morris
Battery Engle and Peck
North Pond
North Beach
Gunnison Beach
NIKE Launch Site
Fishing Beach
Horseshoe Cove
NIKE Radar Site
Battery Kingman
Battery Mills
U. S. Coast Guard Reservation
U. S. Coast Guard Wharf
Guardian Park
Battery Arrowsmith (Fragment)
SANDY HOOK BAY

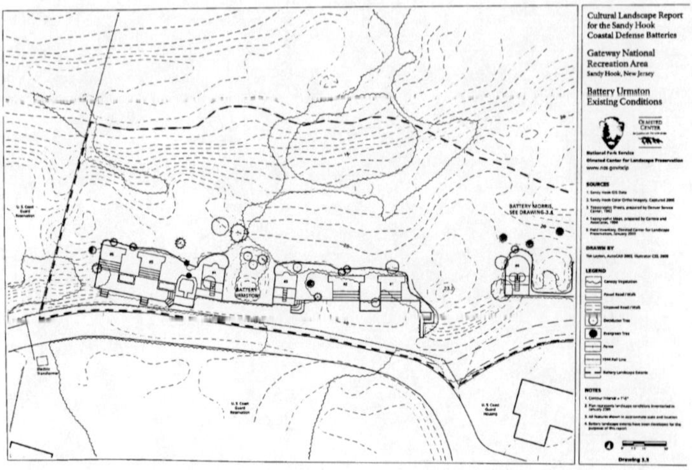
U. S. Coast Guard Reservation
BATTERY URMSTON
BATTERY MORRIS, SEE DRAWING 3.6
Electric Transformer
U. S. Coast Guard Reservation
U. S. Coast Guard Housing
Cultural Landscape Report for the Sandy Hook Coastal Defense Batteries
Gateway National Recreation Area
Sandy Hook, New Jersey
Battery Urmston Existing Conditions
National Park Service
Olmsted Center for Landscape Preservation
www.nps.gov/oclp
SOURCES
DRAWN BY
LEGEND
Canopy Vegetation
Paved Road / Walk
Unpaved Road / Walk
Deciduous Tree
Evergreen Tree
Fence
1944 Rail Line
Battery Landscape Extents
NOTES
Drawing 3.5

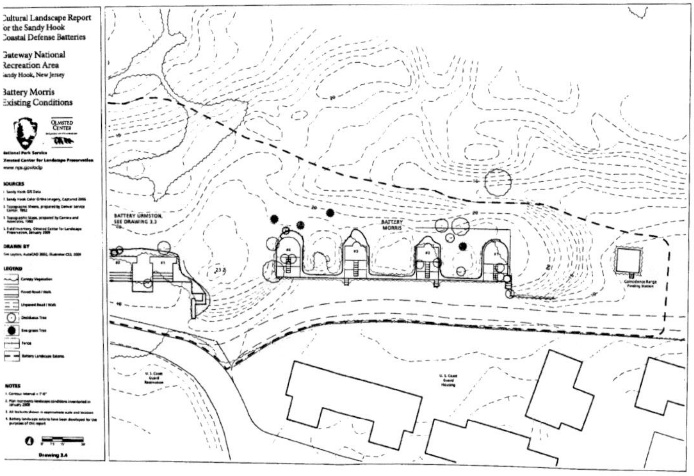

Cultural Landscape Report for the Sandy Hook Coastal Defense Batteries
Gateway National Recreation Area
Sandy Hook, New Jersey
Battery Morris Existing Conditions
National Park Service
Olmsted Center for Landscape Preservation
www.nps.gov/oclp
SOURCES
DRAWN BY
LEGEND
NOTES
Drawing 3.4
BATTERY URMSTON, SEE DRAWING 3.3
BATTERY MORRIS

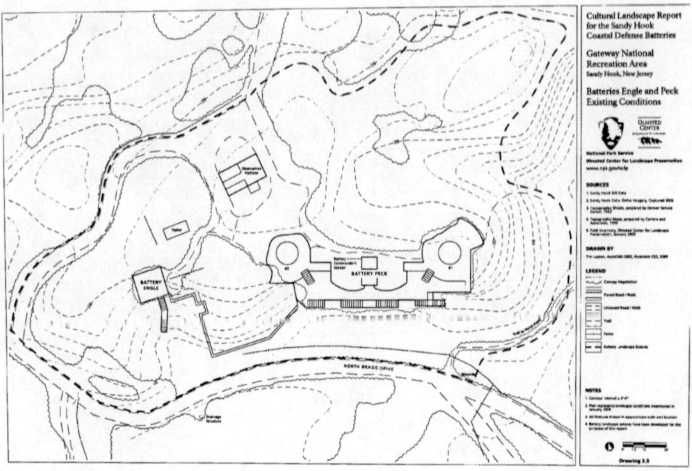
Cultural Landscape Report
for the Sandy Hook
Coastal Defense Batteries
Gateway National
Recreation Area
Sandy Hook, New Jersey
Batteries Engle and Peck
Existing Conditions
National Park Service
Olmsted Center for Landscape Preservation
www.nps.gov/oclp
SOURCES
DRAWN BY
LEGEND
Canopy Vegetation
Paved Road / Walk
Unpaved Road / Walk
Trail
Fence
NOTES
Drawing 3.5
BATTERY ENGLE
BATTERY PECK
NORTH BRAGG DRIVE

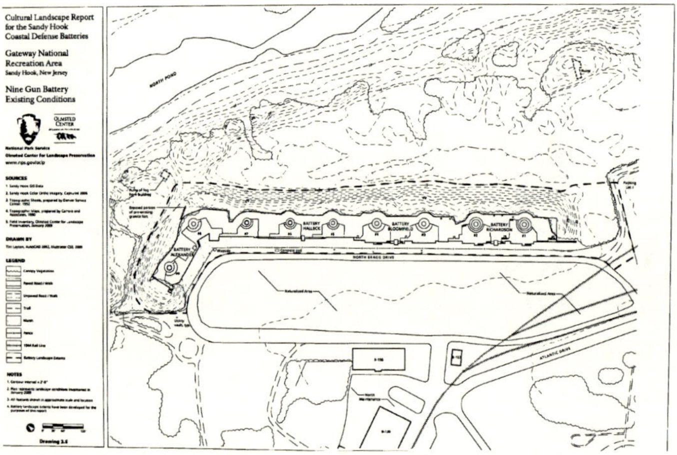
Cultural Landscape Report
for the Sandy Hook
Coastal Defense Batteries
Gateway National
Recreation Area
Sandy Hook, New Jersey
Nine Gun Battery
Existing Conditions
National Park Service
Olmsted Center for Landscape Preservation
www.nps.gov/oclp
SOURCES
DRAWN BY
LEGEND
NOTES
Drawing 3.5
NORTH POND
BATTERY HALLECK
BATTERY BLOOMFIELD
BATTERY RICHARDSON
BATTERY ALEXANDER
NORTH BRAGG DRIVE
ATLANTIC DRIVE

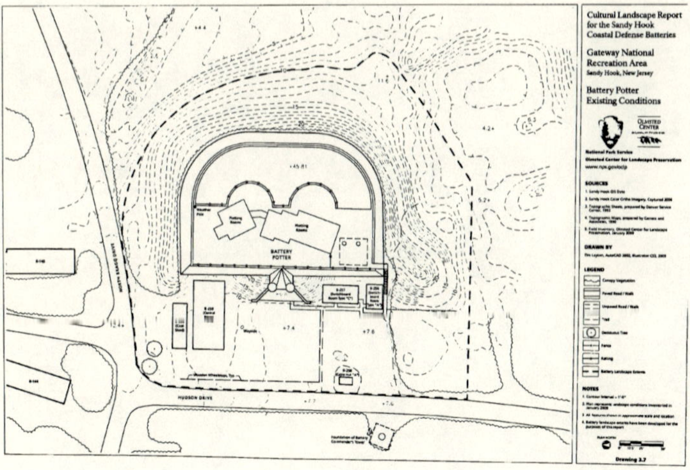
Cultural Landscape Report
for the Sandy Hook
Coastal Defense Batteries
Gateway National
Recreation Area
Sandy Hook, New Jersey
Battery Potter
Existing Conditions
BATTERY POTTER
HUDSON DRIVE
SOURCES
DRAWN BY
LEGEND
NOTES
Drawing 3.7

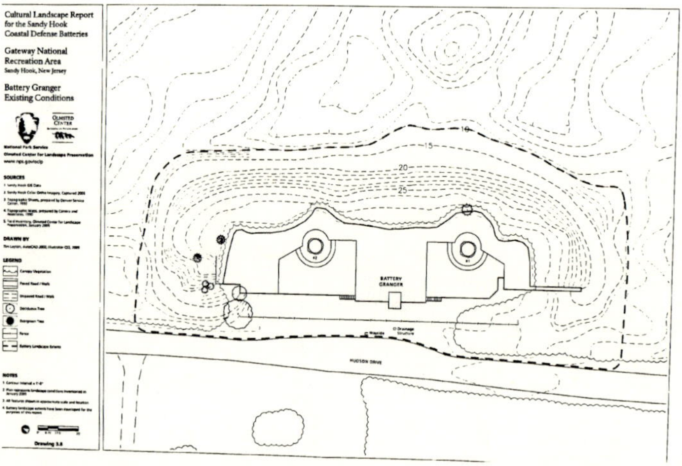
Cultural Landscape Report for the Sandy Hook Coastal Defense Batteries
Gateway National Recreation Area
Sandy Hook, New Jersey
Battery Granger Existing Conditions
National Park Service
Olmsted Center for Landscape Preservation
www.nps.gov/oclp
SOURCES
DRAWN BY
LEGEND
NOTES
10
15
20
25
BATTERY GRANGER
HUDSON DRIVE
Drawing 3.8

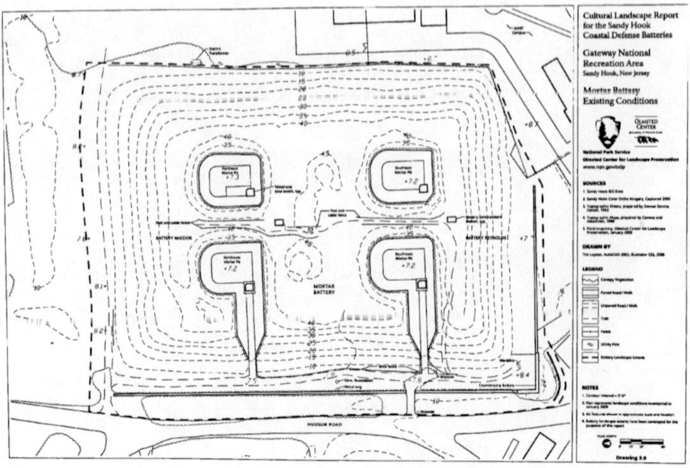

Cultural Landscape Report for the Sandy Hook Coastal Defense Batteries
Gateway National Recreation Area
Sandy Hook, New Jersey
Mortar Battery Existing Conditions
National Park Service
Olmsted Center for Landscape Preservation
SOURCES
DRAWN BY
LEGEND
NOTES
Drawing 3.9
MORTAR BATTERY
BATTERY McCOOK
BATTERY REYNOLDS
HUDSON ROAD

Cultural Landscape Report
for the Sandy Hook
Coastal Defense Batteries

Gateway National
Recreation Area
Sandy Hook, New Jersey

Battery Gunnison
Existing Conditions

National Park Service
Olmsted Center for Landscape Preservation
www.nps.gov/oclp

SOURCES

DRAWN BY

LEGEND

NOTES

Drawing 3.10

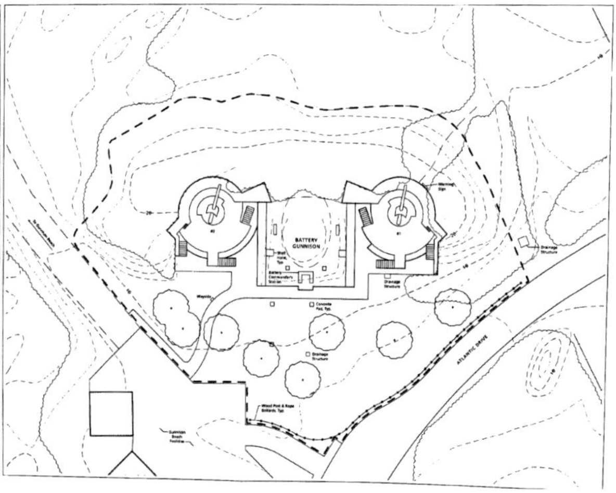

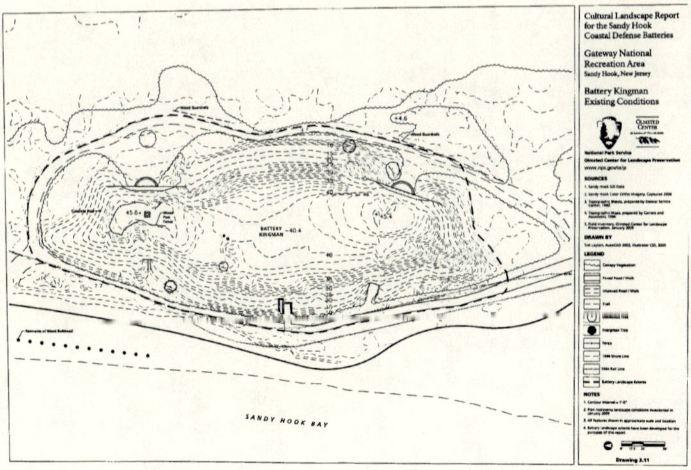

Cultural Landscape Report for the Sandy Hook Coastal Defense Batteries
Gateway National Recreation Area
Sandy Hook, New Jersey
Battery Kingman Existing Conditions
National Park Service
Olmsted Center for Landscape Preservation
SOURCES
DRAWN BY
LEGEND
NOTES
Drawing 3.11
BATTERY KINGMAN
40.4
45.8
SANDY HOOK BAY

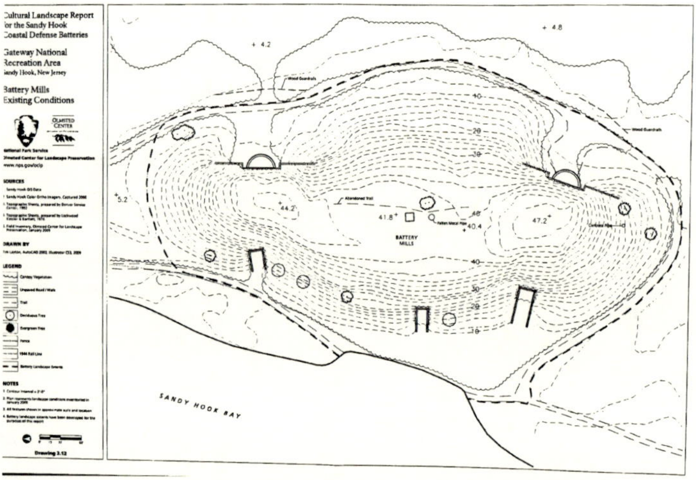
Cultural Landscape Report
for the Sandy Hook
Coastal Defense Batteries
Gateway National
Recreation Area
Sandy Hook, New Jersey
Battery Mills
Existing Conditions
National Park Service
Olmsted Center for Landscape Preservation
www.nps.gov/oclp
SOURCES
DRAWN BY
LEGEND
Deciduous Tree
Evergreen Tree
Fence
NOTES
Drawing 3.12
+ 4.2
+ 4.8
Wood Guardrails
Wood Guardrails
Abandoned Trail
44.2
41.8
BATTERY
MILLS
40.4
47.2
5.2
SANDY HOOK BAY

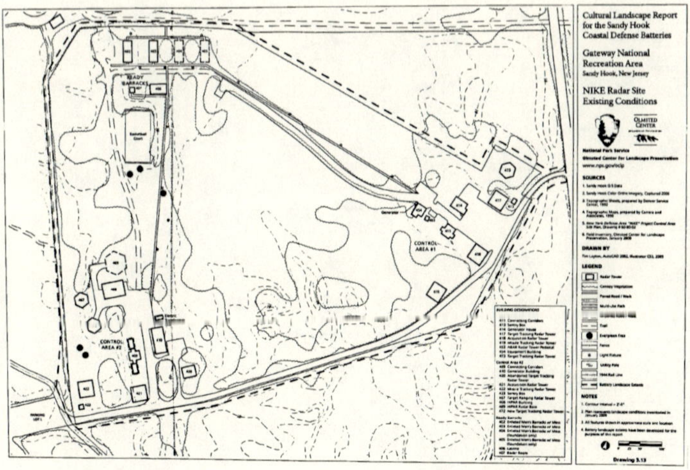
Cultural Landscape Report for the Sandy Hook Coastal Defense Batteries
Gateway National Recreation Area
Sandy Hook, New Jersey
NIKE Radar Site Existing Conditions
National Park Service
SOURCES
DRAWN BY
LEGEND
NOTES
Drawing 3.13
READY BARRACKS
CONTROL AREA #1
CONTROL AREA #2
Generator

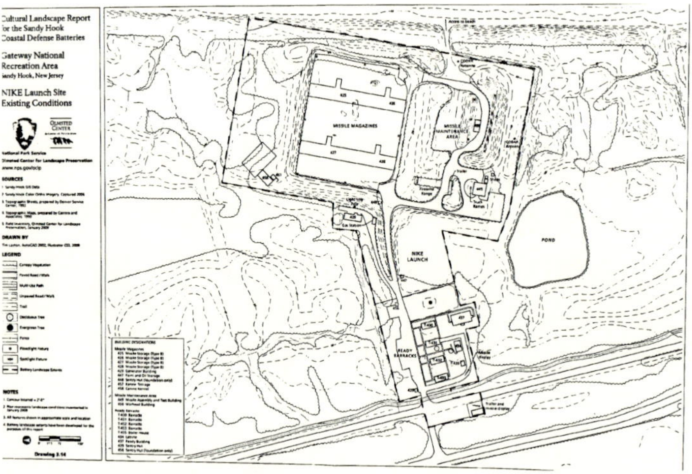
Cultural Landscape Report
for the Sandy Hook
Coastal Defense Batteries
Gateway National
Recreation Area
Sandy Hook, New Jersey
NIKE Launch Site
Existing Conditions
National Park Service
Olmsted Center for Landscape Preservation
www.nps.gov/oclp
SOURCES
DRAWN BY
LEGEND
NOTES
Drawing 3.14
MISSILE MAGAZINES
MISSILE MAINTENANCE AREA
NIKE LAUNCH
POND
READY BARRACKS
BUILDING DESIGNATIONS

ANALYSIS AND EVALUATION

This section provides a summary of the historical significance of Sandy Hook's coastal defense batteries and an evaluation of their historic integrity. The section is divided into two main parts. The first summarizes the National Register status and the significance of Sandy Hook according to National Register of Historic Places criteria. The second is an evaluation of the landscape's historic character at each coastal defense battery according to the cultural landscape methodology outlined in *A Guide to Cultural Landscape Reports: Contents, Process and Techniques* (National Park Service, 1998). This methodology examines general landscape characteristics, such as topography, circulation, and vegetation, comparing existing landscape conditions documented in January 2009 with what is documented or otherwise understood of the historic condition of these landscape characteristics during the period of significance. A summary table of landscape features is provided at the end of the section listing all documented landscape features.

The analysis and evaluation covers eleven extant batteries and the two separate sites that comprise the extant NIKE missile battery. Information is presented in geographical order from north to south starting with Battery Urmston and ending with Batteries Kingman and Mills. The section concludes with the NIKE radar site and the NIKE launch site.

NATIONAL REGISTER STATUS

This analysis and evaluation is based on criteria and aspects of integrity developed by the National Register of Historic Places Program, which lists properties that are significant to our nation's history and prehistory. According to the National Register, historic significance may be present in districts, sites, buildings, structures and objects that possess integrity of location, design, materials, workmanship, feeling, and association which meet at least one of the following criteria:

A. Associated with events that have made a significant contribution to the broad patterns of history.

B. Associated with the lives of persons significant in our past.

C. Embodies the distinctive characteristics of a type, period or method of construction, or that represent the work of a master, or that possess high artistic values, or that represent a significant and distinguishable entity whose components may lack individual distinction.

D. Have yielded, or may be likely to yield, information important in prehistory or history.

The Fort Hancock and Sandy Hook Proving Ground Historic District was listed on the National Register of Historic Places in 1980. This district was comprised of 380 acres in the northern half of the Sandy Hook peninsula bounded by Sandy Hook Bay on the west, portions of Magruder Road, Gunnison Road, and Atlantic Drive on the south, the Atlantic Ocean on the east, and the U. S. Coast Guard property on the north. In addition, the district contained eight noncontiguous sites to the south including Battery Arrowsmith, Battery Kingman, Battery Mills, the Signal Corps radar site, and the NIKE missile sites (Figure 4.1).[1] On November 9, 1982, revised documentation was submitted and the Fort Hancock and Sandy Hook Proving Ground Historic District was listed as a National Historic Landmark (NHL). The boundaries for the 4,584-acre landmark district were expanded to include the majority of the peninsula north of the Route 36 bridge to the northern end of the landform. Only Plum Island, Skeleton Hill Island, and South Island—all extending from the western side of the peninsula—were excluded from the district.[2]

The National Historic Landmark documentation identifies Sandy Hook as significant for its dual roles in United States military history. As a federal military reservation, the peninsula served as the home for the Sandy Hook Proving Ground and Fort Hancock. Additionally, the documentation recognizes Sandy Hook as significant for the Spermaceti Cove Life-Saving Station and the Sandy Hook Lighthouse. The period of significance for the Proving Ground, 1874 to 1919, corresponds to the time period the site served as the nation's testing center for major artillery. For Fort Hancock and the balance of the peninsula, the period of significance spans from 1859 through the 1950s and 1960s Cold War era. Areas of historical significance expressed by the documentation include engineering, military, and social/humanitarian themes.[3]

STATEMENT OF SIGNIFICANCE

Sandy Hook is significant in American history as the site of the federal military reservation that played dual roles in United States military history. The peninsula was home to both the Sandy Hook Proving Ground and Fort Hancock. Between 1874 and 1919, the Proving Ground served as the nation's testing center for major artillery. During this critical time period, the Army developed, tested, and transitioned to rifled artillery that was utilized to protect harbors around the country and in foreign territories. From the 1890s to the Army's divestment of the property in 1974, Fort Hancock and Sandy Hook's coastal defenses were a critical element in a system of fortifications guarding the southern approach to New York City – America's most important harbor and largest metropolis. It was during these years that the United States defeated Spain and emerged as a world power, tipped the scales against the Central Powers in World War I, retreated into the isolation of the 1920s and 30s, and emerged from World War II as a super power.[4]

The Fort Hancock and Sandy Hook Proving Ground Historic District is significant under Criterion A for association with the development of military defenses and the design and testing of artillery that have made a significant contribution to the broad patterns of our history. The site is also significant under Criterion C for military architecture and engineering that embodies the distinctive characteristics of Endicott-Taft period coastal defenses. Sandy Hook's collection of Endicott-Taft batteries includes the first completed, partially armed, and tested coastal defense battery in the United States following the Endicott Board's recommendations and the first concrete mortar battery in the United States. The district may have significance under Criterion D for archeological resources associated with Fort Hancock and the Proving Ground that are likely to yield information important to military history.

The period of significance for Fort Hancock and Sandy Hook's coastal defenses spans from 1859 to 1974. The period begins in 1859 corresponding to the start of construction on the granite Fort at Sandy Hook. In the National Historic Landmark documentation, the narrative statement of significance does not explicitly state the end-date of the period of significance, identifying 1958 as the last specific date corresponding to the introduction of the improved NIKE Hercules missile system.[5] Correspondence between the National Park Service and the New Jersey State Historic Preservation Officer in 1996 relating to the park's List of Classified Structures (LCS) explains that, ". . . because the NIKE missile era identified in the NHL documentation continued almost to the date of transfer between the military and the NPS, December 31, 1974, the deactivation date for Fort Hancock, is used as the end date of the period of significance."[6] Review and concurrence by the New Jersey State Historic Preservation Officer on January 2, 1997 established 1974 as the end date of the period of significance.

EVALUATION OF INTEGRITY

Integrity is the ability of a property to convey its historic identity and significance. While evaluation of integrity is often a subjective judgment, it must be grounded in an understanding of a property's physical features and how these relate to its significance. The National Register identifies seven aspects of integrity comprising location, design, setting, materials, workmanship, feeling and association. Retention of these qualities is essential for a property to convey its significance, though all seven qualities need not be present to convey a sense of past time and place.

Location is the place where the cultural landscape was constructed. The coastal defense batteries continue to occupy the locations where they guarded the southern approach to New York Harbor and the skies over the New York-New Jersey metropolitan area. The coastal defense batteries retain integrity of location.

Design is the combination of elements that create the form, plan, space, structure and style of the cultural landscape. Extant design elements include structural features such as battery commander's stations, auxiliary support buildings, and barracks and vehicular and pedestrian circulation. The primary change to the original design of the coastal defense batteries is the growth of large woody vegetation on the structures, their engineered earthworks, and in immediately adjacent areas that would interfere with historic operations. With the exception of Battery Gunnison, the gun batteries are missing the artillery and carriages that were part of an earth-covered, concrete defensive structure. Similarly, the NIKE radar site lacks the radar units that were mounted on top of the towers for target acquisition and tracking and missile guidance. North of Battery Peck, an observation platform and communications trailer have been added. At most locations, the railroad tracks that supported the construction and provided the projectiles and gunpowder for the batteries are removed. Near Nine Gun Battery, Battery Gunnison, and the NIKE radar site, surface parking areas have been added. The presence of large woody vegetation, addition of some non-historic structures, and changes to circulation features diminishes the integrity of design.

Setting is the physical environment of the cultural landscape. The setting of the coastal defense batteries is defined by topography and vegetation communities that inhabit large, contiguous areas and transitional zones. Contrary to the height of the battery structures and their engineered earthworks, adjacent topography is relatively flat or slightly undulates to form coastal dunes. These topography features are largely intact. Masses of undisturbed vegetation, such as the holly forest east of Batteries Kingman and Mills and the low-growing shrubs and beach grasses on coastal dunes, have also been retained. Although Sandy Hook's function has changed from a strategic military installation to a recreation destination serving a densely-populated region, the coastal defense batteries retain integrity of setting.

Materials are the physical elements that were combined or deposited during the period of significance in a particular pattern or configuration to form the cultural landscape. The coastal defense batteries retain historic built materials of granite, concrete, steel, and sand and earth. The condition of these materials is negatively affected by water infiltration, rust, erosion, and large woody vegetation, however, the materials have not been replaced with non-historic substitutes. Changes have occurred with plant materials on the engineered earthworks and adjacent to the batteries due to succession and the growth of non-native invasive species such as ailanthus. The presence of non-historic plant material can be reversed.

Workmanship is the physical evidence of the crafts of a particular culture or people during the period of significance. The coastal defense batteries demonstrate workmanship of the Army's changing technology in coastal defenses from the late nineteenth to the mid-twentieth century. Masons set granite blocks to form a defensible entrance for Battery Potter. When a land-based attack was no longer a threat and the counterweight gun carriage successfully tested, large caliber gun batteries featured open rear elevations and recessed concrete wells to emplace the guns. Finally, when aerial bombing replaced naval gun fire, Batteries Kingman and Mills were completely casemated in earth-covered concrete to protect artillery and crew. The coastal defense batteries retain integrity of workmanship

Feeling is the cultural landscape's expression of the aesthetic or historic sense of the historic period. Due to their scale, materials, and integration in the landscape with engineered earthworks, the coastal defense batteries are distinct from other buildings and structures at Sandy Hook and retain their historic feeling. At the NIKE missile sites, the perimeter fences convey the security established when the radar and launch sites were operational. Large woody vegetation growing on the batteries, their engineered earthworks, and in surrounding areas diminishes the feeling of a maintained military landscape. Similarly, vegetation along the NIKE fence lines and the poor condition of some sections of fences lessens the integrity of feeling.

Association is the direct link between the important historic event or person and the cultural landscape. The coastal defense batteries have a diminished integrity of association. It is challenging to link the structures with their role in coastal defense due to several factors. Changes in circulation systems and unchecked growth of vegetation make access and therefore recognition of batteries such as Urmston and Morris difficult. Large woody vegetation is the primarily culprit obstructing downrange views from the batteries and impeding an understanding between the battery's location and the water. Finally, vegetation growing on the batteries conveys that the structures are relics and lessens the association of the batteries as vital resources for coastal defense.

The coastal defense batteries at Sandy Hook retain integrity of location, setting, materials, and workmanship. Primarily due to the growth of large woody vegetation, the addition of non-historic structures, and changes to circulation features, the coastal defense batteries have a diminished integrity of design, feeling, and association. The coastal defense batteries retain their overall physical form and addressing the condition of historic details will strengthen the association of the batteries as critical installations for defending the southern approach to New York City and the metropolitan area's airspace.

EVALUATION OF LANDSCAPE CHARACTERISTICS AND FEATURES

Landscape characteristics are the broad patterns, systems, and feature categories that compose the landscape and determine how people interact with it. The analysis of landscape characteristics and features serves to identify the components of the landscape that define the historic character of the landscape and contribute to the landscape's ability to convey its significance. The evaluation entails comparing existing conditions to what was present during the historic period and making an evaluation of whether the landscape characteristic or feature contributes to the landscape's historic character.

The landscape characteristics evaluated for the coastal defense batteries include spatial organization, topography, circulation, buildings and structures, vegetation, tactical views, and small-scale features. The evaluation is organized and presented in two parts. First, characteristics that are common to all battery sites are reviewed in a narrative format with the following components:

Historic Condition: A brief outline of the history of a particular landscape characteristic and associated features.

Existing Condition: A brief description of the current physical condition.

Evaluation: A determination of each landscape characteristic or feature's contribution to the significance of the landscape.

> Contributing - Characteristics and features that contribute to the significance of the coastal defense batteries and that were present during the period of significance, possess historic integrity, and are related to the areas of historic significance.
>
> Non-contributing - Characteristics and features that do not contribute to the significance of the coastal defense batteries and that were not present during the period of significance, do not retain historic integrity, or are unrelated to the area of historic significance.
>
> Undetermined - Characteristics and features that require additional information to determine if they contribute to the significance of the coastal defense batteries.

The second part of the evaluation reviews landscape characteristics and features that are specific to the individual battery sites. The information is presented in geographical order from north to south in separate tables corresponding to the eleven battery sites and two NIKE missile sites. Columns in the table identify the landscape feature, if the feature was extant in 1945, 1974, and during the existing conditions review in January 2009, and concludes with notes and figure references pertaining to the feature. Listing whether a feature was extant in 1974 corresponds to the end of the period of significance for Fort Hancock and the Sandy Hook Proving Ground Historic District. A review of the features in 1945 is provided for the eleven gun batteries because shortly after World War II, American coastal defenses shifted to missile installations to defend against bomber attacks and all of Sandy Hook's gun batteries were disarmed and deactivated. A comparison of the 1945 and 1974 columns serves to identify features—such as large woody vegetation on the engineered earthworks—that emerged during the twenty-nine year interval due to limited maintenance.

SPATIAL ORGANIZATION

Historic Condition: The spatial organization of the coastal defense batteries is defined their role in a larger system of coastal defenses. The gun batteries at Sandy Hook were not isolated, defensive fixtures but components in a system that utilized multiple locations, varying land-based artillery, and underwater controlled mines to defend the south approach to New York. In addition to batteries at Sandy Hook, the Army constructed coastal defenses to the south at Navesink, to the north at Fort Hamilton, Fort Wadsworth, and Fort Lafayette along the Narrows, and to the east at Fort Tilden on the Rockaway peninsula (see Figure 2.31). All of the battery sites were intended to provide defense-in-depth--a redundant system that provided continued resistance against a potential enemy advancing north toward New York City. The NIKE missile battery at Sandy Hook was also part of a redundant system of defenses that incorporated geographically separate radar sites and command centers for coordinating nineteen missile batteries in the New York Defense Area. In addition to Sandy Hook, nearby missile sites included Leonardo and South Plainfield, New Jersey, and Fort Tilden on the Rockaway peninsula.

The individual gun batteries at Sandy Hook were oriented to engage a potential enemy on the water. Consequently, a majority of the batteries faced artillery north or east toward the major shipping channel that followed the Atlantic shoreline of the peninsula. The firing side of the battery was protected by an engineered earthwork that transitioned to a reinforced concrete structure. The structure emplaced the guns, stored ammunition, and housed dedicated spaces for calculating a target's range. The rear elevation of the concrete structure provided personnel access and delivery of ammunition and supplies. If an enemy fired on the battery, the safest place for personnel was under the protective cover of reinforced concrete and engineered earthworks. Recognizing this advantage, the Army converted the covered galleries of the Mortar Battery to house central communications and to serve as a command post during World War II.

Existing Condition: The coastal defense batteries at Sandy Hook have not moved since the end of the period of significance and continue to occupy the locations where they guarded the southern approach to New York Harbor and the skies over the New York-New Jersey metropolitan area. The arrangement of a battery's firing side and engineered earthwork, concrete structure, and rear elevation for access remains unaltered.

Evaluation: Contributing

TOPOGRAPHY

Historic Condition: Mid-nineteenth century improvements to artillery and projectiles coupled with combat experience during the Civil War convinced military engineers that a new generation of coastal defense batteries should rely on constructed earthworks for protection. Batteries shielded with engineered earthworks were constructed at Sandy Hook in the 1890s and designed earthen covered continued to be a feature of batteries until the conclusion of World War II. Compared to masonry and concrete construction, the engineered earthworks were easy and inexpensive to replace if damaged. In addition to protecting a battery, the earthworks offered an added benefit of concealing the concrete structure by blending it into the surrounding coastal topography. Hundreds of thousands of cubic yards of earth and sand were excavated and meticulously placed to complete the coastal defense batteries at Sandy Hook. Engineered earthworks were also constructed at the NIKE launch site to cover the Missile Magazines and to protect adjacent areas from an accidental explosion at the Missile Maintenance Area.

Existing Condition: The engineered earthworks are primarily intact with some erosion occurring since the end of the historic period. At the NIKE launch site, recycling bins cut into a portion of the south earthwork at the Missile Maintenance Area (Figure 4.2). For all sites, social trails across the earthworks advance erosion and threaten these features (see Figure 3.11). Large woody vegetation growing on the earthworks creates the potential for the placed earth and sand to be removed by a toppled tree.

Evaluation: Contributing

CIRCULATION

Historic Condition: Multiple circulation systems and infrastructure developed on Sandy Hook to support various modes of transportation during the historic period. The bay side of the peninsula provided more sheltered waters for anchoring and docking ships and wharves were constructed on the bay side to transport military supplies and to receive recreation seekers. In the mid-nineteenth century, a railroad line met recreational travelers at a Horseshoe Cover ferry landing and continued south through the peninsula to Long Branch, Sea Bright, and other towns along the Atlantic coast. Recognizing the potential for railroads to transport artillery and ammunition, the Army purchased the existing railroad line and extended it north to the Sandy Hook Proving Ground in 1889. Railroads were utilized throughout the Proving Ground's operation and also installed to move materials for the construction of the coastal defense batteries. After construction was completed, railroad lines served to transport artillery and ammunition to the batteries. Railroads also contributed to the coastal defense system by providing the means for positioning artillery and searchlights mounted on flat rail cars. Following World War II, the gun batteries were deactivated and the railroad lines that supported the batteries' construction and operation were allowed to deteriorate.

In addition to the railroads, vehicular routes were established across compacted soil and wood plank roads. As Fort Hancock was developed to support the coastal defense batteries, compacted gravel roads were designed and installed to connect the north and south ends of the peninsula and to provide access around the Fort's semi-circular configuration of officers' quarters, enlisted men's quarters, and auxiliary buildings. In many instances, roads paralleled railroad lines along the rear of the batteries and provided access for personnel. The network of the roads expanded with the increase in personnel during the World Wars and designated parking areas appear on historic maps from 1944. Circulation features also include paved and unpaved pedestrian routes associated with the Proving Ground, Fort Hancock, and the individual batteries. The most formal pedestrian circulation systems were designed and installed at the NIKE missile sites to facilitate access among the barracks, radar towers, magazines, warehouses, and support structures.

Existing Condition: The multiple modes of transportation and their corresponding circulation systems are presently extant at Sandy Hook. A seasonal ferry service operates from Manhattan and brings visitors to the northern end of the peninsula. Vehicular circulation routes provide access throughout Sandy Hook with Hartshorne Drive serving as the major north-south route, Atlantic Drive serving as a secondary north-south route, and Gunnison Road serving as a connecting east-west route between the two. Sidewalks and pedestrian circulation systems connect Fort Hancock's quarters and buildings and provide access among the individual structures that comprise the NIKE missile sites.

Several sections of rail lines and occasional collections of wooden ties are the only remnants of Sandy Hook's railroad system that are present (Figures 4.3 and

4.4). Unmaintained vegetation blocks and obscures some vehicular circulation routes and at other locations, coastal erosion is removing circulation features. New parking lots are present to receive an increasing number of visitors and a multi-use path stretches from the park entrance to the ferry landing to provide dedicated access for jogging, walking, bicycle riding, and roller blading.

Evaluation: Circulation features present from the historic period are contributing. Circulation features added during the National Park Service administration of Sandy Hook, such as the parking lots and the multi-use path, are non-contributing.

BUILDINGS AND STRUCTURES

Historic Condition: The coastal defense batteries represent successive generations of costly buildings and structures constructed in response to the latest offensive weaponry and armament. At Sandy Hook, the Army designed and constructed rapid fire and large caliber batteries to defend the southern entrance to New York Harbor. In addition the Army completed experimental battery designs, such as the Dynamite Gun Battery and Battery Potter, which used different means to fire projectiles and raise large caliber guns. Both rapid fire and large caliber gun batteries were a building system comprised of reinforced concrete structures and protective, engineered earthworks.

The first gun batteries at Sandy Hook incorporated defenses against a land-based attack. At Battery Potter, the main entry resembled a castle and featured gun loops in a pair of flanking towers so soldiers could fire on an advancing enemy. At the Mortar Battery, the structure was surrounded by a perimeter wall and had machine guns set in galleries at opposite corners to fire on intruders inside the wall. With a system of gun batteries and controlled mines defending against a land-based attack, later gun batteries had open, rear elevations that provided personnel access and delivery of ammunition and supplies. Responding to the threat of aerial reconnaissance and bombing, the large caliber gun batteries updated during World War II featured massive concrete canopies over each gun emplacement to protect the artillery and crews.

During the historic period, the gun batteries experienced periods of intensive maintenance and use and also years of minimal care intended to keep the defenses operational ready. Water-repelling coatings and camouflage paints were added to the concrete surfaces to protect the batteries from natural forces and human detection. Architectural features, many of them metal, were important components in security, safety, and communications.

The Army disarmed and deactivated the gun batteries when artillery was no longer effective and when new coastal defenses were operational. The abandoned batteries were not maintained and following World War II, all of the gun batteries were deactivated due to the threat of high-altitude bombers. In response to the new threat, the Army constructed a NIKE missile battery at Sandy Hook. The NIKE missile battery remained operational until new offensive weaponry, the intercontinental ballistic missile (ICBM), eclipsed the NIKE system and defense philosophy shifted to the doctrine of mutually assured destruction. The buildings and structures at the NIKE sites, similar to the gun batteries before them, were abandoned and not maintained.

Existing Condition: The coastal defense batteries are extant and primarily in a stable condition despite decades of little or no maintenance. The reinforced concrete structures and engineered earthworks that comprise the building system are intact. There are instances of erosion on the earthworks and evidence of spalling, cracks, and separation on concrete elements. In addition, efflorescence can be seen on many of the vertical concrete surfaces indicating water has penetrated the concrete and is drawing out salts and other impurities to the surface. Architectural features, particularly metal components, are in a deteriorating condition and missing at some batteries. The concrete block buildings at the NIKE missile sites also show symptoms of water penetration along with corrosion on corrugated metal roofs and metal siding.

Evaluation: Contributing

VEGETATION

Historic Condition: In order to reduce erosion and obscure the gun batteries from enemy identification, small tree, shrub, and grass species were planted on the engineered earthworks. Instructions from the Army detailed acquiring local plant materials from nearby sites, performing infill plantings from season to season to ensure adequate coverage, and watering when conditions were necessary to support the plant growth. Vegetation on the engineered earthworks did not interfere with the operation of the artillery or views to potential targets on the water.

Existing Condition: A mixture of vegetation presently grows on the engineered earthworks and includes native and non-native vines and groundcovers, grasses, shrubs, small trees, and large woody vegetation (see Figure 3.39). The vegetative cover continues to protect the earthworks from erosion and discourages park visitors from walking on and damaging the earthworks.

Evaluation: Vines, groundcovers, grasses, shrubs, and small trees are contributing. Large woody vegetation is non-contributing since this vegetation type interferes with the operation of the artillery or views.

TACTICAL VIEWS

Historic Condition: The concrete gun batteries relied on unobstructed views to the water to sight potential targets and allow unimpeded firing of projectiles. The importance of a clear field of fire is demonstrated by the Army Corps of Engineers' *Report of Completed Works* that recorded information on interference and obstacles for each battery such as adjacent batteries, buildings, and vegetation. In addition to a clear field of fire from an emplacement, unobstructed views were necessary from battery commander's stations and fire control stations. Constructed on top of existing batteries or as independent buildings, battery commander's and fire control stations became dedicated structures for locating and acquiring the range of potential targets (see Figures 2.82 and 2.86).

Tactical views of high-altitude, enemy aircraft were not possible and to counter this strategic advantage, the NIKE missile battery utilized radar to acquire targets and guide missiles to a computed intercept point. Radar and missiles had to be separated by a minimum distance of 3,000 feet for guidance communication to work. Therefore, a tactical view existed between the radar site and launch site so the radar signals could be transmitted without obstruction. The area between the two sites was not stripped of all features but vertical objects that could interfere with the radar signals had to be removed, relocated or managed.

Existing Condition: Tactical views from the emplacements, battery commander's stations, and fire control stations to the water are primarily impeded by woody vegetation growing at the interface of the engineered earthwork and concrete battery structure (Figure 4.5 and see Figures 3.4 and 3.42). Beyond the toe or bottom of the engineered earthwork there may be vegetation that impacts views, however, the impact is difficult to evaluate with obstructing vegetation in close proximity to the start of the view. With the exception of the communications trailer and observation platform at Batteries Engle and Peck, there appears to be no additional buildings or structures that impact views from the emplacements, battery commander's stations, and fire control stations.

From the NIKE radar site, signals traveled over a mile to control vans and individual missiles at the launch site. With these vertical elements absent from the launch site, it is difficult to determine if the tactical view is intact or obstructed.

Evaluation: Contributing at the gun batteries, Undetermined at the NIKE missile battery

SMALL-SCALE FEATURES

Historic Condition: The coastal defense batteries contained numerous small-scale architectural features associated with buildings and structures. Railings and features utilized for lighting, electronic communication, and weather observation were installed on various batteries to improve the operational efficiency of the defenses. In the landscape, small-scale features included fencing and exterior lighting. At the NIKE missile sites, fencing provided security against unauthorized access and served to define the outer boundaries of the radar and launch facilities. The Army added an additional security fence to the launch site as part of upgrades to use Hercules missiles fitted with nuclear warheads. Included in the Hercules upgrades was the installation of floodlights along the newly installed security fence and at the Missile Maintenance Area. Exterior lighting was also a feature at the NIKE radar site. Pedestrian-scale fixtures were installed to illuminate the walkway network between the control areas and Ready Barracks as well as the routes among the barrack buildings.

Existing Condition: Small-scale architectural features associated with the coastal defense batteries and small-scale features in the landscape are presently extant. At the NIKE missile sites, the fencing is in fair to poor condition. Corrosion appears on many components of the fencing and some sections have missing or deteriorated chain-link and barbed wire strands. Vegetation crowds or covers sections of the fencing and makes inspection and routine maintenance difficult. Vegetation also crowds several floodlights at the NIKE launch site and the pedestrian-scale lights at the NIKE radar site. Small-scale features also include remnants of buildings and structures that are no longer extant. At certain locations, concrete footings and collapsed metal pipes are the only items present from observation towers and other structures of the coastal defense system.

Many small-scale features in the landscape are present to support the National Park Service's management of Sandy Hook as a national recreation area. Waysides and signage are located in close proximity to many of the gun batteries to aid interpreting the structures. Additional signage and fencing are installed near some batteries to warn visitors of potentially hazardous conditions and block access to fragile building components and engineered earthworks. Existing small-scale features also include contemporary traffic control devices such as guardrails and bollards.

Evaluation: Small-scale features present from the historic period are contributing. Small-scale features added during the National Park Service administration of Sandy Hook are non-contributing.

Table 4.1: Battery Urmston (LCS# SH-540)
Disarmed 1920 (#1, #2, #5, and #6) and 1942 (#3 and #4), Deactivated 1942

Feature	Extant 1945	Extant 1974	Extant 2009	Contributing	Notes
Spatial Organization	Yes	Yes	Yes	Yes	The spatial organization of Battery Urmston is defined by its role in a larger system of coastal defenses. With other rapid fire gun batteries, Urmston provided a field of fire to protect minefields outside the major shipping channel from shallow-draft boats.
Topography					
Engineered earthwork	Yes	Yes	Yes	Yes	The battery's emplacements and magazines were protected by earthen cover that sloped down from the north facade and merged with existing grades. See Figure 2.48, sections.
High point over central storeroom	Yes	Yes	Yes	Yes	The battery contains a central storeroom constructed between emplacements #3 and #4. The *Report of Completed Works* show four feet of earth cover over the top of this concrete structure and the earthwork is still present. See Figure 2.48, rear elevation.
High point between Battery Urmston and Battery Morris	Yes	Yes	Yes	Yes	Sixty-five feet separate Battery Urmston and Battery Morris and in this transitional area, the engineered earthwork of the two batteries merge and form a high point.
Circulation					
Paved road south of battery	Yes	Yes	Yes	Yes	A 1907 map shows a road paralleled the battery's south facade to provide access for personnel and delivery of munitions. Figure 4.6. The road is presently extant but separated from the battery by the Coast Guard perimeter fence.
Buildings and Structures					
Six emplacement, rapid fire gun battery	Yes	Yes	Yes	Yes	The battery was constructed in phased with emplacements #1 and #2 competed first at the east end, emplacements #5 and #6 completed at the west end, and finally emplacements #3 and #4 in the middle.
Coincidence range finder station between emplacements #4 and #5	Yes	Yes	Yes	Yes	An open style station, lacking a permanent roof, was added to the battery 1919.
Vegetation					
Mixed native and non-native vegetative ground cover on engineered earthwork	Yes	Yes	Yes	Yes	Vegetative cover was an essential component of concealing the battery and limiting erosion and dust. Vegetation was not permitted to interfere with the battery's operation or threaten the structural integrity of the earthwork. See Figure 2.49.
Large woody vegetation south of battery	No	No	Yes	No	In a triangular area between the Coast Guard perimeter fence and battery, woody vegetation overruns the space and makes pedestrian access difficult.
Tactical Views					
Downrange views from the emplacements and coincidence range finder station	Yes	Un-determined	No	Yes	Views are presently obstructed by large woody vegetation, especially tall vegetation growing at the interface of the engineered earthwork and concrete battery structure. See Figure 3.4.

Feature	Extant 1945	Extant 1974	Extant 2009	Contrib-uting	Notes
Small-Scale Features					
U. S. Coast Guard perimeter fence	No	Yes	Yes	No	The fence appears on a 1976 survey south of paved road paralleling the battery's south facade. Presently, the fence is on the north side of the road and creates a narrow space south of the battery that makes pedestrian access difficult. The fence consists of six-foot tall chain-link sections topped with barbed wire.
Wood-slat fence east of battery	No	Yes	Yes	No	Erected by the Army in the early 1970s and presently in fair condition.

Table 4.2: Battery Morris (LCS# SH-539)

Disarmed 1946, Deactivated 1946

Feature	Extant 1945	Extant 1974	Extant 2009	Contributing	Notes
Spatial Organization	Yes	Yes	Yes	Yes	The spatial organization of Battery Morris is defined by its role in a larger system of coastal defenses. With other rapid fire gun batteries, Morris provided a field of fire to protect minefields outside the major shipping channel from shallow-draft boats.
Topography					
Engineered earthwork	Yes	Yes	Yes	Yes	The battery's emplacements and magazines were protected by earthen cover that sloped down from the north facade and merged with existing grades. See Figure 2.51, sections.
High point over magazines	Yes	Yes	Yes	Yes	The battery contains three concrete magazines with each located between the gun emplacements. The *Report of Completed Works* show four feet of earth cover over the top of these concrete structures and the earthwork is still present. See Figure 2.51, rear elevation.
Swale north of engineered slope	Un-determined	Un-determined	Yes	Un-determined	The toe or northern end of the engineered slope forms one side of a swale that flows from west to east. No information was discovered on the construction, intent, or date of this feature.
Circulation					
North Bragg Drive	Yes	Yes	Yes	Yes	A 1907 map shows a road paralleled the south facade of the battery. Today, the road is present as a variable-width trail. The asphalt surface of the road is in poor condition. See Figure 3.5.
Buildings and Structures					
Four emplacement, rapid fire gun battery	Yes	Yes	Yes	Yes	Battery Morris consists of four concrete gun platforms separated by three magazines.
Coincidence range finder station (LCS# SH-K)	Yes	Yes	Yes	Yes	Separate concrete structure added in 1920 east of the battery. The station is a square and supported by four concrete legs that raise the structure approximately ten feet above the ground. See Figure 2.86.
Vegetation					
Mixed native and non-native vegetative ground cover on engineered earthwork	Yes	Yes	Yes	Yes	Vegetative cover was an essential component of concealing the battery and limiting erosion and dust. Vegetation was not permitted to interfere with the battery's operation or threaten the structural integrity of the earthwork.
Large woody vegetation south of battery	No	No	Yes	No	Woody vegetation is growing in close proximity to the battery and makes pedestrian access difficult. See Figures 3.5, 3.6, and 3.8.
Tactical Views					
Downrange views from the emplacements and coincidence range finder station	Yes	Un-determined	No	Yes	Views are presently obstructed by large woody vegetation, especially tall vegetation growing at the interface of the engineered earthwork and concrete battery structure. The coincidence range finder station is completely surrounded by vegetation and barely visible from North Bragg Drive.

Feature	Extant 1945	Extant 1974	Extant 2009	Contrib-uting	Notes
Small-Scale Features					
U. S. Coast Guard perimeter fence	No	Yes	Yes	No	Immediately south of North Bragg Drive, the Coast Guard has erected a six-foot tall chain-link fence topped with barbed wire. See Figure 3.5.
Wood-slat fence north and east of battery	No	Yes	Yes	No	Erected by the Army in the early 1970s and presently in poor condition. See Figure 3.8.
Wood two-by-four guard panels	No	Yes	Yes	No	Erected by the Army in the early 1970s and presently in poor condition. See Figure 3.6.

Table 4.3: Batteries Engle and Peck (LCS# SH-189A and SH-180) **Disarmed 1918 (Engle), 1943 (6-inch guns), and 1946 (90mm guns); Deactivated 1946**					
Feature	**Extant 1945**	**Extant 1974**	**Extant 2009**	**Contrib-uting**	**Notes**
Spatial Organization	Yes	Yes	Yes	Yes	The spatial organization of Batteries Engle and Peck is defined by their role in a larger system of coastal defenses. With other rapid fire gun batteries, Engle and Peck provided a field of fire to protect minefields outside the major shipping channel from shallow-draft boats. The Army disarmed Engle in 1918 and constructed a coincidence range finder station for Peck over the abandoned gun platform.
Topography					
Engineered earthwork	Yes	Yes	Yes	Yes	The battery's emplacements, plotting room, and magazines were protected by earthen cover. The *Report of Completed Works* show an engineered slope away from the battery. See Figure 2.52, sections. Today, a raised landform extends 100 feet north of the battery and then gradually descends down and merges with the undulating coastal dunes.
Circulation					
North Bragg Drive	Yes	Yes	Yes	Yes	A 1907 map shows a road paralleled the south facades of Batteries Engle and Peck and continued west to Batteries Morris Urmston. Presently the road is extant and merges with an unpaved road west of Battery Engle that proceeds north into the dunes.
Unpaved vehicular access to observation platform	No	No	Yes	No	A spur off the unpaved road heads east and terminates in an open area around an observation platform.
Social trails among batteries and observation platform	No	No	Yes	No	Pedestrians follow North Bragg Drive and the unpaved roads to the observation platform and proceed south along social trails to the batteries. See Figure 3.11.
Buildings and Structures					
Two emplacement, rapid fire gun battery	Yes	Yes	Yes	Yes	Battery Peck consists of two circular gun platforms, a concrete commander's station, and magazines accessed from the ground level on the south side of the structure.
Coincidence range finder station west of Battery Peck	Yes	Yes	Yes	Yes	The concrete coincidence range finder station constructed on top of Battery Engle is nineteen feet square and covered with a low-pitched concrete roof. See Figure 3.11.
Communications trailer	No	Yes	Yes	No	Abandoned trailer located northeast of Battery Engle. The trailer appears on a 1976 survey and blocks views from the batteries. See Figure 3.12.
Observation Platform	No	No	Yes	No	North of both batteries, the platform was built over a one story, wood-frame structure. The building and platform block views from the batteries but are regularly used for bird watching and as a higher vantage point to take in views across Lower New York Harbor. See Figure 3.13.

Feature	Extant 1945	Extant 1974	Extant 2009	Contrib-uting	Notes
Vegetation					
Mixed native and non-native vegetative ground cover on engineered earthwork	Yes	Yes	Yes	Yes	Vegetative cover was an essential component of concealing the battery and limiting erosion and dust. Vegetation was not permitted to interfere with the battery's operation or threaten the structural integrity of the earthwork.
Large woody vegetation south of batteries	No	Yes	Yes	No	The south elevation of the batteries was open during the historic period for access to the gun platforms and magazines. Presently, vegetation is very dense and the area is nearly impassable. See Figure 3.14.
Tactical Views					
Downrange views from the emplacements, commander's station, and coincidence range finder station	Yes	Un-determined	No	Yes	Views are presently obstructed by large woody vegetation, especially tall vegetation growing at the interface of the engineered earthwork and concrete battery structure. Views are further obstructed by the communications trailer and observation platform north of the batteries.
Small-Scale Features					
Chain-link fence south of Battery Peck	No	No	Yes	No	The National Park Service installed a chain-link fence and signage to warn visitors of potentially hazardous conditions and block access to Battery Peck's south elevation.
Wooden split-rail fence east of Battery Engle	No	No	Yes	No	The National Park Service installed a wooden split-rail fence to limit social trails and erosion on the engineered earthwork. See Figure 3.11.
Barbed wire fence section west of communications trailer	No	Yes	Yes	No	A 1976 survey shows a continuous fence enclosing a rectangular area around the trailer. Presently, an approximate twenty-foot section of chain-link fence is located in dense vegetation.
Wayside east of Battery Peck	No	No	Yes	No	The National Park Service installed an interpretive wayside east of Battery Peck.

Table 4.4: Nine Gun Battery (LCS# SH-181)

Disarmed 1942-43, Deactivated 1943

Feature	Extant 1945	Extant 1974	Extant 2009	Contrib-uting	Notes
Spatial Organization	Yes	Yes	Yes	Yes	The spatial organization of Nine Gun Battery is defined by its role in a larger system of coastal defenses. Working in concert with the other large caliber gun batteries, Nine Gun was constructed to engage battleships in the main shipping channel and built on top of the Civil War-era Fort at Sandy Hook. Nine Gun and the former Fort paralleled the channel along the eastern coastline and included emplacements to the north to follow the channel around the northern end of the peninsula.
Topography					
Engineered earthwork	Yes	Yes	Yes	Yes	The battery's emplacements and magazines were protected by earthen cover that sloped down from the east and north facades and merged with existing grades.
Circulation					
North Bragg Drive	Yes	Yes	Yes	Yes	A 1907 map shows a road paralleled the west facade of Nine Gun Battery and wrapped around the battery's northern end to provide a route to Batteries Engle and Peck. The road is extant and in good to fair condition.
Social trail from emplacement #8	No	Yes	Yes	No	Aerial photographs from 1933, 1942, and 1962 show social trails leading from various emplacements down the engineered earthwork. Figure 4.7. Although present during the historic period, social trails should be closed in order to preserve the engineered earthwork.
Buildings and Structures					
Nine emplacement, large caliber gun battery	Yes	Yes	Yes	Yes	Nine Gun Battery was constructed in phases between 1898 and 1904 and designated as four batteries that featured 10- and 12-inch caliber guns. From north to south, the four batteries are Battery Alexander, Battery Halleck, Battery Bloomfield, and Battery Richardson. See Figure 3.15.
Remnant of granite fort	Yes	Yes	Yes	Yes	Northeast of emplacement #8, large granite blocks are visible immediately beyond the concrete terreplein. See Figure 3.16.
Vegetation					
Mixed native and non-native vegetative ground cover on engineered earthwork	Yes	Yes	Yes	Yes	Vegetative cover was an essential component of concealing the battery and limiting erosion and dust. Vegetation was not permitted to interfere with the battery's operation or threaten the structural integrity of the earthwork.
Phragmites growing in gun wells	No	No	Yes	No	Phragmites (*Phragmites* sp.) is growing in the gun wells at emplacements #6, #7, and #9. See Figure 3.22.

Feature	Extant 1945	Extant 1974	Extant 2009	Contributing	Notes
Tactical Views					
Downrange views from the gun carriage and battery commander's stations	Yes	Undetermined	No	Yes	A raised platform on the gun carriage allowed an artillery officer views over the concrete structure to a potential target. Figure 4.8. Although the gun carriages are not extant, views from a comparable vantage point and from the battery commander's stations are presently obstructed by large woody vegetation, especially tall vegetation growing on the concrete terreplein and at the interface of the engineered earthwork and concrete battery structure. See Figure 3.21.
Small-Scale Features					
Chain-link fence west of Nine Gun Battery	No	No	Yes	No	The National Park Service installed a chain-link fence and signage to warn visitors of potentially hazardous conditions and block access to Nine Gun Battery's west elevation.
Wayside west of emplacement #8	No	No	Yes	No	The National Park Service installed an interpretive wayside west of Nine Gun Battery.

Table 4.5: Battery Potter (LCS# SH-264)

Disarmed 1906, Deactivated 1945

Feature	Extant 1945	Extant 1974	Extant 2009	Contributing	Notes
Spatial Organization	Yes	Yes	Yes	Yes	The spatial organization of Battery Potter is defined by its role in a larger system of coastal defenses. The battery had a 360-degree field of fire, however, it was located on the eastern half of the peninsula and paralleled the main shipping channel. Following the introduction of new artillery, Potter was disarmed and its raised terreplein used for fire control and coordinating New York Harbor defenses.
Topography					
Engineered earthwork	Yes	Yes	Yes	Yes	The 12-inch guns at Battery Potter were raised into firing position by a steam-powered lift. To protect and reload the artillery, the guns were lowered inside a massive concrete structure. An engineered earthwork wrapped around all sides of the battery to shield the concrete and to blend the conspicuous structure into the coastal landscape. See Figure 2.13.
Engineered slope along west facade	No	No	No	Yes	The construction of the Coal Shed and Central Power Plant (1901-03), and Switchboard Rooms (1907), removed the majority of the engineered slope along Battery Potter's west facade. See Figures 2.17 and 2.27.
High point at southwest corner of Battery Potter	Yes	Yes	Yes	Yes	The engineered earthwork juts away from the battery at the southwest corner and rises to a high point. The high point is more pronounced with the loss of the earthwork along the west facade.
Circulation					
North Bragg Drive and Hudson Drive	Yes	Yes	Yes	Yes	North Bragg Drive and Hudson Drive appear on a 1907 map of Fort Hancock and their intersection continues to define the northwest corner of Battery Potter's site.
Unpaved parking area	Yes	Yes	Yes	No	An aerial photograph from 1942 and photographs from 1951 and 1977 show an informally defined area west of the battery used for parking and as a vehicular turnaround. Figure 4.9. The National Park Service has established a gravel parking area south of the main entry and in front of the switchboard rooms.
Paved landing at main entry	Yes	Yes	Yes	Yes	Bluestone was salvaged from the Fort at Sandy Hook and laid in a random rectangular pattern between the octagonal towers that flanked the main door.
Sidewalks to switchboard rooms	Yes	Yes	Yes	Yes	Concrete sidewalks present in a circa 1907 photograph connect the main entry to the switchboard rooms. See Figure 2.30. The sidewalks are extant and presently in good to fair condition.
Trail at southwest corner of Battery Potter	No	No	Yes	No	A social trail begins south of the switchboard rooms, leads up the battery's engineered earthwork, and disappears on the downhill side. The trail cannot be seen on historic aerial photographs.

Feature	Extant 1945	Extant 1974	Extant 2009	Contributing	Notes
Building and Structures					
Two emplacement, steam-powered, gun lift battery	Yes	Yes	Yes	Yes	D-shaped concrete structure with the curved facade facing east and main entry on the west. The main entry is through an arched opening flanked by defensive granite towers. The top structure, known as the terreplein, contained two openings that were used to raise and lower 12-inch caliber guns. After the battery's artillery was removed, several structures were constructed on the terreplein for fire control and coordinating New York Harbor defenses.
Central Power Plant (LCS# SH-259)	Yes	Yes	Yes	Yes	One story, rectangular, brick building that housed generators to produce electricity for the coastal defense batteries and numerous Fort Hancock buildings. The building is extant and in good condition.
Coal Shed (LCS# SH-260)	Yes	Yes	Yes	Yes	One story, rectangular, brick building that stored coal for the Central Power Plant. The building is extant and in good condition.
Switchboard Room "A" (LCS# SH-256)	Yes	Yes	Yes	Yes	One story, rectangular, rusticated concrete block building that housed a telephone operator room linking fire control stations atop Battery Potter with batteries around Sandy Hook. The building is extant and in good condition.
Switchboard Room "C" (LCS# SH-257)	Yes	Yes	Yes	Yes	One story, rectangular, rusticated concrete block building that housed a telephone operator room linking fire control stations atop Battery Potter with batteries around Sandy Hook. The building is extant and in good condition.
Conduit Hut "A" (LCS# SH-258)	Yes	Yes	Yes	Yes	Rectangular concrete building that held conduit for the fire control telephone line network. The building is extant and in fair condition.
Primary Fire Control Stations	Yes	Yes	Yes	Yes	Nine buildings constructed on the terreplein divided into a set of two connected structures on the south end, two connected structures on the north end, and five connected structures in the middle. Concrete remnants mark the location of the southern building and the remaining seven structures are in poor condition.
Vegetation					
Mixed native and non-native vegetative ground cover on engineered earthwork	Yes	Yes	Yes	Yes	In 1893, after sections of the engineered earthwork were completed, cedar trees, small shrubs, and low growing sod were planted to limit erosion and camouflage the earthwork with the surrounding dunes. Vegetation was not permitted to interfere with the battery's operation or threaten the structural integrity of the earthwork.
Tactical Views					
Downrange views from the emplacements and Primary Fire Control Stations	Yes	Un-determined	No	Yes	Battery Potter's height above the surrounding area provides relatively open views to the water, however, there is some interference from vegetation growing on the engineered earthwork. See Figure 3.25.

Feature	Extant 1945	Extant 1974	Extant 2009	Contributing	Notes
Small-Scale Features					
Metal weather pole	Yes	Yes	Yes	Yes	The northernmost Primary Fire Control station was converted into a meteorological station during World War II. A metal tether was installed north of the building to attach weather balloons for recording wind speeds and direction. A T-shaped metal pole is presently located near the north end of the battery. See Figure 3.31.
Wooden wheelstops	No	No	Yes	No	In order to prevent cars from driving too close or parking in front of Battery Potter, the National Park Service set wooden telephone poles along Hudson Drive and the parking area. See Figure 3.24.
Wayside west of structure	No	No	Yes	No	The National Park Service installed an interpretive wayside west of Battery Potter.

Table 4.6: Battery Granger (LCS# SH-266) Disarmed 1943, Deactivated 1943					
Feature	**Extant 1945**	**Extant 1974**	**Extant 2009**	**Contributing**	**Notes**
Spatial Organization	Yes	Yes	Yes	Yes	The spatial organization of Battery Granger is defined by its role in a larger system of coastal defenses. Battery Granger and other large caliber gun batteries were intended to engage battleships in the main shipping channel that provided a southern approach to New York Harbor.
Topography					
Engineered earthwork	Yes	Yes	Yes	Yes	The battery's emplacements and magazines were protected by earthen cover that sloped down from the east facade and merged with existing grades. See Figure 2.32, sections.
Circulation					
Hudson Drive	Yes	Yes	Yes	Yes	Hudson Drive appears on a 1907 map of Fort Hancock paralleling the west facade of Battery Granger. The road is extant and in good condition.
Vehicular pull-off east of Hudson Drive	No	No	Yes	No	The National Park Service installed a pull-off for cars to stop at Battery Granger.
Buildings and Structures					
Two emplacement, large caliber gun battery	Yes	Yes	Yes	Yes	Battery Granger was the first large caliber gun battery at Sandy Hook to use the Buffington-Croizer counterweight carriage to lower artillery below a concrete wall for reloading and protection. An engineered earthwork covered the wall and sloped away toward the target area. On the opposite side, the battery structure was relatively open with access points to the gun platforms and covered storage areas for gunpowder and projectiles. See Figure 2.34.
Vegetation					
Mixed native and non-native vegetative ground cover on engineered earthwork	Yes	Yes	Yes	Yes	Vegetative cover was an essential component of concealing the battery and limiting erosion and dust. Vegetation was not permitted to interfere with the battery's operation or threaten the structural integrity of the earthwork.
Phragmites growing in gun wells	No	No	Yes	No	Phragmites (*Phragmites* sp.) is growing in the gun wells at emplacements #1 and #2.
Tactical Views					
Downrange views from the gun carriage and battery commander's stations	Yes	Undetermined	No	Yes	A raised platform on the gun carriage allowed an artillery officer views over the concrete structure to a potential target. Figure 4.10. Although the gun carriages are not extant, views from a comparable vantage point and from the battery commander's stations are presently obstructed by large woody vegetation, especially tall vegetation growing at the interface of the engineered earthwork and concrete battery structure. See Figure 3.35.
Small-Scale Features					
Chain-link fence west of battery	No	No	Yes	No	The National Park Service installed a chain-link fence and signage to warn visitors of potentially hazardous conditions and block access to Battery Granger's west elevation.
Wayside west of battery	No	No	Yes	No	The National Park Service installed an interpretive wayside west of Battery Granger.

Table 4.7: Mortar Battery (LCS# SH-349)

Disarmed 1919-20, Deactivated 1950

Feature	Extant 1945	Extant 1974	Extant 2009	Contrib-uting	Notes
Spatial Organization	Yes	Yes	Yes	Yes	The spatial organization of the Mortar Battery is defined by its role in a larger system of coastal defenses. The Mortar Battery and Battery Potter were simultaneously constructed with the Mortar Battery located further west from the Atlantic coastline. From this location, the battery fired projectiles in a high, arcing trajectory at enemy ships in the main shipping channel.
Topography					
Engineered earthwork	Yes	Yes	Yes	Yes	The mortar pits are protected by an earthen mound that rises almost thirty-five feet above surrounding grades.
Circulation					
Hudson Road	Yes	Yes	Yes	Yes	Hudson Road appears on a 1907 map of Fort Hancock leading north from Officers' Row to Hudson Drive. The road is extant and in good condition.
Parking lot south and east of battery	Yes	Yes	Yes	No	Following World War II, two separate lots were combined into one L-shaped lot.
Pedestrian entrance through west perimeter wall	Yes	Yes	Yes	Yes	A section of the west perimeter wall was demolished in 1938 to create access from Hudson Road to the southwest mortar.
Pedestrian access at northwest corner	Yes	Yes	Yes	Yes	The perimeter wall was constructed with an opening at the northwest corner that has successively allowed train, vehicular, and pedestrian access.
Trail paralleling the inside west perimeter wall	Yes	Yes	Yes	Yes	A circulation route connected the opening at the northwest corner with the galleries to the northwest and southwest mortars. Presently, the route is surfaced with a combination of gravel and wood chips.
Trail up engineered earthwork south of southwest emplacement	No	No	Yes	No	A trail developed from visitors access to the top of the engineered earthwork in the late 1970s.
Trail north of battery	Yes	Yes	Yes	Yes	By 1942, an unpaved road was installed north of the battery. Presently, the road is almost entirely overtaken by vegetation and barely passable as a trail. Figure 4.11.
Buildings and Structures					
Four mortar pits organized into two firing batteries with underground connecting galleries, magazines, and storage rooms.	Yes	Yes	Yes	Yes	The battery contains four mortar pits that are recessed in a protective mound of earth and sand rising to almost thirty-five feet. The earthen mound is bound by a rectangular concrete wall. At the wall's southwest and northeast corners, counterscarp galleries were constructed to defend against a land-based attack. The Army designated the two north mortars Battery McCook and the south mortars Battery Reynolds.
Telephone data booths	Yes	Yes	Yes	Yes	One story, rectangular, concrete building located above the southwest corner of each mortar pit and supported by arched, concrete spans. The booths received instructions on aiming artillery and relayed the information to the mortar pits. See Figure 3.37.

Feature	Extant 1945	Extant 1974	Extant 2009	Contributing	Notes
Buildings and Structures continued					
Battery commander's stations	Yes	Yes	Yes	Yes	One story, rectangular, concrete building located on top of the engineered earthwork to direct the firing of each battery. One structure was centered between the northwest and northeast mortars and the other between the southwest and southeast mortars.
Perimeter wall	Yes	Yes	Yes	Yes	The north, the east, and a portion of the south perimeter wall were demolished in 1938.
Counterscarp galleries	Yes	Yes	Yes	Yes	The northeast gallery was demolished in 1938.
Vegetation					
Mixed native and non-native vegetative ground cover on engineered earthwork	Yes	Yes	Yes	Yes	In 1893, after sections of the engineered earthwork were completed, records indicate sod cut from a nearby marsh, native heather, cedar boughs, and oats were planted to limit erosion and camouflage the earthwork. Vegetation was not permitted to interfere with the battery's operation or threaten the structural integrity of the earthwork.
Large woody vegetation along west perimeter wall	No	No	Yes	No	The interior of the west perimeter wall was kept free of large woody vegetation in order to defend the space against a ground attack and to facilitate the addition of structures like the weather station. Presently, large woody vegetation is growing in close proximity to the wall. See Figure 3.38.
Tactical Views					
View from gun emplacements to water	No	No	No	No	Artillery crews at the Mortar Battery did not directly sight targets on the water
View from battery commander's stations to water	Yes	Un-determined	No	Yes	Views are presently obstructed by large woody vegetation growing immediately adjacent to the structures and on the highest points of the engineered earthwork.
Small-Scale Features					
Chain-link fence east of battery	No	Yes	Yes	No	The fence appears on a 1976 survey and was likely installed by the Army to separate development east of the battery from the engineered earthwork.
Woven-wire fence along west side of engineered earthwork	No	No	Yes	No	The National Park Service installed the fence to block access on to the engineered earthwork. The fencing is in good to fair condition. See Figure 3.39.
Wood post and wire cable fence at top of engineered earthwork	No	No	Yes	No	In the late 1970s, the National Park Service installed fencing along a path at the top of engineered earthwork. The fencing is in fair to poor condition. See Figure 3.40.
Concrete footing and metal ring	Yes	Yes	Yes	Yes	The footing and ring are remnants of an early twentieth century steel tower used as a battery commander's station and later, a weather station.
Two signs outside perimeter wall	No	No	Yes	No	The National Park Service installed signs on the north and south sides of the pedestrian entrance through west perimeter wall.
Wayside west of battery	No	No	Yes	No	The National Park Service installed an interpretive wayside west of the Mortar Battery. See Figure 3.41.

Table 4.8: Battery Gunnison (LCS# SH-337)					
Disarmed 1943 (6-inch disappearing guns) and 1947 (6-inch pedestal guns), Deactivated 1947					
Feature	**Extant 1945**	**Extant 1974**	**Extant 2009**	**Contrib-uting**	**Notes**
Spatial Organization	Yes	Yes	Yes	Yes	The spatial organization of Battery Gunnison is defined by its role in a larger system of coastal defenses. Originally planned for a location immediately south of Nine Gun Battery, conflicts with the Proving Ground shifted this rapid fire gun battery further south than any coastal defense at the time. Battery Gunnison is the only rapid fire gun battery facing east and protected minefields outside the major shipping channel from shallow-draft boats.
Topography					
Engineered earthwork	Yes	Yes	Yes	Yes	The battery's emplacements and magazines were protected by earthen cover that sloped down from the east facade and merged with existing grades. See Figure 2.53, sections.
High point over central structure	Yes	Yes	Yes	Yes	The battery contains a central structure that housed the magazine and plotting room. The *Report of Completed Works* show over four and a half feet of earth cover over the top of this concrete structure and the earthwork is still present. See Figure 2.53, rear elevation.
Circulation					
Atlantic Drive	Yes	Yes	Yes	Yes	Atlantic Drive appears on a 1907 map of Fort Hancock. The road is extant and in good condition.
Concrete walk from beach facility to battery	No	No	Yes	No	The concrete walk was added after a 1990 survey as part of the Gunnison Beach facilities.
Social trail heading southeast from emplacement #1	No	Yes	Yes	No	A 1962 aerial photograph shows a social trail starting from emplacement #1, heading down the engineered earthwork, and connecting to an open access route that runs between Atlantic Drive and the beach. Figure 4.12. The current trail terminates at the toe of the engineered slope and does not connect to another circulation feature.
Social trail between emplacements and on top of central structure	No	No	Yes	No	A circa 1940 photograph shows soldiers on top of the earthwork but does not reveal if there were defined circulation routes. Figure 4.13. Today, visitors have formed a trail between the emplacements that also loops around the shell hoists and battery commander's station.
Buildings and Structures					
Two emplacement, rapid fire gun battery	Yes	Yes	Yes	Yes	Battery Gunnison consists of two concrete gun platforms separated by a central structure that housed the magazine and plotting room. The originally emplaced 6-inch guns on counterweight carriages were removed in 1943 and the gun wells filled with concrete. The newly raised concrete platforms received 6-inch pedestal mounted guns that remained through World War II.

Feature	Extant 1945	Extant 1974	Extant 2009	Contributing	Notes
Vegetation					
Mixed native and non-native vegetative ground cover on engineered earthwork	Yes	Yes	Yes	Yes	Vegetative cover was an essential component of concealing the battery and limiting erosion and dust. A 1920 aerial photograph shows exposed sand immediately east of both parapets with vegetation growing on the engineered slope in between. Low-growing vegetation, probably a grass species, is present over the central structure. Vegetation was not permitted to interfere with the battery's operation or threaten the structural integrity of the earthwork.
Deciduous trees in open lawn west of battery	No	Yes	Yes	No	A tree appears west of the central structure in a 1956 photograph and several trees are present in a 1976 photograph. Figure 4.14. Eight trees are presently located west of the battery in a staggered arrangement.
Tactical Views					
Downrange views from the emplacements and battery commander's station	Yes	Un-determined	No	Yes	Views are presently obstructed by large woody vegetation, especially individual eastern red cedars growing at the interface of the engineered earthwork and concrete battery structure. See Figure 3.42.
Small-Scale Features					
Wood post and rope bollards	No	No	Yes	No	The wood post and rope bollards were added after a 1990 survey. The bollards parallel the eastern edge of Atlantic Drive.
Wayside west of battery	No	No	Yes	No	The National Park Service installed an interpretive wayside west of the battery.

Table 4.9: Battery Kingman (LCS# SH-441)

Disarmed 1948, Deactivated 1948

Feature	Extant 1945	Extant 1974	Extant 2009	Contributing	Notes
Spatial Organization	Yes	Yes	Yes	Yes	The spatial organization of Battery Kingman is defined by its role in a larger system of coastal defenses. The battery was constructed along the western shoreline of peninsula with open, concrete platforms that emplaced high-angle, 12-inch caliber guns. The battery's distance from potential targets was a primary means of protection. During World War II, the battery was casemated to provide protection against aerial reconnaissance and bombing and worked with large caliber guns at the Navesink Highlands and Rockaway peninsula to defend the southern approach to New York Harbor.
Topography					
Engineered earthwork	Yes	Yes	Yes	Yes	The battery's guns and central structure for magazines and storage were protected by earthen cover that formed a roughly oval-shaped mound over 700 hundred feet across and forty feet high. See Figure 2.76.
High point over each gun emplacement	Yes	Yes	Yes	Yes	Between 1941 and 1942 the open gun platforms were casemated with concrete and an engineered earthwork. The *Report of Completed Works* show an additional three feet of earth cover each emplacement and these high points are still present.
Circulation					
Access road from Hartshorne Drive	Yes	Yes	Yes	Yes	A 1920 aerial photograph shows an access road leading west from Hartshorne Drive to Batteries Kingman and Mills. The road is extant and closed to the general public by a locked vehicular gate.
Vehicular route circumscribing battery	No	Yes	Yes	No	At the end of World War II, a vehicular route was present along west side of battery only. A 1962 aerial photograph shows the route circumscribing the battery and this circulation feature is presently extant. Figure 4.15.
Buildings and Structures					
Two emplacement, large caliber gun battery casemated in earth and concrete	Yes	Yes	Yes	Yes	Two concrete gun platforms that emplaced high-angle carriages are located on either side of a central concrete structure that housed the magazines and storage areas. Concrete canopies extend over the each gun platform to shield the artillery from overhead fire. The guns and central structure are covered with earth, a two-foot thick concrete "buster course," and a final layer of earth cover.
Concrete box south of emplacement #2	Yes	Yes	Yes	Yes	Approximately thirty-inch concrete cube most likely associated with ventilation or serving as flues for furnaces. See Figure 3.50.
Concrete pipe southwest of emplacement #2	Yes	Yes	Yes	Yes	Concrete pipe protruding from the surface of the engineered earthwork most likely associated with ventilation. See Figure 3.51.

Feature	Extant 1945	Extant 1974	Extant 2009	Contributing	Notes
Buildings and Structures continued					
Horseshoe Cove Wood Bulkhead (LCS# SH-G)	Yes	Yes	Yes	Yes	Between 1937 and 1938, the Army constructed a wood bulkhead in Sandy Hook Bay to stabilize the shoreline west of Batteries Kingman and Mills. A line of wood pilings is presently extant approximately fifty feet west from the shoreline.
Vegetation					
Mixed native and non-native vegetative ground cover on engineered earthwork	Yes	Yes	Yes	Yes	In World War II-era correspondence concerning planting for "obscurement" and erosion and dust control, groundsel bush, rugosa roses, poplars, seedling pine trees, and naturalized or planted grass species are cited as vegetative cover for the engineered earthwork.
Scrub pine (*Pinus virginiana*) on engineered earthwork	Undetermined	Undetermined	Yes	Undetermined	In January 1944 correspondence, "seedling pine trees" were identified for infill planting at Batteries Kingman and Mills. By May 1944, concealment planting at the batteries was halted and none of the work identified earlier in the year may have been accomplished. Today, scrubs pines are present in several locations on the engineered earthwork.
Tactical Views					
View from gun emplacements to water	No	No	No	No	Artillery crews at Battery Kingman did not directly sight targets on the water.
Small-Scale Features					
Chain-link fence above concrete canopy for each emplacement	No	No	Yes	No	The National Park Service installed a six-foot high chain-link fence to prevent access to the concrete canopies above each emplacement. The fences appear to be in good to fair condition with vines twining their way through the chain-link mesh. See Figure 3.48.
Wood post and wire cable fence at top of engineered earthwork	No	No	Yes	No	The National Park Service installed fencing along a path at the top of engineered earthwork. The fencing is in fair to poor condition. See Figure 3.56.
Wood guardrails east of vehicular route	No	No	Yes	No	The wood guardrails appear on a 1990 survey and are presently in fair to poor condition. See Figure 3.57.

Table 4.10: Battery Mills (LCS# SH-440)

Disarmed 1948, Deactivated 1948

Feature	Extant 1945	Extant 1974	Extant 2009	Contributing	Notes
Spatial Organization	Yes	Yes	Yes	Yes	The spatial organization of Battery Mills is defined by its role in a larger system of coastal defenses. The battery was constructed along the western shoreline of peninsula with open, concrete platforms that emplaced high-angle, 12-inch caliber guns. The battery's distance from potential targets was a primary means of protection. During World War II, the battery was casemated to provide protection against aerial reconnaissance and bombing and worked with large caliber guns at the Navesink Highlands and Rockaway peninsula to defend the southern approach to New York Harbor.
Topography					
Engineered earthwork	Yes	Yes	Yes	Yes	The battery's guns and central structure for magazines and storage were protected by earthen cover that formed a roughly oval-shaped mound over 700 hundred feet across and forty feet high. See Figure 2.77.
High point over each gun emplacement	Yes	Yes	Yes	Yes	Between 1941 and 1942 the open gun platforms were casemated with concrete and an engineered earthwork. The *Report of Completed Works* show an additional three feet of earth cover each emplacement and these high points are still present.
Circulation					
Access road from Hartshorne Drive	Yes	Yes	Yes	Yes	A 1920 aerial photograph shows an access road leading west from Hartshorne Drive to Batteries Kingman and Mills. The road is extant and closed to the general public by a locked vehicular gate.
Vehicular route circumscribing battery	No	Yes	Yes	No	At the end of World War II, a vehicular route was present along west side of battery only. A 1962 aerial photograph shows the route circumscribing the battery and this circulation feature is presently extant.
Trail on top of engineered earthwork	No	No	Yes	No	A 1962 aerial photograph shows a social trail leading from the east side of the engineered earthwork up to the top. See Figure 4.15. A trail across the top of the earthwork is recorded on a 1976 survey. Presently, a small section of trail remains along the top of the earthwork but there is no connection to other circulation features.
Buildings and Structures					
Two emplacement, large caliber gun battery casemated in earth and concrete	Yes	Yes	Yes	Yes	Two concrete gun platforms that emplaced high-angle carriages are located on either side of a central concrete structure that housed the magazines and storage areas. Concrete canopies extend over the each gun platform to shield the artillery from overhead fire. The guns and central structure are covered with earth, a two-foot thick concrete "buster course," and a final layer of earth cover.

Feature	Extant 1945	Extant 1974	Extant 2009	Contrib-uting	Notes
Buildings and Structures continued					
Concrete box and metal pipe near center top of the engineered earthwork	Yes	Yes	Yes	Yes	A tapered concrete box and with a collapsed metal pipe is located near the center top of the earthwork. The feature is most likely associated with ventilation or served as a flue for furnaces. See Figure 3.52.
Concrete pipe southwest of emplacement #1	Yes	Yes	Yes	Yes	Concrete pipe protruding from the surface of the engineered earthwork most likely associated with ventilation. See Figure 3.53.
Vegetation					
Mixed native and non-native vegetative ground cover on engineered earthwork	Yes	Yes	Yes	Yes	In World War II-era correspondence concerning planting for "obscurement" and erosion and dust control, groundsel bush, rugosa roses, poplars, seedling pine trees, and naturalized or planted grass species are cited as vegetative cover for the engineered earthwork.
Scrub pine (*Pinus virginiana*) on engineered earthwork	Un-deter-mined	Un-deter-mined	Yes	Un-deter-mined	In January 1944 correspondence, "seedling pine trees" were identified for infill planting at Batteries Kingman and Mills. By May 1944, concealment planting at the batteries was halted and none of the work identified earlier in the year may have been accomplished. Today, scrubs pines are present in several locations on the engineered earthwork. See Figure 3.55.
Planetrees (*Platanus × acerifolia*) on engineered earthwork	Un-deter-mined	Un-deter-mined	Yes	Un-deter-mined	Planetrees are not identified in historic correspondence regarding concealment or erosion control at the batteries. Today, three planetrees are present on the west side of the engineered earthwork.
Tactical Views					
View from gun emplacements to water	No	No	No	No	Artillery crews at Battery Mills did not directly sight targets on the water.
Small-Scale Features					
Chain-link fence above concrete canopy for each emplacement	No	No	Yes	No	The National Park Service installed a six-foot high chain-link fence to prevent access to the concrete canopies above each emplacement. The fences appear to be in good to fair condition with vines twining their way through the chain-link mesh. See Figure 3.49.
Wood guardrails east of vehicular route	No	No	Yes	No	The wood guardrails appear on a 1990 survey and are presently in fair to poor condition. See Figure 3.58.

Table 4.11: NIKE Radar Site Deactivated 1971				
Feature	**Extant 1974**	**Extant 2009**	**Contributing**	**Notes**
Spatial Organization	Yes	Yes	Yes	The spatial organization of NIKE radar site is defined by its role in a larger system of coastal defenses. At Sandy Hook, the radar site worked in conjunction with the launch site to fire radar guided, land-based missiles at potential enemy aircraft over seventy-five miles away. The NIKE battery was one of nineteen missile batteries dispersed around the metropolitan New York area that defended the region from high altitude bomber attacks. At the radar site the arrangement of buildings, circulation routes, and vegetation form three distinct areas—Control Area #1, Control Area #2, and the Ready Barracks. The organization of and distinction among these three separate areas is legible at the site today. Figure 4.16.
Topography	Yes	Yes	Yes	Topography at the NIKE radar site is consistent with the slight variations seen in other interior locations on the Sandy Hook peninsula. Areas have been modified to create level surfaces for buildings, radar towers, and circulation features. Other than those modifications, there are no major engineered or constructed topography features.
Circulation				
Hartshorne Drive	Yes	Yes	Yes	Hartshorne Drive appears on a 1907 map of Fort Hancock. The road is extant and in good condition.
Parking Lot L	Un-determined	Yes	Un-determined	The current parking area west of Control Area #2 does not appear on 1950s plans for the NIKE radar site or plans from the early 1960s when the "Improved Hercules" system was implemented. See Figure 2.101. The parking area is shown on a 1976 survey and today is in good condition.
Multi-use Path (MUP)	No	Yes	No	The first phase of the multi-use path stretches from the park entrance to the ferry landing near the northern end of the Fort Hancock Historic District. Phase one opened to the public in 2006 and a portion runs between Parking Lot L and the radar site perimeter fence.
Paved vehicular route between Control Area #1 and #2	Yes	Yes	Yes	Based on a review of construction drawings for the site, a vehicular route connecting the control areas was constructed between October 1955 and January 1960. The plan calls for a compacted gravel road. Presently, the road is asphalt and in good to fair condition.
Vehicular routes between control areas and Ready Barracks	Yes	Yes	Yes	The current vehicular routes between the control areas and Ready Barracks do not appear on 1950s plans for the radar site. Plans and photographs from the early 1960s show the routes. See Figures 2.102 and 4.16. A present, the route between Control Area #1 and the barracks is asphalt and the route between Control Area #2 and the barracks is unpaved.
Parking area west of Ready Barracks	Yes	Yes	Yes	A 1954 plan for the radar site shows a sixty by eighty foot parking area accessed from Sheldon Road. Presently, the extents of the parking area are poorly defined and the space is used to store bricks and construction materials.

Feature	Extant 1974	Extant 2009	Contributing	Notes
Circulation continued				
Walkway network (LCS# SH-P)	Yes	Yes	Yes	Concrete sidewalks provide pedestrian access between the control areas and Ready Barracks and also among the buildings that comprise the Ready Barracks. A 1954 plan for the radar site shows the walkway network among the Ready Barracks. Based on a review of construction drawings for the site, the walkways from the control areas to the Ready Barracks were constructed between October 1955 and January 1960. See Figure 2.95. The walkways are presently extant and in fair condition. Some portions of the sidewalks are being covered by encroaching woody vegetation. Figure 4.17.
Buildings and Structures				
Control Area #1 Structures	Yes	Yes	Yes	Control Area #1 is comprised of radar towers, support buildings, and concrete foundations that include: 411 Connecting Corridors, 413 Sentry Box, 414 Generator House, 417 Target Tracking Radar Tower, 418 Acquisition Radar Tower, 419 Missile Tracking Radar Tower, 453 ABAR Radar Tower Pedestal, 454 Equipment Building, and 473 Target Tracking Radar Tower. See Drawing 3.13.
Control Area #2 Structures	Yes	Yes	Yes	Control Area #2 is comprised of radar towers, support buildings, and concrete foundations that include: 409 Connecting Corridors, 410 Generator Building, 420 Abandoned Target Tracking Radar Tower, 421 Acquisition Radar Tower, 422 Missile Tracking Radar Tower, 423 Sentry Box, 467 Target Ranging Radar Tower, 468 HIPAR Building, 469 HIPAR Radar Base, and 472 New Target Tracking Radar Tower. See Drawing 3.13.
Ready Barracks Structures	Yes	Yes	Yes	The Ready Barracks is comprised of barracks, support buildings, and concrete foundations that include: 402 Enlisted Men's Barracks with Mess, 403 Enlisted Men's Barracks with Mess, 404 Enlisted Men's Barracks with Mess (foundation only), 405 Enlisted Men's Barracks with Mess (foundation only), 406 Latrine, and 407 Boiler Room. See Drawing 3.13.
Vegetation				
Maintained vegetation among radar towers, support buildings, and barracks	Yes	No	Yes	Historic photographs indicate that a combination of bare sand and grass species was typical around the buildings and structures at the radar site. Figure 4.18. Following the site's closure woody species, especially eastern red cedars, have emerged and are growing in close proximity to the buildings. See Figure 3.63.
Fire breaks along perimeter fence	Yes	No	Yes	Notes added to a 1950s plan for the perimeter fence installation specify a thirty-foot wide firebreak inside the fence line. See Figure 2.92. There is presently no firebreak along the perimeter fence and unmanaged vegetation grows in close proximity to the feature.

Feature	Extant 1974	Extant 2009	Contributing	Notes
Vegetation continued				
Undisturbed area in the center of site	Yes	Yes	Yes	Construction of the radar towers, support buildings and barracks necessitated the removal of existing vegetation. In addition to this clearing, vegetation was removed for firebreaks along the perimeter fence and to permit unobstructed radar signals to the boring masts. The combined vegetation removals resulted in a triangular area in the center of the site where existing, native vegetation remained undisturbed. See Figures 2.97 and 4.16. Today, native vegetation is present in the same area but surrounded by woody vegetation that has grown since the closure of the site.
Tactical Views				
View between each Missile Tracking Radar and the control vans and individual missiles at the launch site	Yes	Undetermined	Undetermined	Between the radar and launch sites, the Army maintained vegetation at a low height to allow unobstructed radar signals between the Missile Tracking Radar, control vans, and individual missiles. Figure 4.19 and see Figures 2.91 and 2.92.
Small-Scale Features				
Perimeter fence (LCS# SH-S)	Yes	Yes	Yes	Construction drawings for the site list the fence as type FE-6 which designates chain-link fence with a single extension arm supporting continuous strands of barbed wire. The fence was to be installed with a consistent top elevation that did not interfere with the transmission of the radar. The perimeter fence is presently extant with chain-link sections attached to H-shaped posts. The fence is in fair to poor condition.
Basketball court	Yes	Yes	Yes	A 1955 plan for the radar site shows a rectangular athletic court south of the Ready Barracks. Presently, an asphalt basketball court is extant with the long axis of the court oriented north to south. Sections of chain-link fence enclose the north and south ends. The court served as a small recreation amenity when personnel staffed the site and was a common feature at NIKE installations across the country.
Pedestrian lighting (LCS# SH-R)	Yes	Yes	Yes	Pedestrian-scale lights line both walkways from the control areas to the Ready Barracks. The lights are also located along walkways to the north and south of the barrack buildings. The lights are mounted on ten-foot tall metal poles and topped with a bell-shaped metal reflector shade. Both pole and reflector have a green, baked enamel finish. The lights are presently extant and in good to fair condition. See Figure 3.60.

Table 4.12: NIKE Launch Site

Disarmed 1971, Deactivated 1971

Feature	Extant 1974	Extant 2009	Contributing	Notes
Spatial Organization	Yes	Yes	Yes	The spatial organization of NIKE launch site is defined by its role in a larger system of coastal defenses. At Sandy Hook, the launch site worked in conjunction with the radar site to fire radar guided, land-based missiles at potential enemy aircraft over seventy-five miles away. The NIKE battery was one of nineteen missile batteries dispersed around the metropolitan New York area that defended the region from high altitude bomber attacks. At the launch site the arrangement of engineered earthworks, buildings, and circulation routes form three distinct areas--the Missile Magazines, the Missile Maintenance Area, and the Ready Barracks. The organization of and distinction among these three separate areas is legible at the site today.
Topography				
Engineered plateau for Missile Magazines	Yes	Yes	Yes	Due to groundwater close to the surface throughout the peninsula, the Army did not excavate for the underground the missile magazines. Instead, a roughly five hundred-foot square, elevated plateau was constructed over the magazines. Elevators carried missiles from the magazines to the racks and launchers on the top of the landform. See Figure 2.104. The engineered plateau is presently extant and in good condition. A major storm event could damage the Atlantic facing side of the earthwork.
Engineered earthwork north of Warhead Building	Yes	Yes	Yes	North of the Warhead Building, a narrow, elliptical earthwork rises to an elevation of twenty feet. The engineered earthwork is presently extant and in good condition.
Engineered earthwork south of Warhead Building	Yes	Yes	Yes	South of the Warhead Building, a crescent-shaped earthwork rises to an elevation of twenty feet. The tips of the crescent wrap around the building to the north and almost form a continuous landform with the northern earthwork. The engineered earthwork is presently extant and in fair condition. See Figure 3.66. Storage bins and containers for recycling are located at the eastern end of earthwork and are damaging the base of the feature.
Circulation				
Hartshorne Drive	Yes	Yes	Yes	Hartshorne Drive appears on a 1907 map of Fort Hancock. The road is extant and in good condition.
Parking area	Yes	Yes	Yes	West of the Hartshorne Drive's northbound lanes is an approximate 50-foot by 180-foot asphalt parking area. The parking area does not appear on historic plans reviewed for this project, however, a historic photograph shows the lot and several parked cars. A Hercules missile is in the background of the photograph dating the image to 1958 or later. Figure 4.20.
Multi-use Path (MUP)	No	Yes	No	The first phase of the multi-use path stretches from the park entrance to the ferry landing near the northern end of the Fort Hancock Historic District. Phase one opened to the public in 2006 and a portion runs between Hartshorne Drive and the launch site's outer fence.

Feature	Extant 1974	Extant 2009	Contrib-uting	Notes
Circulation continued				
Paved central access road	Yes	Yes	Yes	A 1954 plan shows a compacted gravel access road that heads east from Hartshorne Drive, continues past the Ready Barracks, and terminates at routes to the Missile Magazines and Missile Maintenance Area. The access road was paved with asphalt as part of alterations to the launch site for the Hercules missile. Figure 4.21. The road is presently extant and in good condition.
Paved road spur to Generator Building (429)	Yes	Yes	Yes	A 1954 plan shows a compacted gravel road that branches northeast off the central access road and terminates in a small parking area east of the Generator Building (429). The road was paved with asphalt as part of alterations to the launch site for the Hercules missile and is presently extant and in good condition.
Paved vehicular routes and dolly route at Missile Maintenance Area	Yes	Yes	Yes	A 1954 plan shows compacted gravel roads connecting the Missile Assembly and Test Building (449) and Warhead Building (450). In addition, a concrete walk was added so personnel could transport missiles on a dolly between the two buildings. As part of alterations to the launch site for the Hercules missile, the gravel roads were paved with asphalt and the concrete walk was widened to accommodate the larger missile. Figure 4.22. The vehicular routes and dolly route are presently extant and in good condition.
Walkway network at Ready Barracks	Yes	Yes	Yes	A 1954 plan shows a system of narrow walkways for the Ready Barracks that were not in the contract for constructing the launch site. Figure 4.23. The Army presumably added the walkways following major construction activities in a slightly different configuration than shown on the plan. The walkways appear in a historic photograph and are presently extant and in good condition. Figure 4.24.
Unpaved route around inner security fence	Yes	Yes	Yes	A 1954 plan shows a compacted gravel road around the Missile Magazines. When the magazines were modified for the Hercules missile and the inner security fence added, the route remained unpaved and followed the fence line. See Figure 4.19. The unpaved route is presently extant, however, woody vegetation is encroaching on the edges of the circulation feature.
Unpaved area north of Warhead Building (450) and access to beach	No	Yes	No	During the past decade, a New Jersey state beach cleaning program established an unpaved area to store and clean their vehicles north of the Warhead Building. The program also created an unpaved route from the staging area to the beach. Neither the staging area nor the route to the beach was present during the launch site's operation.
Path to Canine Kennel (458)	No	Yes	No	The Army constructed the Canine Kennel (458) near the northwest corner of the Missile Magazines. Prior to the construction, the northwest corner contained bare sand and low-growing vegetation. See Figure 4.19. Occupying a relatively open area, no defined walkway or path developed in association with the kennel. The current path is a result of contemporary access to the building through an area filled with woody vegetation.

Feature	Extant 1974	Extant 2009	Contributing	Notes
Buildings and Structures				
Missile Magazines	Yes	Yes	Yes	The Missile Magazines are comprised of underground storage areas, support buildings, and concrete foundations that include: 425 Missile Storage (Type B), 426 Missile Storage (Type B), 427 Missile Storage (Type B), 428 Missile Storage (Type B), 429 Generator Building, 447 Paint and Oil Storage, 448 Sentry Hut (foundation only), 457 Kennel Storage, and 458 Canine Kennel. See Drawing 3.14.
Missile Maintenance Area	Yes	Yes	Yes	The Missile Maintenance Area is comprised of two workshop buildings—449 Missile Assembly and Test Building and 450 Warhead Building. See Drawing 3.14.
Ready Barracks Structures	Yes	Yes	Yes	The Ready Barracks is comprised of barracks, support buildings, and concrete foundations that include: T-430 Barracks, T-431 Barracks, T-432 Barracks, T-433 Barracks, T-435 Boiler House, 434 Latrine, 437 Ready Building, 439 Sentry Hut, and 456 Sentry Hut (foundation only). The "T" prefix is an Army designation for a temporary structure. See Drawing 3.14.
Vegetation				
Maintained vegetation at the Missile Magazines, Missile Maintenance Area, and Ready Barracks	Yes	No	Yes	Historic photographs indicate that the area around the Missile Magazines was devoid of vegetation. See Figure 4.19. No large woody vegetation can be seen in a photograph looking towards the Missile Maintenance Area. Figure 4.25. Finally, the Ready Barracks featured lawn panels located between the buildings and walkways with an occasional tree planted in a panel. See Figure 4.24. Following the site's closure woody species, especially eastern red cedars, have emerged and are growing in close proximity to the buildings. Figure 4.26.
Firebreaks along perimeter fence	Yes	No	Yes	A 1954 plan identifies a twenty-foot firebreak outside the fence. South of the Missile Maintenance Area, the same plan identifies a thirty-foot firebreak inside the fence along with the twenty feet outside. It is unclear if the thirty-foot interior firebreak continued around the entire fence or was only cleared for the Missile Maintenance Area. There are presently no firebreaks along the perimeter fence and unmanaged vegetation grows in close proximity to the feature. See Figure 3.70.
Low-growing groundcover on engineered earthworks	Yes	No	Yes	Construction drawings for the engineered earthworks in the Missile Maintenance Area call for the slopes to be seeded. A seed mix is not specified, however, based on a 1962 aerial photograph the earthworks appear covered in low-growing vegetation, most likely a grass species. Figure 4.27. Following the site's closure woody species, especially eastern red cedars, have emerged and are growing on the earthworks. See Figure 3.68.
Tactical Views				
View from the control vans and individual missiles to the Missile Tracking Radars at the radar site	Yes	Undetermined	Undetermined	Between the launch and radar sites, the Army maintained vegetation at a low height to allow unobstructed radar signals between the control vans, individual missiles, and the Missile Tracking Radars. See Figures 2.91, 2.92, and 4.19.

Feature	Extant 1974	Extant 2009	Contrib-uting	Notes
Small-Scale Features				
Inner security fence (LCS# SH-S)	Yes	Yes	Yes	The Army installed a chain-link fence around the Missile Magazines as a component of the launch site's security upgrades to use Hercules missiles fitted with nuclear warheads. The top of the fence featured a single extension arm that supported continuous strands of barbed wire. See Figure 4.19. The inner fence is presently extant with chain-link sections attached to H-shaped posts. The fence is in fair to poor condition. Figure 4.28.
Outer security fence (LCS# SH-S)	Yes	Yes	Yes	During the initial construction of the launch site, the Army installed a perimeter security fence. The outer fence is identical in construction to the inner fence listed above. East of the Missile Maintenance Area, the National Park Service replaced a section of the outer fence with a gate for access to the beach. The outer fence is presently in fair to poor condition. See Figure 3.69.[7]
Floodlights along inner security fence (LCS# SH-Q)	Yes	Yes	Yes	A 1958 electrical plan for the launch site shows eight floodlights positioned along the inner fence at the Missile Magazines. Each light features a twenty-four inch parabolic fixture mounted with a metal bracket to a twelve-foot tall wood pole. See Figure 2.109. The eight floodlights are presently extant and in good to fair condition. Many of the floodlights are surrounded by woody vegetation that has grown since the site's closure. See Figure 3.71.
Floodlights at the Missile Maintenance Area (LCS# SH-Q)	Yes	Yes	Yes	Six floodlights, identical to the ones at the Missile Magazines, are located at the Missile Maintenance Area. Three of the lights are located on the northern engineered earthwork and the other three are on the southern engineered earthwork. Vegetation encroaches on many of the floodlights, however, they are in good to fair condition. See Figure 3.68.[8]
Spotlights in the Missile Magazine area	Yes	Yes	Yes	By the end of the historic period, four wood poles were erected with one located near each of the missile magazines. From ground level, the first eight to ten feet of the poles were painted yellow and a red letter was added to the yellow field to denote the magazine section. Spotlights were mounted at the top of each pole. See Figure 3.72. The pole and light fixtures near the Section B magazine (427) are presently extant and the other three poles were removed after the National Park Service acquired the site.
CODAR antenna	No	Yes	No	After the transfer of Sandy Hook to the National Park Service, an antenna and monitoring equipment were set up east of the Missile Maintenance Area and approaching the outer fence. The equipment collects weather and tide information. See Figure 3.73.
CODAR antenna	No	Yes	No	After the transfer of Sandy Hook to the National Park Service, an antenna was set up south of the Missile Maintenance Area and approaching the outer fence. The antenna collects weather and tide information. See Figure 3.74.
Missile display southwest of Ready Barracks	No	Yes	No	The National Park Service installed a NIKE missile display in the southwest corner of the Ready Barracks.

ENDNOTES

[1] Richard F. Greenwood, "National Register of Historic Places Inventory - Nomination Form, Fort Hancock and the Sandy Hook Proving Ground Historic District," June 28, 1976, sect. 7, 1.

[2] Harry Butowsky, "National Register of Historic Places Inventory - Nomination Form, Fort Hancock and the Sandy Hook Proving Ground Historic District," revised November 9, 1982, sect. 10, 1-2.

[3] Ibid., sect. 8, 1.

[4] Ibid.

[5] Ibid., sect. 8, 5.

[6] Savage to Pfoutz, November 5, 1996. From correspondence in reference to "List of Classified Structures," countersigned by Dorothy Guzzo, NJ SHPO, January 2, 1997. NPS, National Register Files, Northeast Region, Boston Office.

[7] The LCS only lists NIKE site fencing and does not distinguish between an inner and outer security fence at the launch site. Identifying an inner and outer fence is important to the history of the site. The outer fence was initially installed and approximately four years later, with the introduction of Hercules missiles fitted with nuclear warheads, the inner fence was added.

[8] The LCS does not distinguish between floodlights at the Missile Magazines and the Missile Maintenance Area.

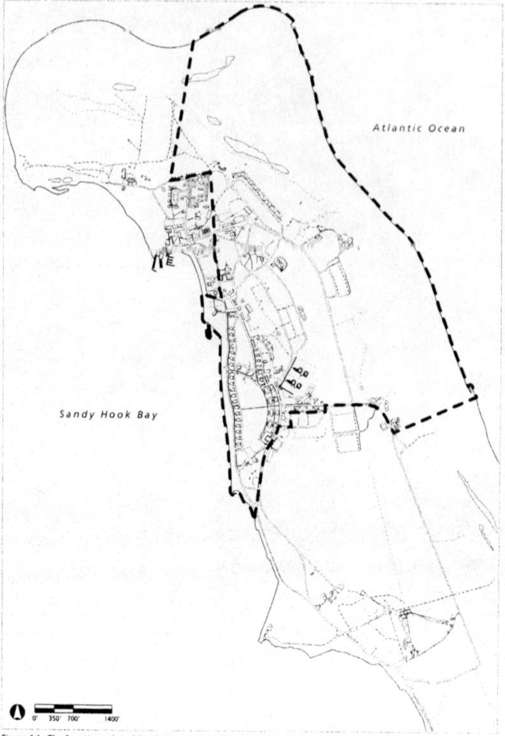

Figure 4.1. The Fort Hancock and Sandy Hook Proving Ground Historic District, 1980. When the district was first listed on the National Register of Historic Places, the boundaries (dashed outline) were defined by Sandy Hook Bay on the west, portions of Magruder Road, Gunnison Road, and Atlantic Drive on the south, the Atlantic Ocean on the east, and the U. S. Coast Guard property on the north. Boundaries for the National Historic Landmark accepted in 1982 include the majority of the peninsula north of the Route 36 bridge (Olmsted Center, 2009).

Figure 4.2. View looking east at the south earthwork, Missile Maintenance Area, NIKE launch site. The railroad tie retaining structure and recycling containers cut into a portion of the engineered earthwork (Olmsted Center, April 2008).

Figure 4.3. Railroad tracks crossing asphalt road near Nine Gun Battery. The tracks are remnants of the historic railroad circulation system that transported ammunition to the batteries (Olmsted Center, January 2009).

Figure 4.4. View looking northwest at Battery Kingman. South of Battery Kingman, coastal erosion has exposed wooden railroad ties. The ties are remnants of a railroad system that delivered ammunition to the coastal defense batteries throughout Sandy Hook. After this picture was taken, continuing coastal erosion completely removed the railroad ties (Olmsted Center, January 2009).

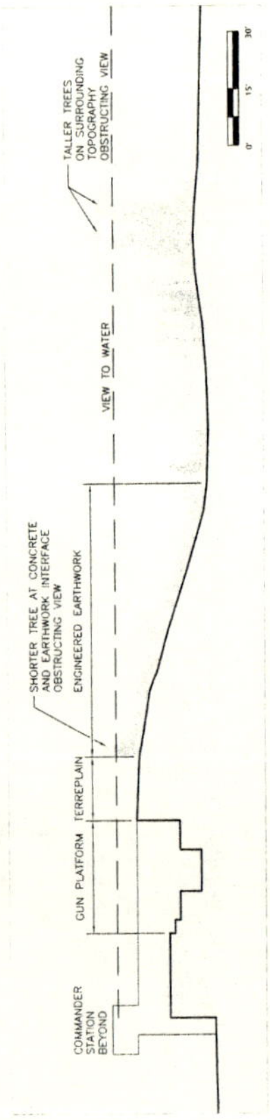

Figure 4.5. Conceptual section through a disappearing gun battery. The section is drawn through a gun emplacement for a concrete battery such as Battery Granger or Nine Gun Battery. Tactical views from the emplacements, battery commander's stations, and fire control stations to the water are primarily impeded by woody vegetation growing at the interface of the engineered earthwork and concrete battery structure (Olmsted Center, 2009).

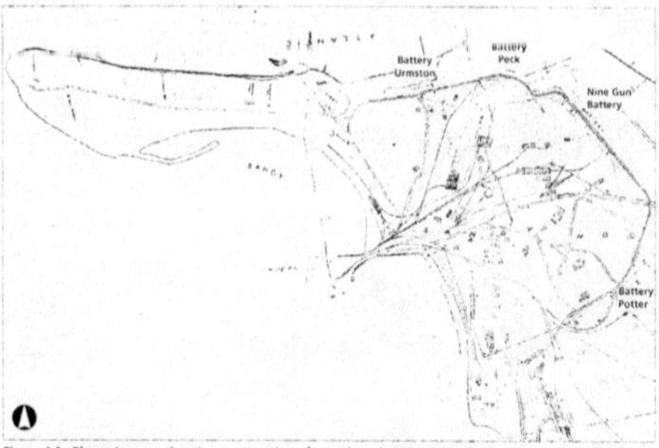

Figure 4.6. Blue print map showing construction of gravel roads at Ft. Hancock, N.J., August 31, 1907. The Army constructed a gravel road, highlighted in red, paralleling the rear facades of the Nine Gun Battery, Battery Peck, and Battery Urmston in order to provide access for personnel and delivery of munitions (GATE GIS and Olmsted Center).

Figure 4.7. Oblique aerial photograph of Nine Gun Battery, 1942. Although the photograph shows social trails leading from various emplacements down the engineered earthwork, social trails should be closed in order to preserve the earthwork (National Archives, Record Group 661 S, Philip S. Gage Collection, Fort Hancock Folder).

Figure 4.8. View looking southeast at artillery firing, Battery Richardson, Nine Gun Battery, circa 1905–10. A raised platform on the gun carriage allowed an artillery officer views over the concrete structure to a potential target. Although the gun carriages are not extant, views from a comparable vantage point and from the battery commander's stations are presently obstructed by large woody vegetation (Thomas Hoffman, *Fort Hancock*, Charleston, SC: Arcadia Publishing, 2007).

Figure 4.9. View looking north at Battery Potter, 1951. By 1942, an informally defined area west of Battery Potter was used for parking and as a vehicular turnaround. The National Park Service presently maintains a gravel parking area southwest of the main entry and in front of the switchboard rooms (GATE 3610).

Figure 4.10. View looking northeast at emplacement #1, Battery Granger, 1899. A raised platform on the gun carriage allowed an artillery officer views over the concrete structure to a potential target. Although the gun carriages are not extant, views from a comparable vantage point and from the battery commander's stations are presently obstructed by large woody vegetation (GATE 7778).

Figure 4.11. View looking northwest at trail north of the Mortar Battery. By 1942, an unpaved road was installed north of the Mortar Battery that presently is overtaken by vegetation and is barely passable as a trail (Olmsted Center, January 2009).

Figure 4.12. Aerial photograph of Battery Gunnison, 1962. A social trail starts from emplacement #1, heads down the engineered earthwork, and connects to an open access route that runs between Atlantic Drive and the beach. Today, a trail starts from emplacement #1 and terminates at the toe of the engineered slope. The social trail does not connect to another circulation feature (Army Corps of Engineers Coastal and Hydraulics Laboratory).

Figure 4.13. View looking north from emplacement #1 at commander's station, shell hoist, and central structure, Battery Gunnison, circa 1940. Soldiers are seen on top of the earthwork in front of the commander's station, however, the photograph does not reveal defined circulation routes. Today, visitors have formed a trail between the emplacements that also loops around the shell hoists and battery commander's station (GATE 13708).

Figure 4.14. View looking northeast at central structure, Battery Gunnison, 1956. A tree appears west of the central structure and today, eight trees are located west of the battery in a staggered arrangement (GATE 11217).

Figure 4.15. Aerial photograph of Batteries Kingman and Mills, 1962. At the end of World War II, a vehicular route was present only along west side of batteries. By the time of this photograph, the route circumscribes the battery and this circulation feature is presently extant (Army Corps of Engineers Coastal and Hydraulics Laboratory).

Figure 4.16. Oblique aerial of the NIKE radar site, circa 1962. At the radar site the arrangement of buildings, circulation routes, and vegetation form three distinct areas—Control Area #1, foreground, Control Area #2, left background, and the Ready Barracks, right background. The organization of and distinction among these three separate areas is legible at the site today (GATE 20818).

Figure 4.17. View looking northwest at pedestrian walkway, Control Area #1, NIKE radar site. The concrete walkways connecting the control areas and Ready Barracks are presently extant and in fair condition. Some portions of the sidewalks are being covered by encroaching woody vegetation (Olmsted Center, January 2009).

Figure 4.18. View looking west at target tracking radars (417 and 473), Control Area #1, NIKE radar site, circa 1962. A combination of bare sand and grass species was typical around the buildings and structures at the radar site. The vegetation in the foreground is in front of the perimeter fence and therefore outside the radar site (GATE 22043).

Figure 4.19. View looking northwest at the Missile Magazines, NIKE launch site, circa 1958. The Army maintained vegetation at a low height, highlighted by the red lines, to allow unobstructed radar signals between the radar and launch sites. Also note that the inner fence surrounding the magazines completely lacked any trace of vegetation when the NIKE facility was operational (GATE 8067 and Olmsted Center).

Figure 4.20. View from Hartshorne Drive looking east at Ready Barracks, NIKE launch site, circa 1958. A parking lot and several parked cars are seen west of the Hartshorne Drive's northbound lanes. An approximate 50-foot by 180-foot asphalt parking area is presently extant in this location (GATE 20157).

Figure 4.21. View looking east at the Missile Magazines and Missile Maintenance Area, circa 1958. The access road to the Missile Magazines and Missile Maintenance Area was paved with asphalt as part of alterations to the launch site for the Hercules missile. The road is presently extant and in good condition (GATE 22042).

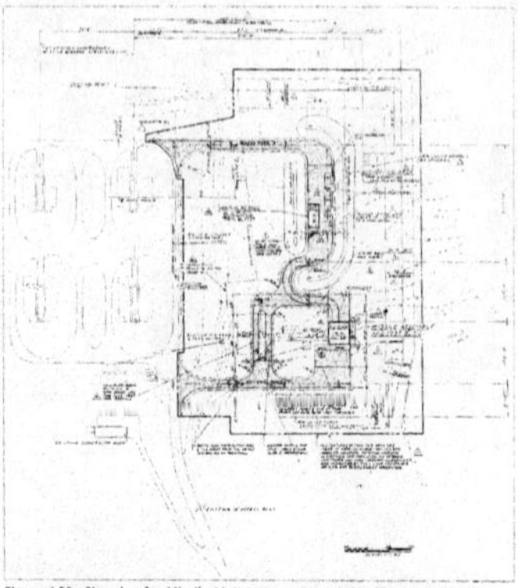

Figure 4.22. Site plan for Missile Maintenance Area, 1958. The gray tone has been added to show vehicular circulation present during the historic period (GATE 7620-2983 and Olmsted Center).

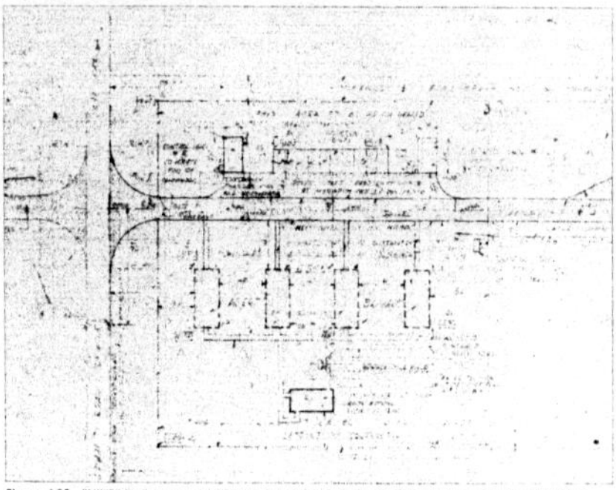

Figure 4.23. "NIKE" Project, Launching Area, Access Road to Launching Area. A system of narrow walkways for the Ready Barracks are labeled "not in the contract" on this drawing for constructing the launch site. The Army presumably added the walkways following major construction activities in a slightly different configuration than shown on the plan (GATE 11040m).

Figure 4.24. Aerial view of the Ready Barracks, NIKE launch site, circa 1958. This photograph shows trees growing in the barrack's lawn panels in contrast to bare earth maintained on either side of the fence lines (GATE 5781).

Figure 4.25. View looking northeast at the Missile Magazines, NIKE launch site, circa 1968. During the historic period, vegetation was maintained at the launch site and no large woody vegetation can be seen in the Missile Maintenance Area. The Paint and Oil Storage shed (447) can be seen on the left foreground (GATE 22041).

Figure 4.26. View looking northeast at access gate to Missile Magazines and Missile Maintenance Area, NIKE launch site. Following the site's closure woody species, especially eastern red cedars, have emerged and are growing in close proximity to the buildings. The Paint and Oil Storage shed (447) can be seen on the right foreground surrounded by eastern red cedars (Olmsted Center, January 2009).

Figure 4.27. Aerial photograph of the NIKE launch site, 1962. The construction drawings for the engineered earthworks in the Missile Maintenance Area call for the slopes to be seeded. A seed mix was not specified, however, the earthworks appear covered in low-growing vegetation, most likely a grass species, compared to the surrounding vegetation (Army Corps of Engineers Coastal and Hydraulics Laboratory).

Figure 4.28. View looking southeast across Missile Magazines, NIKE launch site. The Army installed an inner security fence around the Missile Magazines as a component of the launch site's security upgrades to use Hercules missiles fitted with nuclear warheads. The inner fence is presently extant with chain-link sections attached to H-shaped posts and is in fair to poor condition (Olmsted Center, April 2008).

TREATMENT

The National Park Service defines landscape treatment as historic preservation efforts focused on the goal of enhancing the historic character of a cultural landscape within the context of its contemporary function.[1] Treatment essentially describes how the landscape should look in the future. While fundamentally focused on historic preservation, landscape treatment also addresses other park management goals, such as public access, natural resource conservation, and interpretation. Landscape treatment does not address routine and cyclical measures, such as tree pruning and lawn mowing, necessary to maintain the existing character of a landscape.[2]

The surviving defense infrastructure at Sandy Hook and Fort Hancock are of national significance, being part of the extensive Fort Hancock and Sandy Hook Proving Ground National Historic Landmark. Two of Fort Hancock's batteries, Battery Potter and the Mortar Battery were the first of their type in the United States. The district was listed on the National Register of Historic Places on April 24, 1980, identifying a period of significance spanning from 1859, through the 1950s and 1960s Cold War Era, and ending in 1974. The National Register nomination recognizes the importance of the defense installations at Sandy Hook in guarding New York City (Figure 5.1).[3]

This chapter begins by presenting a framework for treatment based on the park's enabling legislation, National Park Service standards and guidelines, and current park planning documents. The framework is followed by a treatment philosophy that emphasizes stabilizing and rehabilitating the coastal defense batteries to enhance historic character. A summary of preservation issues is provided and followed by the treatment goals and approach for common-to-all and specific treatment tasks. The narrative presentation of tasks is accompanied by graphics and a treatment plan for each battery site.

Recognizing that the rich history of coastal defense work at Sandy Hook includes the survival of subtle remnants of searchlight emplacements, radar installations, mobile gun batteries, isolated concrete magazines, and pill-boxes, the following recommendations are of a more limited scope (Figures 5.2 and 5.3). The following recommendations are constrained largely to the more obvious large gun and missile battery features remaining on site as the many isolated and incidental remnants of Sandy Hook's military past may be better addressed through individual historic structure and archeological documentation.

FRAMEWORK FOR TREATMENT

Signed into law on October 27, 1972, the enabling legislation for the Gateway National Recreation Area guides the framework for treatment for the coastal defense batteries at Sandy Hook. For the Sandy Hook Unit, the act specifically directs that the Secretary of the Interior "...shall inventory and evaluate all sites and structures having present and potential historical, cultural, or architectural significance and shall provide for appropriate programs for the preservation, restoration, interpretation, and utilization of them."[4] As stated in planning documents for Gateway National Recreation Area, the goal for historic structures and cultural landscapes within the Fort Hancock and the Sandy Hook Proving Ground Historic District is rehabilitation and interpretation. It is recommended that the surviving coastal defense batteries be rehabilitated in accordance with the Gateway National Recreation Area General Management Plan, completed in 1979, and with the fundamental historic preservation values expressed in *The Secretary of the Interior's Standards for the Treatment of Historic Properties: Rehabilitation*. Furthermore, as stated in the park's 1990 General Management Plan Amendment, it is recommended that the batteries be interpreted to the public with a focus on their historic functions, and the technological changes in coastal defenses during Fort Hancock's history.[5] Presently, the Gateway National Recreation Area is in the process of preparing a new General Management Plan to guide planning and management at the park for the next twenty years. This on-going effort has identified the coastal defense batteries as fundamental resources of the park based on the enabling legislation.[6]

The National Park Service bears stewardship responsibilities for cultural as well as natural resources, maintaining the National Register of Historic Places as the official list of the Nation's historic places worthy of preservation. Fort Hancock and the Sandy Hook Proving Ground were first nominated to the National Register of Historic Places as a district in 1980, (*NJ 36, Fort Hancock and vicinity, NHL, NPS-80002505*). This nomination was later amended in 1982 to enlarge the district and include the entire Sandy Hook Peninsula and to designate it as a National Historic Landmark (NHL) District. This documentation focused on the property's significance under National Register "Criteria A" for its association with the military defense of the United States for over a period of two hundred years. In the documentation, multiple periods of significance are defined for this district. The period from 1874–1919 is given as the period of significance for the facilities of the Sandy Hook Proving Ground. The period from 1895–1949 is given for the Spermaceti Cove #2 Life Saving Station (southern portion of peninsula). Fort Hancock's period of significance is defined in the 1982 amended documentation as the period from 1859–1950s. This period begins in 1859 due to the existence of remnants of a granite fort dating to this period. The narrative statement of significance does not explicitly state the end-date of the period of significance, identifying 1958 as the last specific date attendant to the introduction of the improved NIKE Hercules missile system. However because the NIKE missile era identified in the NHL documentation continued almost to the date of transfer between the Department of Defense and the Department of the Interior, the deactivation date for Fort Hancock is used as the end date of the period of significance. The New Jersey State Historic Preservation Officer has concurred with this finding through correspondence related to the NPS List of Classified Structures (LCS).[7]

Rehabilitation of the Sandy Hook gun and missile batteries would entail the removal of non-historic invasive vegetation as well as an extensive condition and structural analysis of each structure. At a minimum, preserving and rehabilitating these batteries will involve the stabilization and repair of the concrete structures, treatment of deteriorating metal elements at the batteries, the addition of lighting, and the repair and construction of safe railing systems, walkways, and accessible routes. Accomplishing these tasks would greatly increase the park's ability to provide safe public access and effective interpretation of the Endicott System of defense installations at Sandy Hook, and to make available the dynamic history of Sandy Hook's coastal defenses.[8]

TREATMENT PHILOSOPHY

Wordlessly referencing the importance of the urban skyline to the northwest, the surviving coastal defenses at Sandy Hook, New Jersey are remnants of a vast nationwide program that deployed generations of the most costly arms technology imaginable upon the slender landform. Consistent with both park enabling legislation and current park planning documents, Sandy Hook's surviving coastal defense batteries will be stabilized and otherwise treated so as to slow the deterioration of the historic defenses. Where it is judged safe and appropriate to do so, coastal defense sites will be rehabilitated to enhance historic character and in order to make the sites accessible for the education and enjoyment of the public. Structural battery features will be considered as part of the larger coastal battery sites that are components of Sandy Hook's cultural landscape. Vegetation will be managed within the boundaries of Sandy Hook's battery sites to make it possible to preserve and observe the historic structures and to understand both the operation of the individual historic batteries and system of batteries.

Preservation measures recommended in this cultural landscape report are consistent with fundamental historic preservation values expressed in *The Secretary of the Interior's Standards for the Treatment of Historic Properties*.

Recommendations speaking to purely structural concerns are intended to be consistent with recommendations of architectural conservators and historians presented in the *Historic Structure Report for Battery Potter, Mortar Battery and Battery Gunnison* (2007), and with the *Historic Fortification Preservation Handbook*, prepared by the National Park Service, the University of Oregon and the Washington State Parks and Recreation Commission as part of the Pacific Northwest Preservation Partnership (2003).

PRESERVATION ISSUES

Several preservation issues for the costal defense batteries were identified by previous cultural resource studies and through consultant with park staff. Properly addressing these issues will result in preserving the historic character of the batteries and improving their interpretation as critical elements in a defensive system protecting New York City.

Coastal Erosion

As the meandering shoreline of Sandy Hook Bay has made the preservation of Battery Arrowsmith impossible, in time coastal erosion has the potential to make the continued preservation and public access of other coastal defense sites impractical and the continued investment in maintenance difficult. In addition to Battery Arrowsmith, beach erosion and rising ocean levels already threaten Battery Kingman, Battery Mills, and the NIKE launch site. At Battery Kingman, storm events and bayside erosion have advanced toward the western edge of the battery landscape extents and have removed portions of a historic railroad bed. At Battery Mills, erosion has removed a portion of the vehicular route that circumscribes the battery. At the NIKE launch site, the Atlantic shoreline has advanced toward the eastern perimeter of the missile facility and a future storm event could remove portions of the perimeter fence and circulation features.

Water Infiltration

Coastal defenses were located and designed to fulfill a defensive purpose, rather than to stand as monuments for all time. They were often constructed in less-than-ideal locations, and sometimes constructed with less-than-perfect materials and workmanship. Occupying coastal areas, these structures were often built on low boggy ground, or on eroding bluffs where wind-blown mist carries a freight of corrosive salt. Water—in the ground, in the air, or precipitated as rain—serves as the common element at work undermining these structures over time.[9] Water infiltration, combined with seasonal freeze-thaw cycles, results in concrete spalling and cracks. Accumulation of water in battery interiors and deterioration of metal elements further degrade the historic battery structures.

Unmanaged Woody Vegetation

After the Army deactivated coastal defense batteries, routine vegetation maintenance to support tactical operations, to provide camouflage, and to promote security ceased. In the subsequent decades, the unmanaged growth of large woody vegetation has become a common feature at the battery sites. The vegetation threatens the batteries' historic earthworks due to the potential for uprooting in a storm event. In addition, vegetation growing near and on concrete structures accelerates deterioration of the concrete. Large woody vegetation on the structures, the earthworks, and within tactical views to the water obscures the visual connection between the defense and potential targets. Finally, unmanaged woody vegetation blocks access to coastal defense batteries such as batteries Urmston and Morris.

TREATMENT GOALS AND APPROACH

Laying to one side the threat posed by rising sea levels, coastal defense sites are inherently transient. Effective preservation must aim to slow deterioration rather than arrest it. Further providing some benefit for public investment in these preservation measures, modifications to the historic defense sites are justified where it is reasonable to provide safe visitor access. That the public may learn something meaningful during the course of a visit, it is also reasonable to implement modest changes to help visitors better understand the park's cultural resources. These goals, clearly supported by park planning documents and the enabling legislation creating Gateway National Recreation Area, suggest *Rehabilitation* as the most appropriate choice among the four sanctioned approaches to treatments identified in the *Secretary of the Interior's Standards for the Treatment of Historic Properties*. However, it must be clearly understood, that it is a relatively short list of fundamental preservation measures that comprise the core of the *Rehabilitation* program prescribed for the Sandy Hook coastal defenses. Of primary concern to the defense sites as cultural landscapes, beginning and implementing effective management of vegetation serves as the central task proposed by this report. Recommendations propose treatment measures aimed at preserving historic structures and their features, yet these are not intended to supersede, but rather to support recommendations found in historic structure reports.

The following landscape treatment recommendations are presented below relative to Sandy Hook's eleven extant batteries; including batteries Urmston, Morris, Engle, Peck, Nine Gun, Potter, Granger, Mortar, Gunnison, Kingman and Mills. The extant Fort Hancock NIKE missile battery, consisting of two separate sites, a radar site for acquiring targets and tracking outgoing missiles and its partner site designed for launching the missiles, is also included in the following recommendations.

The following recommendations do not address the Mining Casemate, owing to the presence of this structure within the active U. S. Coast Guard reservation, and beyond National Park Service management responsibilities. Similarly, Battery Arrowsmith is left out of the following discussion. The battery is in an extremely ruinous state and coastal storms continue to break apart the remaining structure and the peninsula upon which it sits (Figure 5.4). Finally, coastal defenses constructed prior to the recommendations of the Endicott Board, such as the Civil War-era Fort at Sandy Hook, are not addressed in this treatment section.

Treatment recommendations are outlined and presented below in two ways. Treatment tasks common to all sites are presented first, providing an opportunity to explore the rationale behind these common approaches with some depth. This is followed by a site-by-site presentation of treatment tasks, beginning with treatment measures recommended independently for Battery Urmston to the extreme northwest, to the NIKE missile launch site to the extreme southern end of the study area. Recognizing an element of redundancy in this approach, the choice of presenting landscape treatment recommendations in this way is intended as a convenience to those who care for these historic resources and who will implement these recommendations over time on a site-by-site basis. Evaluating these coastal defense sites as cultural landscapes for the first time, this report's recommendations have clearly demarcated the physical geographic scope of treatment for these cultural resources.

The preparation of the following treatment recommendations has been greatly aided by the *Historic Fortification Preservation Handbook*, prepared in 2003, through a partnership between the National Park Service, the University of Oregon, and the Washington State Parks and Recreation Commission. This comprehensive document examines the issues facing historic fortifications from an international perspective, offering a range of treatment approaches with a breadth and depth well beyond the scope of this cultural landscape report. Owing to its excellence, the *Historic Fortification Preservation Handbook* should be considered "incorporated by reference" into the following landscape treatment recommendations, and should appropriately serve as the primary reference to those confronting specific issues related to structures, masonry, metals, wood, and other architectural materials.

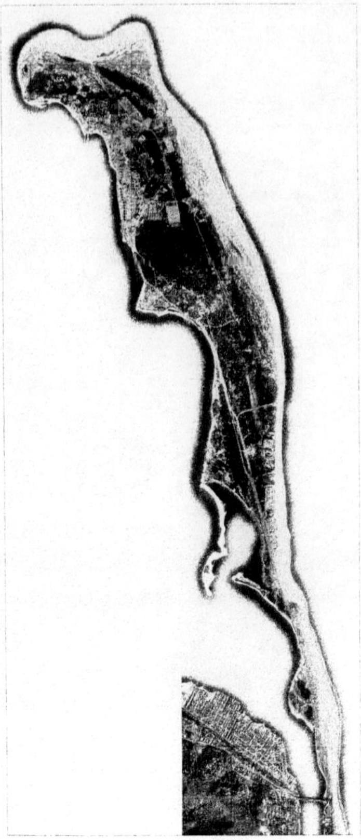

Figure 5.1. Aerial photograph of Sandy Hook landform, 2006. Prior to the National Park Service's administration, Sandy Hook was a highly secured Army reservation that featured successive generations of coastal defenses which guarded the southern approach to New York City (GATE GIS).

Figure 5.2. Mobile railway gun, circa 1939-1940. Mobile artillery, such as this 8-inch caliber gun, played an important role in coastal defenses at Sandy Hook, however, the treatment recommendations will focus on the concrete gun batteries and NIKE missile installation (Thomas Hoffman, *Fort Hancock*, Charleston, SC: Arcadia Publishing, 2007).

Figure 5.3. Collapsible railway searchlight, no date. Similar to mobile artillery, mobile searchlights as well as small, auxiliary structures were features of Sandy Hook's landscape that played a role in defending the southern approach to New York Harbor. These mobile and sometimes temporary structures will not be addressed in the treatment section (Thomas Hoffman, *Fort Hancock*, Charleston, SC: Arcadia Publishing, 2007).

Figure 5.4. View looking northwest at Battery Arrowsmith. Coastal storms continue to break apart Battery Arrowsmith and the peninsula along Horseshoe Cove (Olmsted Center, January 2009).

TREATMENT TASKS COMMON TO ALL SITES

The fundamental purposes behind all treatment tasks prescribed for Sandy Hook's surviving coastal defense sites include preserving historic structures, landscapes, and providing safe and informative visitor access. Park planning documents do not recommend that these sites be returned to the condition in which they were in during military operation, nor to a state of nature. Therefore, a program of straightforward preservation measures, readily achieved, becomes more desirable than spelling out an "ideal" treatment program that would be impossible to realize.

Management of vegetation serves as the foremost preservation task that will prolong the life of the historic concrete and earthen structures. Additionally, vegetation management will reestablish historic downrange views to the water that are critical to understanding the historic purpose and function of these sites. Following vegetation management tasks, repairs and maintenance of concrete surfaces, including repairing voids and cracks, and sealing the porous concrete surfaces against water infiltration will extend the number of years that the ruined structures can be made safely accessible to the public. In conjunction with limiting water infiltration on the concrete structures, exposed, corroding metal components at the batteries should be stabilized to preserve the metal and minimize deterioration to the concrete caused by metal corrosion. Providing safe and informative visitor access involves repairing, retrofitting and replacing deteriorated stairways, walkways, and accompanying safety railings. Providing safe access also involves repairing doors and erecting fences and other barriers to prevent visitors from accessing unsafe locations within these sites.

The following common tasks are presented below.

MANAGE VEGETATION TO PRESERVE AND INTERPRET PARK RESOURCES

The following vegetation management recommendations are intended to preserve historic battery sites. These recommendations address three components of the battery sites and are not influenced by the aesthetic or environmental criteria of plant material. First, recommendations respond to the threats posed by large trees that could uproot in a storm event and displace historic engineered landforms. Second, tasks address woody vegetation established in cracks and voids in the historic concrete structures, or otherwise taking root in accumulated organic matter on concrete surfaces. Finally, measures provide for managing vegetation in perpetuation of historic views, critical to the historic operation of the ordnance. The essence of the following recommendations might be conveniently remembered as "***4-by-4-by-Fore***." The first of the two "4's" standing for eliminating trees greater than four-inches, measured at breast height, from engineered landforms; the second of the two

"4's" representing eliminating woody vegetation from within four-feet of buildings and structures. The third "Fore" refers to managing vegetation forward of battery sites that blocks historic downrange views and hinders public interpretation and understanding of these sites.

As is the case throughout the Sandy Hook peninsula, non-native invasive species are an endemic product of three hundred and fifty years of European settlement. This report recommends the careful, selective removal of out-of-scale vegetation to preserve cultural features, and discourages the creation of large areas of newly cleared soil, that would become prone to additional erosion or otherwise the colonization by non-native invasive species. Where non-native species are present and are effective in stabilizing engineered landforms from erosion, it is recommended that the protection afforded by these non-natives be provisionally retained until such time when they can be removed in concert with a robust revegetation program utilizing plants with a proven ability to prevent soil erosion and protect the integrity of the cultural resource.

Manage Woody Vegetation on Engineered Slopes

With the exception of the NIKE radar site, all of the batteries reviewed for the cultural landscape report contain engineered slopes. At the gun batteries, engineers covered concrete structures with earth to absorb the impact and explosion of enemy fire (Figure 5.5). In the case of the NIKE launch site, earthen berms and traverses were constructed to shield the area where missiles were armed with explosives.

Engineered slopes historically supported vegetation as part of a concealment strategy. However, large trees were not permitted to grow to an extent where they compromised the integrity of the engineered landform, or obstructed the effective field-of-fire. Since their period of active service, unmanaged woody vegetation has obstructed views and threatens the long-term preservation of the earthworks and structures below them. The root systems of these woody species have penetrated the earthwork and have the potential to exploit and damage pores in the concrete structures. As the canopies of these woody species continue to grow, there is a risk that snow, ice, and wind could topple a tree and a major portion of the engineered earthwork would be removed with the tree's roots (Figure 5.6).

In order to prevent further damage to the earthworks and structures below them, all woody vegetation greater than four-inches diameter at breast height should be selectively removed from the engineered slope. After the woody vegetation has been cut, the stumps of deciduous species need to be treated to prevent sprouting and regrowth. Since grubbing out or grinding the woody stumps would cause damage to the historic earthwork and possibly the concrete structure below or nearby, the stumps should be treated with a triclopyr herbicide (*Garlon*™ brand or approved equal) to kill the root system and prevent resprouting. The herbicide treatment is especially important for non-native invasive species such as ailanthus (*Ailanthus altissima*) that will sprout vigorously once the main stem is cut (Figures 5.7 and 5.8). The selectively removed vegetation should be chipped and the chips and any remaining debris should be removed from the park and legally disposed. Removing wood chips and debris from the park is the preferred approach to limit the spread of non-native invasive species and undesirable plants such as poison ivy.

Manage Woody Vegetation Growing Near Buildings and Structures

All of the battery sites need to have woody vegetation removed that is growing on and near structural and landscape features. At the NIKE sites, woody vegetation is growing near radar platforms, barracks, and other auxiliary buildings. The root systems threaten footings and foundations. The plants block light and air movement accelerating the deterioration of painted surfaces, siding, and roofing.

During the historic period, the Army concealed the concrete battery structures with camouflage surface treatments, paints, and overhead netting, however, vegetation was never permitted to grow on the concrete structures. Since the batteries were deactivated following World War II, low points such as stairwells and flat areas such as roofs of battery commander's stations have accumulated soil, leaf litter, and moisture. These conditions have resulted in the growth of woody vegetation. Left untreated, this vegetation can grow to a considerable size (Figure 5.9). The vegetation threatens to further deteriorate the historic battery's concrete features and surfaces and should be removed.

Separation between individually cast concrete elements provides another opportunity for woody vegetation to become established. A void is created between concrete elements due to differential settling creating an opportunity for plant material (Figure 5.10). Even if woody vegetation is not growing on a structure or in a crack or void, the expanding root system of nearby vegetation can find and exploit weaknesses in concrete structures. In addition, as nearby vegetation grows ever larger, there will be an increase in the amount of leaf litter and debris on the concrete structure that will support secondary plants and cause greater moisture retention within the structure surfaces.[19]

As a conservative measure aimed at mitigating structural problems caused or exacerbated by woody vegetation and the concrete structures, all woody vegetation growing on or within four-feet of concrete features should be removed. Both deciduous and evergreen stumps should be treated with a triclopyr herbicide (*Garlon*™ brand or approved equal) on the historic concrete structures since removing the live roots and stumps would cause further structural damage. After the root systems are dead and decayed, the stumps should be carefully removed to the greatest extent practicable, and following this, appropriate concrete repairs should be completed.[11]

Manage Downrange Water Views

Where battery commander's stations or range finding positions were located in close proximity to a battery, soldiers stationed at Sandy Hook's batteries could effectively identify, track, and engage an enemy target. This would not have been possible if the view from the battery to the water was obstructed by tall vegetation. The downrange views to targets on the water from the gun platforms and battery commander's stations are significant in understanding the historic operation of the battery and should be reestablished wherever possible. Reestablishing historic visual connections to the water is crucial for interpretive and visitor access programs and to explain the tactical relationship of the battery to the coastline.[12]

However, not all batteries relied upon a direct view to the target for their effective operation. Most notably, the fire of the Mortar Battery and batteries Kingman and Mills were directed from elevated positions and control towers located some distance from the gun positions. Rather than a visual link to the water, the NIKE missile battery relied on an in-line visual connection between the radar site and the launch site. This was critical in order that the tracking radar equipment could "lock" onto the nose of the missile prior to launch so that the outbound trajectory could be monitored.

Managing downrange view comprises a third and final step in managing the woody vegetation growing on or near historic coastal defenses. After removing woody vegetation growing on the engineered slopes and from voids in the battery structure itself, the resulting views to the water must be evaluated. Additional cutting may not be needed once woody vegetation has been managed on the structures and slopes. However, in some instances tall, individual woody vegetation that blocks the view shed can be identified and removed (Figure 5.11). Following removal, as is recommended in the prior two vegetation management recommendations, deciduous stumps should be treated with a triclopyr herbicide to discourage root sprouts and suckering. Cut material must be removed for proper disposal.

PROVIDE SAFE VISITOR ACCESS

Repair, Retrofit, and Replace Safety Railings

Handrails located along steps and ramps and guardrails are positioned near the open sides of elevated areas at many of the batteries at Sandy Hook. The majority of these rails are made from pipe railings with cast ball joint connectors. Repair and replacement priority should be given to the batteries that are part of the park's interpretive program or are planned to be made open and accessible to the public in the foreseeable future (Figure 5.12). These include the Nine Gun Battery, Battery Potter, and the NIKE radar site.

Where railings survive, all of the current railings have large openings below the top or intermediate horizontal rails that would not adequately protect all visitors. In order to provide a consistent level of protection and satisfy applicable building codes, the existing railings should be repaired, retrofitted, and replaced where necessary. Retrofitting existing railings or installing new railings to comply with life safety codes is necessary when a battery is opened for public access. The panels should be installed where there is a vertical change equal to or greater than thirty inches.

At Golden Gate National Recreation Area in California's Bay Area, historic architects have successfully retrofitted railing systems on historic buildings with mesh infill panels. This approach inserts panels of steel mesh or woven-wire fabric into the large voids of railing out of compliance with life safety codes (Figure 5.13).

A less costly alternative to the infill approach to retrofitting safety railing may be accomplished with simple tools and readily available building materials. This alternative utilizes applied materials such as black vinyl-coated woven-wire fabric, or chain-link, fastened with corrosion resistant fittings common to the fencing industry. These materials, tensioned and clamped to the inboard side of historic and repaired handrailings adjacent to pedestrian traffic, will satisfy safety requirements, result in a similar modest visual appearance, and may be installed, repaired, or replaced conveniently.

Prior to choosing either an infill or an applied approach for repairing and retrofitting safety railings, a detailed inspection and evaluation of existing railings must be undertaken. Those sections of surviving historic railings found in good to fair condition may only need minor repairs and the addition of an infill or applied treatment. Other sections of safety railing may need to have missing sections of railing replaced, and loose paint removed and recoated with primer and paint to match the historic black finish. Railings in good condition without rust may be treated with corrosion inhibitors, however, these products are typically a wax coating and should not be used in places where the railing would be handled.[13]

Railings in fair condition with visible rust should be chemically treated to halt the corrosion process. Rust converters should be applied that react with the iron oxide to render a more stable compound that will accept primer and paint. Immediately after this treatment, the metal should be primed and painted to match the historic finish.[14]

Damaged or severely deteriorated railings and components should be removed and replaced with new components that match the original as close as possible. To reduce future maintenance requirements, the new railings may be finished with a color-galvanized coating that matches the historic paint finish. The color-galvanized coating, especially in a waterfront setting, will last longer and require less maintenance than traditional prime and paint finishes. Duncan Galvanizing and Voigt and Schweitzer Galvanizing are two national companies that offer color-galvanizing services.

Existing railings were screwed into threaded escutcheon plates and the plates bolted to the concrete structures. For added strength against lateral loads, new railing components should be core drilled and set in non-shrink epoxy grout. An escutcheon plate that closely matching the historic plates should be fitted around the vertical member before the rail is set and lowered into position to cover the epoxy interface (Figure 5.14).[15]

Infill panels or applied meshes covering for the large openings in the existing railings should consider several factors. To prevent a small child from falling through a railing, most building codes require that a four-inch sphere must not be able to pass through any opening in the railing design. In addition to this criterion, using an infill pattern of horizontal members or wide-spaced meshes creates a ladder effect that potentially encourages climbing. Adding vertical members creates a balustrade appearance that detracts from the historic form of the simple pipe rail guards. Therefore, the preferred option for visitor safety and to retain the historic form of the pipe rails is to add tightly-spaced mesh panels (Figure 5.15).

The infill or applied retrofit material should be attached to the rails with non-corrosive vinyl-coated hardware clamps permitting convenient replacement or removal without damaging the historic railings. The mesh, either as infill or as applied, should feature a matte black finish or other protective coating that will recede from view when seen from the inboard side of the battery. The mesh should be either a welded wire fabric or a coated chain-link made from nine-gauge or heavier wire.

Repair and Secure Interior Access Points

Metal and wood doors and metal gates, windows, and grating are located on gun and missile batteries throughout Sandy Hook. All of these building features require a detailed evaluation that is beyond the scope of this cultural landscape report. However in general terms, sound material with minor corrosion or decay should be treated in place. Loose paint and rust should be removed immediately followed by priming and painting to match the historic finish. A moderate level of repair may also be conducted in place. For example, an operational gate with a missing a hinge spindle should be repaired in place with a new hinge spindle that matches the historic dimensions and finish. If a component is damaged or severely deteriorated, it should be removed and repaired at an off-site shop or newly fabricated to match the existing (Figure 5.16).[16]

As was highlighted in the discussion of newly fabricated railings, new metal doors, gates, windows, and gratings may be finished with a color-galvanized coating that resembles the historic paint finish. The color-galvanized coating will last longer and require less maintenance than traditional prime and paint finishes.

A final recommendation for doors and gates addresses their hinge hardware. Bronze or brass hinge hardware may be cast into the concrete structure to receive a door or gate. Either bronze or brass, in contact with the iron in the steel door, reacts quickly with air and moisture to produce corrosion. To prevent this accelerated reaction, a hard plastic washer should be installed to separate the two metals.[17]

Close Hazardous Social Trails and Repair Eroded Paths

During a review of existing conditions of Sandy Hook's historic gun and missile the batteries in January 2009, steep and unsafe social trails were observed at Battery Engle, Battery Gunnison, Battery Potter and the Mortar Battery. Many of these trails lead up or across a historic engineered earthwork. Due to the steep elevation changes on the earthworks, the effect of these trails is to channelize stormwater and promote additional soil erosion.

Despite the presence of fences and signs forbidding access and warning of dangers, visual evidence of unauthorized trail use encourages others to follow. Low-growing native shrubs should be planted at the top and bottom of a social trail to block access. Appropriate native species would include fragrant sumac (*Rhus aromatica*) and bayberry (*Myrica pensylvanica*). Access to a social trail can be further obscured by placing cut branches—three to four feet in length—at the trail's top and bottom.

To manage erosion, straw or coir fiber wattles should be installed at approximately ten-foot intervals along the trail to be closed. The wattles are commercially available in a 1-foot diameter size and are packaged in long lengths. The wattles will need to be cut and should extend beyond the width of the trail. They should be secured with two-inch square wood stakes. A porous, biodegradable erosion control fabric—woven from jute, straw or wood fibers—should be added between the wattles on slopes greater than 4:1. Low-growing native shrubs should be planted to secure the soil and discourage future access (Figure 5.17). Before installation of the wattles, nearby leaf duff and organic matter should be collected. After installation, the duff should be spread over the former trail to help disguise and revegetate the trail bed.

As part of closing hazardous social trails and repairing eroded paths, the park should continue to use fences to restrict access to closed battery sites and manage pedestrian circulation. In order to reduce a variety non-historic fence types and to make future replacements and repairs more efficient, the park should use three fence types at the batteries. First, the tall chain-link fencing should remain and continued to be used at sites that are not open to public access. Second, a wood post and poultry wire fence, such as the one at the Mortar Battery, should be installed to prevent access on historic earthworks. This second fence type should not be installed at every battery, but only added where patterns of unauthorized visitor access need to be changed. Third, wooden split-rail fence should be installed to reinforce designated pedestrian routes and direct circulation. The park currently uses split-rail fence along trails leading to the North Pond near batteries Engle and Peck and the Nine Gun Battery. All three fence types are readily available from commercial companies, relatively inexpensive to purchase, install, and maintain, and identifiable as a contemporary introduction to the historic battery sites.

PRESERVE BATTERY STRUCTURES

Repair Voids and Cracks in Concrete Surfaces

Concrete is subject to expansion and contraction caused by temperature fluctuations. In addition, concrete will absorb small amounts of water especially on horizontal surfaces where water may not drain quickly. The infiltration of water, combined with seasonal freezing and thawing, results in spalling and cracking of concrete surfaces. Even small cracks in concrete create locations where organic matter can accumulate, and where seeds can lodge and vegetation can take root to further damaging the structure. In order to protect the concrete battery structures, spalling concrete surfaces should be stabilized and cracks repaired.

Spalling surfaces should be removed until sound concrete is encountered. If reinforcing steel is exposed, additional concrete should be removed so the steel is ½-inch clear minimum on all sides. The steel should be cleaned and have an anticorrosion coating applied. In consultation with a structural engineer, new reinforcing may be required and this material should be epoxy coated to inhibit corrosion.

The removed area should be mechanically cleaned and patching material applied according to the manufacturer's directions. Deep patches will require dowels, welded wire fabric, and other reinforcing. These should be installed using specific items certified for horizontal, vertical, and overhead applications. Finally, the texture and contour of the finished patch should be compatible with the character of the historic concrete (Figure 5.18).[18]

Similar to spalling concrete surfaces, cracks will allow water into the concrete substrate where further damage will occur. Cracks should be repaired and for small cracks, the preferred treatment is grouting and sealing. This method involves removing an area slightly larger than the crack with a hand or power chisel. The void should be mechanically cleaned and dry prior to installing the sealant. The sealant should be a non-epoxy compound and have the same properties as the material around it in terms of bonding strength and water exchange. If the sealant is stronger and has a different porosity, it will lead to cracks and deterioration at new locations away from the repair.[19]

Large, structural cracks will require extensive repair and a preferred method for their repair should be determined with a structural engineer. Small and large crack repairs should be compatible with the character of the historic concrete (Figure 5.19).

Seal Horizontal Concrete Battery Surfaces

After spalling and cracked concrete surfaces are repaired, maintenance coatings are required on the exposed concrete of the gun and missile batteries to slow ongoing decay. Challenging environmental factors that lead to concrete deterioration will always be at work against the best-intentioned preservation measures. In order to reduce water infiltration and to protect the concrete battery structures, a surface coating must be applied periodically to the horizontal surfaces.

It is important to emphasize that concrete surface defects that pool and collect rainwater must be repaired before the application of a maintenance coating. The two broad categories of coatings available are penetrating sealers and surface sealers.

Concrete Surface Sealers and Membranes

Surface sealers form a protective water repellent layer above the concrete surface. The most readily-available sealer is latex paint. Although the Army used latex paint at certain coastal defense batteries across the country, historic photographs of Sandy Hook batteries indicate they were finished with an asphalt emulsion paint—a product comparable to present-day driveway sealers (Figure 5.20). Latex paint may also be tinted for aesthetics, including tints that mimic the look of weathered concrete.

Other surface sealers that provide thicker and more durable protective coatings compared to paint include Portland cement coatings modified with latex, acrylic latex, or polyvinyl acetate, stucco, and cement-based paints.[20] A preferable surface sealer that would be in keeping with the asphalt emulsion paint is a bitumen coating. Worthy of consideration for the expansive horizontal concrete surface of the NIKE launch site, the materials and installation can be readily provided by a roofing contractor and additional protection could be achieved by laying gravel into the bitumen coating. After installation, the horizontal concrete surfaces will be protected with a sacrificial layer and regularly scheduled maintenance requirements will be reduced.

An advantage of a bitumen coating over paints or penetrating sealers is that it can be built up to correct minor imperfections of the surface concrete. The coating should be finished to preventing ponding of accumulated water and to pitch water away from the structure. With the application of a bitumen coatings, water vapor will only be apply to escape through exposed vertical surfaces. Before a bitumen coating is applied, vapor transfer and its potential impact on the concrete structure should be reviewed by qualified professionals.[21]

Another alternative providing an effective and durable barrier to water infiltration are the various engineered membranes commonly used in the roofing industry. "Modified Bitumen" roofing membranes are rubberized bituminous (tar) sheets that have been reinforced with fiberglass.[22] Some of these roofing systems and products are rated for use over weathered concrete, following the application of a sealant product.

Penetrating Sealers

The two generic types of penetrating sealers employ silane and siloxane, which are silicone-based compounds that penetrate into the concrete surface. These compounds react with concrete to form microscopic pores that are too small for water to pass through, yet the pores are large enough that water vapor may transpire. These products do not generally produce a surface sheen and, migrating into the concrete surface, penetrating sealers are able to resist abrasion when walked upon. In fact, these products are used commercially to seal sidewalks and other landscape paving. Penetrating sealers are susceptible to ultraviolet rays, salt spray, acid rain, and airborne pollutants over time, and need to be reapplied every four to five years in order to maintain an effective water repellent coating.[23] Despite their relativity short service life, penetrating type sealers are generally preferable over surface sealers and are recommended for widespread use on the Sandy Hook coastal defense batteries. These products may be applied either by park staff or by contractors without specialized skills or equipment, and they are comparatively inexpensive. Available in 55-gallon drums for less than $1,500, similar to the unit cost of high-quality paint, this amount of product will seal up to 10,000 square feet (approximately one-quarter acre) of exposed concrete surface.

Repair Roofing Material on Free-Standing Buildings

The Battery Potter site and the NIKE Radar and Launch sites are host to numerous free-standing historic buildings that stand apart from the central battery infrastructure. These buildings were once used as workshops, storehouses, sentry posts, magazines, kennels, and barracks and are now underutilized as informal storage of cast-off materials. These fundamentally abandoned buildings are neglected and in disrepair. Water being the primary agent leading to building failure, maintaining effective roof coverings is the most cost-effective measure for the continued preservation of these historic resources.

Figure 5.5. Sand being hauled into place in front of the terreplein, Nine Gun Battery, 1928. Engineers covered the concrete structures with sand and earth for concealment and to help absorb the impact of enemy fire (GATE 7009).

Figure 5.6. Storm-thrown tree, Union Fort Fisher, Petersburg National Battlefield. Permitting large trees to grow on engineered slopes, increases risks that wind, could topple the tree and displace a large volumes of the earthwork with its roots. Falling trees also pose impact risks to structural features (Olmsted Center, 1998).

Figure 5.7. Ailanthus stump at Battery Mills. If stumps are not treated after cutting, species like ailanthus (*Ailanthus altissima*) will produce root sprouts and develop into a denser, more vigorous stand of vegetation. Stumps should be cut as flush to ground level as possible and treated with a triclopyr herbicide following the specific manufacturer's label instructions (Olmsted Center, January 2009).

Figure 5.8. Application of triclopyr herbicide to a cut stump. Instructions from this particular manufacturer state to treat the outer two inches of the stump with herbicide. Note that the stump has been cut as flush to ground level as possible (Olmsted Center, May 2007).

Figure 5.9. View looking northwest across gun platform #4, Battery Urmston. Low and flat areas like this gun platform have accumulated soil, leaf litter, and moisture. These conditions have resulted in the growth of woody vegetation that should be removed from the structure (Olmsted Center, January 2009).

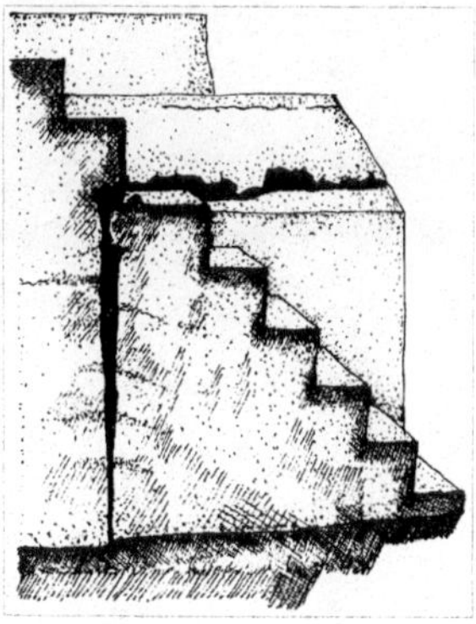

Figure 5.10. Concrete separation at unreinforced steps. Separation between individually cast concrete elements provides another opportunity for woody vegetation to emerge. The voids can also be exacerbated by growing woody material (Joe C. Freeman et al., *Seacoast Fortifications Preservation Manual, Golden Gate National Recreation Area, San Francisco, California*, United States Department of the Interior, National Park Service and KEA Environmental, July 1999, 148).

Figure 5.11. View east from south gun platform, Battery Gunnison. The downrange views from gun emplacements and battery commander's stations are significant to the historic operation of the batteries and should be reestablished to greatest extent practicable. The evergreens located closest to the gun in this image are growing upon the engineered slope. Once these have been removed, downrange water views can be evaluated and in limited instances tall, individual woody vegetation removed on a case-by-case basis (Olmsted Center, January 2009).

Figure 5.12. View looking west at safety railings, Battery Granger. The existing railing system at Battery Granger displays successive generations of railing components and repairs (Olmsted Center, January 2009).

Figure 5.13. Example of the infill approach to retrofitting railing systems for compliance with life-safety codes. In the wide openings between the horizontal pipe rail members, a mesh panel framed by square bar stock has been added. The frame is connected to the existing pipe rails by welding metal tabs between the two (Barbara Judy, Golden Gate National Recreation Area).

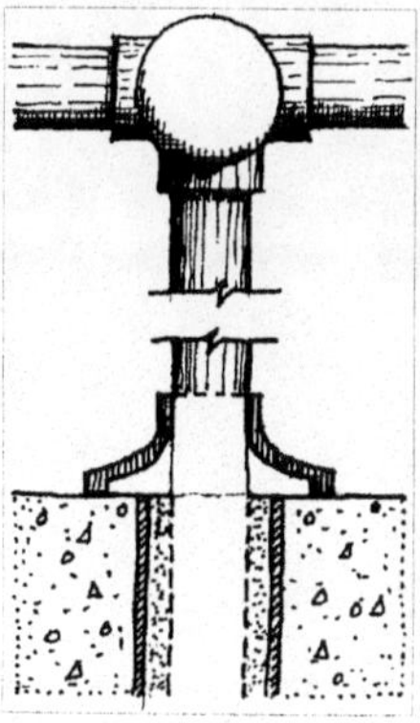

Figure 5.14. Cross-section, new railing installation. New guardrails and handrails should be attached by core drilling into the existing concrete and setting the rail in non-shrink epoxy grout. An escutcheon plate matching the historic plates should be fitted around the vertical member before the rail is set and lowered into position to cover the epoxy interface (Freeman et al., *Seacoast Fortifications Preservation Manual*, 160).

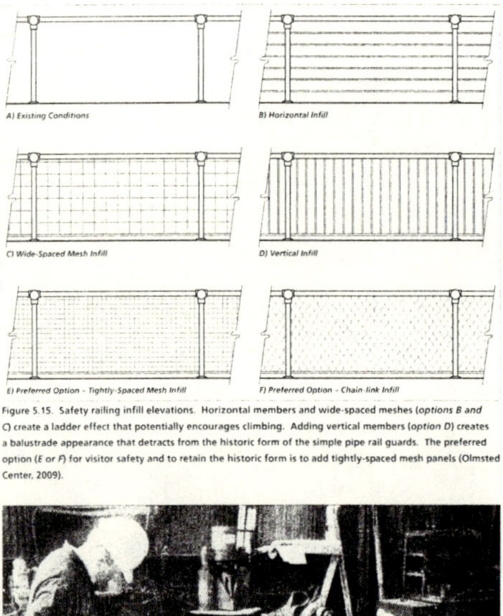

Figure 5.15. Safety railing infill elevations. Horizontal members and wide-spaced meshes (*options B and C*) create a ladder effect that potentially encourages climbing. Adding vertical members (*option D*) creates a balustrade appearance that detracts from the historic form of the simple pipe rail guards. The preferred option (*E or F*) for visitor safety and to retain the historic form is to add tightly-spaced mesh panels (Olmsted Center, 2009).

Figure 5.16. Off-site repair of historic metal door for Battery Worth, Fort Casey, Washington. Standing water resulted in the bottom portion of this door being severely deteriorated. The door was removed and is shown being repaired with a new steel plate and angles (From, David M. Hansen, Kimberly Keagle, and Deborah Rehn, *Historic Fortification Preservation Handbook*, Olympia, WA: Washington State Parks and Recreation Commission, 2003, 3.102).

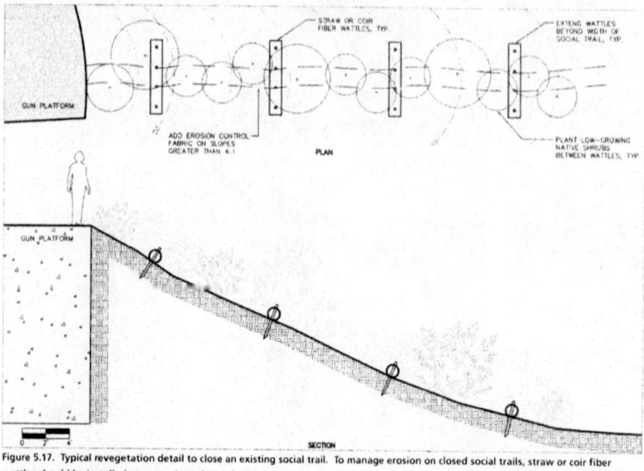

Figure 5.17. Typical revegetation detail to close an existing social trail. To manage erosion on closed social trails, straw or coir fiber wattles should be installed at approximately ten-foot intervals. Low-growing native shrubs should be planted between the wattles to discourage future use (Olmsted Center, 2009).

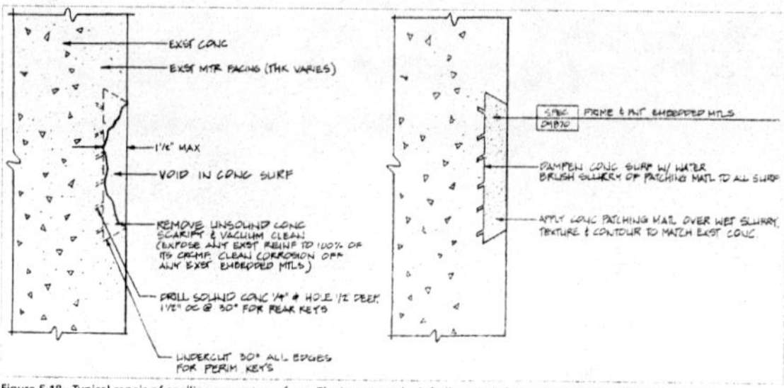

Figure 5.18. Typical repair of spalling concrete surface. The image on the left illustrates the removal of unsound concrete and preparation of the area to receive patching material. On the right, the patch is in place and has been finished to be compatible with the character of the historic concrete. In addition, the prepared area may be lightly coated with an approved bonding agent to promote greater adhesion of the new concrete (Hansen, Keagle, and Rehn, *Historic Fortification Preservation Handbook*, 3.78-3.79).

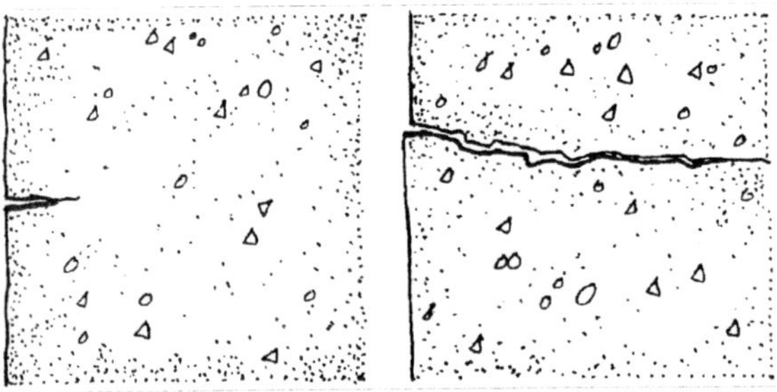

Figure 5.19. Typical concrete cracks. The image on the left illustrates a small, surface crack that can be repaired by grouting and sealing. The image on the right illustrates a large, structural crack that will require extensive repairs. Consultation with a structural engineer is recommended to determine a preferred method of repair (Freeman et al., *Seacoast Fortifications Preservation Manual*, 147).

Figure 5.20. Oblique aerial view of Nine Gun Battery, 1942. This World War II-era photograph of Nine Gun Battery, and a portion of Battery Peck (*left*), indicate they were both finished with an asphalt emulsion paint (also refer to cover photograph). This surface treatment has worn away from gun platforms #3 and #4 (*center*) and the brighter appearance of the concrete underneath is visible (National Archives, Record Group 661 S, Philip S. Gage Collection, Fort Hancock Folder).

SITE-BY-SITE TREATMENT RECOMMENDATIONS

The following treatment recommendations are organized site-by-site, presented in order, beginning with Battery Urmston, at the northwestern extremity of National Park Service property on Sandy Hook, toward the south, concluding with the NIKE launch site. Many of the treatment tasks identified in the following site-by-site breakdown are common to all of Sandy Hook's surviving coastal defense sites, and have been presented and explained in some detail previously in this report. Acknowledging a redundancy with material presented above, these common tasks are reiterated briefly below, organizing all relevant treatment tasks associated with a single site for the convenience of those using this report.

BATTERY URMSTON (LCS SH-540)

The Army began construction of Battery Urmston in 1899 as a smaller rapid-fire battery operating in concert with the large caliber gun batteries guarding the approach to New York Harbor. By 1900, four gun emplacements at Battery Urmston were fitted with balanced pillar mounted guns. When not in use, the guns could swing ninety degrees to the shoreline and rest their barrels in a notch in the concrete gun platform. The final phase of construction was completed in June 1904 with the completion of two additional gun emplacements in between the prior four emplacements (Figure 5.21). The disarming of this battery took place in the reverse order of its construction. Four of the six gun emplacements, the two outside pairs, were disarmed following World War I. Emplacements #3 and #4 at the center of the battery remained in service until 1942, when the two guns here were relocated to a temporary emplacement in the dunes north of Battery Gunnison. These two relocated guns continued to serve as "New Battery Urmston" until September 1946.

Battery Urmston survives in poor condition. Access to the battery site is made difficult by the unmanaged growth of woody vegetation, including especially vigorous growths of poison ivy. Downrange views are blocked by trees. Concrete surfaces display widespread spalling and metal fixtures such as handrails and door and window hardware are severely corroded.

TREATMENT TASKS

Vegetation Management Treatment Tasks

UR-1: Remove woody vegetation greater than four-inches diameter growing on engineered slopes

Large woody vegetation growing on the north-facing engineered slopes of Battery Urmston consists primarily of eastern red cedar (*Juniperus virginiana*), beach plum (*Prunus maritima*), hackberry (*Celtis occidentalis*), and ailanthus (*Ailanthus altissima*) (Figure 5.22). To protect the earthwork and the concrete structures below, woody vegetation greater than four-inches diameter at breast height should be removed following the guidelines in the general treatment recommendations. Due to their close proximity, it is difficult to prescribe a line that divides the engineered earthworks of Battery Urmston and Battery Morris. Looking at both batteries as a single unit, the area to be selectively cleared would be approximately 1.2 acres (Drawing 5.1, scope of treatment).

UR-2: Remove all woody vegetation growing on or within four-feet of concrete features

Untreated vegetation on Battery Urmston has grown to a considerable size and threatens to further deteriorate the historic battery's concrete features. Consistent with treatment recommendations offered for all of Sandy Hook's coastal defense sites, vegetation growing on or within four-feet of concrete features should be removed. As highlighted in the general treatment recommendations, both deciduous and evergreen stumps should be treated with a triclopyr herbicide to inhibit resprouting and to promote root decay. After the root systems deteriorate, the stumps should be carefully removed to the greatest extent practicable, and appropriate concrete repairs should be undertaken.

UR-3: Remove vegetation blocking historic downrange views

Historic photographs indicate a clear line of sight and field of fire at Battery Urmston to defend against fast moving, shallow-draft boats (Figure 5.23). Vegetation removals on the engineered slope and structure itself will greatly improve an unobstructed view to the water. After these removals, it will be necessary to evaluate the views and determine if select, tall woody vegetation beyond the engineered slope should be removed (Figure 5.24). In addition to vegetation, the introduction of new buildings and structures can impact the visual connection to the water. No buildings or accessory structures should be constructed within the downrange view from Battery Urmston to the water.

UR-4: Remove all woody vegetation six-feet north of the U. S. Coast Guard perimeter fence

Immediately south of Battery Urmston is U. S. Coast Guard property separated by a six-foot high chain-link fence topped with barbed wire. The north side of the fence, closest to Battery Urmston, is becoming overrun with ailanthus (*Ailanthus altissima*), Virginia creeper (*Parthenocissus quinquefolia*), poison ivy (*Toxicodendron radicans*), and honey locust saplings (*Gleditsia triacanthos*). If not treated and maintained, this area will soon be impassable. Once the large woody vegetation has been removed, the six-foot width can be easily maintained with a small tractor and brush hog mowing deck (Figure 5.25).

Visitor Access Treatment Tasks

UR-5: Construct New Visitor Access Trail

During the historic period, a road paralleled Battery Urmston's south facade and provided access for personnel and delivery of ammunition (see Figure 5.21). The road is presently extant but separated from the battery by the U. S. Coast Guard perimeter fence. Visitors and park staff currently walk to the battery in the area between the fence and concrete structure. At present, that area is becoming overrun with vegetation that makes access difficult. After the vegetation is removed north of the perimeter fence, the park should construct trail to Battery Urmston. Since regular mowing will be required to maintain vegetation along the fence, a practical method for defining and maintaining the trail is to mow a four-foot wide route at a lower height.

UR-6: Repair, retrofit, and replace safety railings

Historic safety railings are typically located at stairwells on the south side of the battery and a handrail is installed along an external set of stairs to the commander's station. Both are typically constructed from pipe railings with the individual sections connected by ball joint fixtures (Figure 5.26). Safety railings and handrailings should be treated to stop the corrosion process followed by priming and painting to match the historic finish. Infill panels should be installed where there is a vertical change equal to or greater than thirty inches in order to provide greater safety at the large openings below the top rails.

UR-7: Repair and secure doors and grating to prevent unauthorized access

Although operational during Battery Urmston's years of service, the doors leading to the magazine and bomb proofs should be properly mounted and locked to prevent unauthorized access to interior spaces. Specific treatments should follow the procedures detailed in the general treatment recommendations, beginning with a case-by-case evaluation of the condition of each door or grille. At openings where an outer solid door and inner metal gate are installed, the gate should be securely locked and the solid door left open to permit air circulation and lessen the accumulation of moisture inside the battery structure.

Battery Structures Treatment Tasks

UR-8: Stabilize spalling concrete surfaces and repair cracks

Spalling and cracks appear in both the vertical and horizontal concrete surfaces at Battery Urmston. Due to their lower elevation and an increased exposure to standing water, spalling is greater in the gun platforms. The tops of magazines and bomb proofs show less evidence of spalling concrete but substantial cracks are present (Figure 5.27). Both the spalling concrete and cracks should be repaired to reduce water infiltration, vegetation growth, and the further deterioration of the concrete. Detailed treatment information is provided in the general treatment recommendations.

UR-9: Repair and seal horizontal concrete surfaces to reduce water infiltration

Historic photographs indicate that Battery Urmston, unlike nearby Battery Peck and Nine Gun Battery, did not have an asphalt emulsion surface treatment (Figure 5.28). After concrete surface defects have been repaired, two options are possible to treat Battery Urmston without creating a non-historic appearance. First, penetrating sealers could be used with the understanding that to achieve the best protection, they should be applied every few years. The other option, providing a more durable coating, is to apply bitumen with light-colored gravel laid into the coating. The gravel should match the color of the existing concrete. At Battery Urmston, approximately 3,130 square feet of concrete will need a surface coating.

UR-10: Repair and repaint ferrous metal fixtures

A variety of ferrous metal fixtures were incorporated into the construction of Battery Urmston. Metal fixtures in fair condition with visible rust should be chemically treated, primed, and painted to match the historic finish. Damaged or severely deteriorated fixtures should be removed and replaced with new components that match the original as close as possible. Additional information on ferrous metal treatments can be found in the Safety Railings section of the treatment tasks common to all battery sites and in the *Historic Fortification Preservation Handbook* (Washington State Parks and Recreation Commission, 2003).

UR-11: Replace wood-slat fence east of battery

At the eastern end of the Battery Urmston, an engineered earthwork rises up between the battery and Battery Morris. The earthwork ends abruptly at a retaining wall that extends from Urmston. Immediately east of the retaining wall, a four-foot high, wood-slat fence meanders up the earthwork and wraps around toward the gun platform. The fence is in fair condition but is not a historic feature of the battery. Removing the fence will help facilitate the vegetation removals on the engineered earthwork (Drawing 5.1).

If upon the judgment of park staff, this location warrants the installation of a non-historic safety railing, then a metal safety railing should be installed. The metal safety railing should be visually compatible with repaired and retrofitted historic safety railings recommended for widespread use throughout Sandy Hook's coastal defense batteries.

TABLE 5.1: SUMMARY OF TREATMENT RECOMMENDATIONS, BATTERY URMSTON		
Rehabilitation Task	Notes	Priority for Action 1 - high priority 2 - medium priority 3 - low priority, but requires ongoing monitoring 4 - no action
UR-1: Remove woody vegetation greater than four-inches diameter growing on engineered slopes		1 - high priority for action
UR-2: Remove all woody vegetation growing on or within four-feet of concrete features		1 - high priority for action
UR-3: Remove vegetation blocking historic downrange views		1 - high priority for action
UR-4: Remove all woody vegetation six-feet north of the U. S. Coast Guard perimeter fence		1 - high priority for action
UR-5: Construct New Visitor Access Trail	A trail needs to be established on the south side of the battery in order to provide access for routine maintenance, implementing other treatment tasks, and visitor access	1 – high priority for action
UR-6: Repair, retrofit, and replace safety railings	Can be implemented as part of a multiple battery or park-wide battery project	2 – plan for future action
UR-7: Repair and secure doors and grating to prevent unauthorized access		1 - high priority for action
UR-8: Stabilize spalling concrete surfaces and repair cracks		1 - high priority for action
UR-9: Repair and seal horizontal concrete surfaces to reduce water infiltration	Implement after concrete surface defects have been repaired	1 – high priority for action
UR-10: Repair and repaint ferrous metal fixtures		2 – plan for future action
UR-11: Replace wood-slat fence east of battery	Coordinate with future plans to open battery site to public visitation	2 – plan for future action

Figure 5.21. View looking northeast at Battery Urmston, circa 1900. In contrast to its appearance today, the south side of Battery Urmston contained no woody vegetation (GATE 7882).

Figure 5.22. View looking west at gun platforms #5 and #6, Battery Urmston. The engineered slope meeting the concrete structure on the west and north sides contains woody vegetation growing on, or within, four feet of concrete structures and should be removed (Olmsted Center, January 2009).

Figure 5.23. View looking northwest, Battery Urmston, circa 1906. The battery commander (*center*) did not have a shielded structure but stood between the two gun platforms. There could be no large woody vegetation obstructing the commander's view or the field of fire for safe and effective operation of the gun battery (Thomas Hoffman, *Fort Hancock*, Charleston, SC: Arcadia Publishing, 2007).

Figure 5.24. View looking east toward water from Battery Urmston. Once woody vegetation larger than 4-inches diameter growing on engineered slopes, and vegetation growing on or within four-feet of concrete features is removed, downrange views should be evaluated to identify additional vegetation to be removed to in order to perpetuate historic views. Lower growing woody vegetation should be retained (Olmsted Center, January 2009).

Figure 5.25. U. S. Coast Guard perimeter fence south of Battery Urmston and Morris. After the large woody vegetation has been removed along the perimeter fence, a six-foot wide swath from the fence can be easily maintained with a small tractor and brush hog mowing deck. The mowed swath will provide a convenient route for visitor access to these batteries (Olmsted Center, January 2009).

Figure 5.26. Existing historic safety railing at Battery Urmston is fabricated of pipe rail sections and ball joint connectors. After treating corrosion and restoring the historic finish, infill panels should be installed where there is a vertical change equal to or greater than thirty inches in order to provide greater safety at the large openings below the top rails (Olmsted Center, January 2009).

Figure 5.27. View looking down at gun platform #5, Battery Urmston. The tops of the magazines and bomb proofs show less evidence of spalling concrete, yet substantial cracks are present (Olmsted Center, January 2009).

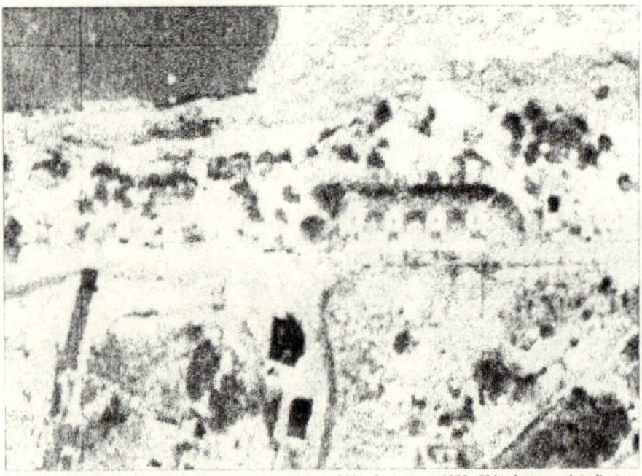

Figure 5.28. Aerial photograph of Batteries Urmston and Morris, January 1933. This photograph indicates that at this time, the concrete surfaces belonging to Batteries Urmston and Morris did not feature a paint, asphalt emulsion, or another darkly hued surface treatment (Coastal and Hydraulics Laboratory, Engineer Research and Development Center).

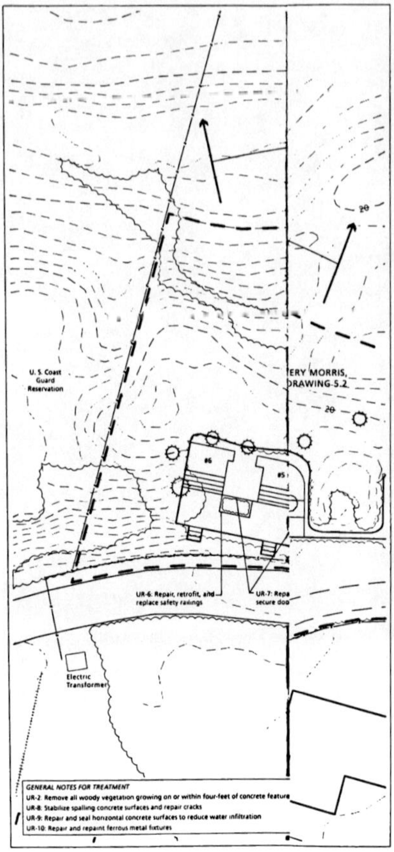

Cultural Landscape Report for the Sandy Hook Coastal Defense Batteries

Gateway National Recreation Area

Sandy Hook, New Jersey

Battery Urmston Treatment Plan

Olmsted Center

National Park Service

Olmsted Center for Landscape Preservation

www.nps.gov/oclp

SOURCES

1. Sandy Hook GIS Data
2. Sandy Hook Color Ortho Imagery, Captured 2006
3. Topographic Sheets, prepared by Denver Service Center, 1992
4. Topographic Maps, prepared by Carrera and Associates, 1990
5. Field Inventory, Olmsted Center for Landscape Preservation, January 2009

DRAWN BY

Tim Layton, AutoCAD 2002, Illustrator CS3, 2009

LEGEND

Canopy Vegetation

Paved Road / Walk

Unpaved Road / Walk

Deciduous Tree

Evergreen Tree

Fence

1944 Rail Line

Scope of Treatment

NOTES

1. Contour Interval = 1'-0"
2. Plan represents landscape conditions inventoried in January 2009
3. All features shown in approximate scale and location

0' 7.5' 15' 30'

Drawing 5.1

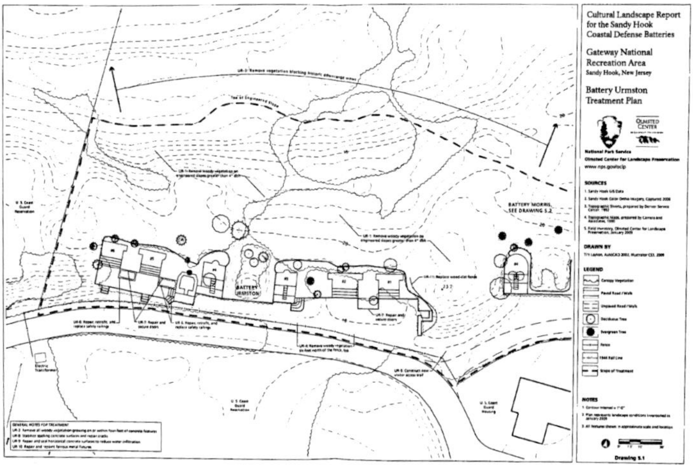
Cultural Landscape Report for the Sandy Hook Coastal Defense Batteries
Gateway National Recreation Area
Sandy Hook, New Jersey
Battery Urmston Treatment Plan
National Park Service
Olmsted Center for Landscape Preservation
SOURCES
DRAWN BY
LEGEND
NOTES
BATTERY URMSTON
BATTERY MORRIS, SEE DRAWING 5.2
Drawing 5.1

BATTERY MORRIS (LCS SH-539)

The Army completed construction of Battery Morris in 1903 as a small-caliber, rapid-fire supplement to adjacent batteries Urmston and Engle. The four gun emplacements built at Battery Morris remained unarmed until 1909. In 1920, the fire from Battery Morris was directed by a newly constructed coincidence range finder located near its eastern end (Figure 5.29). This battery remained in service throughout World War II, and was disarmed in 1946.

Battery Morris survives in a greatly deteriorated condition (Figure 5.30). Dense growth of vines and trees makes access difficult and blocks downrange views (Figure 5.31). The presence of leaf litter and plant debris perpetuate a damp environment hastening deterioration of concrete and metal surfaces. A wooden non-historic fence, apparently located here for reasons of safety, has deteriorated beyond repair. Concrete surfaces display widespread spalling, and metal fixtures such as handrails and door and window hardware are severely corroded.

TREATMENT TASKS

Vegetation Management Treatment Tasks

MO-1: Remove woody vegetation greater than four-inches diameter growing on engineered slopes

The existing topography of Battery Morris suggests that the north-facing engineered slopes of both Batteries Morris and Urmston were considered as a single element during the construction process to create a continuous protective feature. Since there is no discernable break or interruption in the landform, it is difficult to prescribe a line that divides the engineered earthworks of the two batteries. Considering the earthen shielding protecting both batteries as a single unit, the area subjected to selective vegetation removal is approximately 1.2 acres. Within this area, trees greater than four inches diameter at breast height should be carefully removed. The purpose of this recommendation is two-fold. First, smaller trees to not present as much canopy exposure to the wind, and are of less risk in toppling and displacing the engineered landform during a wind storm. Second, large trees were not permitted to obstruct the battery field of fire during the historic period. Managing vegetation to discourage the growth of large trees, while encouraging the growth of smaller trees and shrubs is historically accurate, and will perpetuate historic downrange views critical to interpreting the historic function of the historic batteries to visitors (Drawing 5.2, scope of treatment). Removed woody vegetation should be chipped and any remaining debris should be removed from the park and legally disposed. Both deciduous and evergreen stumps must be carefully treated with a triclopyr herbicide to prevent resprouting according to label directions.

MO-2: Remove all woody vegetation growing on or within four-feet of concrete features

Battery Morris has a large amount of woody vegetation growing directly upon its concrete gun platforms, including dense stands of hackberry (*Celtis occidentalis*) along the south face of the structure. The vegetation, taking root in accumulated leaf litter and sprouting from voids and cracks in the concrete, threatens the long-term preservation of the battery and must be removed. In addition to the battery structure, the freestanding range finding station nearby should have all woody vegetation growing within four-feet removed. The vegetation removals around the range finding station will begin to return this structure to the prominent, open setting it once occupied.

Both deciduous and evergreen stumps must be carefully treated with a triclopyr herbicide to prevent resprouting according to label directions. After the root system has deteriorated, the stumps should be carefully removed and appropriate concrete repairs undertaken.

MO-3: Remove vegetation blocking historic downrange views

North of Battery Morris's engineered slope, the topography rises up to a height comparable to the gun platforms. After vegetation has been removed from the engineered slope and concrete structure, views from the battery to the water should be evaluated. Selectively clearing may be necessary since the ground level elevation of certain trees would be close to the elevation of the gun positions.

MO-4: Remove all woody vegetation six-feet north of the U. S. Coast Guard perimeter fence

The U. S. Coast Guard perimeter fence runs south of Battery Urmston and continues east past Battery Morris. The fence is a six-foot high chain-link topped with barbed wire. The north side of the fence, closest to Battery Morris, is becoming overrun with ailanthus (*Ailanthus altissima*), Virginia creeper (*Parthenocissus quinquefolia*), poison ivy (*Toxicodendron radicans*), and honey locust saplings (*Gleditsia triacanthos*). If not treated and maintained, this area will soon be impassable. Also observed between the fence and Battery Morris is yard waste, most likely from the nearby Coast Guard properties. Managing a six-foot width of vegetation along the fence improves security, provides easier access for future maintenance work at the batteries, and demonstrates to abutters that the National Park Service is a responsible neighbor. Once the large woody vegetation has been removed, the six-foot width can be easily maintained with a small tractor and brush hog mowing deck.

Visitor Access Treatment Tasks

MU-5: Rehabilitate existing road trace as visitor access trail

During the historic period, a road paralleled Battery Morris's south facade and provided access for personnel and delivery of ammunition. Today, the road is present as a variable-width trace north of the Coast Guard perimeter fence. The asphalt surface of the road contains numerous large cracks and is in poor condition. Large woody vegetation is growing in the cracks and makes visitor and staff access to Battery Morris difficult. In conjunction with removing vegetation north of the perimeter fence, the park should rehabilitate the road trace for access to the battery. Large woody vegetation emerging from the roadbed should be removed along with the deteriorated asphalt surface. After removing the asphalt, the exposed base course should be compacted. If the base course contains clay, organic matter, and other material that would not provide a stable surface, the existing base course should be removed and replaced with a hard, durable stone aggregate. A new asphalt surface should be installed over the base course with the width and alignment matching the existing roadbed.

MO-6: Repair and secure doors and grating to prevent unauthorized access

Based on field observations in January 2009, the doors on the south side of Battery Morris appeared to be in good to fair condition (Figure 5.32). Accumulated leaf litter and debris should be removed from the front of the doors in order to remove a source of moisture that will accelerate corrosion.

MO-7: Replace wood guard panels on gun platforms

At the eastern most gun platform of Battery Morris, wood guard panels have been installed due to the difference in elevation between the platform levels. The panels are constructed from two-by-fours, and have peeling, maroon paint (Figure 5.33).

Metal pipe railing was historically used for safety railing on coastal batteries while wood was generally limited to light framing, doors, windows, decking, and siding.[24] The wood panels are not a historic feature and do not comply with safety codes due to the excessive space between the rails and cross brace. The wood guard panels should be removed and great care should be exercised not to damage the historic concrete structures removing fasteners that secured the wood to the concrete.

Presently the vegetation growing close to and on the battery provides more of a barrier to access than the wood panels. After vegetation removal and if the park intends to open Battery Morris to the public, wherever judged appropriate, the park should add pipe rail safety railings with metal mesh infill panels as discussed in the general treatment guidelines.

MO-8: Replace wood picket fence north and east of battery

Similar to the wood guard panels, a wood picket fence was installed at Battery Morris to the north and east of the eastern most gun platform. The fence is painted maroon and appears to be in place to keep people from walking up the eastern historic earthwork and falling into the gun platform (Figure 5.34).

The fence is not a historic feature and conveys a false sense of security. Only a little force would need to be applied to topple the fence. The entire length of fence should be removed and great care should be exercised not to damage the historic concrete structures removing fasteners that secured the wood to the concrete. Great care should also be exercised not to damage the historic earthwork north of the battery when posts are removed. Any depressions left from the posts should be filled with soil from a sterile source that does not have the potential to damage archaeological information.[25] If there is concern about safety in the vicinity of Battery Morris, the existing deteriorated wooden fencing can be replaced with chain-link fence similar to that used elsewhere at Sandy Hook's battery sites.

Battery Structures Treatment Tasks

MO-9: Stabilize spalling concrete surfaces and repair cracks

The extent of concrete deterioration was not clear in the field due to the amount of vegetation on structure. After vegetation removals and following the procedures highlighted in the general treatment recommendations, spalling concrete surfaces and cracks should be repaired.

MO-10: Repair and seal horizontal concrete surfaces to reduce water infiltration

Like Battery Urmston, historic photographs indicate that Battery Morris did not have paint, asphalt emulsion, or another dark colored surface treatment (see Figure 5.28). After concrete surface defects have been repaired, two options are possible to seal horizontal concrete surfaces without creating a non-historic appearance. First, penetrating sealers could be used with the understanding that to achieve the best protection, they should be applied every few years. The other option, providing a more durable coating, is to apply bitumen with light-colored gravel laid into the coating. The gravel should match the color of the existing concrete. At Battery Morris, approximately 1,580 square feet of concrete will need a surface coating.

MO-11: Repair and repaint ferrous metal fixtures

A variety of ferrous metal fixtures were incorporated into the construction of Battery Morris. Metal fixtures in fair condition with visible rust should be chemically treated, primed, and painted to match the historic finish. Damaged or severely deteriorated fixtures should be removed and replaced with new components that match the original as close as possible. Additional information on ferrous metal treatments can be found in the Safety Railings section of the treatment tasks common to all battery sites and in the *Historic Fortification Preservation Handbook* (Washington State Parks and Recreation Commission, 2003).

TABLE 5.2: SUMMARY OF TREATMENT RECOMMENDATIONS, BATTERY MORRIS		
Rehabilitation Task	**Notes**	**Priority for Action** 1 - high priority 2 - medium priority 3 - low priority, but requires ongoing monitoring 4 - no action
MO-1: Remove woody vegetation greater than four-inches diameter growing on engineered slopes		1 - high priority for action
MO-2: Remove all woody vegetation growing on or within four-feet of concrete features		1 - high priority for action
MO-3: Remove vegetation blocking historic downrange views		1 - high priority for action
MO-4: Remove all woody vegetation six-feet north of the U. S. Coast Guard perimeter fence		1 - high priority for action
MO-5: Rehabilitate existing road trace as visitor access trail	A trail needs to be established on the south side of the battery in order to provide access for routine maintenance, implementing other treatment tasks, and visitor access.	1 - high priority for action
MO-6: Repair and secure doors and grating to prevent unauthorized access		1 - high priority for action
MO-7: Replace wood guard panels on gun platforms	Coordinate with future plans to open battery site to public visitation	2 - plan for future action
MO-8: Replace wood picket fence north and east of battery	Coordinate with future plans to open battery site to public visitation	2 - plan for future action
MO-9: Stabilize spalling concrete surfaces and repair cracks		1 - high priority for action
MO-10: Repair and seal horizontal concrete surfaces to reduce water infiltration	Implement after concrete surface defects have been repaired	1 - high priority for action
MO-11: Repair and repaint ferrous metal fixtures		2 - plan for future action

Figure 5.29. Coincidence range finder station, Battery Morris, circa 1920. Note the open character of the adjacent landscape. Woody vegetation should be removed within four feet of the freestanding structure (GATE 7893).

Figure 5.30. View looking northeast at Battery Morris. This image shows dense stands of hackberry (*Celtis occidentalis*) growing directly along the south face of the concrete structure (Olmsted Center, January 2009).

Figure 5.31. Large hackberry growing in the accumulated leaf litter on top of Battery Morris (Olmsted Center, January 2009).

Figure 5.32. View looking northwest at south facade, Battery Morris. Accumulated leaf litter and debris should be removed from the front of the doors in order to remove a source of moisture that accelerates corrosion (Olmsted Center, January 2009).

Figure 5.33. Wood guard panels at Battery Morris. The wood panels are not a historic feature and do not comply with safety codes due to the excessive space between the rails and cross brace. The wood guard panels should be removed and great care should be exercised not to damage the historic concrete structures removing fasteners that secured the wood to the concrete (Olmsted Center, January 2009).

Figure 5.34. Wood picket fence on top of Battery Morris. The entire length of the pictured non-historic fence should be removed. Great care should be exercised not to damage the historic concrete structures and the historic earthwork north of the battery when the posts are removed (Olmsted Center, January 2009).

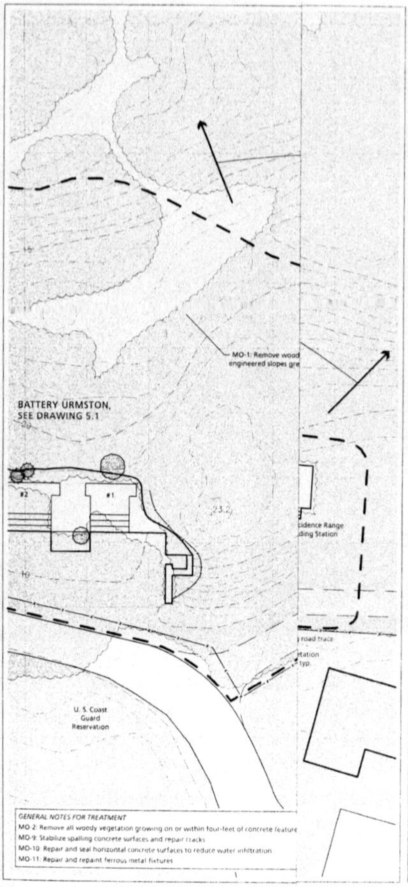

Cultural Landscape Report for the Sandy Hook Coastal Defense Batteries

Gateway National Recreation Area

Sandy Hook, New Jersey

Battery Morris Treatment Plan

National Park Service
Olmsted Center for Landscape Preservation
www.nps.gov/oclp

SOURCES

1. Sandy Hook GIS Data
2. Sandy Hook Color Ortho Imagery, Captured 2006
3. Topographic Sheets, prepared by Denver Service Center, 1992
4. Topographic Maps, prepared by Carrera and Associates, 1990
5. Field Inventory, Olmsted Center for Landscape Preservation, January 2009

DRAWN BY

Tim Layton, AutoCAD 2002, Illustrator CS3, 2009

LEGEND

Canopy Vegetation
Paved Road / Walk
Unpaved Road / Walk
Deciduous Tree
Evergreen Tree
Fence
Scope of Treatment

NOTES

1. Contour Interval = 1'0"
2. Plan represents landscape conditions inventoried in January 2009
3. All features shown in approximate scale and location

0' 7.5' 15' 30'

Drawing 5.2

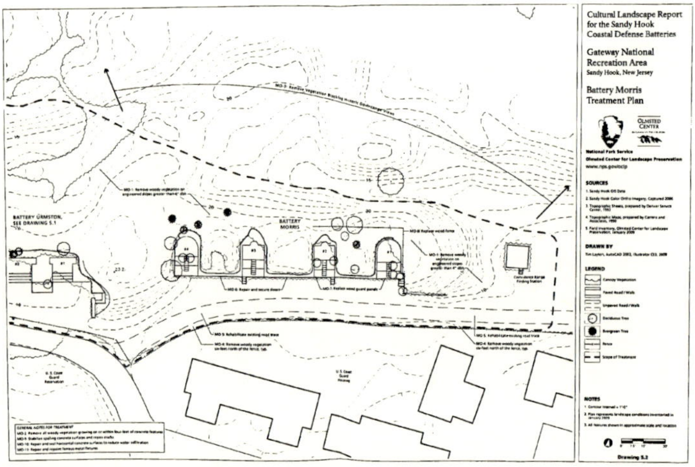

Cultural Landscape Report for the Sandy Hook Coastal Defense Batteries
Gateway National Recreation Area
Sandy Hook, New Jersey
Battery Morris Treatment Plan
Olmsted Center
National Park Service
Olmsted Center for Landscape Preservation
www.nps.gov/oclp
SOURCES
DRAWN BY
LEGEND
NOTES
Drawing 5.2
BATTERY MORRIS
BATTERY ORMSTON, SEE DRAWING 5.1
GENERAL NOTES FOR TREATMENT

BATTERIES ENGLE AND PECK (SH-189A AND SH-180)

Although batteries Engle and Peck each have their own individual histories, because they lay immediately adjacent, they are considered together for the purpose of this cultural landscape report. The Army constructed and armed Battery Engle in 1898 with a single five-inch gun. The non-standard five-inch gun was deemed obsolete and the emplacement was disarmed in 1918. A rangefinding station was soon constructed over the former gun emplacement in 1920, directing the fire of nearby Battery Peck (Figure 5.35).

Battery Peck was completed and armed in 1903, joining Batteries Urmston, Morris and Engle in defending the shipping channel directly offshore Sandy Hook's northern extremity. Battery Peck's original armament consisted of two 6-inch barbette mount guns shielded with semi-circular armor plating. Owing to its ability to fire rapidly, Battery Peck's guns were removed used to replace the slower operating armament at Battery Gunnison in 1943 during World War II. Battery Peck was in turn refitted four with "Dual-Purpose" guns capable of engaging either aircraft or surface ships at a high rate of fire, and was redesignated as "Battery Number 8." The former Battery Peck site served throughout World War II, and was disarmed in 1946.[26]

Batteries Engle and Peck survive in deteriorated condition. Downrange views from gun emplacements and range finder stations have been blocked by the growth of woody vegetation (Figures 5.36 and 5.37). Accumulation of windblown sand, organic matter and the growth of vines and other plants hinder access throughout the battery site. Concrete surfaces display widespread spalling, and metal fixtures such as handrails and door and window hardware are severely corroded.

TREATMENT TASKS

Vegetation Management Treatment Tasks

EN/PE-1: Remove woody vegetation greater than four-inches diameter growing on engineered slopes

The existing topography of the Battery Engle and Peck site suggests that the engineered slopes and terrain of both batteries Engle and Peck were considered as a single element during the construction process to create a continuous protective feature. Since there is no discernable break or interruption in the landform, it is difficult to prescribe a line that divides the engineered earthworks of the two batteries. Within this area, trees greater than four inches diameter at breast height should be carefully removed. The purpose of this recommendation is two-fold. First, smaller trees do not present as much canopy to the wind, and are of less risk in toppling and displacing the historic landform during a storm.

Second, large trees were not permitted to obstruct the battery field of fire during the historic period. Managing vegetation to discourage the growth of large trees, while encouraging the growth of smaller trees and shrubs is historically accurate, and will perpetuate historic downrange views critical to interpreting the historic function of the batteries to visitors (Drawing 5.3, scope of treatment). Removed woody vegetation should be chipped and any remaining debris should be removed from the park and legally disposed. Both deciduous and evergreen stumps must be carefully treated with a triclopyr herbicide to prevent resprouting according to label directions.

EN/PE-2: Remove all woody vegetation growing on or within four-feet of concrete features

Unmanaged vegetation on batteries Engle and Peck has grown to a considerable size and threatens to further deteriorate the historic battery's concrete features. Vegetation growing on or within four-feet of concrete features should be removed. As highlighted previously in the treatment tasks common to all battery sites, both deciduous and evergreen stumps should be treated with a triclopyr herbicide to prevent resprouting and accelerate root decay. After the root systems deteriorate, the stumps should be carefully removed to the greatest extent practicable and appropriate concrete repairs should be made.

EN/PE-3: Remove vegetation blocking historic downrange views

North of Battery Engle and Peck's engineered slope, the topography of the adjacent dunes rises up to a height comparable to the gun platforms. After vegetation has been removed from the immediacy of the engineered slopes and concrete structures, downrange views from the batteries Engle and Peck to the water should be evaluated. Selectively clearing may be necessary since the ground level elevation of certain trees would be close to the elevation of the gun positions.

EN/PE-4: Remove vegetation blocking access to rear of Battery Peck

During the historic period, North Bragg Drive turned west past Nine Gun Battery and paralleled the south facade Battery Peck. The south facade provided access for personnel and ammunition and located opposite the firing direction of the artillery, served as the rear of the battery. The rear of Battery Peck was kept free of vegetation to expedite deliveries and changes in personnel (Figure 5.38).

Today the area between the rear of Battery Peck and North Bragg Drive is filled with dense vegetation and is nearly impassable (Figure 5.39). In order to provide staff and visitor access, the vegetation growing between North Bragg Drive and the rear of Battery Peck should be removed. Removing the vegetation also rehabilitates the rear of Battery Peck to resemble the open character present during the battery's years of operation.

Visitor Access Treatment Tasks

EN/PE-5: Close social trail and improve eroded pathway east of battery

East of Battery Engle, a social trail winds up an engineered slope and connects to a series of trails around Battery Peck that lead to the observation platform. Although a spilt-rail fence has been installed, users have worn a path that squeezes between the fence and the historic structure (see Figure 5.36). In order to protect the historic engineered earthwork and limit potential erosion, the social trail should be closed. Low-growing native shrubs should be planted at the top and bottom of the trail to block access. Additional information on appropriate species and installing erosion control materials is presented in the treatment tasks common to all battery sites section.

EN/PE-6: Install new split-rail fence around observation platform and direct pedestrian circulation via a new trail to the North Pond.

Due to Battery Peck's current hazardous conditions, a chain-link fence restricts visitor access to the structure from North Bragg Drive. Visitors arrive at batteries Engle and Peck by following an unpaved road to the observation platform and then heading south along a series of social trails to the batteries (Drawing 5.3). The social trails trod across the batteries' engineered earthworks and lead visitors to structures that have not been rehabilitated for public access.

In order to curtail unauthorized access to the batteries, preserve the engineered earthworks, and provide visitors with a continuous route to other attractions at the park, a new split-rail fence should be installed around the observation platform and a new trail established that unites with the existing trail to the North Pond. Split-rail fence is currently in place north of the observation platform to direct pedestrians and protect natural resource areas. Additional fencing should clearly define a space around the observation platform and contain an opening at the head of the new trail. The trail should proceed north of the engineered earthworks and gradually descend a steep slope before uniting with the existing trail to the North Pond (Drawing 5.3). After vegetation and battery structure tasks are completed, visitors should access batteries Engle and Peck from North Bragg Drive. This route allows visitors to approach the batteries in the same manner as soldiers did during the historic period.

EN/PE-7: Repair, retrofit, and replace safety railings

At batteries Engle and Peck, metal handrails line the steps that provided access from the ground level to the batteries. Metal guardrails are also installed near the open sides of elevated areas such as gun platforms (Figure 5.40). Metal railings in fair condition with visible rust should be chemically treated, primed, and painted to match the historic finish. Damaged or severely deteriorated railings should be removed and replaced with new components that match the original as close as possible. Additional information on metal treatments and adding infill or applied materials to comply with life safety codes can be found in the treatment tasks common to all battery sites.

Battery Structures Treatment Tasks

EN/PE-8: Repair and repaint ferrous metal fixtures

In addition to the repair work needed for the metal guardrails and handrails, Battery Peck has a metal antenna and mounting brackets that attached it to the commander's station (Figure 5.41).

This specific metal fixture is not present at the other batteries. A measured drawing of the antenna and brackets should be prepared to document these features. At a later date, these components may need to be replaced and fabricated based on the measured drawings.

The existing corrosion should be removed or made inert with a chemical treatment and immediately followed with priming and painting to match the historic finish.[27]

ENPE-9: Repair and secure doors and grating to prevent unauthorized access

Existing metal doors at batteries Engle and Peck should be inventoried and evaluated to determine a proper level of treatment. Minor corrosion and replacing small functional or decorative components should be performed with the door in place. If a component is damaged or severely deteriorated, it should be removed and repaired at an off-site shop or newly fabricated to match the existing. Additional information on repairing and securing doors can be found in the treatment tasks common to all battery sites and in the *Historic Fortification Preservation Handbook* (Washington State Parks and Recreation Commission, 2003).

EN/PE-10: Stabilize spalling concrete surfaces

Concrete surfaces at batteries Engle and Peck exhibit spalling areas and cracks resulting from water infiltration and freeze-thaw cycles. In order to limit further damage to the concrete, spalling surfaces should be removed, mechanically cleaned, and patched to match the character of the historic material. Small cracks should be dried and prepared to receive a sealant that is compatible with the character of the historic concrete. The treatment of large, structural cracks should be determined by a structural engineer. Additional information addressing the repair of spalling areas and cracks can be found in the treatment tasks common to all battery sites and in the *Historic Fortification Preservation Handbook* (Washington State Parks and Recreation Commission, 2003).

EN/PE-11: Repair and seal horizontal concrete surfaces to reduce water infiltration

In order to reduce water infiltration and to protect the concrete structures at batteries Engle and Peck, a surface coating should be applied to the horizontal surfaces. Application of a surface coating must occur after spalling and cracked concrete surfaces are repaired and defected surfaces that collect and pool rainwater are corrected. Additional information penetrating sealers and surface sealers can be found in the treatment tasks common to all battery sites. At Battery Engle, approximately 415 square feet of concrete should be sealed. The area to be sealed at Battery Peck is approximately 4,100 square feet.

EN/PE-12: Remove metal trailer and section of 12-foot chain-link fence

West of Battery Peck and in close proximity to the CRF station (Battery Engle), the Army set a communications trailer for the NIKE system (Figure 5.42). As recently as 1990, a map of Battery Peck indicated in addition to the trailer, a twelve-foot high chain-link fence topped with barbed wire surrounded much of the trailer and observation deck.

Based on field observations in January 2009, only a small portion of the chain-link fence remains. The fence is overrun with Japanese honeysuckle (*Lonicera japonica*) and other vines and the trailer is a frequent target for graffiti. Although the NIKE system is part of the coastal defenses deployed throughout Sandy Hook's history, the location of the trailer and fence so close to Battery Peck detract from understanding the spatial relationship of the gun emplacements, commander's station, CRF station, and the water in the distance. The trailer and section of fence should be removed to improve and visual and spatial connection of these elements.

Prior to removing the trailer, the structure should be thoroughly documented including its interior configuration, remaining equipment, and any surviving papers. Removing the trailer should be accomplished by disassembling it and carrying pieces out via the trail to the observation deck. Large machinery should not be brought in the vicinity of the trailer as machinery will have the potential to damage Battery Peck's historic concrete structures and earthworks.

TABLE 5.3: SUMMARY OF TREATMENT RECOMMENDATIONS, BATTERIES ENGLE AND PECK		
Rehabilitation Task	**Notes**	**Priority for Action** 1 - high priority 2 - medium priority 3 - low priority, but requires ongoing monitoring 4 - no action
EN/PE-1: Remove woody vegetation greater than four-inches diameter growing on engineered slopes		1 – high priority for action
EN/PE-2: Remove all woody vegetation growing on or within four-feet of concrete features		1 – high priority for action
EN/PE-3: Remove vegetation blocking historic downrange views		1 – high priority for action
EN/PE-4: Remove vegetation blocking access to rear of Battery Peck		1 – high priority for action
EN/PE-5: Close social trail and improve eroded pathway east of battery		1 – high priority for action
EN/PE-6: Install new split-rail fence around observation platform and direct pedestrian circulation via a new trail to the North Pond.		1 – high priority for action
EN/PE-7: Repair, retrofit, and replace safety railings	Can be implemented as part of a multiple battery or park-wide battery project	2 – plan for future action
EN/PE-8: Repair and repaint ferrous metal fixtures		2 – plan for future action
EN/PE-9: Repair and secure doors and grating to prevent unauthorized access		1 – high priority for action
EN/PE-10: Stabilize spalling concrete surfaces		1 – high priority for action
EN/PE-11: Repair and seal horizontal concrete surfaces to reduce water infiltration	Implement after concrete surface defects have been repaired	1 – high priority for action
EN/PE-12: Remove metal trailer and section of 12-foot chain-link fence		2 – plan for future action

Figure 5.35. Batteries Engle and Peck circa 1920. The battery commander's station for Battery Peck is seen in the foreground. The low concrete structure seen in the background is the coincidence range finder station built into the former gun emplacement of Battery Engle in 1920. Note the low-growing vegetation in this photograph, making possible downrange views and effective operation of the batteries (GATE 7892).

Figure 5.36. View looking northwest at Battery Engle (CRF Station Peck). Although a split-rail fence has been installed as a safety measure, park visitors have trod a path that squeezes between the fence and the historic structure. Low-growing native shrubs should be planted at the top and bottom of the trail to block access (Olmsted Center, January 2009).

Figure 5.37. Blocked downrange view looking northwest from the Battery Peck battery commander's station. Blocked views such as these may be readily reestablished by selectively removing out-of-scale woody vegetation. Views to the water from coastal batteries are critical in understanding the historic purpose and operation of the coastal defense system (Olmsted Center, January 2009).

Figure 5.38. View looking northwest at Battery Peck, circa 1905-10. The south facade or rear of the battery provided access for personnel and ammunition and was kept free of vegetation to expedite those functions (Thomas Hoffman, *Fort Hancock*, Charleston, SC: Arcadia Publishing, 2007).

Figure 5.39. View looking northwest at Battery Peck. Today the area south of Battery Peck is filled with dense vegetation and is nearly impassable. Existing vegetation should be removed to resemble the open character present during the battery's years of operation and to improve access (Olmsted Center, January 2009).

Figure 5.40. View of historic guardrail south of emplacement #1, Battery Peck. Severely deteriorated railing components, such as the vertical post in the foreground, should be removed and replaced with new components that match the original as close as possible. Final painting or a color-galvanized coating should match the historic railing paint finish (Olmsted Center, January 2009).

Figure 5.41. View of northwest facade of Battery Peck's commander station. The metal antenna and mounting brackets are features of this structure and should be preserved or replaced in kind. Measured drawings should be prepare to document these features followed by corrosion treatment, priming, and painting to match the historic finish (Olmsted Center, January 2009).

Figure 5.42. View looking north at a post World War II trailer located near Batteries Peck and Engle. The trailer is in a seriously deteriorated condition and, along with an accompanying section of fence, should be removed to improve the visual and spatial connection among Battery Peck's gun emplacements, commander station, CRF station, and the water in the distance (Olmsted Center, January 2009).

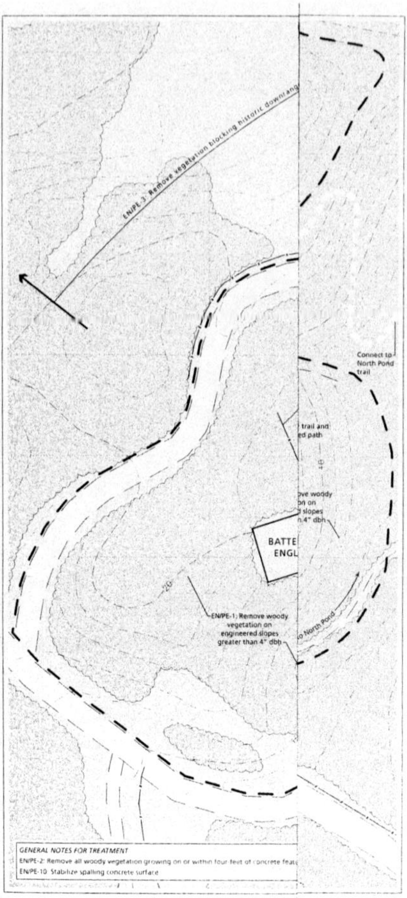

Cultural Landscape Report for the Sandy Hook Coastal Defense Batteries

Gateway National Recreation Area

Sandy Hook, New Jersey

Batteries Engle and Peck Treatment Plan

National Park Service

Olmsted Center for Landscape Preservation

www.nps.gov/oclp

SOURCES

1. Sandy Hook GIS Data
2. Sandy Hook Color Ortho Imagery, Captured 2006
3. Topographic Sheets, prepared by Denver Service Center, 1992
4. Topographic Maps, prepared by Carrera and Associates, 1990
5. Field Inventory, Olmsted Center for Landscape Preservation, January 2009

DRAWN BY

Tim Layton, AutoCAD 2002, Illustrator CS3, 2009

LEGEND

Canopy Vegetation

Paved Road / Walk

Unpaved Road / Walk

Trail

Fence

Scope of Treatment

NOTES

1. Contour interval = 2'-0"
2. Plan represents landscape conditions inventoried in January 2009
3. All features shown in approximate scale and location

0' 7.5' 15' 30'

Drawing 5.3

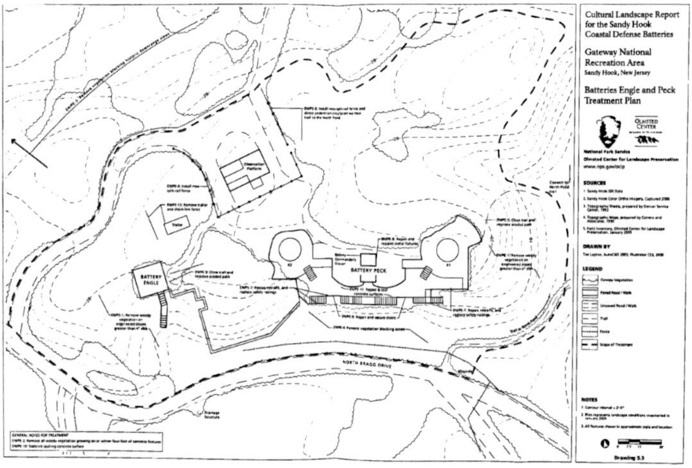
Cultural Landscape Report for the Sandy Hook Coastal Defense Batteries
Gateway National Recreation Area
Sandy Hook, New Jersey
Batteries Engle and Peck Treatment Plan
National Park Service
Olmsted Center for Landscape Preservation
SOURCES
DRAWN BY
LEGEND
NOTES
Drawing 5.3
BATTERY ENGLE
BATTERY PECK
NORTH BRAGG DRIVE

NINE GUN BATTERY (SH-181)

The Army began construction of what has become known as Nine Gun Battery in 1897, the project built astride the curtain walls of an incomplete five-sided granite fort begun in the 1850s. Three gun emplacements were completed and armed in 1898 with 10-inch caliber guns mounted on counterweight carriages. Four additional gun emplacements were completed in 1899 and armed in 1900 when it became commonly known as Seven Gun Battery, yet officially designated as Battery Halleck. Two additional gun emplacements were completed south of the existing arrangement of gun positions in 1902 and later armed in 1904 (Figure 5.43 and cover of report). Improvements to naval artillery eventually provided ships at sea with guns of greater range and destructive force than the coastal artillery mounted at Fort Hancock's Nine Gun Battery. Obsolete before the end of World War II, maps of the post drawn in 1944 indicate that at that time, the armament at the Nine Gun Battery had been dismantled.[28]

Among the most visually prominent and accessible of Sandy Hook's coastal defense sites, the Nine Gun Battery has been the subject of several stabilization efforts during National Park Service stewardship. Despite these efforts, the Nine Gun Battery continues to share common issues with other battery sites throughout Sandy Hook. These include spalling and deteriorating concrete surfaces, including unsafe concrete walkways where concrete has fallen away, leaving only a lattice-work of corroded reinforcing steel; woody vegetation actively growing in expansion joints between concrete surfaces. Metal handrailings at the Nine Gun Battery are in fair to good condition due to recent maintenance, however, corrosion is present in this marine environment and there are many instances of corroded metal fixtures including safety railings and metal doors and windows. Unmanaged growth of young trees, vines, and other woody vegetation on the engineered earthwork obscures downrange views and masks the presence of social trails, animal burrows, and other instances of erosion and disturbance (Figure 5.44).

TREATMENT TASKS

Vegetation Management Treatment Tasks

9G-1: Remove woody vegetation greater than four-inches diameter growing on engineered slopes

A mixture of vegetation presently grows on the engineered earthwork at Nine Gun Battery including native and non-native vines and groundcovers, grasses, shrubs, and large woody vegetation. Large woody vegetation defines any deciduous or evergreen tree that has a trunk size greater than four-inches diameter at breast height. Given this size, a tree that topples over due to wind, rain, snow, or ice is likely to damage a portion of the engineered earthwork. Additionally, the tree roots can damage the concrete structures below the protective earthwork. In order to protect the historic earthwork, woody vegetation greater than four-inches diameter at breast height should be selectively removed and the stumps treated with a triclopyr herbicide. Further information on vegetation removals and treatment can be found in the treatment tasks common to all battery sites.

9G-2: Remove all woody vegetation growing on or within four-feet of concrete features

At Nine Gun Battery, woody vegetation is growing in close proximity to concrete structures and is also emerging from spalling areas, cracks, and where leaf litter and debris have accumulated (see Figure 5.44). The existing woody vegetation is either causing or has the potential to cause structural concrete problems. Given the harmful effect of woody vegetation in this situation, all woody vegetation growing on or within four-feet of concrete features should be removed. After removing the woody material, both deciduous and evergreen stumps should be treated with a triclopyr herbicide. Additional information on removing woody vegetation growing near and on structures can be found in the treatment tasks common to all battery sites.

9G-3: Remove vegetation blocking historic downrange views

Unobstructed views were necessary from the artillery and battery commander's stations at Nine Gun Battery in order to have a clear field of fire and to locate and acquire the range of potential targets (Figure 5.45). After removing woody vegetation growing on the engineered earthwork and from the battery structure itself, the resulting downrange views to the water must be evaluated. In some instances tall, individual woody vegetation that blocks the view shed should be identified and removed. Further information on managing vegetation for downrange views can be found in the treatment tasks common to all battery sites.

9G-4: Remove phragmites (*Phragmites* sp.) from gun platform wells

The gun platforms at Nine Gun Battery feature concentric steps that lead to a lower level and a circular well in which the artillery was emplaced. Over time, water and organic debris have accumulated in several wells and colonies of phragmites (*Phragmites* sp.) have emerged.

Similar to the woody vegetation growing on the concrete structures, the phragmites threatens to further degrade the historic battery's concrete and should be removed. In addition, the phragmites distracts from the interpretive goal of opening sections of Nine Gun Battery to visitors and conveying the purpose and intent of this coastal defense system (Figure 5.46).

Since phragmites reproduces vegetatively, some mechanical control methods such as mowing, disking, and cutting can actually increase its spread. If phragmites is cut just after tasseling—usually before the end of July—most of the food reserves produced that season are removed with the aerial portion of the plant thereby reducing the plant's vigor.

In addition to timely cutting and removal of the culms, the remaining stems should be treated with a hand-swiped application of a glyphosate herbicide. The phragmites will need to be monitored and the process repeated for several seasons until the stand is removed.[29]

After the phragmites has been successfully removed, the circular wells at each gun platform should be inspected, cleaned out if debris has built up, and monitored to prevent the future accumulation of water and debris. If a drain in the gun well is failing and causing water and debris to collect, the structure should be cleaned out. Drainage lines should be flushed with pressurized water (150 psi) to remove any accumulated debris. Additional repairs, improvements, and supplements to the existing historic drainage system should be designed by a qualified engineer advised by a historical architect.

Visitor Access Treatment Tasks

9G-5: Repair and secure doors and grating to prevent unauthorized access

The existing metal doors and grates at Nine Gun Battery have been inventoried and evaluated by park staff to determine a proper level of treatment (Figures 5.47 and 5.48). Missing doors and grates are presently being fabricated as part of opening Nine Gun Battery for visitor access. In addition to off-site fabrication, repairing minor corrosion and replacing small functional or decorative components should be performed with the door in place. Additional information on repairing and securing doors can be found in the treatment tasks common to all battery sites and in the *Historic Fortification Preservation Handbook* (Washington State Parks and Recreation Commission, 2003).

9G-6: Install chain-link fence outside cantilevered structure at gun platforms #5 through #7 to mitigate hazards

As covered previously, door and window openings will require repaired elements or to otherwise be properly secured to prevent unauthorized access inside the battery. After this has been completed, the existing chain-link fence to the rear (land-side) of the Nine Gun Battery should be removed making it possible for visitors to walk about the ground level of the batteries.

Between gun platforms #5 and #7, a new chain-link fence should be installed outside a cantilevered structure to protect visitors (Drawing 5.4). This component of the batteries will not be accessible to visitors from the gun platform level and it is possible that material from above could injure a visitor on the ground level.

9G-7: Rehabilitate metal stairs and handrails from ground level to gun platforms #1 and #2

The next six treatment tasks for Nine Gun Battery address topics raised in the *Nine Gun Battery Visitor Access Plan*. Many of the topics, such as rehabilitating handrails, are discussed for multiple batteries at Sandy Hook and should be included as part of the specific tasks for Nine Gun.

The *Visitor Access Plan* proposes to open gun platforms #1, #2, and #9. These three platforms will be accessible from the ground level and a pedestrian route between platforms #2 and #9 will be provided across the terreplein.

In order to access platforms #1, handrails should be installed on the existing concrete ramp (Figure 5.49). The ramp already has escutcheon plates on its outside edge. The escutcheons should be inspected and have their fasteners tightly secured or new fastening hardware installed. If the plates are not in good condition, a new handrail should be installed that is core drilled into the ramp's concrete structure.

The new handrail components should match the original pipe railings and ball joint connectors at Nine Gun. To reduce future maintenance requirements, the new handrails should be finished with a color-galvanized coating that matches the historic paint finish. The color-galvanized coating, especially in a waterfront setting, will last longer and require less maintenance than traditional prime and paint finishes.

In addition to the concrete ramp, individual metal stairs lead directly to gun platforms #1 and #2. Damaged or severely deteriorated treads and stringers should be removed and replaced with new components that match the original. The joints and connections should be inspected and properly tightened and secured. Corrosion should be removed or made inert with a chemical treatment and immediately followed with priming and painting to match the historic finish.

For both the concrete ramp and metal stair handrails, wire mesh panels should be added to the existing openings to provide a higher level of protection. The mesh should have a matte black finish or coating that will recede in front of the batteries.

9G-8: Construct handrails on existing concrete stairs from gun platforms #1 and #2 to terreplein

Visitors will access the terreplein from gun platforms #1 and #2 via existing concrete stairs north of each gun emplacement (Drawing 5.4). The stairs should have new handrails added with a mesh infill on their outside edge. There is approximately ten-feet of elevation difference between the gun platform level and terreplein. Due to this change in elevation, the handrails need to have mesh infill in order to act like a guardrail and provide a greater level of visitor protection.

The new handrails should be installed by core drilling into the steps' concrete structure and should match the original pipe railings and ball joint connectors at Nine Gun. Each vertical member should be fitted with an escutcheon plate to match the existing. To reduce future maintenance requirements, the new handrails should be finished with a color-galvanized coating that matches the historic paint finish.

9G-9: Install boardwalk at perimeter of terreplein forward slope for access between gun platform #2 to gun platform #9

As presented in the *Nine Gun Battery Visitor Access Plan*, the visitor route between gun platforms #2 and #9 will be on top of the terreplein. The terreplein will be marked with yellow paint to demarcate a six-foot wide route visitors should adhere to.

The currently proposed visitor route between gun platforms #2 and #9 presents two problems. There is an approximate ten feet of elevation change between the terreplein and the gun platform level and no proposed protective measure to prevent an accident. In addition, there is no measure to prevent or discourage visitors from exiting the route and proceeding down the historic earthwork. Without some measure in place, visitors will develop trails down and across the historic earthwork and the foot traffic will damage this resource.

In order to provide greater visitor safety and protect the historic earthwork, a boardwalk should be installed with simple pipe rail guards. The guards will indicate to visitors not to deviate from the boardwalk route and will be compatible with historic pipe railings currently in place (Figures 5.50 and 5.51).

9G-10: Install wood stairway from terreplein level to gun platform #9

Unlike gun platforms #1 and #2, there are no concrete stairs from the terreplein level to gun platform #9. In order to provide visitor access, a wood stairway should be constructed and installed. Wood construction was seldom used at the gun batteries and due to this fact, visitors will be better able to distinguish new, non-historic construction from the historic fabric (Drawing 5.4).

The stairway should have uniform riser and tread dimensions with a maximum riser height of seven-inches and a minimum tread depth of eleven-inches. Guardrails and handrails need to be provided due to the ten-feet or more of elevation change. Finally the stairway should terminate on gun platform #9 in a direction that positions visitors' path of travel away from the gun pit.

9G-11: Rehabilitate concrete stairs and install handrails from gun platform #9 to ground level

The final component to creating a pedestrian circulation loop across Nine Gun is to rehabilitate the concrete stairs in the west corner gun platform and install new handrails to the ground level (Drawing 5.4). After the vegetation removals have been completed, access to the stairs will be greatly improved. At this time, the existing concrete should be inspected and repairs made on any spalling or cracks.

The stairs should have new handrails added with a mesh infill on their outside edge. The new handrails should be installed by core drilling into the steps' concrete structure and should match the original pipe railings and ball joint connectors at Nine Gun. Each vertical member should be fitted with an escutcheon plate to match the existing. To reduce future maintenance requirements, the new handrails should be finished with a color-galvanized coating that matches the historic paint finish.

9G-12: Provide picnic area at southern flank of Nine Gun Battery

South of Nine Gun Battery, Parking Lot J provides a central location where visitors can leave their vehicles and walk to the North Beach area, Battery Potter, and Nine Gun. Around 2000, the park removed picnic grounds from the North Beach and is currently interested in establishing a new picnic area to address visitor demand. Between Nine Gun Battery and Lot J, a picnic area should be created at a node where recreation opportunities and historic resources meet (Drawing 5.4).

The picnic area should be located south of Nine Gun's engineered slope and large vegetation should remain between the picnic area and earthwork to discourage visitor access on the historic resource. Selective clearing will be needed to provide a sufficient open area for tables.

9G-13: Eliminate existing social trail and construct new visitor trail from gun emplacement #8 toward North Pond

Historic aerial photographs indicate that informal trails lead from Nine Gun Battery's emplacements down the engineered earthwork to the surrounding land north and east of the battery. An existing social trail is present starting at emplacement #8 that traverses the earthwork below emplacements #8 and #9. The existing trail is steep, hastens erosion of the earthwork, and is dangerous for visitors to properly use. The existing social trail should be closed and revegetated and a better option provided for visitors wanting to connect to existing trails in the vicinity of the North Pond. Additional information on appropriate native species to block trail access and erosion control materials is presented in the treatment tasks common to all battery sites section.

After the existing social trail has been closed and revegetated, a new trial should be constructed that follows shallower grades down the engineered earthwork. Cribbing, check dams, and other trail stabilizing features should be installed as needed to facilitate access and limit erosion. At the toe or bottom of the engineered slope, the trail should lead across relatively level ground and avoid existing depressions and dunes. The new trail should unite with the existing trail west of the North Pond (Drawing 5.4).

Battery Structures Treatment Tasks

9G-14: Stabilize spalling concrete surfaces and repair cracks

The extent of concrete deterioration was not clear in the field due to the amount of vegetation on structure. After vegetation removals and following the procedures highlighted in the general treatment recommendations, spalling concrete surfaces and cracks should be repaired.

9G-15: Repair and seal horizontal concrete surfaces to reduce water infiltration

Like Battery Urmston, historic photographs indicate that Battery Morris did not have paint, asphalt emulsion, or another dark colored surface treatment. After concrete surface defects have been repaired, two options are possible to seal horizontal concrete surfaces without creating a non-historic appearance. First, penetrating sealers could be used with the understanding that to achieve the best protection, they should be applied every few years. The other option, providing a more durable coating, is to apply bitumen with light-colored gravel laid into the coating. The gravel should match the color of the existing concrete. At Battery Morris, approximately 1,580 square feet of concrete will need a surface coating.

9G-16: Repair and repaint ferrous metal fixtures

A variety of ferrous metal fixtures were incorporated into the construction of Nine Gun Battery (see Figure 5.48). Metal fixtures in fair condition with visible rust should be chemically treated, primed, and painted to match the historic finish. Damaged or severely deteriorated fixtures should be removed and replaced with new components that match the original as close as possible. Additional information on ferrous metal treatments can be found in the Safety Railings section of the treatment tasks common to all battery sites and in the *Historic Fortification Preservation Handbook* (Washington State Parks and Recreation Commission, 2003).

Interpretive Treatments

9G-17: Restore section of railroad track and locate flatcar to interpret the handling of heavy ordnance and munitions

When Sandy Hook's gun batteries were operational, a railroad transported the large guns and their ordnance from docks located near the northern tip of the peninsula to the various batteries. Although present-day roads and trails have been constructed over some former rail lines, the location and importance of the railroad to coastal defenses has become difficult to perceive. In conjunction with plans to open the Nine Gun Battery to greater visitor access, an opportunity exists to restore a short section of railroad track and locate a flatcar upon it to interpret the transportation of shells and other heavy materials.

South of gun platform #1, a rail line connected the docks to the west with the proving ground to the east. This section of track ran through an area west of the battery that had been used for overflow parking. The track continued east crossing the present-day Parking Lot J before terminating at the proving ground (Figure 5.52).

Although the railroad bed and ties are not visible, the tracks do appear in a section of asphalt pavement west of Nine Gun (Figure 5.53). From this location, the tracks should be extended roughly eighty-feet east to meet Lot J and west into the field for a sufficient length to locate a flatcar. The park no longer plans to use the field for overflow parking and as a result, there will be no conflict between parking requirements and adding this interpretive element. Extending the tracks to Lot J will help to physically draw visitors to the interpretive display and reveal a small part of a historic transportation system that is largely obscured.

9G-18: Excavate and interpret exposed portions of the northeast bastion and curtain wall of the pre-existing granite fort

Prior to Nine Gun Battery's construction, a granite block-constructed fort occupied the northern end of Sandy Hook. Roughly trapezoidal in shape with projecting bastions at the northeast, southeast, southwest and northwest corners, the structure was known as the Fort at Sandy Hook. The Fort was constructed between 1859 and 1867, yet never completed as powerful rifled artillery made the brittle qualities of stone and brick masonry obsolete for future use in coastal defense sites.[30]

Construction began on Nine Gun in 1897 and the concrete battery structure was built over the pre-existing granite structure's eastern wall (Figure 5.54). The layout and angled position of Nine Gun Battery's northernmost two gun positions was not capricious, but matched the salient angle of the earlier granite fort (Figure 5.55).

North of gun platform #8, evidence can be seen of granite blocks that comprised the northeast bastion of the Fort (Figure 5.56). In consultation with a regional archaeologist, an extant section of the bastion should be excavated and exposed. With a piece of the granite fort revealed, the proposed *Nine Gun Battery Visitor Access Plan* should incorporate interpretation of this prior structure as part of the continuum of Sandy Hook's coastal defenses.

TABLE 5.4: SUMMARY OF TREATMENT RECOMMENDATIONS, NINE GUN BATTERY		
Rehabilitation Task	**Notes**	**Priority for Action** 1 - high priority 2 - medium priority 3 - low priority, but requires ongoing monitoring 4 - no action
9G-1: Remove woody vegetation greater than four-inches diameter growing on engineered slopes		1 – high priority for action
9G-2: Remove all woody vegetation growing on or within four-feet of concrete features		1 – high priority for action
9G-3: Remove vegetation blocking historic downrange views		1 – high priority for action
9G-4: Remove phragmites (*Phragmites* sp.) from gun platform wells		1 – high priority for action
9G-5: Repair and secure doors and grating to prevent unauthorized access	Coordinate with plans to open the battery for visitor access	1 – high priority for action
9G-6: Install chain-link fence outside cantilevered structure at gun platforms #5 through #7 to mitigate hazards	Coordinate with plans to open the battery for visitor access	1 – high priority for action
9G-7: Rehabilitate metal stairs and handrails from ground level to gun platforms #1 and #2	Coordinate with plans to open the battery for visitor access	1 – high priority for action
9G-8: Construct handrails on existing concrete stairs from gun platforms #1 and #2 to terreplein	Coordinate with plans to open the battery for visitor access	1 – high priority for action
9G-9: Install boardwalk at perimeter of terreplein forward slope for access between gun platform #2 to gun platform #9	Coordinate with plans to open the battery for visitor access	1 – high priority for action
9G-10: Install wood stairway from terreplein level to gun platform #9	Coordinate with plans to open the battery for visitor access	1 – high priority for action
9G-11: Rehabilitate concrete stairs and install handrails from gun platform #9 to ground level	Coordinate with plans to open the battery for visitor access	1 – high priority for action
9G-12: Provide picnic area at southern flank of Nine Gun Battery		2 – plan for future action
9G-13: Eliminate existing social trail and construct new visitor trail from gun position #8 to North Pond	Coordinate with plans to open the battery for visitor access	1 – high priority for action
9G-14: Stabilize spalling concrete surfaces and repair cracks		1 – high priority for action
9G-15: Repair and seal horizontal concrete surfaces to reduce water infiltration	Implement after concrete surface defects have been repaired	1 – high priority for action
9G-16: Repair and repaint ferrous metal fixtures		2 – plan for future action
9G-17: Restore section of railroad track and locate flatcar to interpret the handling of heavy ordnance and munitions		3 – low priority
9G-18: Excavate and interpret exposed portions of the northeast bastion and curtain wall of the pre-existing granite fort	Coordinate with plans to open the battery for visitor access	1 – high priority for action

Figure 5.43. Aerial photograph of Nine Gun Battery, January 1933. This photograph shows the engineered slope of Nine Gun Battery with limited vegetation. To protect the earthwork, all woody vegetation greater than four-inches diameter at breast height should selectively removed. The area north of Battery Alexander appears darker in this image because it is the north slope and in shadows (Coastal and Hydraulics Laboratory, Engineer Research and Development Center).

Figure 5.44. View looking west toward battery commander's station Bloomfield, Nine Gun Battery. Eastern red cedars (*Juniperus virginiana*) have become established in the joints of the concrete terreplein and should be removed (Olmsted Center, January 2009).

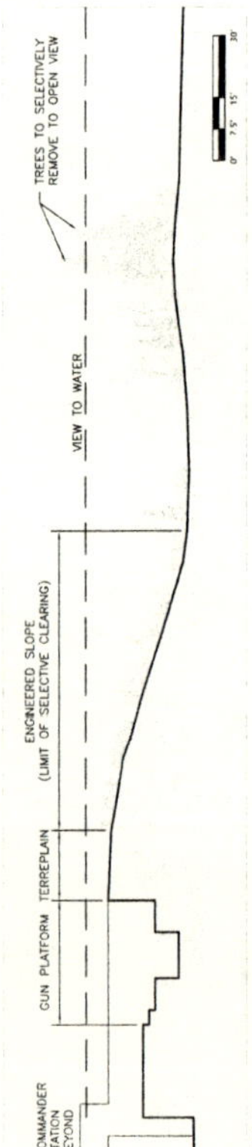

Figure 5.45. Conceptual section through Nine Gun Battery. After vegetation is selectively removed from concrete structures and from engineered slopes, the historic downrange views from the battery commander's station should be evaluated. The batteries could not defend New York Harbor if they did not have an unobstructed view to the water. Restoring the view and visual connection to the water is important in communicating the history and mission of these defenses to the public (Olmsted Center, 2009).

Figure 5.46. View of phragmites in gun well #6, Nine Gun Battery. Phragmites should be cut just after tasseling and the remaining stems should be treated with a hand-swiped application of a glyphosate herbicide (Olmsted Center, January 2009).

Figure 5.47. View of failing metal door, Nine Gun Battery. Doors and windows should be properly mounted and locked to prevent unauthorized access to interior spaces. While the door in view may be repaired, when a door is damaged or severely deteriorated, a new door should be fabricated to match the existing in materials and finish (Olmsted Center, January 2009).

Figure 5.48. View of shell hoist metal door, Nine Gun Battery. Doors and windows should be properly mounted and locked to prevent unauthorized access. If a door is damaged or severely deteriorated, a new door should be fabricated to match the existing in materials and finish (Olmsted Center, January 2009).

Figure 5.49. View looking northwest at the concrete ramp to gun platform #1, Nine Gun Battery. New safety railings should be installed on the ramp to facilitate visitor access. The rails should either attach to the existing escutcheon plates or be core drilled into the ramp's concrete structure. The new handrail components should match the original pipe railings and ball joint connectors at Nine Gun Battery to the greatest extent practicable (Olmsted Center, January 2009).

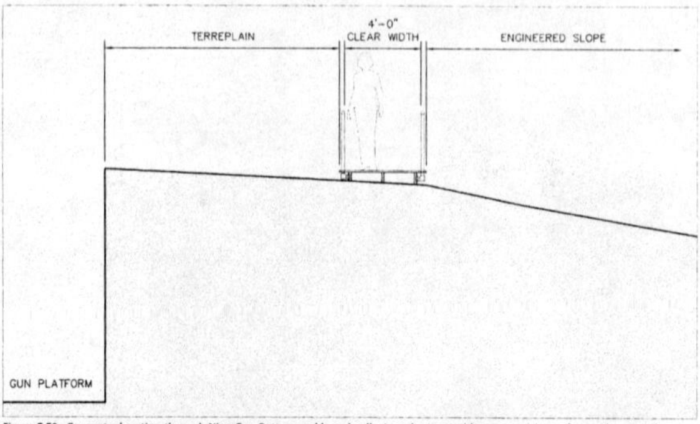

Figure 5.50. Conceptual section through Nine Gun Battery and boardwalk. In order to provide greater visitor safety and protect the historic earthwork, a boardwalk should be installed for visitor access across the terreplein (Olmsted Center, 2009).

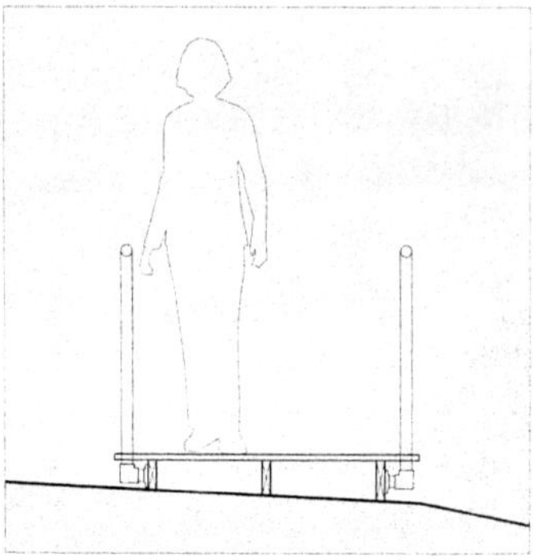

Figure 5.51. Detail section of decking and handrails, Nine Gun Battery. The handrails will indicate to visitors not to deviate from the boardwalk route and will be compatible with the historic pipe railings currently in place (Olmsted Center, 2009).

Figure 5.52. Aerial photograph of Nine Gun Battery, January 1933. The red dashed line has been added to highlight the rail line from the docks to the proving ground. Two rail cars can be seen in the image. A section of track near Nine Gun should be restored and a flatcar located there to interpret the handling of heavy ordnance and munitions (Coastal and Hydraulics Laboratory, Engineer Research and Development Center).

Figure 5.53. View of extant railroad track, Nine Gun Battery. From this location, the tracks should be extended roughly eighty-feet east to meet parking lot J and west into the field for a sufficient length to locate a flatcar for interpretive purposes (Olmsted Center, January 2009).

Figure 5.54. Construction of Nine Gun Battery, 1897. The concrete battery structure was built over a Civil War-era granite block fort. The fort's bastions can be seen in the image as the forming of the battery occurs over the fort's eastern wall (GATE 7880).

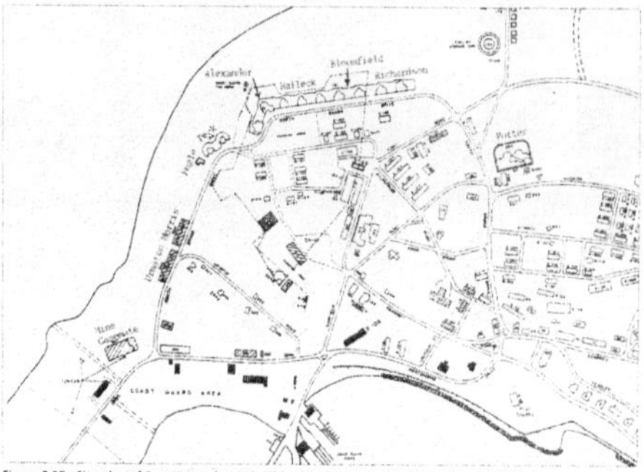

Figure 5.55. Site plan of Fort Hancock, 1967. This plan shows the location of the mid-19th century granite fortress (*dashed outline*) in relation to Nine Gun Battery. A portion of the northeast curtain wall and bastion is visible above the ground surface, though greatly obscured by vegetation (Thomas Hoffman, *Fort Hancock*, Charleston, SC: Arcadia Publishing, 2007).

Figure 5.56. Portion of the northeast curtain wall belonging to the former granite fort. This large granite block is located north of gun platform #8. A longer section of the curtain wall and northeast bastion could be carefully exposed to help park visitors understand and appreciate the multiple layers of coastal defenses at Sandy Hook (Olmsted Center, January 2009).

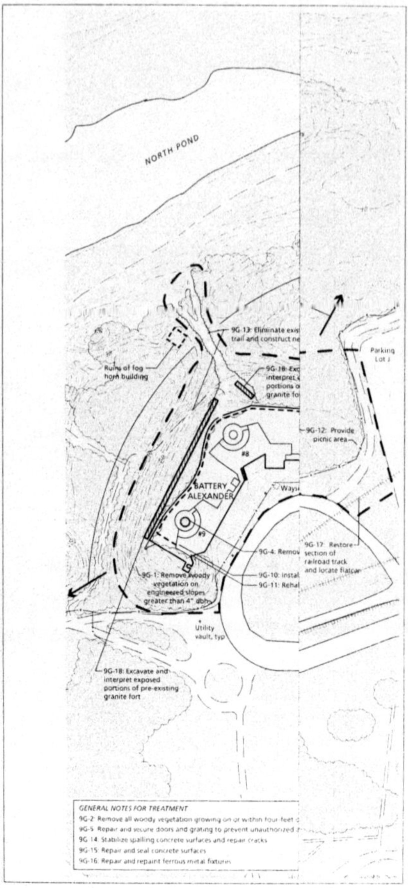

Cultural Landscape Report for the Sandy Hook Coastal Defense Batteries

Gateway National Recreation Area

Sandy Hook, New Jersey

Nine Gun Battery Treatment Plan

OLMSTED CENTER

National Park Service

Olmsted Center for Landscape Preservation

www.nps.gov/oclp

SOURCES

1. Sandy Hook GIS Data
2. Sandy Hook Color Ortho Imagery, Captured 2006
3. Topographic Sheets, prepared by Denver Service Center, 1992
4. Topographic Maps, prepared by Carrora and Associates, 1990
5. Field Inventory, Olmsted Center for Landscape Preservation, January 2009

DRAWN BY

Tim Layton, AutoCAD 2002, Illustrator CS3, 2009

LEGEND

Canopy Vegetation

Paved Road / Walk

Unpaved Road / Walk

Trail

Marsh

Fence

1944 Rail Line

Scope of Treatment

NOTES

1. Contour interval = 2'-0"
2. Plan represents landscape conditions inventoried in January 2009
3. All features shown in approximate scale and location

0' 30' 60' 120'

Drawing 5.4

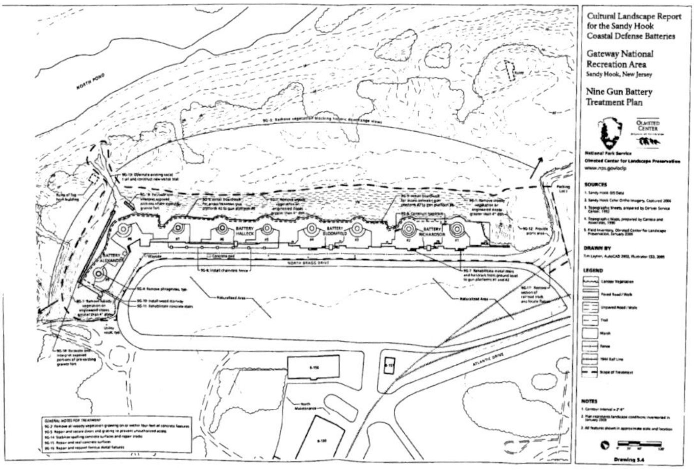
Cultural Landscape Report for the Sandy Hook Coastal Defense Batteries
Gateway National Recreation Area
Sandy Hook, New Jersey
Nine Gun Battery Treatment Plan
National Park Service
SOURCES
DRAWN BY
LEGEND
Paved Road / Walk
Trail
Marsh
Fence
Scope of Treatment
NOTES
Drawing 5.4
NORTH POND
BATTERY HALLECK
BATTERY BLOOMFIELD
BATTERY RICHARDSON
NORTH BRAGG DRIVE
ATLANTIC DRIVE

BATTERY POTTER (SH-264)

The Army began construction of "Lift-Gun Battery #1" in 1891 and the first of its two 12-inch guns was emplaced and test fired the following year. This unusual gun battery is the only example of a steam-powered hydraulic lift that raised the guns into firing position from behind a protective earth-shielded concrete fortification. This technology made possible a 360 degree field of fire. Masonry construction was completed in 1893 and a second gun was emplaced in 1895. The battery site was designated as Battery Potter in 1903 (Figure 5.57). However the battery's usefulness was short-lived, as the innovative development of the depressing-type counterweight gun carriages led the Army to disarm Battery Potter in 1906. Immediately prior to its being disarmed, the Army had conceived of a new role for Battery Potter, using its elevated terreplein to locate a primary fire control structure organizing the concerted fire of the entire system of coastal artillery on Sandy Hook. Initially, a wooden structure was added to Battery Potter's terreplein in 1905 to coordinate firing at the Mortar Battery. Two years later, a series of concrete structures were added to coordinate firing at Nine Gun Battery, Battery Granger, Battery Peck, and Battery Gunnison.[31] In addition to these control structures, switchboard rooms for telephone communications among the batteries were added near the front entry of Battery Potter in 1907. During World War II, Battery Potter continued its service as an element of the Advanced Harbor Entrance Control Post. This use was discontinued after the war's end.

Battery Potter survives in deteriorated condition and is host to preservation issues common to historic battery sites throughout Sandy Hook (Figure 5.58). These include unmanaged woody vegetation growing upon the engineered earthwork designed to absorb the impact of enemy fire, and also obscuring downrange views from the gun positions and from the battery commander's station. The roots of adjacent woody vegetation penetrate cracks and voids within the concrete structure exacerbating poor conditions. While Battery Potter has recently been equipped with safety railings surrounding the rooftop wells that once held the steam driven machinery that lifted the guns, metal fittings and fixtures such as railings, stairways, and doors and windows are subjected to ongoing corrosion. The large openings present in both historic and modern railing systems do not meet life-safety code requirements.

TREATMENT TASKS

Vegetation Management Treatment Tasks

PO-1: Remove woody vegetation greater than four-inches diameter growing on engineered slopes

A mixture of vegetation presently grows on the engineered earthwork at Battery Potter including native and non-native vines and groundcovers, grasses, shrubs, and large woody vegetation. Large woody vegetation defines any deciduous or evergreen tree that has a trunk size greater than four-inches diameter at breast height. Given this size, a tree that topples over due to wind, rain, snow, or ice is likely to damage a portion of the engineered earthwork. Additionally, the tree roots can damage the concrete structures below the protective earthwork. In order to protect the historic earthwork, woody vegetation greater than four-inches diameter at breast height should be selectively removed and the stumps treated with a triclopyr herbicide. For Battery Potter, the area to be selectively cleared would be approximately 0.9 acres (Drawing 5.5, scope of treatment). Further information on vegetation removals and treatment can be found in the treatment tasks common to all battery sites.

PO-2: Remove all woody vegetation growing on or within four-feet of concrete features

At Battery Potter, woody vegetation is growing in close proximity to concrete structures and is also emerging from spalling areas, cracks, and where leaf litter and debris have accumulated (Figure 5.59). The existing woody vegetation is either causing or has the potential to cause structural concrete problems. Given the harmful effect of woody vegetation in this situation, all woody vegetation growing on or within four-feet of concrete features should be removed. After removing the woody material, both deciduous and evergreen stumps should be treated with a triclopyr herbicide. Additional information on removing woody vegetation growing near and on structures can be found in the treatment tasks common to all battery sites.

PO-3: Remove vegetation blocking historic downrange views

Unobstructed views were necessary from the artillery and fire control stations at Battery Potter in order to have a clear field of fire and to locate and acquire the range of potential targets (Figure 5.60). After removing woody vegetation growing on the engineered earthwork and from the battery structure itself, the resulting downrange views to the water must be evaluated. In some instances tall, individual woody vegetation that blocks the view shed should be identified and removed. Further information on managing vegetation for downrange views can be found in the treatment tasks common to all battery sites.

Visitor Access Treatment Tasks

PO-4: Repair, retrofit, and replace safety railings

At Battery Potter, metal guardrails are installed between the superior slope and the terreplein where the guns were emplaced and along open sides of elevated areas (Figure 5.61). Metal railings in fair condition with visible rust should be chemically treated, primed, and painted to match the historic finish. Damaged or severely deteriorated railings should be removed and replaced with new components that match the original as close as possible. Additional information on metal treatments and adding infill or applied materials to comply with life safety codes can be found in the treatment tasks common to all battery sites.

PO-5: Formalize and relocate visitor parking

While there should be no increase in number of parking spaces serving Battery Potter, the existing informal parking area is ill-defined and poorly drained. Visually, the presence of visitor parking in its current configuration detracts from the formality of the rear approach to the castellated granite defensible entrance. A new parking area, surfaced in crushed stone, and of an area no greater in size than the current parking area, should be designed and constructed to facilitate convenient visitor access to this unique coastal battery structure and landscape. This recommendation amounts to shifting the existing informal parking area approximately fifty-feet southward (Drawing 5.5).

PO-6: Install Accessible Route from Parking Level to Battery Potter terreplein

An unmet need has been expressed by park staff, park partners, and the public for an accessible elevated location where visitors might take in a panoramic view and where the entire coastal defense system can be explained and understood. The Sandy Hook Lighthouse provides an elevated location but it is constrained by three factors. First, the Lighthouse is only open April through October. Second, its narrow stairway limits the number of people who can ascend to the top and observe the view. Finally, it would be impossible to make the Lighthouse accessible to those with mobility issues. Seeking a more practical alternative, interest has been expressed in making the summit of the Mortar Battery accessible to the public in order to both explain the operation of the Mortar Battery and the surrounding defensive system. Another option often mentioned is the elevated terreplein of Battery Potter.

Site visits to both the Mortar Battery site and Battery Potter site, followed by discussions with park staff, suggest that Battery Potter appears to be the most promising and practical location on which to accommodate this unmet need. This recommendation is based on observing the dangerously steep earthen slopes of the Mortar Battery, where new non-historic stairways and safety railings, ramps, viewing platforms and corresponding safety barriers would be required before inviting the public to the summit. These modifications to the historic battery would also be prominently in view, greatly distracting from the historic conditions that the park hopes to perpetuate.

Interestingly, directions communicated from the observation point atop Battery Potter were used to direct the systematic fire of gun batteries defending the southern approach to New York Harbor, including the Mortar Battery. While anti-aircraft guns occupied the summit of the Mortar Battery after the large guns were removed, soldiers originally operating the guns in the pits relied on instructions telephoned in from off-site observation towers, such as the position atop Battery Potter to aim the guns and track a potential enemy.

Battery Potter currently features pedestrian routes to the top of the battery structure from both an exterior steel staircase and an interior concrete stairway. The terreplein provides a generous viewing area that is already minimally equipped with safety railings. These existing safety railings could be easily supplemented and modified for improved safety with comparatively little impact to the historic character of the structure or its corresponding landscape.

Elsewhere in the National Park system, former military sites have made historic battery structures accessible through sensitive rehabilitation efforts. Battery Huger, an Endicott period concrete structure, rests atop Fort Sumter in Charleston, South Carolina (FOSU), at the center of perhaps the most historically significant coastal battery site in the United States. Battery Huger has been made accessible with the addition of three small wheelchair lifts. The former bombproof Joint Operations Center located in the dry moat of fortress San Cristobal in San Juan, Puerto Rico (SAJU) has been retrofitted with an interior elevator, making viable use of this World War II-era concrete structure for visitor services, museum storage, and administrative needs.

The qualities of the Battery Potter site provide the superior circumstances required to develop a successful design for universal access to the summit of Battery Potter. Designing and constructing a new ramp, supported in part by concrete piers, may be designed into the wooded site immediately south-east of Battery Potter (Drawing 5.5). Located in this position, sight of the lengthy ramp from the vantage point of Hudson Road would be obscured by the surrounding vegetation and the flare of the engineered earthen slope adjacent to freestanding switchboard building (B-256).

Battery Structures Treatment Tasks

PO-7: Stabilize spalling concrete surfaces and repair cracks and voids

Concrete surfaces at Battery Potter exhibit spalling areas and cracks resulting from water infiltration and freeze-thaw cycles. In order to limit further damage to the concrete, spalling surfaces should be removed, mechanically cleaned, and patched to match the character of the historic material. Small cracks should be dried and prepared to receive a sealant that is compatible with the character of the historic concrete. The treatment of large, structural cracks should be determined by a structural engineer. Additional information addressing the repair of spalling areas and cracks can be found in the treatment tasks common to all battery sites and in the *Historic Fortification Preservation Handbook* (Washington State Parks and Recreation Commission, 2003).

PO-8: Repair and seal horizontal concrete surfaces to reduce water infiltration

In order to reduce water infiltration and to protect the concrete structures at Battery Potter, a surface coating should be applied to the horizontal surfaces. Application of a surface coating must occur after spalling and cracked concrete surfaces are repaired and defected surfaces that collect and pool rainwater are corrected. Additional information penetrating sealers and surface sealers can be found in the treatment tasks common to all battery sites. At Battery Potter, approximately 32,000 square feet of concrete should be sealed.

PO-9: Repair and repaint ferrous metal fixtures

A variety of ferrous metal fixtures were incorporated into the construction of Battery Potter. Metal fixtures in fair condition with visible rust should be chemically treated, primed, and painted to match the historic finish. Damaged or severely deteriorated fixtures should be removed and replaced with new components that match the original as close as possible. Additional information on ferrous metal treatments can be found in the Safety Railings section of the treatment tasks common to all battery sites and in the *Historic Fortification Preservation Handbook* (Washington State Parks and Recreation Commission, 2003).

PO-10: Restore roofs of plotting rooms

In 1907, the Army added two concrete buildings on top of Battery Potter's terreplein to improve the targeting of enemy ships. One building was configured as a grouping of five distinct, interconnected structures and the other building was designed as a grouping of two. The buildings served the large caliber guns at Nine Gun Battery and Battery Granger as well as the rapid fire guns at Battery Peck and Battery Gunnison.

Today, the concrete structures are in poor condition primarily due to exposure to the elements. Deteriorating wooden rafters and trusses are present on top of the buildings and no roofing material or other covering is present (Figure 5.62). In order to stabilize the plotting room buildings, the roofs should be restored based on the research presented in the *Historic Structure Report for Battery Potter, Mortar Battery and Battery Gunnison* and following the *Secretary of the Interior's Standards for the Treatment of Historic Properties*. Once the roofs are restored, the interiors may be used to house durable exhibitry and help interpret the coastal defense system at Sandy Hook.

TABLE 5.5: SUMMARY OF TREATMENT RECOMMENDATIONS, BATTERY POTTER		
Rehabilitation Task	**Notes**	**Priority for Action** 1 - high priority 2 - medium priority 3 - low priority, but requires ongoing monitoring 4 - no action
PO-1: Remove woody vegetation greater than four-inches diameter growing on engineered slopes		1 – high priority for action
PO-2: Remove all woody vegetation growing on or within four-feet of concrete features		1 – high priority for action
PO-3: Remove vegetation blocking historic downrange views		1 – high priority for action
PO-4: Repair, retrofit, and replace safety railings	Coordinate with installing accessible route to terreplein	2 – plan for future action
PO-5: Formalize and relocate visitor parking		1 – high priority for action
PO-6: Install accessible route from parking level to Battery Potter terreplein	Coordinate with safety railing treatment	2 – plan for future action
PO-7: Stabilize spalling concrete surfaces and repair cracks and voids		1 – high priority for action
PO-8: Repair and seal horizontal concrete surfaces to reduce water infiltration	Implement after concrete surface defects have been repaired	1 – high priority for action
PO-9: Repair and repaint ferrous metal fixtures		2 – plan for future action
PO-10: Restore roofs of plotting rooms		1 – high priority for action

Figure 5.57. View looking southeast at Battery Potter, 1893. The Lift-Gun Battery #1, designated Battery Potter in 1903, was the only coastal defense battery constructed that used a steam-powered hydraulic lift to raise the guns up into firing position after they were loaded behind the protection of a massive concrete fortification (GATE 7811).

Figure 5.58. View looking north at defensible main entry, Battery Potter. The main entry is through an arched opening flanked by defensive stone towers. Each tower had gun loop slots so machine guns could fire on potential attackers. The entry facade resembles a castle and was constructed from granite blocks salvaged from Sandy Hook's Civil War-era fort (Olmsted Center, January 2009).

Figure 5.59. View looking east at the *chemin de ronde*, Battery Potter. Woody vegetation is growing in the *chemin de ronde*, a designed sentry route located north, south, and east of Battery Potter's superior slope. The vegetation threatens the historic battery's concrete features and surfaces and should be removed. After vegetation removals, the *chemin de ronde* should be regularly inspected and leaf litter and accumulated debris should be removed to prevent future vegetation growth and to protect the concrete surface (Olmsted Center, January 2009).

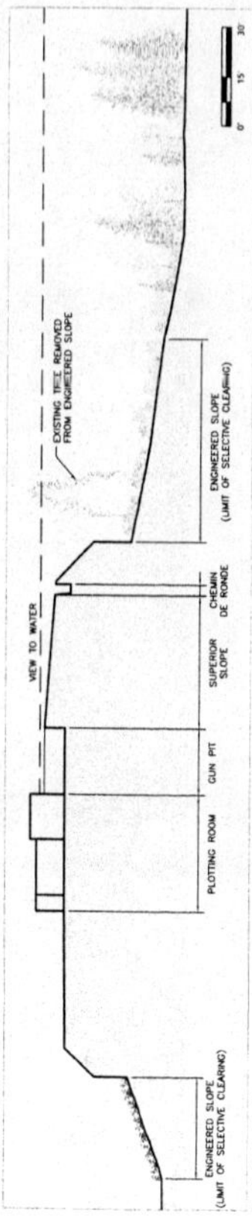

Figure 5.60. Conceptual section through Battery Potter. Existing, large woody vegetation on the engineered slope obstructs downrange views from the plotting rooms and terreplein to the water. Large woody vegetation on the engineered slope should be removed to restore views and protect the historic earthwork from potential damage due to thrown trees. Existing vegetation beyond the toe of the engineered slope may not impact views due to the viewing height on Battery Potter (Olmsted Center, 2009).

Figure 5.61. Recently installed contemporary safety railing, Battery Potter. Woven-wire may be either installed as infill panel, or the mesh applied with clamps to satisfy life-safety codes (Olmsted Center, January 2009).

Figure 5.62. Plotting rooms, Battery Potter. In improving physical access to the upper level of Battery Potter for use as an elevated prospect, rehabilitating the deteriorated plotting rooms shown here may be of some value for interpretive purposes. Once the roofs of these buildings are replaced, the interiors may be used to house durable exhibitry. Enamelled interpretive wayside panels may effectively substitute for missing window frames, offering detailed graphic interpretation of Battery Potter and the entire coastal defense system (Olmsted Center, January 2009).

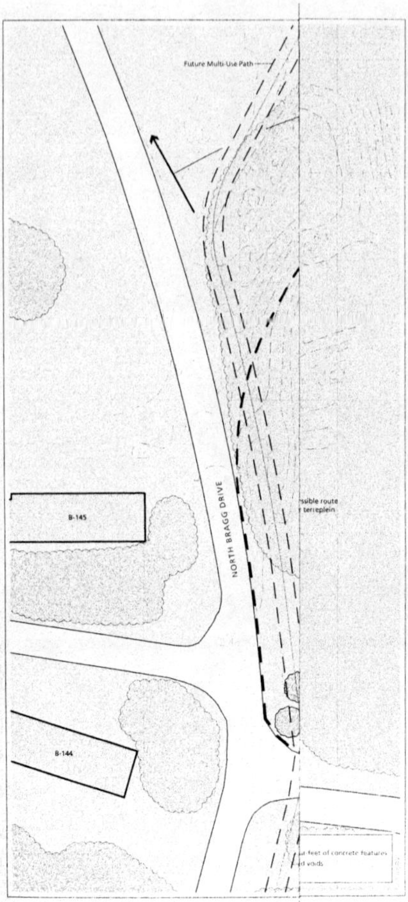

Cultural Landscape Report for the Sandy Hook Coastal Defense Batteries

Gateway National Recreation Area
Sandy Hook, New Jersey

Battery Potter Treatment Plan

National Park Service

Olmsted Center for Landscape Preservation

www.nps.gov/oclp

SOURCES

1. Sandy Hook GIS Data
2. Sandy Hook Color Ortho Imagery, Captured 2006
3. Topographic Sheets, prepared by Denver Service Center, 1992
4. Topographic Maps, prepared by Carrera and Associates, 1990
5. Field Inventory, Olmsted Center for Landscape Preservation, January 2009

DRAWN BY

Tim Layton, AutoCAD 2002, Illustrator CS3, 2009

LEGEND

Canopy Vegetation
Paved Road / Walk
Unpaved Road / Walk
Trail
Deciduous Tree
Fence
Railing
Scope of Treatment

NOTES

1. Contour Interval = 1'-0"
2. Plan represents landscape conditions inventoried in January 2009
3. All features shown in approximate scale and location

PLAN NORTH

0' 12.5' 25' 50'

Drawing 5.5

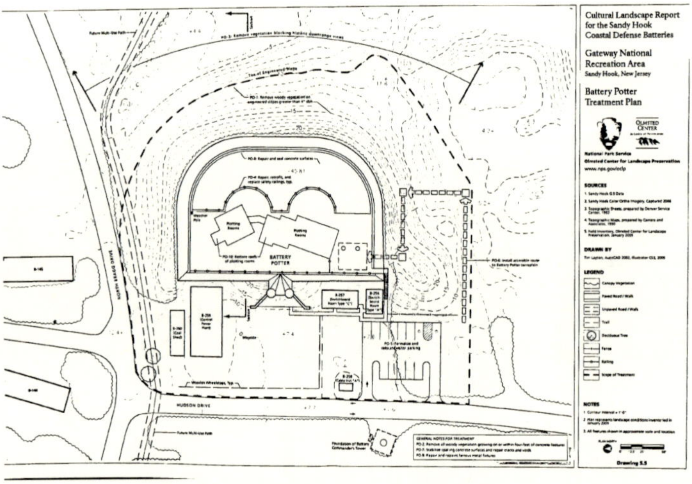
Cultural Landscape Report for the Sandy Hook Coastal Defense Batteries
Gateway National Recreation Area
Sandy Hook, New Jersey
Battery Potter Treatment Plan
National Park Service
Olmsted Center for Landscape Preservation
www.nps.gov/oclp
SOURCES
DRAWN BY
LEGEND
NOTES
Drawing 5.5
BATTERY POTTER
HUDSON DRIVE

BATTERY GRANGER (SH-266)

Battery Granger was the first large caliber gun battery at Sandy Hook to use the Buffington-Croizer counterweight gun carriage. Located between Battery Potter to the north and Mortar Battery to the south, construction on Battery Granger was completed in 1896 and it was armed with two ten-inch guns in 1897 (Figure 5.63). A decade after the guns were emplaced, the Army updated Battery Granger by extending the platforms behind the guns in order to allow for more convenient loading of munitions. In addition, they added an enclosed, concrete battery commander's station between the two gun emplacements providing a central location and greater protection for the commanding officer. After decades of standing ready, Battery Granger was declared obsolete and disarmed in 1942.

Battery Granger stands east of Hudson Drive and is presently not open to visitors. The park has installed a chain-link fence and signage between the road and battery to warn visitors of potentially hazardous conditions (Figure 5.64). Efflorescence can be seen on some vertical concrete surfaces and small spalling areas are present on both horizontal and vertical surfaces. The views from the commander's station to the water are blocked by woody vegetation first encountered at the edge of the terreplein and continuing on the engineered earthwork. Phragmites, also called common reed, is growing in the wells at both gun platforms. Guardrails are located along the terreplein on either side of the commander's station. The railings are in good to fair condition showing limited corrosion, however, they contain large openings that do not provide safety for all visitors.

TREATMENT TASKS

Vegetation Management Treatment Tasks

GR-1: Remove woody vegetation greater than four-inches diameter growing on engineered slopes

Images from the historic period indicate the Army managed vegetation on the engineered slopes (Figure 5.65). Presently, a mixture of vegetation grows on the earthwork including native and non-native vines and groundcovers, grasses, shrubs, and large woody vegetation (Figure 5.66). Large woody vegetation defines any deciduous or evergreen tree that has a trunk size greater than four-inches diameter at breast height. Given this size, a tree that topples over due to wind, rain, snow, or ice is likely to damage a portion of the engineered earthwork. Additionally, the tree roots can damage the concrete structures below the protective earthwork. In order to protect the historic earthwork, woody vegetation greater than four-inches diameter at breast height should be selectively removed and the stumps treated with a triclopyr herbicide. For

Battery Granger, the area to be selectively cleared would be approximately 0.8 acres (Drawing 5.6, scope of treatment). Further information on vegetation removals and treatment can be found in the treatment tasks common to all battery sites.

GR-2: Remove all woody vegetation growing on or within four-feet of concrete features

At Battery Granger, woody vegetation is growing in close proximity to concrete structures and is also emerging from spalling areas, cracks, and where leaf litter and debris have accumulated (Figure 5.67). The existing woody vegetation is either causing or has the potential to cause structural concrete problems. Given the harmful effect of woody vegetation in this situation, all woody vegetation growing on or within four-feet of concrete features should be removed. After removing the woody material, both deciduous and evergreen stumps should be treated with a triclopyr herbicide. Additional information on removing woody vegetation growing near and on structures can be found in the treatment tasks common to all battery sites.

GR-3: Remove vegetation blocking historic downrange views

Unobstructed views were necessary from the artillery and battery commander's stations at Battery Granger in order to have a clear field of fire and to locate and acquire the range of potential targets (Figure 5.68). After removing woody vegetation growing on the engineered earthwork and from the battery structure itself, the resulting downrange views to the water must be evaluated. In some instances tall, individual woody vegetation that blocks the view shed should be identified and removed. Further information on managing vegetation for downrange views can be found in the treatment tasks common to all battery sites.

GR-4: Remove phragmites (*Phragmites* sp.) from gun platform wells

Being similar in design to the gun emplacements utilized at the nearby Nine Gun Battery, the two gun emplacements located at Battery Granger feature a depressed, circular well in which the artillery was once secured. Over time, water and organic debris have accumulated in the two wells and colonies of phragmites (*Phragmites* sp.), a species of large grass, have become well established.

Similar to the woody vegetation growing on the concrete structures, the phragmites threatens to further degrade the historic battery's concrete and should be removed. Since phragmites reproduces vegetatively, some mechanical control methods such as mowing, disking, and cutting can actually increase its vigor and accelerates its growth. If phragmites is cut just after tasseling—usually before the end of July—most of the food reserves produced that season are removed with the aerial portion of the plant thereby reducing the plant's vigor.

In addition to timely cutting and removal of the culms, the remaining stems should be treated with a hand-swiped application of a glyphosate herbicide. The phragmites will need to be monitored and the process repeated for several seasons until the stand is removed.

After the phragmites has been successfully removed, the circular wells at each gun platform should be inspected, cleaned out if blocked, and monitored to prevent the buildup of water and debris. If a drain in the gun well is failing and causing water and debris to collect, the structure should be cleaned out. Drainage lines should be flushed with pressurized water (150 psi) to remove any accumulated debris. Additional repairs, improvements, and supplements to the existing historic drainage system should be designed by a qualified engineer advised by a historical architect.

Visitor Access Treatment Tasks

GR-5: Repair, retrofit, and replace safety railings

At Battery Granger, metal guardrails are installed near the open sides of the gun platforms (Figure 5.69). Metal railings in fair condition with visible rust should be chemically treated, primed, and painted to match the historic finish. Damaged or severely deteriorated railings should be removed and replaced with new components that match the original as close as possible. Additional information on metal treatments and adding infill or applied materials to comply with life safety codes can be found in the treatment tasks common to all battery sites.

GR-6: Repair and secure doors and grating to prevent unauthorized access

Existing metal doors and grating at Battery Granger should be inventoried and evaluated to determine a proper level of treatment. Minor corrosion and replacing small functional or decorative components should be performed with the door in place. If a component is damaged or severely deteriorated, it should be removed and repaired at an off-site shop or newly fabricated to match the existing. Additional information on repairing and securing doors can be found in the treatment tasks common to all battery sites and in the *Historic Fortification Preservation Handbook* (Washington State Parks and Recreation Commission, 2003).

GR-7: Install accessible route from road level to Battery Granger terreplein

In addition to the visitor access plan for the Nine Gun Battery and treatment recommendations for an accessible route to Battery Potter's terreplein, an accessible route should be installed from the road level to Battery Granger's terreplein. The accessible route should begin south of emplacement #1 and following a series of designed switchbacks at a 12:1 slope, the route should ascend the engineered earthwork and arrive at a flush transition on top of the terreplein (Drawing 5.6). Ramps supported in part by concrete piers should elevate the accessible route above the engineered earthwork and minimize disturbance to this historic feature. Landings will be required along the route at every change in direction and also after traveling at a continuous 12:1 slope for thirty feet. Existing vegetation between Hudson Road and the battery and also south of the battery should be retained to screen the accessible route and to minimize the visual impact of ramps needed to negotiate the existing elevation change. Existing railings on top of Battery Granger should be inspected and supplemented for visitor safety. Modifications to address existing, wide openings and the addition of new railings if needed will create relatively little impact to the historic character of the historic structure or its corresponding landscape.

Battery Structures Treatment Tasks

GR-8: Stabilize spalling concrete surfaces and repair cracks and voids

Concrete surfaces at Battery Granger exhibit spalling areas and cracks resulting from water infiltration and freeze-thaw cycles. In order to limit further damage to the concrete, spalling surfaces should be removed, mechanically cleaned, and patched to match the character of the historic material. Small cracks should be dried and prepared to receive a sealant that is compatible with the character of the historic concrete. The treatment of large, structural cracks should be determined by a structural engineer. Additional information addressing the repair of spalling areas and cracks can be found in the treatment tasks common to all battery sites and in the *Historic Fortification Preservation Handbook* (Washington State Parks and Recreation Commission, 2003).

GR-9: Repair and seal horizontal concrete surfaces to reduce water infiltration

The concrete terreplein at Battery Granger shows evidence of an asphalt-based product either used to fill joints or remaining in the joints after use as part of a larger concrete surface treatment (Figure 5.70 and see Figure 5.65). Cement grout was also used to fill cracks for concrete batteries from the 1890s to early 1900s.[32] In order to reduce water infiltration and to protect the concrete structures at Battery Granger, a surface coating should be applied to the horizontal surfaces. Application of a surface coating must occur after spalling and cracked concrete surfaces are repaired and defected surfaces that collect and pool rainwater are corrected. Additional information penetrating sealers and surface sealers can be found in the treatment tasks common to all battery sites. At Battery Granger, approximately 14,000 square feet of concrete should be sealed.

GR-10: Repair and repaint ferrous metal fixtures

A variety of ferrous metal fixtures were incorporated into the construction of Battery Granger. Metal fixtures in fair condition with visible rust should be chemically treated, primed, and painted to match the historic finish. Damaged or severely deteriorated fixtures should be removed and replaced with new components that match the original as close as possible. Additional information on ferrous metal treatments can be found in the Safety Railings section of the treatment tasks common to all battery sites and in the *Historic Fortification Preservation Handbook* (Washington State Parks and Recreation Commission, 2003).

TABLE 5.6: SUMMARY OF TREATMENT RECOMMENDATIONS, BATTERY GRANGER		
Rehabilitation Task	Notes	Priority for Action 1 - high priority 2 - medium priority 3 - low priority, but requires ongoing monitoring 4 - no action
GR-1: Remove woody vegetation greater than four-inches diameter growing on engineered slopes		1 - high priority for action
GR-2: Remove all woody vegetation growing on or within four-feet of concrete features		1 - high priority for action
GR-3: Remove vegetation blocking historic downrange views		1 - high priority for action
GR-4: Remove phragmites (*Phragmites* sp.) from gun platform wells		1 - high priority for action
GR-5: Repair, retrofit, and replace safety railings	Coordinate with installing accessible route to terreplein	2 - plan for future action
GR-6: Repair and secure doors and grating to prevent unauthorized access		1 - high priority for action
GR-7: Install Accessible Route from Road Level to Battery Granger terreplein	Coordinate with safety railing treatment	2 - plan for future action
GR-8: Stabilize spalling concrete surfaces and repair cracks and voids		1 - high priority for action
GR-9: Repair and seal horizontal concrete surfaces to reduce water infiltration	Implement after concrete surface defects have been repaired	1 - high priority for action
GR-10: Repair and repaint ferrous metal fixtures		2 - plan for future action

Figure 5.63. Battery Granger, circa 1900. Note the growth of woody vegetation beyond the limits of the engineered slopes. Great effort was made to disturb as little pre-existing vegetation in front of the battery as possible in order to conceal the structure from enemy fire (GATE 7778).

Figure 5.64. View looking north at emplacement #1 and battery commander's station, Battery Granger. Battery Granger is accessed via Hudson Drive, left, and a chain-link fence and signage have been installed between the road and battery to warn visitors of potentially hazardous conditions. Eastern red cedars, right, are heavily concentrated at the interface of the engineered slope and the battery's concrete terreplein (Olmsted Center, January 2009).

Figure 5.65. Aerial photograph of Battery Granger, January 1933. This photograph indicates management of woody vegetation growing on the engineered slope forward of the battery (Coastal and Hydraulics Laboratory, Engineer Research and Development Center).

Figure 5.66. View looking northwest at engineered slope to rear of Battery Granger, host to large unmanaged woody vegetation (Olmsted Center, January 2009).

Figure 5.67. View looking southeast at Battery Granger. This image shows three large hackberry (*Celtis occidentalis*) trees growing directly adjacent to the corner of the concrete structure (Olmsted Center, January 2009).

Figure 5.68. Blocked view northeastward from the battery commander's station at Battery Granger. Blocked downrange views to the water makes it difficult for park visitors to understand the historic operation of these coastal defense sites. Note corrosion of ferrous metal building features (Olmsted Center, January 2009).

Figure 5.69. Existing safety railings, Battery Granger. At this location and elsewhere throughout Sandy Hook's coastal defense sites, one can see the tangible history of maintenance and repair. This simple railing may be retrofitted with either infill mesh panels or otherwise with woven wire mesh applied with clamps and hardware to satisfy life-safety codes (Olmsted Center, January 2009).

Figure 5.70. Close-up view of existing concrete terreplein, Battery Granger. Existing conditions indicate that joints between concrete panels were once sealed with bituminous material. With the passage of time, this sealant material requires maintenance (Olmsted Center, January 2009).

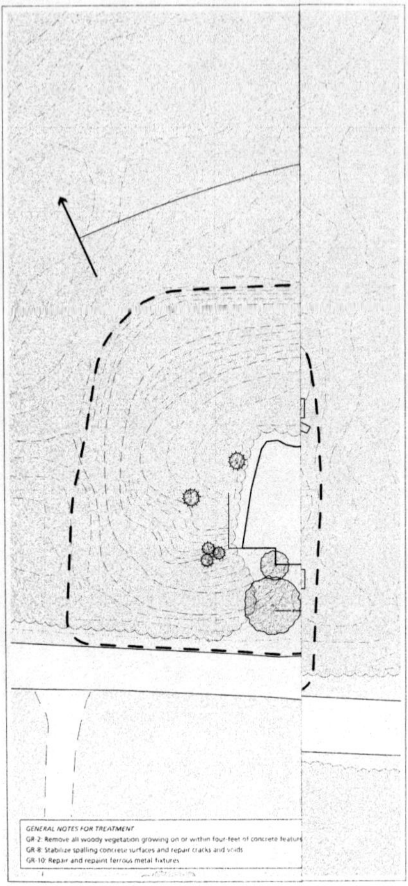

Cultural Landscape Report for the Sandy Hook Coastal Defense Batteries

Gateway National Recreation Area
Sandy Hook, New Jersey

Battery Granger Treatment Plan

Olmsted Center

National Park Service
Olmsted Center for Landscape Preservation
www.nps.gov/oclp

SOURCES

1. Sandy Hook GIS Data
2. Sandy Hook Color Ortho Imagery, Captured 2006
3. Topographic Sheets, prepared by Denver Service Center, 1992
4. Topographic Maps, prepared by Carrera and Associates, 1990
5. Field Inventory, Olmsted Center for Landscape Preservation, January 2009

DRAWN BY

Tim Layton, AutoCAD 2002, Illustrator CS3, 2009

LEGEND

Canopy Vegetation
Paved Road / Walk
Unpaved Road / Walk
Deciduous Tree
Evergreen Tree
Fence
Scope of Treatment

NOTES

1. Contour interval = 1'-0"
2. Plan represents landscape conditions inventoried in January 2009
3. All features shown in approximate scale and location

0' 8.75' 17.5' 35'

Drawing 5.6

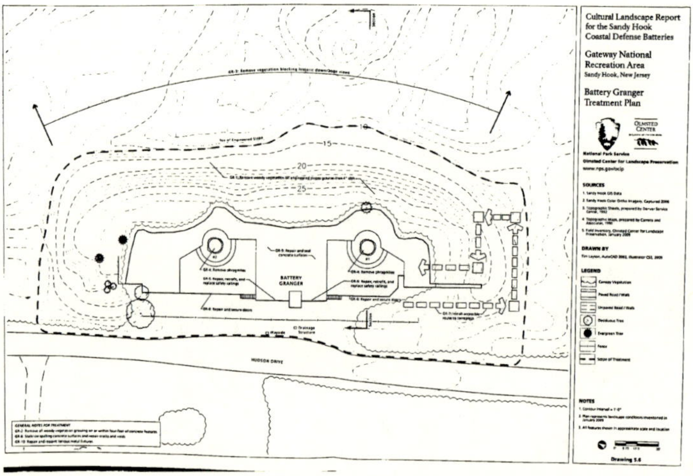
Cultural Landscape Report for the Sandy Hook Coastal Defense Batteries
Gateway National Recreation Area
Sandy Hook, New Jersey
Battery Granger Treatment Plan
Olmsted Center
National Park Service
SOURCES
DRAWN BY
LEGEND
NOTES
BATTERY GRANGER
HUDSON DRIVE
15
20
25
Drawing 5.6

MORTAR BATTERY (SH-349)

Construction began in 1890 on the Mortar Battery, the first completed and operational concrete mortar battery in United States.[33] The battery contained four mortar pits, each with four twelve-inch mortars, protected by earth and sand that rose almost thirty-five feet above them (Figure 5.71). Lacking a direct view to their targets on the water, the Army constructed telephone data booths above each of the four mortar pits in 1905.[34] The booths received instructions from control structures on top of Battery Potter and relayed the information to artillery crews who positioned the mortars accordingly.

Following World War I, the Mortar Battery was disarmed because the range of its artillery could not engage ships equipped with more powerful guns. Between 1922 and 1923, two anti-aircraft guns were mounted on top of the engineered earthwork and a third was added circa 1937. During World War II, the tunnels that connected the mortars and stored ammunition were converted into the New York Harbor Defense Command Post (HDCP). The HDCP coordinated coastal defenses from Long Island to Atlantic City, New Jersey.

Located east of Hudson Road and opposite the Sandy Hook Lighthouse, the Mortar Battery is accessed through an opening in the perimeter wall that leads to the southwest battery. A gravel and wood-chip surfaced trail parallels the perimeter wall and offers access to the northwest battery as well. Efflorescence can be seen on some of the vertical surfaces and spalling is present on both horizontal and vertical surfaces of the mortars. Vegetation emerges from the broken and cracked concrete surfaces and large woody vegetation is present on the engineered earthwork. The park has installed fencing to discourage visitors from climbing up the engineered earthwork and fencing is also located along closed trails at the top of the structure.

TREATMENT TASKS

Vegetation Management Treatment Tasks

MB-1: Remove woody vegetation greater than four-inches diameter growing on engineered slopes

A mixture of vegetation presently grows on the engineered earthwork at the Mortar Battery including native and non-native vines and groundcovers, grasses, shrubs, and large woody vegetation (Figures 5.72 and 5.73). Large woody vegetation defines any deciduous or evergreen tree that has a trunk size greater than four-inches diameter at breast height. Given this size, a tree that topples over due to wind, rain, snow, or ice is likely to damage a portion of the engineered earthwork. Additionally, the tree roots can damage the concrete structures below the protective earthwork. In order to protect the historic earthwork, woody vegetation greater than four-inches diameter at breast height should be selectively removed and the stumps treated with a triclopyr herbicide. For the Mortar Battery, the area to be selectively cleared would be approximately 4.8 acres. Further information on vegetation removals and treatment can be found in the treatment tasks common to all battery sites.

MB-2: Remove all woody vegetation growing on or within four-feet of concrete structures and features

At the Mortar Battery, woody vegetation is growing in close proximity to concrete structures and is also emerging from spalling areas, cracks, and where leaf litter and debris have accumulated (Figures 5.74 and 5.75). The existing woody vegetation is either causing or has the potential to cause structural concrete problems. Given the harmful effect of woody vegetation in this situation, all woody vegetation growing on or within four-feet of concrete features should be removed. After removing the woody material, both deciduous and evergreen stumps should be treated with a triclopyr herbicide. Additional information on removing woody vegetation growing near and on structures can be found in the treatment tasks common to all battery sites.

Visitor Access Treatment Tasks

MB-3: Repair, retrofit, and replace safety railings

At the Mortar Battery, metal handrails line the steps that provided access to the telephone data booths. Metal railings in fair condition with visible rust should be chemically treated, primed, and painted to match the historic finish. Damaged or severely deteriorated railings should be removed and replaced with new components that match the original as close as possible. Additional information on metal treatments and adding infill or applied materials to comply with life safety codes can be found in the treatment tasks common to all battery sites.

MB-4: Close social trails and stabilize the eroded path south of southwest mortar

An eroded path presently heads up the engineered earthwork south of the gallery to the southwest mortar pit. Additional social trails lead up and across the engineered earthwork. Both the path and trails should be closed in order to limit erosion and preserve the historic structure. Low-growing native shrubs should be planted at the top and bottom of a social trail to block access. Branches cut three to four feet in length should also be placed at the top and bottom of a trail to obscure the route. Additional information on appropriate plant species and erosion control measures can be found in the treatment tasks common to all battery sites.

MB-5: Install at-grade boardwalks in exterior access galleries to mortar pits

From the interior trail along the west perimeter wall, visitors may access the northwest or southwest mortar pits via concrete galleries. After heavy rains, standing water can be an issue in the galleries because the drainage system is not properly functioning. Please see treatment task MB-10 for additional information on improving the drainage system.

In order to improve visitor access to the northwest or southwest mortar pits, an at-grade boardwalk should be installed in the galleries. The boardwalk should be similar in construction to the boardwalk presented in treatment task 9G-9 for Nine Gun Battery (see Figure 5.51). However, since the walk will be six inches or less above the current surface and tall, concrete walls separate the galleries from the engineered earthworks, there is no need for a handrail.

For the base of the boardwalk, two-by-six pressure treated joists should be set on the existing concrete walkways to the mortar pits. The bottom of the joists may need to be scribed and cut to match the concrete surface and provide a level platform to attach the decking. The decking should be pressure treated or a wood or synthetic lumber product that resists rot. Deck boards should be set perpendicular to the joists and nailed or screwed with galvanized fasteners. At either edge of the decking, a two-inch tall wood bumper should be attached to delineate the extents of the walking surface. The boardwalk should only be a temporary solution to providing safe access in wet conditions to the mortar pits. After the drainage system is improved and standing water is no longer present, the boardwalk should be removed.

MB-6: Clear vegetation from former north access road

By 1942, an unpaved road was installed north of the Mortar Battery. The road proceeded east from Hudson Road and provided access to temporary structures located north and east of the battery. Presently, the road is almost entirely overtaken by vegetation and is barely passable as a trail (Figure 5.76). In order to rehabilitate a circulation feature from the historic period, vegetation should be cleared from the former access road and an unobstructed, twelve-foot wide route maintained. Woody vegetation should be cut as flush to ground level as possible. Since the trees are not growing on a historic engineered earthwork, the remaining stumps should be ground with a stump grinder to a depth of three inches below grade to minimize potential archeological disturbance. After the woody vegetation has been removed, the twelve-foot width can be easily maintained with a small tractor and brush hog mowing deck. Rehabilitating the access road will aid in accomplishing other treatment tasks at the Mortar Battery by providing an area away from primary circulation routes for vehicles and staging.

Battery Structures Treatment Tasks

MB-7: Stabilize spalling concrete surfaces and repair cracks and voids

Concrete surfaces at the Mortar Battery exhibit spalling areas and cracks resulting from water infiltration and freeze-thaw cycles (see Figure 5.75). In order to limit further damage to the concrete, spalling surfaces should be removed, mechanically cleaned, and patched to match the character of the historic material. Small cracks should be dried and prepared to receive a sealant that is compatible with the character of the historic concrete. The treatment of large, structural cracks should be determined by a structural engineer. Additional information addressing the repair of spalling areas and cracks can be found in the treatment tasks common to all battery sites and in the *Historic Fortification Preservation Handbook* (Washington State Parks and Recreation Commission, 2003).

MB-8: Repair and seal horizontal concrete surfaces to reduce water infiltration

In order to reduce water infiltration and to protect the concrete structures at the Mortar Battery, a surface coating should be applied to the horizontal surfaces. Application of a surface coating must occur after spalling and cracked concrete surfaces are repaired and defected surfaces that collect and pool rainwater are corrected. Additional information penetrating sealers and surface sealers can be found in the treatment tasks common to all battery sites. At the Mortar Battery, approximately 8,900 square feet of concrete should be sealed.

MB-9: Repair and repaint ferrous metal fixtures

A variety of ferrous metal fixtures were incorporated into the construction of the Mortar Battery. Metal fixtures in fair condition with visible rust should be chemically treated, primed, and painted to match the historic finish. Damaged or severely deteriorated fixtures should be removed and replaced with new components that match the original as close as possible. Additional information on ferrous metal treatments can be found in the Safety Railings section of the treatment tasks common to all battery sites and in the *Historic Fortification Preservation Handbook* (Washington State Parks and Recreation Commission, 2003).

MB-10: Improve drainage to minimize standing water in mortar pits and access ways

The four mortar pits were recessed into an engineered earthwork that rose approximately thirty-five feet above each pit's concrete platform. As a result, the mortar pits were low points that could collect water and surface runoff. In order to remove any water, the Army designed and installed a system of drain inlets, catch basins, and the underground lines. Today, the drainage system is not properly functioning and standing water in the mortar pits and access ways damages the historic structure and limits visitor access.

In order to improve drainage and minimize standing water, the existing drain inlets and structures should be cleaned out. Drainage lines should be flushed with pressurized water at 150 psi to remove any accumulated debris. If existing cast iron or vitrified clay pipes have collapsed, the area of the identified failure should be carefully excavated and the pipe replaced with schedule 40 PVC or ADS N-12 pipe. Both schedule 40 PVC and ADS N-12 are designed to withstand vehicular loads and are commonly used in drainage applications. Repairs, improvements, and supplements to the existing historic drainage system should be designed by a qualified engineer advised by a historical architect.

TABLE 5.7: SUMMARY OF TREATMENT RECOMMENDATIONS, THE MORTAR BATTERY		
Rehabilitation Task	**Notes**	**Priority for Action** 1 - high priority 2 - medium priority 3 - low priority, but requires ongoing monitoring 4 - no action
MB-1: Remove woody vegetation greater than four-inches diameter growing on engineered slopes		1 – high priority for action
MB-2: Remove all woody vegetation growing on or within four-feet of concrete features		1 – high priority for action
MB-3: Repair, retrofit, and replace safety railings	Can be implemented as part of a multiple battery or park-wide battery project	2 – plan for future action
MB-4: Close social trails and stabilize the eroded path west of southwest battery		1 – high priority for action
MB-5: Install at-grade boardwalk in exterior access corridor	Provides immediate improvement for visitor access. Boardwalk should be removed if drainage tasks detailed in MB-10 eliminate standing water	1 – high priority for action
MB-6: Clear vegetation from former north access road		2 – plan for future action
MB-7: Stabilize spalling concrete surfaces and repair cracks and voids		1 – high priority for action
MB-8: Repair and seal horizontal concrete surfaces to reduce water infiltration	Implement after concrete surface defects have been repaired	1 - high priority for action
MB-9: Repair and repaint ferrous metal fixtures		2 – plan for future action
MB-10: Improve drainage to minimize standing water in gun pits and access ways		1 - high priority for action

Figure 5.71. Oblique aerial photograph of the Mortar Battery, circa 1917, taken from an Army Signal Corps balloon. Note the low, scrub vegetation growing on the Mortar Battery's engineered landform (GATE 7870).

Figure 5.72. View looking northwest above mortar pit, the Mortar Battery. Woody vegetation greater than four-inches diameter should be removed from engineered slopes, and all woody trees and shrubs must not be allowed to grow upon, or within four-feet of a concrete structure or feature (Olmsted Center, January 2009).

Figure 5.73. View looking northeast along interior trail, the Mortar Battery. In order to protect the historic earthwork, woody vegetation greater than four-inches diameter at breast height should be selectively removed (Olmsted Center, January 2009).

Figure 5.74. View looking northwest along interior trail, the Mortar Battery. Given the harmful effect of woody vegetation growing in close proximity to concrete structures, all woody vegetation growing on or within four feet of concrete features should be removed (Olmsted Center, January 2009).

Figure 5.75. View looking southeast at concrete glacis, the Mortar Battery. Here, a tree greater than four-inches in diameter is seen growing directly upon the concrete battery surfaces. Such vegetation must be removed in the interest of long-term preservation of the battery structures (Olmsted Center, April 2008).

Figure 5.76. View looking northwest at trail north of the Mortar Battery. By 1942, an unpaved road was installed north of the Mortar Battery that presently is overtaken by vegetation and is barely passable as a trail. Vegetation should be cleared from this former access road and an unobstructed route maintained (Olmsted Center, January 2009).

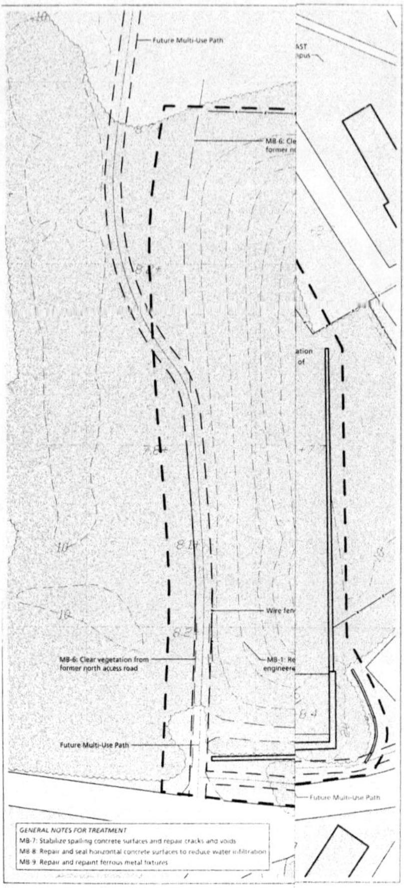

Cultural Landscape Report for the Sandy Hook Coastal Defense Batteries

Gateway National Recreation Area

Sandy Hook, New Jersey

Mortar Battery Treatment Plan

National Park Service

Olmsted Center for Landscape Preservation

www.nps.gov/oclp

SOURCES

1. Sandy Hook GIS Data
2. Sandy Hook Color Ortho Imagery, Captured 2006
3. Topographic Sheets, prepared by Denver Service Center, 1992
4. Topographic Maps, prepared by Carrera and Associates, 1990
5. Field Inventory, Olmsted Center for Landscape Preservation, January 2009

DRAWN BY

Tim Layton, AutoCAD 2002, Illustrator CS3, 2009

LEGEND

Canopy Vegetation

Paved Road / Walk

Unpaved Road / Walk

Trail

Fence

Utility Pole

Scope of Treatment

NOTES

1. Contour interval = 5'-0"
2. Plan represents landscape conditions inventoried in January 2009
3. All features shown in approximate scale and location

PLAN NORTH

0' 15' 30' 60'

Drawing 5.7

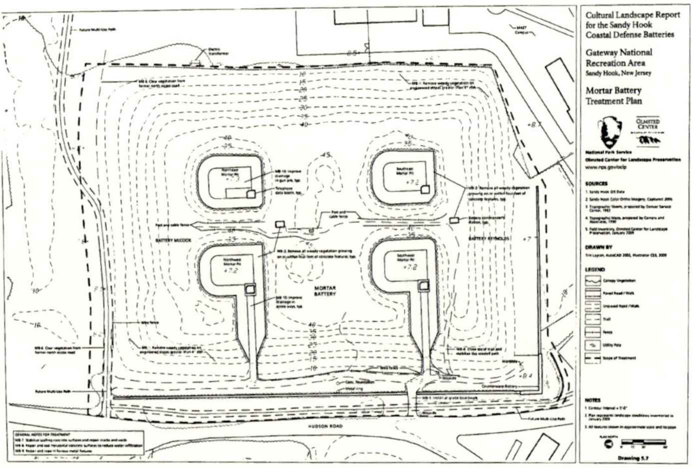
Cultural Landscape Report
for the Sandy Hook
Coastal Defense Batteries
Gateway National
Recreation Area
Sandy Hook, New Jersey
Mortar Battery
Treatment Plan
National Park Service
Olmsted Center for Landscape Preservation
www.nps.gov/oclp
SOURCES
DRAWN BY
LEGEND
NOTES
MORTAR BATTERY
BATTERY MCCOOK
BATTERY REYNOLDS
HUDSON ROAD
Drawing 5.7

BATTERY GUNNISON (SH-337)

Battery Gunnison joined Battery Urmston, Morris, Engle, and Peck as the fifth rapid-fire gun battery at Sandy Hook. The Army completed construction in 1904 and the following year, emplaced two six-inch guns that were mounted on counterweight carriages (Figure 5.77). In 1943, the Army decided to install the faster-firing barbette carriages and guns from Battery Peck at Battery Gunnison. In order to mount Battery Peck's guns, concrete was added to fill the gun platform area to the top of the parapet wall. Once the new guns were installed, Battery Granger was re-designated New Battery Peck. Following World War II, the battery was deactivated. The six-inch guns were replaced in 1948 with similar artillery that remains in place today.[35]

Presently, park infrastructure is located in close proximity to Battery Gunnison and includes Parking Lot G and a trio of buildings for visitors heading to Gunnison Beach. A concrete walk parallels the route to the beach and gently winds towards Battery Gunnison's gun platform #2. Recent vegetation clearing has been conducted near the battery, however, large woody vegetation remains on the engineered earthwork and obscures downrange views. Concrete surfaces display efflorescence and spalling areas consistent with long-term water infiltration. Handrails are installed along the stairs leading up to the guns platforms and guardrails are located around platforms themselves. The railings are in good condition, but contain large openings that do not provide safety for all visitors (Figure 5.78).

TREATMENT TASKS

Vegetation Management Treatment Tasks

GU-1: Remove woody vegetation greater than four-inches diameter growing on engineered slopes

A mixture of vegetation presently grows on the engineered earthwork at Battery Gunnison including native and non-native vines and groundcovers, grasses, shrubs, and large woody vegetation. Large woody vegetation defines any deciduous or evergreen tree that has a trunk size greater than four-inches diameter at breast height. Given this size, a tree that topples over due to wind, rain, snow, or ice is likely to damage a portion of the engineered earthwork. Additionally, the tree roots can damage the concrete structures below the protective earthwork. In order to protect the historic earthwork, woody vegetation greater than four-inches diameter at breast height should be selectively removed and the stumps treated with a triclopyr herbicide. For Battery Gunnison, the area to be selectively cleared would be approximately 0.5

acres. Further information on vegetation removals and treatment can be found in the treatment tasks common to all battery sites.

GU-2: Remove all woody vegetation growing on or within four-feet of concrete features

At Battery Gunnison, woody vegetation is growing in close proximity to concrete structures. The existing woody vegetation is either causing or has the potential to cause structural concrete problems. Given the harmful effect of woody vegetation in this situation, all woody vegetation growing on or within four-feet of concrete features should be removed. After removing the woody material, both deciduous and evergreen stumps should be treated with a triclopyr herbicide. Additional information on removing woody vegetation growing near and on structures can be found in the treatment tasks common to all battery sites.

GU-3: Remove vegetation blocking historic downrange views

Unobstructed views were necessary from the artillery and battery commander's stations at Battery Gunnison in order to have a clear field of fire and to locate and acquire the range of potential targets. After removing woody vegetation growing on the engineered earthwork and from the battery structure itself, the resulting downrange views to the water must be evaluated (see Figure 5.78). In some instances tall, individual woody vegetation that blocks the view shed should be identified and removed. Further information on managing vegetation for downrange views can be found in the treatment tasks common to all battery sites.

GU-4: Close social trail and stabilize erosion southeast of emplacement #1

A social trail heads southeast from emplacement #1 and terminates at the toe of the engineered slope. The trail does not connect to another circulation feature and should be closed in order to limit erosion and preserve the historic earthwork. Low-growing native shrubs should be planted at the top and bottom of a social trail to block access. Branches cut three to four feet in length should also be placed at the top and bottom of a trail to obscure the route. Additional information on appropriate plant species and erosion control measures can be found in the treatment tasks common to all battery sites.

Visitor Access Treatment Tasks

GU-5: Repair, retrofit, and replace safety railings

At Battery Gunnison, metal handrails line the steps that provided access from the ground level to the batteries. Metal guardrails are also installed near the open sides of elevated areas such as gun platforms (see Figure 5.78). Metal railings in fair condition with visible rust should be chemically treated, primed, and painted to match the historic finish. Damaged or severely deteriorated railings should be removed and replaced with new components that match the original as close as possible. Additional information on metal treatments and adding infill or applied materials to comply with life safety codes can be found in the treatment tasks common to all battery sites.

GU-6: Construct new visitor trail between emplacements #1 and #2

Visitors viewing the artillery at either emplacement #1 or #2 currently have to retrace their steps and walk down from a gun platform, cross behind the battery, and climb up a set of stairs in order to view the opposite emplacement. In order to create a continuous route for visitors at Battery Gunnison, a new trail should be constructed between emplacements #1 and #2. Starting at emplacement #1, the trail should begin at the parapet wall south of a raised concrete apron. The trail should continue in a gentle arc approximately five feet east of the battery and meet the parapet wall at emplacement #2 north of a raised concrete apron. The east side of the new trail should be heavily planted with low-growing native shrubs to discourage visitors from exiting the designated route and creating new social trails across the engineered earthwork (Drawing 5.8).

Battery Structures Treatment Tasks

GU-7: Stabilize spalling concrete surfaces and repair cracks and voids

Concrete surfaces at Battery Gunnison exhibit spalling areas and cracks resulting from water infiltration and freeze-thaw cycles. In order to limit further damage to the concrete, spalling surfaces should be removed, mechanically cleaned, and patched to match the character of the historic material. Small cracks should be dried and prepared to receive a sealant that is compatible with the character of the historic concrete. The treatment of large, structural cracks should be determined by a structural engineer. Additional information addressing the repair of spalling areas and cracks can be found in the treatment tasks common to all battery sites and in the *Historic Fortification Preservation Handbook* (Washington State Parks and Recreation Commission, 2003).

GU-8: Repair and seal horizontal concrete surfaces to reduce water infiltration

In order to reduce water infiltration and to protect the concrete structures at Battery Gunnison, a surface coating should be applied to the horizontal surfaces. Application of a surface coating must occur after spalling and cracked concrete surfaces are repaired and defected surfaces that collect and pool rainwater are corrected. Additional information penetrating sealers and surface sealers can be found in the treatment tasks common to all battery sites. At Battery Gunnison, approximately 5,200 square feet of concrete should be sealed.

GU-9: Repair and repaint ferrous metal fixtures

A variety of ferrous metal fixtures were incorporated into the construction of Battery Gunnison. Metal fixtures in fair condition with visible rust should be chemically treated, primed, and painted to match the historic finish. Damaged or severely deteriorated fixtures should be removed and replaced with new components that match the original as close as possible. Additional information on ferrous metal treatments can be found in the Safety Railings section of the treatment tasks common to all battery sites and in the *Historic Fortification Preservation Handbook* (Washington State Parks and Recreation Commission, 2003).

TABLE 5.8: SUMMARY OF TREATMENT RECOMMENDATIONS, BATTERY GUNNISON		
Rehabilitation Task	**Notes**	**Priority for Action** 1 - high priority 2 - medium priority 3 - low priority, but requires ongoing monitoring 4 - no action
GU-1: Remove woody vegetation greater than four-inches diameter growing on engineered slopes		1 – high priority for action
GU-2: Remove all woody vegetation growing on or within four-feet of concrete features		1 – high priority for action
GU-3: Remove vegetation blocking historic downrange views		1 – high priority for action
GU-4: Stabilize erosion south of south gun platform		1 – high priority for action
GU-5: Repair, retrofit, and replace safety railings	Battery Gunnison is a good case study for safety railing treatment due to the battery's high visibility and potential for visitation from those accessing Gunnison Beach	1 – high priority for action
GU-6: Construct new visitor trail between emplacements #1 and #2		1 – high priority for action
GU-7: Stabilize spalling concrete surfaces and repair cracks and voids		1 – high priority for action
GU-8: Repair and seal horizontal concrete surfaces to reduce water infiltration	Implement after concrete surface defects have been repaired	1 – high priority for action
GU-9: Repair and repaint ferrous metal fixtures		2 – plan for future action

Figure 5.77. Battery Gunnison, circa 1941 prior to converting the battery to barbette mounted guns. Note the predominance of herbaceous vegetation at this time. Also note the weathered black paint on the concrete surfaces (GATE 7834).

Figure 5.78. View looking northeast at emplacement #2, Battery Gunnison. The Battery Gunnison landscape survives in a superior state of preservation compared with other battery sites on Sandy Hook. Open downrange views convey the character of the cultural landscape and the historic purpose of these defenses to visitors (Olmsted Center, January 2009).

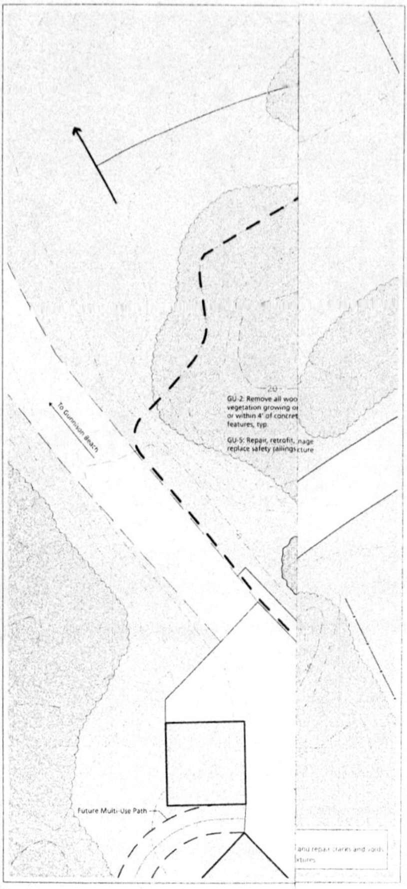

Cultural Landscape Report for the Sandy Hook Coastal Defense Batteries

Gateway National Recreation Area

Sandy Hook, New Jersey

Battery Gunnison Treatment Plan

OLMSTED CENTER

National Park Service

Olmsted Center for Landscape Preservation

www.nps.gov/oclp

SOURCES

1. Sandy Hook GIS Data
2. Sandy Hook Color Ortho Imagery, Captured 2006
3. Topographic Sheets, prepared by Denver Service Center, 1992
4. Topographic Maps, prepared by Carrera and Associates, 1990
5. Field Inventory, Olmsted Center for Landscape Preservation, January 2009

DRAWN BY

Tim Layton, AutoCAD 2002, Illustrator CS3, 2009

LEGEND

- Canopy Vegetation
- Paved Road / Walk
- Unpaved Road / Walk
- Trail
- Deciduous Tree
- Fence
- Scope of Treatment

NOTES

1. Contour interval = 2'-0"
2. Plan represents landscape conditions inventoried in January 2009
3. All features shown in approximate scale and location

0' 7.5' 15' 30'

Drawing 5.8

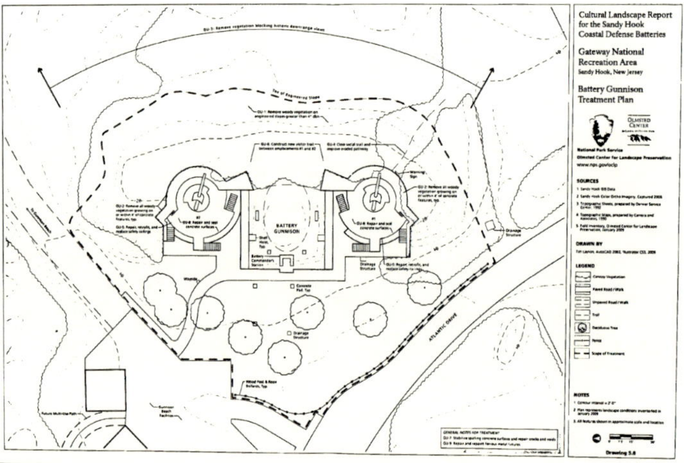
BATTERY GUNNISON
ATLANTIC DRIVE
Cultural Landscape Report for the Sandy Hook Coastal Defense Batteries
Gateway National Recreation Area
Sandy Hook, New Jersey
Battery Gunnison Treatment Plan
National Park Service
Olmsted Center for Landscape Preservation
www.nps.gov/oclp
SOURCES
DRAWN BY
LEGEND
NOTES
Drawing 5.8

BATTERIES KINGMAN AND MILLS (SH-441 AND 440)

The last large caliber gun batteries constructed at Sandy Hook were batteries Kingman and Mills. The Army completed masonry construction of the batteries 1917 and armed them in 1919 with twelve-inch guns. The guns were emplaced on open, circular platforms and had a 360-degree field of fire (Figure 5.79). The artillery more than doubled the range of earlier large caliber guns and stood on the western side of the peninsula, further away from potential enemy fire.[16] Between 1941 and 1942, the open gun platforms at batteries Kingman and Mills were casemated to protect the guns from aerial bombing (Figure 5.80). The casemated dates appear inscribed on concrete bulkheads even though the batteries were originally constructed twenty-five years earlier. Following World War II, both batteries were disarmed in 1948.

Currently, the most striking feature of the two batteries is their forty-foot tall earthen mounds that rise in stark contrast to the flat, slightly undulating coastal topography around them (Figure 5.81). Large woody vegetation and a thick understory of vines cover the engineered earthen casemates. Above the gun emplacements at batteries Kingman and Mills, concrete canopies were constructed to shield the artillery from overhead fire. The canopies and concrete facades around the emplacement openings show efflorescence and in some cases, large spalling areas. The park has installed a six-foot high chain-link fence above each gun emplacement to prevent unauthorized access to the concrete canopies and injury from a fall.

BATTERY KINGMAN TREATMENT TASKS

Vegetation Management Treatment Tasks

KI-1: Remove woody vegetation greater than four-inches diameter growing on engineered slopes

The two 12-inch guns at Battery Kingman were originally emplaced on open platforms that permitted 360-degrees of rotation and firing (see Figure 5.79). Between 1941 and 1942, the emplacements were casemated with concrete structures and covered with enough protective sand and earth to cover a three-story building. World War II-era photographs show the vegetation immediately around the gun and on the earthen casemate above was a low growing turf mixture.

Restoring the earthen casemate to a turf mixture is not a practical treatment and would create new maintenance challenges for the park. In order to preserve the historic earthwork and concrete structures below, all woody vegetation greater than four-inches diameter at breast height should be removed. For Battery Kingman, the area to be selectively cleared would be approximately 3.7 acres (Drawing 5.9, scope of treatment).

KI-2: Remove all woody vegetation growing on or within four-feet of concrete features

In comparison to the disappearing gun batteries, Battery Kingman does not as high a quantity of exposed concrete structures. Concrete facades, canopies to shield the gun emplacements, sloped glacises that meet the earthen casement, and bulkhead entries on the west side are all present and threatened by woody vegetation growing on them or nearby (Figure 5.82). As discussed in the general treatment recommendations, all woody vegetation growing on or within four-feet of concrete features should be removed and treated with a triclopyr herbicide to inhibit resprouting and kill the root system.

KI-3: Clear overgrowth external to gun battery in area of gun traverse/field of fire

Two 12-inch guns were emplaced at Battery Kingman and the barrel of each gun was nearly forty feet long. In order to rotate the gun into position and set its firing trajectory, the vegetation immediately around the platform had to be low growing. A 1940s photograph of the north gun platform shows the vegetation immediately around the gun and on the earthen casemate above was a low growing turf mixture (Figure 5.83).

Restoring a turf mix across the entire earthwork is not a practical treatment and would create new maintenance challenges for the park. To visually convey the space required to operate the battery's 12-inch guns, the recommendation is to clear tree and shrub vegetation immediately around the gun platform. This clearing effort needs to focus on the slopes against the battery's concrete facades as the level area in front of the guns is relatively free of tree and shrub vegetation (Figure 5.84).

To remove Japanese honeysuckle (*Lonicera japonica*), greenbrier (*Smilax* sp.), and poison ivy (*Toxicodendron radicans*), the park may consider using tended or supervised goats enclosed within temporary fencing that the herbivores may consume the vines and other vegetation. Gateway National Recreation Area has successfully used goats at Battery Duane in the Staten Island Unit and the same treatment could be considered at batteries Kingman and Mills.

With the overgrown vegetation removed, a low-maintenance, perennial, native grass such as switch grass (*Panicum virgatum*) should be planted. Once established, switch grass competes very well against invasive species and provides excellent food and cover for wildlife. To help establish the new plantings, erosion control fabric should be used on slopes greater than 4:1.

Visitor Access Treatment Tasks

KI-4: Maintain chain-link fences above casemate canopies to prevent unauthorized access and visitor injuries

Above both gun emplacements at Battery Kingman, concrete canopies shield the artillery from overhead fire. The canopies emerge from a concrete facade constructed in front of the emplacement. The engineered earthwork meets the top of the concrete facade and continues to rise at a 2:1 slope to an elevation approximately thirty-five feet above most of the surrounding area.

To prevent unauthorized access to the canopy and avoid injury due to the steep slope of the earthwork, the National Park Service installed a six-foot high chain-link fence above the concrete facade (Figure 5.85). As previously mentioned, visitor access is not planned for Battery Kingman. Although visitors are not supposed to have access, the chain-link fence should be maintained for added safety. Regular inspections should make sure the line posts are solid and securely anchored to the ground. The chain-link mesh should be inspected for any holes or other deficiencies. Both the posts and mesh should be repaired or replaced as conditions merit.

Battery Structures Treatment Tasks

KI-5: Stabilize spalling concrete surfaces and repair cracks and voids

Concrete surfaces at Battery Kingman exhibit spalling areas and cracks resulting from water infiltration and freeze-thaw cycles (see Figures 5.84 and 5.85). In order to limit further damage to the concrete, spalling surfaces should be removed, mechanically cleaned, and patched to match the character of the historic material. Small cracks should be dried and prepared to receive a sealant that is compatible with the character of the historic concrete. The treatment of large, structural cracks should be determined by a structural engineer. Additional information addressing the repair of spalling areas and cracks can be found in the treatment tasks common to all battery sites and in the *Historic Fortification Preservation Handbook* (Washington State Parks and Recreation Commission, 2003).

KI-6: Repair and seal horizontal concrete surfaces to reduce water infiltration

In order to reduce water infiltration and to protect the concrete structures at Battery Kingman, a surface coating should be applied to the horizontal surfaces. Application of a surface coating must occur after spalling and cracked concrete surfaces are repaired and defected surfaces that collect and pool rainwater are corrected. Additional information penetrating sealers and surface sealers can be found in the treatment tasks common to all battery sites. At Battery Kingman, approximately 975 square feet of concrete should be sealed.

KI-7: Repair and repaint ferrous metal fixtures

A variety of ferrous metal fixtures were incorporated into the construction of Battery Kingman. Metal fixtures in fair condition with visible rust should be chemically treated, primed, and painted to match the historic finish. Damaged or severely deteriorated fixtures should be removed and replaced with new components that match the original as close as possible. Additional information on ferrous metal treatments can be found in the Safety Railings section of the treatment tasks common to all battery sites and in the *Historic Fortification Preservation Handbook* (Washington State Parks and Recreation Commission, 2003).

KI-8: Cap and seal concrete pipe on northern end of battery to prevent injury and reduce water damage

In addition to the animal burrow, a vertically set concrete pipe was observed on the northern end of Battery Kingman. The pipe protruded slightly above finish grade and was positioned north of the north gun emplacement (Figure 5.86). A 1944 plan prepared for the Army Corps of Engineers's *Report of Completed Works* does not show a structure or below-ground room that would correspond to this concrete pipe (see Figure 2.76). It may have served as a ventilation shaft and based on observations during the field review, appears to run down a considerable distance from finish grade.

Even though visitor access is not planned for Battery Kingman, the concrete pipe should be capped and sealed to prevent possible injury and reduce water entering into or around the underground structures. An ABS plastic cap with non-corrosive, vandal-resistant hardware should be fitted over and secured to the concrete pipe. The top of the cap should be pitched to prevent water and ice from building up (Figure 5.87).

KI-9: Repair animal burrow on northern end of battery

During on-site review of the gun batteries at Sandy Hook, no evidence was observed of animal disturbance to the historic earthworks accept at Battery Kingman. On the northern end of the battery, a burrow with excavated earth in front of it was discovered (Figure 5.88). Most likely a groundhog burrow, the animal's activities have destroyed a small portion of the historic earthwork. The damage should be repaired and efforts made to stop future damage to the earthwork.

The preferred management recommendation for groundhogs and burrowing animals is to humanely trap the animal and relocate it to an area away from the historic earthwork. If this remedy does not work, extermination is the next option to pursue.[57] The burrow should be filled with soil from a sterile source that does not have the potential to damage archaeological information.[58]

BATTERY MILLS TREATMENT TASKS

Vegetation Management Treatment Tasks

MI-1: Remove woody vegetation greater than four-inches diameter growing on engineered slopes

Park staff recently undertook a woody vegetation removal project on the south end of Battery Mills. Their work targeted ailanthus (*Ailanthus altissima*)--the predominant woody species on this section of the battery. After cutting down the trees, the trunks and limbs were left in place on the historic earthwork (Figure 5.89). The fallen debris needs to be removed and any future removals should allow proper time and equipment for the trunks and limbs to be removed. The long-term preservation of the historic earthworks will require future inspection and removal of woody species greater than four-inches diameter. The frequency of inspections and removals should be increased to manage invasive non-native plant species such as ailanthus. In order to safely and effectively permit future inspections and removals, the trunks and limbs have to be removed. For Battery Mills, the area to be selectively cleared would be approximately 3.9 acres (Drawing 5.10, scope of treatment).

MI-2: Remove all woody vegetation growing on or within four-feet of concrete features

Like Battery Kingman, the concrete features at Battery Mills include concrete facades, canopies to shield the gun emplacements, sloped glacises that meet the earthen casement, and bulkhead entries on the west side (Figure 5.90). All woody vegetation growing on or within four-feet of these concrete features should be removed and treated with a triclopyr herbicide to kill the root system.

MI-3: Clear overgrowth external to gun battery in area of gun traverse/field of fire

Like Battery Kingman, Battery Mills once emplaced two 12-inch guns that required an unobstructed arc for positioning and setting their firing trajectory. A World War II-era photograph of Battery Mills has not been found to confirm the vegetation immediately around the gun and on the earthen casemate. However, Battery Mills and Kingman both appear on a 1943 plan entitled "Batteries Kingman and Mills, Alterations to Electrical Systems, General Plan and Index" and have identical layouts. Since their design is the same and not wanting to distinguish and draw attention to either battery, they arguably shared the same vegetation treatment. A 1940s photograph of Battery Kingman shows the vegetation immediately around the gun and on the earthen casemate above was a low growing turf mixture.

Restoring a turf mix across the entire earthwork is not a practical treatment and would create new maintenance challenges for the park. To visually convey the space required to operate the battery's 12-inch guns, the recommendation is to clear tree and shrub vegetation immediately around the gun platform. This clearing effort needs to focus on the slopes against the battery's concrete facades as the level area in front of the guns is relatively free of tree and shrub vegetation

To remove Japanese honeysuckle (*Lonicera japonica*), greenbrier (*Smilax* sp.), and poison ivy (*Toxicodendron radicans*), the park may consider using introduced goats in fenced areas to consume the vines and other vegetation. Gateway National Recreation Area has successfully used goats at Battery Duane in the Staten Island Unit and the same treatment might be effectively used at Battery Mills.

With the overgrown vegetation removed, a low-maintenance, perennial, native grass such as switch grass (*Panicum virgatum*) should be cultivated. Once established, switch grass competes very well against invasive species and provides excellent food and cover for wildlife. To help establish the new plantings, erosion control fabric should be used on slopes greater than 4:1.

MI-4: Remove Japanese knotweed (*Polygonum cuspidatum*) between northwestern side of battery and coastline

Recent storm activity has advanced the coastline towards the western side of Battery Mills. On the northwest side of the battery, the eroded and recently disturbed area has been colonized by Japanese knotweed (*Polygonum cuspidatum*) (Figure 5.91). Japanese knotweed has been identified as an invasive non-indigenous plant species by the New Jersey Department of Environmental Protection. Knotweed's smooth stalks are chambered and similar in appearance to bamboo. The stalks emerge in early spring and their dense growth prevents indigenous species from establishing. As a result, plant species diversity and wildlife habitat are reduced.[39]

The Japanese knotweed should be removed and one of the most effective strategies is to inject glyphosate herbicide into the lower nodes of the stalks. Stem injection has demonstrated better control of knotweed than other herbicide application methods and mechanical methods.[40] The injection method greatly reduces the possibility of herbicide drift that could occur with a foliar application and several companies offer injection tools (Figure 5.92). After initial treatment, the Japanese knotweed will need to be monitored and the process repeated for several seasons until the stand is removed.

Visitor Access Treatment Tasks

MI-5: Maintain chain-link fences above casemate canopies to prevent unauthorized access and injury

Between the first and second World Wars, Battery Mills and Kingman were improved with earthen casemates constructed over the gun emplacements. Like Battery Kingman, Battery Mills features concrete canopies that shielded the emplaced guns from overhead fire. The canopies project from a concrete facade and at the top of the facade, the engineered earthwork rises at a steep rate to an elevation approximately thirty-five feet above most of the surrounding area.

To prevent unauthorized access to the canopy and avoid injury due to the steep slope of the earthwork, the National Park Service installed a six-foot high chain-link fence above the concrete facade. Although visitors are not supposed to have access to Battery Mills, the chain-link fence should be maintained for added safety. Regular inspections should make sure the line posts are solid and securely anchored to the ground. The chain-link mesh should be inspected for any holes or other deficiencies. Both the posts and mesh should be repaired or replaced as conditions merit.

Battery Structures Treatment Tasks

MI-6: Stabilize spalling concrete surfaces and repair cracks and voids

Concrete surfaces at Battery Mills exhibit spalling areas and cracks resulting from water infiltration and freeze-thaw cycles. In order to limit further damage to the concrete, spalling surfaces should be removed, mechanically cleaned, and patched to match the character of the historic material. Small cracks should be dried and prepared to receive a sealant that is compatible with the character of the historic concrete. The treatment of large, structural cracks should be determined by a structural engineer. Additional information addressing the repair of spalling areas and cracks can be found in the treatment tasks common to all battery sites and in the *Historic Fortification Preservation Handbook* (Washington State Parks and Recreation Commission, 2003).

MI-7: Repair and seal horizontal concrete surfaces to reduce water infiltration

In order to reduce water infiltration and to protect the concrete structures at Battery Mills, a surface coating should be applied to the horizontal surfaces. Application of a surface coating must occur after spalling and cracked concrete surfaces are repaired and defected surfaces that collect and pool rainwater are corrected. Additional information penetrating sealers and surface sealers can be found in the treatment tasks common to all battery sites. At Battery Mills, approximately 975 square feet of concrete should be sealed.

MI-8: Repair and repaint ferrous metal fixtures

A variety of ferrous metal fixtures were incorporated into the construction of Battery Mills. Metal fixtures in fair condition with visible rust should be chemically treated, primed, and painted to match the historic finish. Damaged or severely deteriorated fixtures should be removed and replaced with new components that match the original as close as possible. Additional information on ferrous metal treatments can be found in the Safety Railings section of the treatment tasks common to all battery sites and in the *Historic Fortification Preservation Handbook* (Washington State Parks and Recreation Commission, 2003).

MI-9: Cap and seal concrete pipe on southern end of battery to prevent injury and reduce water damage

Similar to Battery Kingman, a vertically set concrete pipe was observed on the southern end of Battery Mills. The pipe protruded slightly above finish grade and was positioned south of the south gun emplacement. Unlike Battery Kingman, the concrete pipe at Battery Mills had a flanged end (Figure 5.93). A 1944 plan prepared for the Army Corps of Engineers's *Report of Completed Works* does not show a structure or below-ground room that would correspond to this concrete pipe (see Figure 2.77). It may have served as a ventilation shaft and based on observations during the field review, appears to run down a considerable distance from finish grade.

Even though visitor access is not planned for Battery Mills, the concrete pipe should be capped and sealed to prevent possible injury and reduce water entering into or around the underground structures. An ABS plastic cap with non-corrosive, vandal-resistant hardware should be fitted over and secured to the concrete pipe. The top of the cap should be pitched to prevent water and ice from building up.

MI-10: Install course stone soil revetment at the toe of the engineered slope on the battery's western side

Aerial photographs from 2002, 2003, and 2006 indicate a narrow road looping around Battery Mills. The western portion of this road, closest to Sandy Hook Bay, aligns with a railroad line that delivered ordnance to the battery and is shown on a 1944 Army Corps of Engineers map of Fort Hancock.

In the past three years, storm activity has eroded the western portion of the loop road and the coastline is advancing toward the engineered slope and concrete bulkheads that enter the battery (Figures 5.94).

To better respond to beach erosion, the park is currently installing and testing a sand-slurry system that can replenish eroded areas. Current plans are to deposit sand-slurry from the testing phase of the system on the western edge of Battery Mills. The addition of the sand-slurry will be helpful, however, to better protect the concrete structure and historic earthworks of Battery Mills randomly and loosely placed course stones should be installed at the toe of the battery's slope.

Placed at the toe of the slope, the course stones would be located at a minimum approximately thirty-five feet from the shore line observed in January 2009 (Drawing 5.10). Since the course stones would be inland from the shore, they would not interfere with normal tidal actions. The course stones would provide a needed layer of protection to the concrete structure and historic earthwork in the event of a major storm event or hurricane. Finally, placed course stones would be consistent with a component of the battery's historic appearance. A 1950s photograph indicates stacked stone walls were constructed near one of the battery's entries (Figure 5.95).

TABLE 5.9: SUMMARY OF TREATMENT RECOMMENDATIONS, BATTERY KINGMAN		
Rehabilitation Task	Notes	Priority for Action 1 - high priority 2 - medium priority 3 - low priority, but requires ongoing monitoring 4 - no action
KI-1: Remove woody vegetation greater than four-inches diameter growing on engineered slopes		1 – high priority for action
KI-2: Remove all woody vegetation growing on or within four-feet of concrete features		1 – high priority for action
KI-3: Clear overgrowth external to gun battery in area of gun traverse/ field of fire		1 – high priority for action
KI-4: Maintain chain-link fences above casemate canopies to prevent unauthorized access and visitor injuries		3 – requires ongoing monitoring of condition
KI-5: Stabilize spalling concrete surfaces and repair cracks and voids		1 – high priority for action
KI-6: Repair and seal horizontal concrete surfaces to reduce water infiltration	Implement after concrete surface defects have been repaired	1 - high priority for action
KI-7: Repair and repaint ferrous metal fixtures		2 – plan for future action
KI-8: Cap and seal concrete pipe on northern end of battery to prevent injury and reduce water damage		1 – high priority for action
KI-9: Repair animal burrow on northern end of battery		1 - high priority for action

TABLE 5.10: SUMMARY OF TREATMENT RECOMMENDATIONS, BATTERY MILLS		
Rehabilitation Task	**Notes**	**Priority for Action** 1 - high priority 2 - medium priority 3 - low priority, but requires ongoing monitoring 4 - no action
MI-1: Remove woody vegetation greater than four-inches diameter growing on engineered slopes		1 – high priority for action
MI-2: Remove all woody vegetation growing on or within four-feet of concrete features		1 – high priority for action
MI-3: Clear overgrowth external to gun battery in area of gun traverse/ field of fire		1 – high priority for action
MI-4: Remove Japanese knotweed (*Polygonum cuspidatum*) between northwestern side of battery and coastline		1 – high priority for action
MI-5: Maintain chain-link fences above casemate canopies to prevent unauthorized access and injury		3 – requires ongoing monitoring of condition
MI-6: Stabilize spalling concrete surfaces and repair cracks and voids		1 – high priority for action
MI-7: Repair and seal horizontal concrete surfaces to reduce water infiltration	Implement after concrete surface defects have been repaired	1 – high priority for action
MI-8: Repair and repaint ferrous metal fixtures		2 – plan for future action
MI-9: Cap and seal concrete pipe on southern end of battery to prevent injury and reduce water damage		1 – high priority for action
MI-10: Install course stone soil revetment at the toe of the engineered slope on the battery's western side	The next major storm event could irrevocably damage the historic earthwork	1 – high priority for action

Figure 5.79. View looking north of gun emplacements at Batteries Kingman and Mills. Prior to 1941, the guns were emplaced on open platforms that permitted 360-degrees of rotation and firing. The north emplacement at Mills is in the foreground and beyond that the south emplacement at Kingman (GATE 938).

Figure 5.80. View looking southwest at gun emplacement, Battery Kingman, circa 1940s. During World War II, the vegetation immediately in front of and directly above the casemate was maintained at a low height (GATE 8084).

Figure 5.81. View looking northeast at the Battery Kingman engineered landform. This photograph shows the size and quantity of woody vegetation growing on Battery Kingman's engineered slope. All woody vegetation greater than four-inches diameter at breast height should be selectively removed to preserve the historic structure and its sheltering earthwork (Olmsted Center, January 2009).

Figure 5.82. View looking south atop of the engineered slope, Battery Kingman. Here, a large tree is seen growing near an exposed concrete feature seen at the left foreground. Woody vegetation should not be permitted to grow on, or within four-feet of concrete battery structures and features (Olmsted Center, January 2009).

Figure 5.83. North gun emplacement, Battery Kingman, circa 1940s. This photograph shows the vegetation immediately around the gun emplacement and on the earthen casemate above was a low growing turf mixture ensuring the field of fire would not be obstructed (GATE 8085).

Figure 5.84. View looking northwest at the south gun emplacement, Battery Kingman. Vegetation removal to restore the historic field of fire should focus on the slopes against the battery's concrete facades as the level area in front of the guns is relatively free of tree and shrub vegetation (Olmsted Center, January 2009).

Figure 5.85. View looking southwest at north gun emplacement, Battery Kingman. Although visitors are warned of the hazards of accessing the summit of these batteries, existing chain-link fencing located above the concrete casemate canopies should be maintained for added safety at both Battery Kingman and Battery Mills (Olmsted Center, January 2009).

Figure 5.86. Concrete pipe on north slope of Battery Kingman. The concrete pipe should be capped to prevent possible injury and reduce water entering into or around the underground structures (Olmsted Center, January 2009).

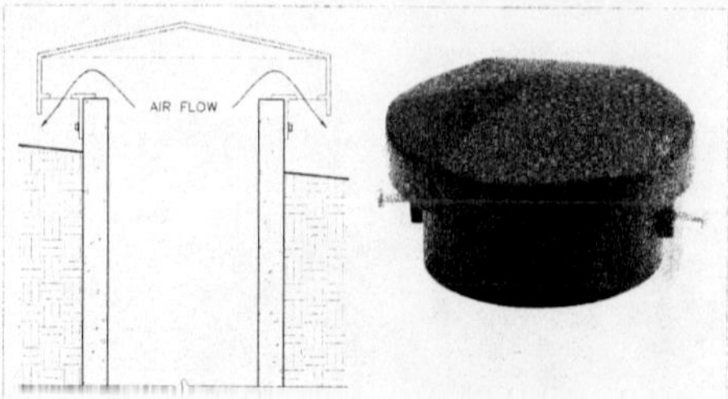

Figure 5.87. Installation of cap over concrete pipe and ABS plastic ventilation cap. The top of the cap should be pitched to prevent water and ice from building up. It should also be vented to allow air flow (Olmsted Center and http://www.toolstation.com/images/library/stock/webbig/22205.jpg).

Figure 5.88. Animal burrow on north slope of Battery Kingman. The preferred management recommendation for burrowing animals is to humanely trap the animal and relocate it to an area away from the historic earthwork. The burrow should be filled with soil from a sterile source that does not have the potential to damage archaeological information (Olmsted Center, January 2009).

Figure 5.89. View looking east at southern end of Battery Mills. After recent cutting to manage invasive non-indigenous plant species, trunks, limbs, and other fallen debris were not removed. In order to safely and effectively permit future inspections and removals, the trunks and limbs have to be removed (Olmsted Center, January 2009).

Figure 5.90. View looking east at a bulkhead entry, Battery Mills. All woody vegetation growing on or within four-feet of concrete features like the bulkhead entries should be removed (Olmsted Center, January 2009).

Figure 5.91. Japanese knotweed growing on western side of Battery Mills. The red dashed outline indicates the area of Japanese knotweed in this image. Japanese knotweed has been identified as an invasive non-indigenous plant species by the New Jersey Department of Environmental Protection and should be removed (Olmsted Center, January 2009).

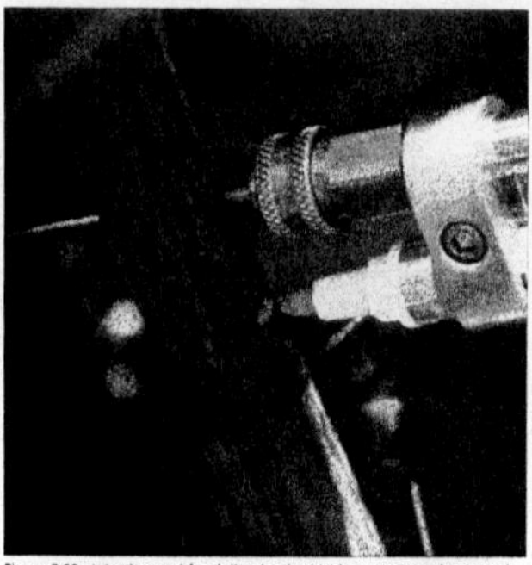

Figure 5.92. Injection tool for delivering herbicide to Japanese knotweed. One of the most effective strategies for controlling knotweed is to inject glyphosate herbicide into the lower nodes of the stalks. This image shows a proprietary injection tool with a marking attachment to indicate which plants have been treated (http://www.jkinjectiontools.com/methodinfo.php?method=steminjection).

Figure 5.93. Concrete pipe on southern slope of Battery Mills. The concrete pipe should be capped to prevent possible injury and reduce water entering into or around the underground structures (Olmsted Center, January 2009).

Figure 5.94. Eroded loop road on western side of Battery Mills. To better protect the concrete structures and historic earthworks of Battery Mills, randomly and loosely placed course stones should be installed at the toe of the battery's slope (Olmsted Center, January 2009).

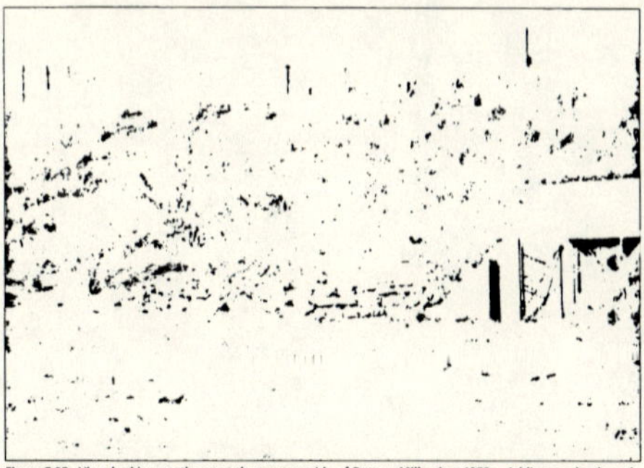

Figure 5.95. View looking northeast at the western side of Battery Mills, circa 1950s. Adding randomly and loosely placed course stones at the toe of the battery's slope would be consistent with a component of its historic appearance. This image shows a stacked stone wall near one of the battery's entries (GATE 20536).

Cultural Landscape Report
for the Sandy Hook
Coastal Defense Batteries

Gateway National
Recreation Area
Sandy Hook, New Jersey

Battery Mills
Treatment Plan

National Park Service

Olmsted Center for Landscape Preservation

SOURCES

1. Sandy Hook GIS Data
2. Sandy Hook Color Ortho Imagery, Captured 2006
3. Topographic Sheets, prepared by Denver Service Center, 1992
4. Topographic Sheets, prepared by Lockwood Kessler & Bartlett, 1976
5. Field Inventory, Olmsted Center for Landscape Preservation, January 2009

DRAWN BY

Tim Layton, AutoCAD 2002, Illustrator CS3, 2009

LEGEND

- Canopy Vegetation
- Unpaved Road / Walk
- Trail
- Deciduous Tree
- Evergreen Tree
- Fence
- 1944 Rail Line
- Scope of Treatment

NOTES

1. Contour Interval = 2'-0"
2. Plan represents landscape conditions inventoried in January 2009
3. All features shown in approximate scale and location

0' 15' 30' 60'

Drawing 5.10

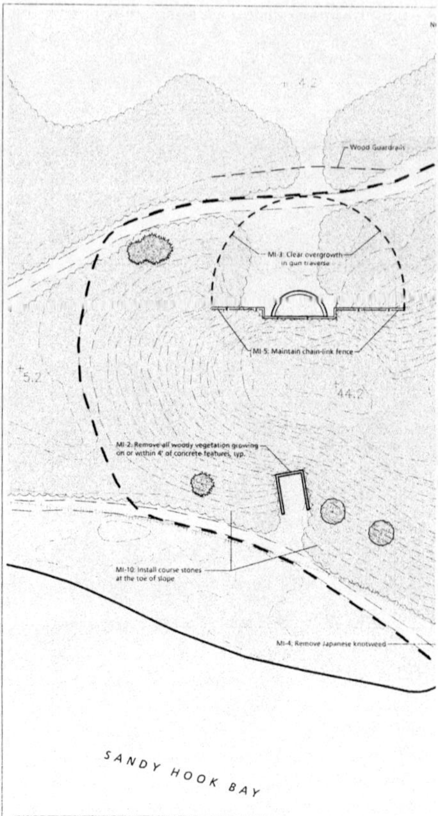

GENERAL NOTES FOR TREATMENT

MI-6: Stabilize spalling concrete surfaces and repair cracks and voids

MI-7: Repair and seal horizontal concrete surfaces to reduce water infiltration

MI-8: Repair and repaint ferrous metal fixtures

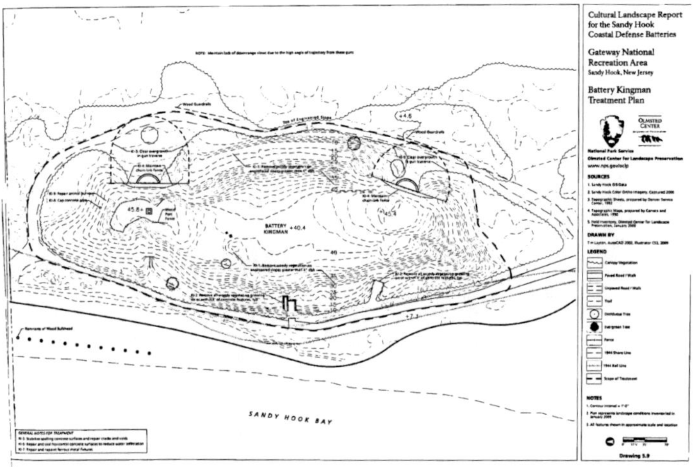
Cultural Landscape Report for the Sandy Hook Coastal Defense Batteries
Gateway National Recreation Area
Sandy Hook, New Jersey
Battery Kingman Treatment Plan
Olmsted Center
National Park Service
Olmsted Center for Landscape Preservation
www.nps.gov/oclp
SOURCES
DRAWN BY
LEGEND
NOTES
Drawing 5.9
BATTERY KINGMAN +40.4
45.8+
+4.6
+7.1
SANDY HOOK BAY

NIKE MISSILE BATTERY

The Army developed the NIKE missile battery to engage long-range bombers that emerged as a threat in the closing years of World War II. Sandy Hook's NIKE missile battery consisted of a launching complex, where the missiles were stored in underground magazines, and a radar tracking and control station with equipment for acquiring targets, tracking targets, and tracking the flight of outbound missiles. Sandy Hook's battery was one of the few dual battery sites built in the United States featuring two rows of missile launchers and two corresponding groups of radar. Construction was completed on the launch site in spring 1955 and on the radar site in 1956 (Figures 5.96 and 5.97).

The Army soon introduced a second-generation NIKE missile, known as the Hercules, and began modifying launch sites in 1958. Sandy Hook received the new missile and related enhancements to the radar site between 1961 and 1962. The development of intercontinental ballistic missiles, or ICBMs, shifted the threat away from the long range bombers the NIKE system was intended to stop. The Army deactivated the NIKE missile battery at Sandy Hook in 1971, concluding a history of coastal defenses that stretched back to the American Revolution.

The NIKE radar and launch sites are approximately a mile apart and located off of Hartshorne Drive, Sandy Hook's major north-south thoroughfare. The buildings and structures at both sites show early to intermediate signs of deterioration in specific building materials that include metal, concrete block, and corrugated siding and roofing (Figure 5.98). The radar towers feature guardrails around the tops of their platforms with large openings that would not adequately protect all visitors.

Beginning with deactivation of the sites, woody vegetation has encroached on buildings, vehicular and pedestrian circulation features, and the perimeter fences (Figure 5.99). Large woody vegetation also covers the majority of the engineered earthworks in the launch site (Figure 5.100). The radar site is open to volunteer-led tours on a regular schedule throughout the year. Tours of the launch site occur three or four times per year. Additionally, the NIKE launch site has become host to a variety of uses including park maintenance and law enforcement, a New Jersey state beach cleaning program, and academic research on weather, tides, and shellfish (Figures 5.101 and 5.102).

NIKE RADAR SITE TREATMENT TASKS

Vegetation Management Treatment Tasks

NR-1: Remove all woody vegetation growing on or within four-feet of buildings and structures

Consistent with the approach to vegetation management recommended for traditional gun battery sites found to the north, all woody vegetation should be removed to a minimum distance of four feet from buildings and structures. Beyond buildings themselves within the boundaries of the NIKE radar site, this recommendation would include fencing, roads, sidewalks and concrete pads.

During the NIKE radar site's years of operation, vegetation was strictly maintained among the buildings and structures in Control Area #1, Control Area #2, and the Ready Barracks (Figure 5.103). Currently, woody vegetation is well established and growing near radar platforms, barracks, and other auxiliary buildings. The vegetation's root systems threaten footings and foundations. Mold, mildew, and the accelerated deterioration of painted surfaces, siding, and roofing all result from vegetation blocking light and air movement at a building or structure.

To protect the buildings and structures at the NIKE radar site, all woody vegetation growing in a zone around Control Area #1, Control Area #2, and the Ready Barracks should be removed (Drawing 5.11). Deciduous stumps should be treated with a triclopyr herbicide to prevent root sprouts from emerging.

NR-2: Remove all woody vegetation six-feet off either side of circulation features

After the army abandoned the NIKE radar site and the property was transferred to the National Park Service, vegetation management that was a routine part of the site's maintenance was not addressed. Consequently, circulation features such as parking lots, access roads, sidewalks and a basketball court have become obscured with overgrown vegetation.

The park has recently removed some vegetation to reveal the historic sidewalks that once provided access between the control areas and the Ready Barracks. Further removal of woody vegetation is needed to protect the circulation features from future incursions. Asphalt and concrete-paved circulation features, as well as gravel-surfaced features, should have vegetation cleared a minimum of six-feet off of all sides of the feature (Figure 5.104). Large woody vegetation, particularly eastern red cedars (*Juniperus virginiana*), should be removed first. Once the large woody vegetation has been removed, the six foot width can be easily maintained with a small tractor and brush hog mowing deck.

NR-3: Remove all woody vegetation four-feet off either side of the perimeter fence

The extent of the NIKE radar site was clearly marked by a perimeter fence topped with barbed wire. The fence not only defined the site but secured it with access strictly controlled at gates located at Control Area #1, Control Area #2, and the Ready Barracks.

To verify security of the radar area, a site plan from 1954 indicates a fire break thirty-feet inside the perimeter fence. No vegetation was allowed to grow within this thirty-foot zone for security as well as fire prevention. Restoring the thirty-foot fire break is not practical and would create additional maintenance workload, however, the fence line and historic boundary of the site should be clearly delineated and maintained by removing all woody vegetation a minimum of four-feet off either side of the perimeter fence (Figure 5.105 and Drawing 5.11).

Large woody vegetation, particularly eastern red cedars (*Juniperus virginiana*), should be removed first. Once the large woody vegetation has been removed, the four-foot width can be easily maintained with a small tractor and brush hog mowing deck.

Visitor Access Treatment Tasks

NR-4: Install compatible stairway for safe access to radar platform

The park has expressed interest in opening up one of the radar platforms to visitors so that from an elevated position, visitors can better understand the layout of the radar site and take in the surrounding landscape. Based on existing elevations, it is recommended that the acquisition radar platform (Building 421) in Control Area #2 be rehabilitated for visitor access. This platform will give visitors the highest point in the radar site for viewing the area. In addition, Building 421 is close to two existing circulation features that presently facilitate, and a proposed project that will enhance convenient visitor access. Building 421 is approximately 200 feet east from Parking Lot L and the recently installed multi-use path. Current park planning proposes to create a loop off of the existing multi-use path that routes visitors through the radar site. The majority of the proposed loop follows existing roads in the radar site and will bring visitors directly to the base of Building 421.

Access to Building 421 is currently provided by a metal ladder running nearly vertical from ground level to the top of the platform. To provide safe access to the platform, a compatible stairway should be installed. The stairway should be designed with metal components matching the tubular railings used on the platform and finished in a matching color. The stairway should be located on the north side of the platform where it will be less conspicuous for visitors viewing the site from the parking lot and multi-use path to the west (Figure 5.106).

NR-5: Repair, retrofit, and replace safety railings

In addition to providing safe access up to the platform, safety needs to be improved for the guardrails at the top. Damaged or severely deteriorated rails and components should be removed and replaced with new components that match the original. The joints and connections of the existing guardrails should be inspected and properly tightened and secured. Corrosion should be removed or made inert with a chemical treatment and immediately followed with priming and painting to match the historic finish.[41]

To provide a higher level of protection, expanded metal mesh should cover the existing guardrail openings. On other radar platforms, expanded metal mesh is present at the lower level of the guardrail (Figure 5.107). The metal gauge and mesh spacing should match the existing sample. The new infill material should cover lower and upper guardrail openings and be attached to the inside of the rails with non-corrosive hardware. The clamps would permit easy replacement or removal and minimize damage to the guardrails.

NR-6: Relocate brick masonry stockpiles to Fort Hancock maintenance yard

Servicemen were not continuously stationed at the radar site but arrived at the facility from their Fort Hancock barracks when called into action. In the northwest corner of the radar site, west of the Ready Barracks, a gravel parking lot was installed to handling parking for the arriving servicemen (Figure 5.108).

Currently, the parking lot is the site of a stockpile of yellow brick of a type widely used in many of Fort Hancock's historic buildings. Since the area was never historically used for material storage and the brick is intended for buildings a mile and a half north of the radar site, the brick should be stacked on to palettes and moved to a storage location within the maintenance yard at Fort Hancock.

Battery Structures Treatment Tasks

NR-7: Stabilize Free-Standing Buildings

The control areas and Ready Barracks are defined by a collection of buildings and accompanying landscape features that were designed to identify, track, and guide NIKE missiles to aerial targets. Presently, the free-standing buildings are in a generally fair condition with some building materials showing signs of deterioration due to inadequate protection from the elements (see Figure 5.98). The radar towers, support buildings and barracks should be thoroughly inventoried in order to assess specific conditions and develop recommendations for building treatments beyond the scope of this report. In the interim, temporary measures to close and secure exterior openings and routine maintenance such as painting can provide short-term protection against the elements and help stabilize free-standing buildings. Equipment from the historic period currently exposed to the elements, such as the generator northwest of the Equipment Building (454), should be moved to a protected, interior location.

NR-8: Repair and replace chain-link fencing site-wide

The chain-link fencing found throughout the NIKE radar site is in serious disrepair, the material and fixtures having reached the end of their useful service life. Removing woody vegetation growing on either side and in many instances though the wire fabric will only make this advanced state of decay more apparent (see Figure 5.105). Owing to the fact that fencing material and hardware of this kind remains available in commerce, the entire fencing system should be replaced in-kind once the adjacent vegetation has been removed.

When replacing sections of the fencing system, new line posts should match the existing H-beam posts. The wire gauge and mesh opening should match the existing chain-link and all material and hardware should be galvanized to match the specifications of the original material.

A site plan from 1954 indicates the perimeter fence was type FE-6—a designation for chain-link with barbed wire on a single extension arm. The plan further illustrates that the fence was installed at roughly ten-feet in height with minor variations to account for existing grades and to maintain unobstructed lines of sight. The contractor was to excavate either side of the fence at a 2:1 slope in order to maintain the specified height (Figure 5.109). When replacing sections of the deteriorated fencing system, new line posts should match the existing H-beam posts. The wire gauge and mesh opening should match the existing chain-link and all material and hardware should be galvanized.

NR-9: Preserve historic light fixtures

Two sidewalks provided pedestrian access from the Ready Barracks to Control Area #1 and #2. Along these walks simple light fixtures—comprised of a tubular pole and metal reflector—were installed. The majority of light fixtures are in good to fair condition and should be periodically assessed (Figure 5.110).

Damaged or severely deteriorated components should be replaced. If necessary, new hardware and connectors should be fabricated to match the existing if a contemporary supplier cannot be found. Corrosion on the metal components should be removed or made inert with a chemical treatment and immediately followed with priming and painting to match the historic finish.

During site inspection, a historic light fixture near the Ready Barracks was seen haven fallen over (Figure 5.111). This fixture is located between buildings 404 and 405 which are presently two concrete slabs. The slabs would have supported barrack structures and therefore have building number designations.

The light fixture should be reset and will most likely require a new concrete footing to accomplish this task. Due to snowy conditions, it was difficult to determine at what point the fixture failed and fell over. Resetting the fixture may require a new tubular pole with adequate length to extend into the footing below ground. The new pole should match the existing in material, dimensions, and finishing. The fixture's other components should be inspected at this time and repaired or replaced based on their condition.

NIKE LAUNCH SITE TREATMENT TASKS

Vegetation Management Treatment Tasks

NL-1: Remove woody vegetation greater than four-inches diameter growing on engineered slopes

Following an approach consistent with to that recommended for the Sandy Hook gun batteries, woody vegetation should be removed a distance of at least four feet from engineered slopes. Rather than the earthen shielding forward of the batteries found to the north, at the NIKE launch site, engineered slopes include the portion of the access road built upon a ramped fill section ascending from the barracks area to the level of the launch platform. At this mid-twentieth century site, engineered slopes also include the earthen traverses surrounding the Warhead Building and the slopes adjacent to the launch area.

NL-2: Remove all woody vegetation growing on or within four-feet of buildings and structures

Also consistent with the approach to vegetation management recommended for more traditional gun battery sites, all woody vegetation should be removed to a minimum distance of four feet from buildings and structures. Beyond buildings themselves, this would include fencing, roads and concrete pads.

When the army actively used launch area, the vehicular connection between the barracks to the west and Missile Magazines and Missile Maintenance Area to the east was maintained on either side with a turf mixture (Figure 5.112). Today, this connection has become overgrown and feels like a tight corridor in contrast to its open, historic feel (Figure 5.113).

The landscape around the Ready Barracks survives in good condition and does not require extensive vegetation removal. In the barracks area, two London planetrees (*Platanus × acerifolia*) are growing in the lawn panels between the buildings and these trees should remain. Historic photographs show that trees were growing in the barrack's lawn panels in contrast to bare earth maintained along other features like fence lines (Figure 5.114). Targeted removals should take place at barracks buildings 430 and 431 were young eastern red cedars (*Juniperus virginiana*) have started to grow near the buildings' foundations. Removal work around buildings should focus on the Generator Building (429) and kennel buildings (457 and 458) as these structures are becoming enveloped by overgrown vegetation (Figure 5.115).

In addition to buildings and structures, vegetation removal should proceed on the historic earthworks in the Missile Maintenance Area (Figure 5.116). The treatment for these earthworks should follow the guidelines established for the park's older batteries. All woody vegetation greater than four-inches diameter at breast height should be selectively removed and the stumps treated with a triclopyr herbicide. For the two earthworks in the Missile Maintenance Area, 0.5 acres will need to be selectively cleared.

NL-3: Remove all woody vegetation four-feet off either side of the inner and outer perimeter fences

The NIKE launch site distinguishes itself from the radar site with both an outer and inner perimeter security fence. The outer fence defines the extent of the site while the inner fence provides an additional layer of security to access the four missile magazines and the launching apparatus. Similar to the radar site, a plowed and harrowed firebreak of bare soil was once maintained along the outer perimeter fence. A plan from 1958 indicates the bare soil of the firebreak was once thirty-feet wide to the inside of the fence and twenty-feet wide to the outside the fence. The inner fence surrounding the magazines and launching apparatus was devoid of all vegetation when the facility was operational (see Figure 5.96).

Currently, extensive vegetation has become established between the inner fence and perimeter road around the magazine and launch area (Figure 5.117). Vegetation also encroaches on the outer perimeter fence. Restoring the firebreak is not practical; however, the fence lines should be clearly delineated and maintained by removing all woody vegetation at least four-feet off either side. Once the large woody vegetation has been removed, the four-foot width can be easily maintained with a small tractor and brush hog mowing deck.

Visitor Access Treatment Tasks

In preparation to have self-guided access and guided tours of the NIKE launch site, park staff has drafted the *Fort Hancock NIKE Launch Area Visitor Access Plan*. The plan addresses proposed circulation routes for visitors as well as site improvements for a safer and more enjoyable experience. As the NIKE launch site is currently used by various park maintenance programs, as well as being the site of a National Park Service law enforcement firearms range, making this site accessible to the public will require displacing these functions elsewhere, or otherwise carefully coordinating dates and times of visitor access in order to provide the public with a safe experience.

NL-4: Relocate staging area for beach cleaning equipment

When the NIKE launch site was operational prior to 1974, there was no circulation route between the northern end of the Missile Maintenance Area and the southern perimeter of the missile magazines (Figure 5.118). During the past decade, a New Jersey state beach cleaning program has established a convenient route to the beach as well as to an area to store and clean their vehicles where historically neither had existed.

The equipment and staging for the state's beach cleaning program should not be relocated within the NIKE launch site, but moved to new location that does not impact historic resources. Relocating the cleaning and staging area out of the launch site will also enhance the guided tours planned for the southwest Missile Magazines. The proposal is for visitors to proceed east on the access road and then head north into a tunnel entry to access the southwest magazine.

NL-5: Remove recycling storage bins from historic earthwork in the Missile Maintenance Area

A component of the park's maintenance activities at NIKE launch includes storage for the park recycling program. Currently, storage bins and containers are located at the eastern end of a historic earthwork in the Missile Maintenance Area (Figure 5.119). Looking in plan view at the site, the earthwork is roughly crescent-shaped and 1958 plans indicate the top of the earthwork rose seven to ten feet higher than the surrounding grade. An existing paved area at the base of the earthwork may provide convenient access to the recycling materials, however, moving, handling, and storage of the recyclables threatens the historic earthwork. The recycling bins and other containers should be removed and any portion of the earthwork that was disturbed should be restored.

The park is currently exploring shifting recycling activities to the north maintenance facility at Fort Hancock. Relocating recycling to the Fort Hancock facility or developing a new recycling area for the south half of the peninsula is a better long-term strategy for preserving the resources at NIKE launch. Utilizing a single facility for collecting recyclables improves operational efficiency by reducing time and energy spent transporting materials. More importantly, NIKE launch is a contributing site to the National Historic Landmark designation and locating recycling collection within the site creates a non-historic, incompatible use. The launch site currently supports a non-historic firearms range for park police and seasonal law enforcement staff. Additional non-historic uses should not be added.

NL-6: Remove beach-cleaning equipment debris from historic earthwork in the Missile Maintenance Area

Located next to the recycling program's storage bins and containers is a debris pile from the state's beach cleaning program. The pile sits at the toe of slope for the historic earthwork in the Missile Maintenance Area (Figure 5.120). The debris obscures the highly engineered shape of the earthwork feature. Furthermore, moving and pushing the pile around exposes the historic earthwork to damage from large equipment. The debris pile should be carefully removed from the historic earthwork with equipment no larger than a skid-steer tractor. As the removal process approaches the historic toe of slope, the last three feet should be removed by hand to minimize possible impacts. Any portion of the historic earthwork that was disturbed by the debris pile should be restored.

NL-7: Relocate park trash and recycling functions to the north maintenance yard

The park is currently exploring options for relocating trash and recycling services to the north maintenance facility at Fort Hancock. Moving trash and recycling out of the NIKE launch site would remove a non-historic, non-compatible use from a resource that contributes to the National Historic Landmark status of Sandy Hook. Additionally, relocating trash and recycling functions will enhance visitors' experience and understanding of the launch site. In the near future, the park is planning to have self-guided and guided tours of the site as outlined in the *Fort Hancock NIKE Launch Area Visitor Access Plan*.

Battery Structures Treatment Tasks

NL-8: Stabilize Free-Standing Buildings

The missile magazine, Missile Maintenance, and Ready Barracks areas all contain buildings that supported the operation, maintenance and security of the NIKE launch site. Presently, the free-standing buildings are in a generally fair condition with some building materials showing signs of deterioration due to inadequate protection from the elements (Figure 5.121). The launch site buildings should be thoroughly inventoried in order to assess specific conditions and develop recommendations for building treatments beyond the scope of this report. In the interim, temporary measures to close and secure exterior openings and routine maintenance such as painting can provide short-term protection against the elements and help stabilize free-standing buildings.

NL-9: Repair and replace chain-link fencing site-wide

The chain-link fencing found throughout the NIKE launch site is in serious disrepair, the material and fixtures having reached the end of their useful service life. Removing woody vegetation growing on either side and in many instances though the wire fabric will only make this advanced state of decay more apparent (Figure 5.122). Owing to the fact that fencing material and hardware of this kind remains available in commerce, the entire fencing system should be replaced in-kind once the adjacent vegetation has been removed.

When replacing sections of the fencing system, new line posts should match the existing H-beam posts. The wire gauge and mesh opening should match the existing chain-link and all material and hardware should be galvanized to match the specifications of the original material.

NL-10: Repair, maintain, and replace missing historic light fixtures

Floodlight and spotlight fixtures at the NIKE launch site are character-defining features of this Cold War defense installation. Each floodlight fixture is comprised of a twenty-four inch diameter light housing attached to a metal bracket and mounted to a pole (Figure 5.123). At the Missile Magazines, the lights are mounted on wood poles and at the Missile Maintenance Area they are mounted on metal poles. Within the Missile Magazine area, four spotlights were erected by the end of the historic period. From ground level, the first eight to ten feet of the poles were painted yellow and a red letter was added to the yellow field to denote the magazine section. Spotlights were mounted at the top of each pole. Three of the poles were removed following transfer to the National Park Service and presently, only the pole and lights at the Section B magazine (427) are extant.

Each extant light fixture should be routinely inspected to make sure the pole is vertically plumb and the material is sound. Poles should be reset to a vertical position and if the pole is damaged, severely deteriorated, or missing, it should be replaced to match the historic material and finish. The mounting hardware and light fixtures should be treated for corrosion, primed, and painted to match the historic finish. The glass lens on the fixture should be replaced to match the existing if it is cracked or broken. The lights were historically either mounted horizontally or angled slightly downward. If the hardware has loosened and the fixtures aim straight down, these should be reset to a horizontal position and securely fastened (see Drawing 5.12 for locations).

NL-11: Provide handicap accessible parking and improve visitor parking lot off of Hartshorne Drive

One of the items in the *Fort Hancock NIKE Launch Area Visitor Access Plan* indicates new handicap accessible parking inside the launch site near the Ready Barracks. Instead of creating separate locations for handicap and standard parking, both can be provided in the same location with a reconfiguration of the existing visitor lot off of Hartshorne Drive (Figure 5.124).

The lot currently has two bays of parking stalls and a resulting central aisle that is too narrow for parked cars backing up. The proposed reconfiguration would place the stalls near the Hartshorne Drive side with a five-foot raised, curbed buffer between the two. Without expanding the existing lot, the aisle behind the new stalls would be wide enough for two-way traffic and cars backing up. Two center stalls would be designated handicap accessible and share a van accessible walkway between them.

NL-12: Install pedestrian crosswalk and signage from visitor parking lot to site via the multi-use path

In addition to providing handicap accessible parking at the current NIKE launch area visitor parking lot, a modest reconfiguration of the existing parking lot would include adding a pedestrian crosswalk from the lot to the multi-use path on the other side of Hartshorne Drive. New Jersey Department of Transportation required signage would also be installed with the crosswalk (see Figure 5.124).

The crosswalk would align with the van accessible walkway in the lot and all visitors would share the circulation system from the lot to the launch site. The crosswalk would be located away from intersections to minimize pedestrian and vehicular conflicts. Once across Hartshorne Drive, visitors would move along the existing multi-use path and follow the path to the gated access at the launch site. This would allow visitors to enter at the same point where servicemen once arrived when the site was on alert.

NL-13: Reconstruct the sentry hut near missile magazines

A component of the *Fort Hancock NIKE Launch Area Visitor Access Plan* calls for reconstructing the missing sentry hut near the missile magazine area. An existing sentry hut survives near the access gate off of Hartshorne Drive. Its missing companion historically guarded access at a second security point and should be reconstructed over a surviving foundation near the missile magazine area (Figure 5.125).

NL-14: Construct access tunnel to southwest missile magazine

One of the more ambitious goals of providing visitor access to the NIKE launch site is a proposal to offer guided tours of the southwest underground missile magazine and show the below ground area where NIKE missiles were stored and raised into a firing position. In order to provide underground access, a tunnel must be designed and constructed to connect the access road to the south with the magazine. Visitors would proceed east on the access road and then turn north into a tunnel entrance providing access the below-grade missile magazine.

Large corrugated metal tubing has been used at the Minute Man National Historical Park to make possible a continuous pedestrian trail below a busy commuter route (Figure 5.126).

In terms of visitor access, the Ready Barracks, immediately adjacent to Hartshorne Drive, could be readily opened to self-guided tours as indicated in the *Fort Hancock NIKE Launch Area Visitor Access Plan*. There is an existing fence and gate between the Ready Barracks and access road to the missile magazines that makes the barracks self-contained and allows for self-guided tours to just outside launch area enclosure. Limiting access to the tunnel and the underground magazine would require that doors be installed on the entrance to the tunnel.

NL-15: Stabilize spalling concrete surfaces and repair cracks and voids

The concrete pads for the former launchers and racks exhibit spalling areas and cracks resulting from water infiltration and freeze-thaw cycles. In order to limit further damage to the concrete, spalling surfaces should be removed, mechanically cleaned, and patched to match the character of the historic material. Small cracks should be dried and prepared to receive a sealant that is compatible with the character of the historic concrete. The treatment of large, structural cracks should be determined by a structural engineer. Additional information addressing the repair of spalling areas and cracks can be found in the treatment tasks common to all battery sites and in the *Historic Fortification Preservation Handbook* (Washington State Parks and Recreation Commission, 2003).

NL-16: Repair and seal horizontal concrete surfaces to reduce water infiltration

In order to reduce water infiltration and to protect the concrete pads at the missile magazines, a surface coating should be applied to the horizontal surfaces. Application of a surface coating must occur after spalling and cracked concrete surfaces are repaired and defected surfaces that collect and pool rainwater are corrected. Additional information penetrating sealers and surface sealers can be found in the treatment tasks common to all battery sites. At the NIKE launch site, approximately 31,000 square feet of concrete should be sealed.

NL-17: Repair and repaint ferrous metal fixtures and surfaces

A variety of ferrous metal fixtures were incorporated into the construction of the NIKE launch site. Metal fixtures in fair condition with visible rust should be chemically treated, primed, and painted to match the historic finish. Damaged or severely deteriorated fixtures should be removed and replaced with new components that match the original as close as possible. Additional information on ferrous metal treatments can be found in the Safety Railings section of the treatment tasks common to all battery sites and in the *Historic Fortification Preservation Handbook* (Washington State Parks and Recreation Commission, 2003).

TABLE 5.11: SUMMARY OF TREATMENT RECOMMENDATIONS, NIKE RADAR SITE		
Rehabilitation Task	**Notes**	**Priority for Action** 1 - high priority 2 - medium priority 3 - low priority, but requires ongoing monitoring 4 - no action
NR-1: Remove all woody vegetation growing on or within four-feet of buildings and structures		1 – high priority for action
NR-2: Remove all woody vegetation six-feet off either side of circulation features		1 – high priority for action
NR-3: Remove all woody vegetation four-feet off either side of the perimeter fence		1 – high priority for action
NR-4: Install compatible stairway for safe access to radar platform	Coordinate with plans to enhance tours at the radar site	1 – high priority for action
NR-5: Repair, retrofit, and replace safety railings	Coordinate with installing access to radar platform	1 – high priority for action
NR-6: Relocate brick masonry stockpiles to Fort Hancock maintenance yard		1 – high priority for action
NR-7: Stabilize Free-Standing Buildings		1 – high priority for action
NR-8: Repair and replace chain-link fencing site-wide	Implement after vegetation removals from both sides of existing fence	2 – plan for future action
NR-9: Preserve historic light fixtures		2 - plan for future action

TABLE 5.12: SUMMARY OF TREATMENT RECOMMENDATIONS, NIKE LAUNCH SITE		
Rehabilitation Task	**Notes**	**Priority for Action** 1 - high priority 2 - medium priority 3 - low priority, but requires ongoing monitoring 4 - no action
NL-1: Remove woody vegetation greater than four-inches diameter growing on engineered slopes		1 – high priority for action
NL-2: Remove all woody vegetation growing on or within four-feet of buildings and structures		1 – high priority for action
NL-3: Remove all woody vegetation four-feet off either side of the inner and outer perimeter fences		1 – high priority for action
NL-4: Relocate staging area for beach cleaning equipment		1 – high priority for action
NL-5: Remove recycling storage bins from historic earthwork in the Missile Maintenance Area		1 – high priority for action
NL-6: Remove beach-cleaning equipment debris from historic earthwork in the Missile Maintenance Area		1 – high priority for action
NL-7: Relocate park trash and recycling functions to the north maintenance yard		1 – high priority for action
NL-8: Stabilize Free-Standing Buildings		1 – high priority for action
NL-9: Repair and replace chain-link fencing site-wide	Implement after vegetation removals from both sides of existing fence	2 - plan for future action
NL-10: Repair, maintain, and replace missing historic light fixtures		2 - plan for future action
NL-11: Provide handicap accessible parking and improve visitor parking lot off of Hartshorne Drive	Coordinate with projects for the *NIKE Launch Area Visitor Access Plan*	1 - high priority for action
NL-12: Install pedestrian crosswalk and signage from visitor parking lot to site via the multi-use path	Coordinate with projects for the *NIKE Launch Area Visitor Access Plan*	1 – high priority for action
NL-13: Reconstruct the sentry hut near Missile Magazines		2 - plan for future action
NL-14: Construct underground access to the southwest Missile Magazines	Coordinate with projects for the *NIKE Launch Area Visitor Access Plan*	3 – low priority
NL-15: Stabilize spalling concrete surfaces and repair cracks and voids		1 - high priority for action
NL-16: Repair and seal horizontal concrete surfaces to reduce water infiltration	Implement after concrete surface defects have been repaired	1 - high priority for action
NL-17: Repair and repaint ferrous metal fixtures and surfaces		2 – plan for future action

ENDNOTES

[1] Robert R. Page, Cathy A. Gilbert, and Susan A. Dolan, *A Guide to Cultural Landscape Reports: Contents, Process and Techniques* (Washington, D.C.: United States. Department of the Interior, National Park Service, 1998), 81.

[2] Such tasks are addressed in a separate cultural landscape document known in the National Park Service as a "Preservation Maintenance Plan." This plan is not included in the scope of this project.

[3] Harry Butowsky, "National Register of Historic Places Inventory - Nomination Form, Fort Hancock and the Sandy Hook Proving Ground Historic District," revised November 9, 1982, sect. 7, 1 and sect. 8, 1.

[4] Enabling legislation, as cited in *General Management Plan, Gateway National Recreation Area, New York/New Jersey* (United States Department of the Interior, National Park Service, August 1979), 163-65.

[5] *General Management Plan Amendment: Development Concept Plan and Interpretation Prospectus: Sandy Hook Unit, Gateway National Recreation Area, New York/New Jersey* (United States. Department of the Interior, National Park Service, January 1990), 13.

[6] Helen Mahan, telephone conversation with the author, August 5, 2010.

[7] Savage to Pfoutz, 5 November 1996, correspondence in reference to "List of Classified Structures," countersigned by Dorothy Guzzo, NJ SHPO, 2 January 1997, NPS, National Register Files, Northeast Regional Office.

[8] James J. Lee III and Lauren Laham, *Historic Structure Report: Battery Potter, Mortar Battery and Battery Gunnison. Fort Hancock, New Jersey, Sandy Hook Unit, Gateway National Recreation Area* (United States. Department of the Interior, National Park Service, 2007), 6-7.

[9] David M. Hansen, Kimberly Keagle, and Deborah Rehn, *Historic Fortification Preservation Handbook* (Olympia, WA: Washington State Parks and Recreation Commission, 2003), 3.3.

[10] Ibid., 3.74.

[11] Ibid., 3.14.

[12] Ibid., 4.8.

[13] Ibid., 3.97.

[14] Ibid., 3.97-3.98.

[15] Joe C. Freeman et al., *Seacoast Fortifications Preservation Manual, Golden Gate National Recreation Area, San Francisco, California* (United States. Department of the Interior, National Park Service and KEA Environmental, July 1999), 160.

[16] Ibid., 169-172.

[17] Ibid., 169.

[18] Hansen, *Historic Fortification Preservation Handbook*, 3.78-3.79.

[19] Ibid., 3.51-3.52.

[20] Ibid., 3.48.

[21] Ibid., 3.48-3.49.

[22] See Johns Manville Corporation, "SBS Modified Bitumen Roofing Membranes," http://www.specjm.com/commercial/roofing/sbsbituminous.asp.

[23] Kenneth Barry, "The Chemistry of Waterproofing," Mason Contractors Association of America, http://www.masonrymagazine.com/11-03/waterproof.html.

[24] Freeman, *Seacoast Fortifications Preservation Manual*, 160, 162.

[25] *Guide to Sustainable Earthworks Management* (United States Department of the Interior, National Park Service, Draft, 1998), 128.

[26] Thomas Hoffman, "Fort Hancock Gun Batteries: Revised Draft Text" (working paper, Sandy Hook Unit, 1999).

[27] For additional information on chemical applications making rust inert, please see Hansen, *Historic Fortification Preservation Handbook*, 3.97.

[28] Hoffman, "Fort Hancock Gun Batteries"; Thomas Hoffman, telephone conversation with the author, February 23, 2009.

[29] Virginia Pitman Barnes, *Identification and Control of Common Reed (Phragmites australis) in Virginia*, 2003.

[30] Thomas Hoffman, *Fort Hancock* (Charleston, SC: Arcadia Publishing, 2007), 7.

[31] Ibid., 79.

[32] Hansen, *Historic Fortification Preservation Handbook*, 3.46.

[33] Hoffman, *Fort Hancock*, 20.

[34] Ibid., 26.

[35] Hoffman, "Fort Hancock Gun Batteries".

[36] Hoffman, *Fort Hancock*, 100.

[37] *Guide to Sustainable Earthworks Management*, 23.

[38] Ibid., 128.

[39] David Snyder and Sylvan R. Kaufman, *An Overview of Nonindigenous Plant Species in New Jersey* (Trenton, NJ: New Jersey Department of Environmental Protection, 2004), 87-89.

[40] Jonathan Soll, *Controlling Knotweed (Polygonum cuspidatum, P. sachalinense, P. polystachyum and hybrids) in the Pacific Northwest* (Portland, OR: The Nature Conservancy, 2004), 10-11.

[41] For additional information on chemical applications making rust inert, please see Hansen, *Historic Fortification Preservation Handbook*, 3.97.

Figure 5.96. View looking northwest at the missile magazines, NIKE launch site, circa 1958. The inner fence surrounding the magazines completely lacked any trace of vegetation when the NIKE facility was operational (GATE 8067).

Figure 5.97. Oblique aerial view, NIKE radar site, circa 1962. In this photograph Control Area #2 is in the foreground with Control Area #1 in the background and the Ready Barracks to the right. In addition to the thirty-foot fire break inside the perimeter fence, most of the vegetation on the site was strictly managed except for a wedge-shaped area in the center (GATE 20818).

Figure 5.98. View looking southeast at the Generator Building (414), Control Area #1, NIKE radar site. The buildings and structures in the radar site show signs of deterioration in specific building materials that include metal, concrete block, and corrugated siding and roofing. Due to damaged windows and doors, the Generator Building lacks a closed building envelope exposing the interior to water and seasonal temperature fluctuations that advance deterioration (Olmsted Center, January 2009).

Figure 5.99. View looking northwest at pedestrian walkway, Control Area #1, NIKE radar site. Following the site's closure woody species, especially eastern red cedars, have emerged and are encroaching on pedestrian circulation features as well as buildings and the perimeter fence (Olmsted Center, January 2009).

Figure 5.100. View looking southeast at engineered earthwork, NIKE launch site. Eastern red cedars (*Juniperus virginiana*) cover the majority of the engineered earthworks in the Missile Maintenance Area (Olmsted Center, January 2009).

Figure 5.101. View looking north at the firearms range, NIKE launch site. Park law enforcement has set up a range in a low lying area north of the access road that leads to the Warhead Building (Olmsted Center, January 2009).

Figure 5.102. View looking northeast at CODAR antenna, NIKE launch site. The launch site has become home to a variety of uses for other institutions. An antenna and monitoring equipment have been set up for collecting weather and tide information. A pile of shells and palettes on the right are for a shellfish seeding program (Olmsted Center, January 2009).

Figure 5.103. View looking west at target tracking radars (417 and 473), Control Area #1, NIKE radar site, circa 1962. The vegetation in the foreground of this image was located in front of the perimeter fence and was outside the site. Beyond the fence and around the radar platforms was bare sand, beachgrass, and no woody vegetation (GATE 22043).

Figure 5.104. View looking north of sidewalk from Control Area #2 to the Ready Barracks, NIKE radar site. Asphalt, concrete, and gravel-surfaced circulation features should be cleared of woody vegetation six-feet off of all sides. Once woody vegetation, like the eastern red cedars seen in this photograph, has been removed, the six foot width can be easily maintained with a small tractor and brush hog mowing deck (Olmsted Center, January 2009).

Figure 5.105. Existing perimeter fence, NIKE launch site. The existing perimeter fence at the radar and launch sites should be clearly delineated and maintained by removing all woody vegetation a minimum of four-feet off either side of the fence. The vegetation removals will also aid in inspection and repairs of the existing fence (Olmsted Center, January 2009).

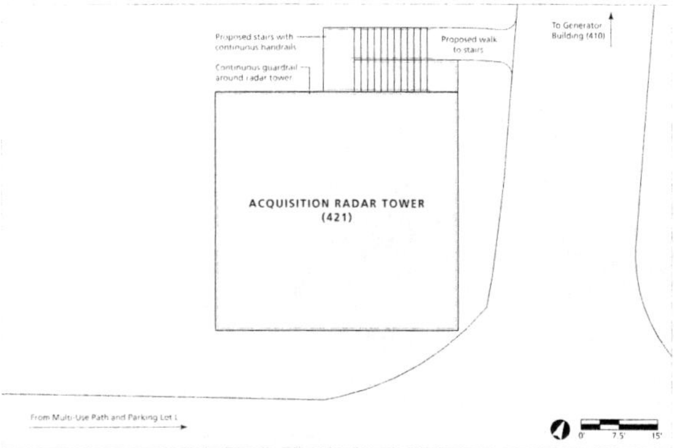

Figure 5.106. Plan of proposed access stairs to acquisition radar tower (Building 421), NIKE radar site. The proposed stairs should be located on the north side of the platform where they will be less conspicuous for visitors viewing the site from the parking lot and multi-use path to the west (Olmsted Center, 2009).

Figure 5.107. Existing expanded metal mesh on guardrails at radar tower, NIKE radar site. New expanded metal mesh should match the existing in this photograph and be applied to the lower and upper openings of the existing guardrails for added safety (Olmsted Center, January 2009).

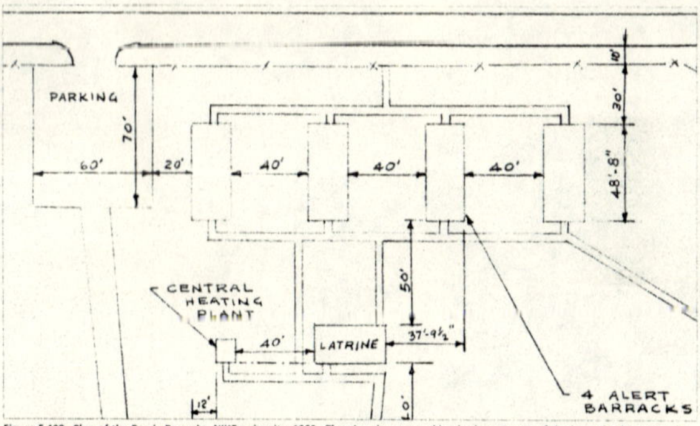

Figure 5.108. Plan of the Ready Barracks, NIKE radar site, 1962. The plan shows a parking lot layout west of the barracks that currently holds a stockpile of yellow brick for Fort Hancock buildings. The brick should be stacked on to palettes and moved to the maintenance yard at Fort Hancock (GATE 11057).

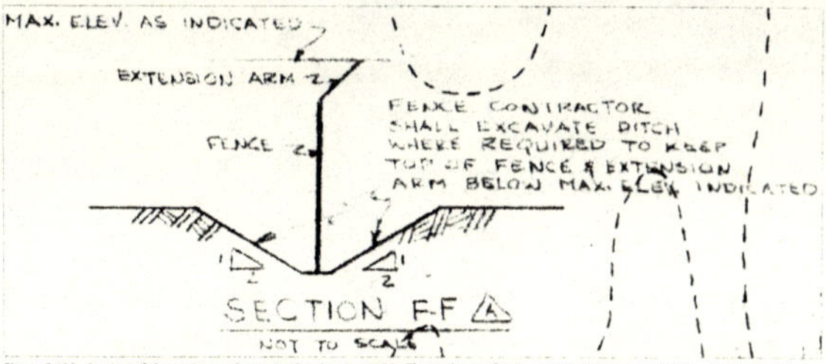

Figure 5.109. Section of the perimeter fence, NIKE radar site, 1954. The perimeter fence was called out as type FE-6—a designation for chain-link with barbed wire on a single extension arm. The contractor was to excavate either side of the fence at a 2:1 slope in order to maintain the specified height (GATE 11052).

Figure 5.110. Existing light fixture, NIKE radar site. The historic light fixtures should be periodically inspected, have components repaired or replaced as needed, and receive corrosion treatment, priming, and painting to match the historic finish. The eastern red cedar in the foreground should be removed as part of vegetation management along the circulation systems (Olmsted Center, January 2009).

Figure 5.111. Existing light fixture between building 404 and 405, NIKE radar site. The fallen fixture should be reset and will most likely require a new concrete footing and tubular pole. The new pole should match the existing in material, dimensions, and finishing. The fixture's other components should be inspected at this time and repaired or replaced based on their condition (Olmsted Center, January 2009).

Figure 5.112. View looking northeast at the missile magazines, NIKE launch site, circa 1968. The vehicular connection between the Ready Barracks and the Missile Magazines and Missile Maintenance Area to the east was maintained on either side with a turf mixture (GATE 22041).

Figure 5.113. View looking northwest toward Ready Barracks, NIKE launch site. This photograph shows the vehicular route has become overgrown and feels like a tight corridor in contrast to the open, low-growing vegetation in the historic image. The overgrown vegetation limits vehicular sight-distances and may put pedestrians at risk if park visitors use this route as a walkway during the hours of active maintenance operations (Olmsted Center, April 2008).

Figure 5.114. Oblique aerial view of the Ready Barracks, NIKE launch site, circa 1958. This photograph shows trees growing in the barrack's lawn panels in contrast to bare earth maintained on either side of the fence lines. The existing trees at the barrack's lawn panels should remain (GATE 5781).

Figure 5.115. View looking northwest at the kennel buildings, NIKE launch site. Vegetation removals around existing buildings should focus on the generator building (429) and kennel buildings (457 and 458) as these structures are becoming enveloped by overgrown vegetation (Olmsted Center, January 2009).

Figure 5.116. View looking southeast at Missile Maintenance Area historic earthwork, NIKE launch site. For the NIKE earthworks, all woody vegetation greater than four-inches diameter at breast height should be selectively removed and the stumps treated with a triclopyr herbicide (Olmsted Center, January 2009).

Figure 5.117. View looking east at the missile magazines, NIKE launch site. In contrast to the historic image, extensive vegetation has grown up between the inner fence and perimeter road around the magazines. The dense vegetation will impede repairs to the historic fence (Olmsted Center, April 2008).

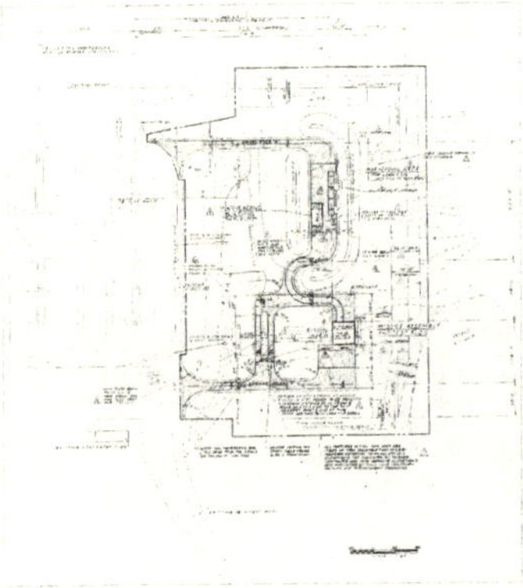

Figure 5.118. Site plan for Missile Maintenance Area, 1958. The gray tone has been added to show vehicular circulation. The current location for beach cleaning equipment (*red outline*) should be relocated to restore an area that was never intended for vehicular use (GATE 7620-2983 and Olmsted Center).

Figure 5.119. View looking east at Missile Maintenance Area historic earthwork, NIKE launch site. The railroad tie retaining structure and recycling containers should be removed from the eastern end of the earthwork (Olmsted Center, April 2008).

Figure 5.120. View looking southeast at Missile Maintenance Area historic earthwork, NIKE launch site. In addition to the recycling containers visible on the left, a debris pile from the state's beach cleaning program sits at the toe of the earthwork. The debris obscures the highly engineered shape of the earthwork and should be carefully removed to avoid damaging this feature (Olmsted Center, January 2009).

Figure 5.121. View looking northwest at Warhead Building (450), NIKE launch site. Routine maintenance procedures will help stabilize free-standing buildings in the launch site. The water damage seen in this image originates from a metal gutter mounted at the top of the wall that needs to be cleaned and reset so water is carried away from the building (Olmsted Center, April 2008).

Figure 5.122. View looking northeast across missile magazines, NIKE launch site. After vegetation removals the inner, outer, and kennel fences should be inspected, repaired where needed, and replaced where damaged or severely deteriorated (Olmsted Center, April 2008).

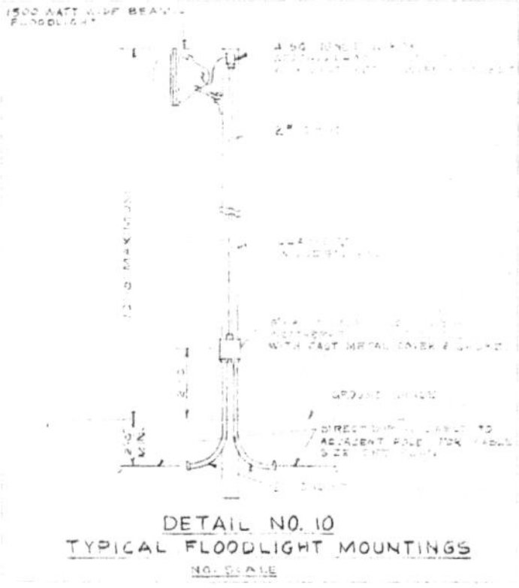

Figure 5.123. Elevation of floodlight, NIKE launch site, 1958. The poles, mounting hardware, light fixtures, and glass lenses should be routinely inspected. Any deficiencies should be corrected and damage components should be replaced to match the existing (GATE 11056).

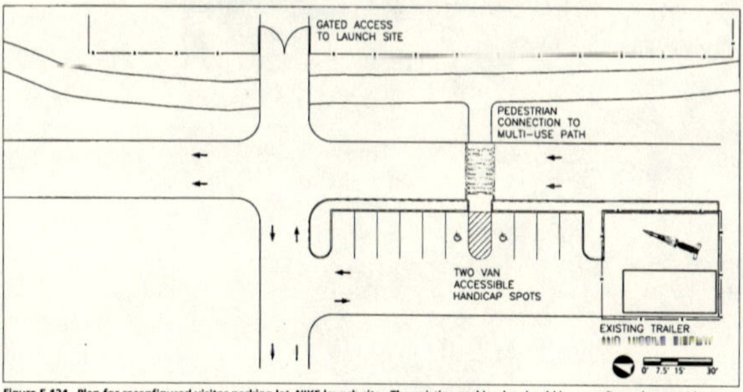

Figure 5.124. Plan for reconfigured visitor parking lot, NIKE launch site. The existing parking lot should be reconfigured to provide handicap accessible parking, a pedestrian crosswalk across Hartshorne Drive, and access to the site via the existing multi-use path (Olmsted Center, 2009).

Figure 5.125. View looking northwest toward the Ready Barracks, NIKE launch site. The sentry hut near the missile magazines should be reconstructed as part of plans to prepare the site for visitor access and interpretation. The concrete foundation for the hut is visible in the right foreground (Olmsted Center, April 2008).

Figure 5.126. Example of a cut and cover tunnel routing the park "Battle Road Trail" below Hanscom Drive, Minute Man National Historical Park. This type of tunnel, installed from prefabricated segments, is under consideration to provide visitor access to one of Sandy Hook's subsurface NIKE missile magazine rooms (January 2009, Minute Man NHP, Massachusetts).

Cultural Landscape Report
or the Sandy Hook
Coastal Defense Batteries

Gateway National
Recreation Area
andy Hook, New Jersey

NIKE Launch Site
Treatment Plan

OLMSTED CENTER for Landscape Preservation

ational Park Service
lmsted Center for Landscape Preservation
www.nps.gov/oclp

OURCES

Sandy Hook GIS Data

Sandy Hook Color Ortho Imagery, Captured 2006

Topographic Sheets, prepared by Denver Service Center, 1992

Topographic Maps, prepared by Carrera and Associates, 1990

Field Inventory, Olmsted Center for Landscape Preservation, January 2009

RAWN BY

m Layton, AutoCAD 2002, Illustrator CS3, 2009

EGEND

- Canopy Vegetation
- Paved Road / Walk
- Multi-Use Path
- Unpaved Road / Walk
- Trail
- Deciduous Tree
- Evergreen Tree
- Fence
- Floodlight Fixture
- Spotlight Fixture
- Scope of Treatment

IOTES

Contour Interval = 2'-0"

Plan represents landscape conditions inventoried in January 2009

All features shown in approximate scale and location

0' 37.5' 75' 150'

Drawing 5.12

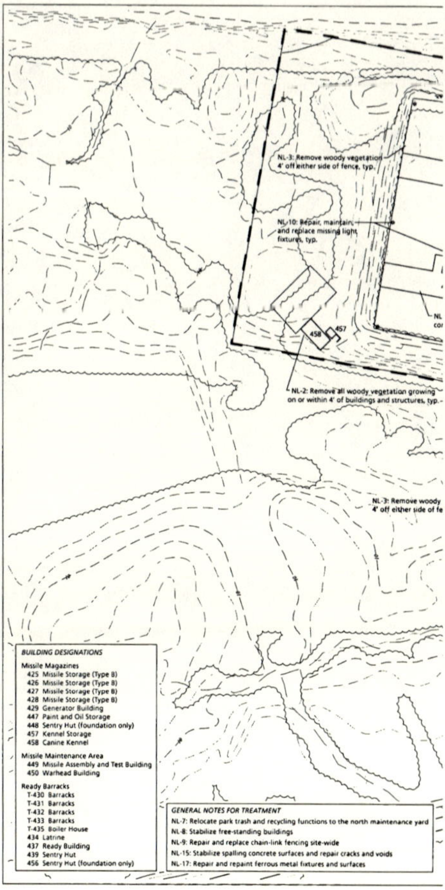

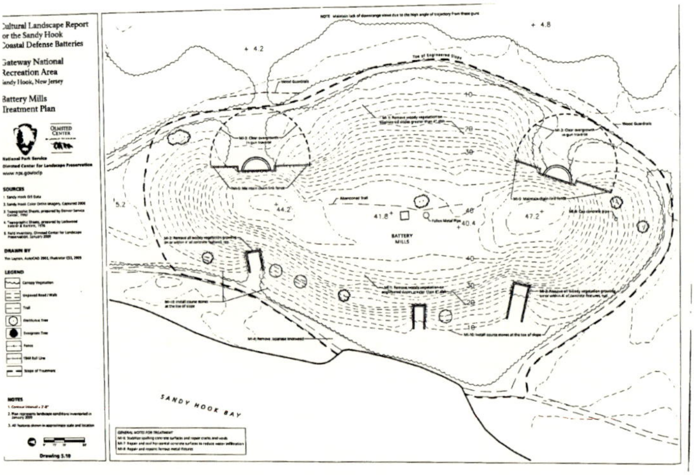
ultural Landscape Report
or the Sandy Hook
oastal Defense Batteries
ateway National
ecreation Area
andy Hook, New Jersey
Battery Mills
reatment Plan
National Park Service
SOURCES
DRAWN BY
LEGEND
NOTES
Drawing 5.10
+ 4.2
+ 4.8
5.2
44.2
41.8
47.2
40.4
BATTERY
MILLS
SANDY HOOK BAY

REFERENCES

PUBLISHED BOOKS AND REPORTS

Barnard, Roy S. *The History of ARADCOM Volume 1: The Gun Era 1950–1955.* United States Department of Defense, Headquarters ARADCOM, [1973?].

Bearss, Edwin C. *Historic Resource Study and Historic Structure Report Historical Data Section Spermaceti Cove Life-Saving Station, Sandy Hook Unit, Gateway National Recreation Area, New York/New Jersey.* United States Department of the Interior, National Park Service, January 1983.

———. *Historic Resource Study Fort Hancock: 1948-1974, Sandy Hook Unit, Gateway National Recreation Area, Monmouth County, New Jersey.* United States Department of the Interior, National Park Service, November 1982.

———. *Historic Resource Study The Sandy Hook Proving Ground 1874-1919. Sandy Hook Unit, Gateway National Recreation Area, New Jersey.* United States Department of the Interior, National Park Service, September 1983.

Berhow, Mark A. *U. S. Strategic and Defensive Missile Systems 1950-2004.* New York: Osprey Publishing Limited, 2005.

Freeman, Joe C., Stephen A. Haller, David M. Hansen, John A. Martini, and Karen J. Weitze. *Seacoast Fortifications Preservation Manual, Golden Gate National Recreation Area, San Francisco, California.* United States Department of the Interior, National Park Service and KEA Environmental, July 1999.

General Management Plan, Gateway National Recreation Area, New York/New Jersey. United States Department of the Interior, National Park Service, August 1979.

General Management Plan Amendment: Development Concept Plan and Interpretation Prospectus: Sandy Hook Unit, Gateway National Recreation Area, New York/New Jersey. United States Department of the Interior, National Park Service, January 1990.

Hansen, David M., Kimberly Keagle, and Deborah Rehn. *Historic Fortification Preservation Handbook.* Olympia, WA: Washington State Parks and Recreation Commission, 2003.

Hoffman, Thomas. *Fort Hancock.* Charleston, SC: Arcadia Publishing, 2007.

Lee, James J. III. *Spermaceti Cove Life-Saving Station Historic Structure Report, Sandy Hook Unit, Gateway National Recreation Area, Fort Hancock, New Jersey.* United States Department of the Interior, National Park Service, 2008.

Lee, James J. III and Lauren Laham. *Historic Structure Report: Battery Potter, Mortar Battery and Battery Gunnison. Fort Hancock, New Jersey, Sandy Hook Unit, Gateway National Recreation Area.* United States Department of the Interior, National Park Service, 2007.

Lewis, Emanuel Raymond. *Seacoast Fortifications of the United States: An Introductory History.* Annapolis, MD: Naval Institute Press, 1993. First published 1970 by Smithsonian Institution Press.

Lonnquest, John C., and David F. Winkler. *To Defend and Deter: The Legacy of the United States Cold War Missile Program.* United States Department of Defense, Army Construction Engineering Research Laboratories, November 1996.

The Louis Berger Group, Inc. *Archeological Investigations of the Magruder Road Demolition and Repaving and Gunnison Road Realignment Project Sandy Hook, New Jersey.* United States Department of the Interior, National Park Service, Denver Service Center, January 2004.

Martini, John A., and Stephen A. Haller. *What We Have We Shall Defend: An Interim History and Preservation Plan for Nike Site SF-88L, Fort Barry, California.* United States Department of the Interior, National Park Service, Golden Gate National Recreation Area, 1998.

McGovern, Terrance, and Bolling Smith. *American Coastal Defenses 1885-1950.* New York: Osprey Publishing Limited, 2006.

Page, Robert R., Cathy A. Gilbert, and Susan A. Dolan. *A Guide to Cultural Landscape Reports: Contents, Process and Techniques.* United States Department of the Interior, National Park Service, 1998.

Rosenbaum, Joel, and Tom Gallo. *Iron Horses Across the Garden State.* Piscataway, NJ: Railpace Company, Inc., 1985.

Sandy Hook: A Study of Alternatives. United States Department of the Interior, National Park Service, 1967.

Snyder, David, and Sylvan R. Kaufman. *An Overview of Nonindigenous Plant Species in New Jersey.* Trenton, NJ: New Jersey Department of Environmental Protection, 2004.

Sullivan, Judith Q. *Building 32 Quartermaster's Storehouse, Fort Hancock, Historic Structure Report, Sandy Hook Unit, Gateway National Recreation Area.* United States Department of the Interior, National Park Service, 2004.

Williams, Norma E. *Cultural Landscape Report for Proving Ground and Wartime Expansion Areas, Sandy Hook Unit, Gateway National Recreation Area.* United States Department of the Interior, National Park Service, July 1999.

Winkler, David F. *Searching the Skies: The Legacy of the United States Cold War Defense Radar Program.* United States Department of Defense, Air Force Air Combat Command, June 1997.

PERIODICALS, ARTICLES, UNPUBLISHED REPORTS, AND WEB SITES

Barnes, Virginia Pitman. *Identification and Control of Common Reed (Phragmites australis) in Virginia.* Virginia Cooperative Extension Fact Sheet number 427-101, 2003.

Barry, Kenneth. "The Chemistry of Waterproofing." Mason Contractors Association of America. http://www.masonrymagazine.com/11-03/waterproof.html.

Berhow, Mark A. "Caretaker Status in the Coast Artillery, 1912-1948." *The Coast Defense Study Group Journal* 14, no. 4 (2000): 48-57.

"Billy Mitchell." Air and Space Power Journal. http://www.airpower.maxwell.af.mil/airchronicles/cc/mitch.html.

"British Navy Ships—HMS Dreadnought 1906-1922." United States Department of the Navy, Naval Historical Center. http://www.history.navy.mil/photos/sh-fornv/uk/uksh-d/drednt9.htm.

Butowsky, Harry. "National Register of Historic Places Inventory - Nomination Form, Fort Hancock and the Sandy Hook Proving Ground Historic District," revised November 9, 1982.

"Chapter 2: American Military History, Volume II." United States Army Center of Military History. http://www.history.army.mil/books/AMH-V2/AMH%20V2/chapter2.htm.

Greenwood, Richard E. "National Register of Historic Places Inventory - Nomination Form, Fort Hancock and the Sandy Hook Proving Ground Historic District," June 28, 1976.

Guide to Sustainable Earthworks Management. United States Department of the Interior, National Park Service, Draft, 1998.

Hoffman, Thomas. "Cold War Defender: Draft Text." Working paper, Sandy Hook Unit, Gateway National Recreation Area, 2005.

———. "Fort Hancock Gun Batteries: Revised Draft Text." Working paper, Sandy Hook Unit, Gateway National Recreation Area, 1999.

Johns Manville Corporation. "SBS Modified Bitumen Roofing Membranes." http://www.specjm.com/commercial/roofing/sbsbituminous.asp.

"Marine Academy of Science and Technology." Monmouth County Vocational School District. http://www.mast.mcvsd.org/.

Maritime Heritage Program. "Sandy Hook Light National Historic Landmark Study." National Park Service. http://www.nps.gov/history/maritime/nhl/sandy.htm.

Morang, Andrew. "Historical Aerial Photographs Made Available by the ERDC Coastal and Hydraulics Laboratory." United States Army Corps of Engineers Coastal and Hydraulics Laboratory. http://chl.wes.army.mil/shore/newjersey/shore1920/.

Northeast Fisheries Science Center. "James J. Howard Marine Sciences Laboratory." National Oceanic and Atmospheric Administration. http://sh.nefsc.noaa.gov/.

Potts, JR. "HMS Dreadnought." Military Factory. http://www.militaryfactory.com/ships/detail.asp?ship_id=HMS-Dreadnought.

"Sandy Hook Bird Observatory." New Jersey Audubon Society. http://www.njaudubon.org/Centers/SHBO/.

Soll, Jonathan. *Controlling Knotweed (Polygonum cuspidatum, P. sachalinense, P. polystachyum and hybrids) in the Pacific Northwest.* Portland, OR: The Nature Conservancy, 2004.

Tobias, James. "Frequently Asked Questions - Naming Army Installations." United States Army Center of Military History. http://www.history.army.mil/html/faq/base_name.html.

U. S. Geological Survey. "NYC Regional Geology – Atlantic Coastal Plain." http://3dparks.wr.usgs.gov/nyc/coastalplain/coastalplain.htm.

———. "Volumetric Change Analysis along Gateway National Recreation Area - Sandy Hook and Fire Island National Seashore." http://ngom.usgs.gov/dsp/mapping/volumetric_change.html.

REPOSITORIES

Center for Military History, Carlisle, PA.

Coastal Defense Study Group, Bel Air, MD.

Engineering and Maintenance Division, Sandy Hook Unit, Gateway National Recreation Area.

Gateway National Recreation Area Museum Collection.

National Archives and Records Administration, College Park, MD.

National Park Service
U.S. Department of the Interior

Olmsted Center for Landscape Preservation
Boston National Historical Park
Charlestown Navy Yard, Quarters C
Boston, Massachusetts 02129
Phone: 617-241-6954
Fax: 617-241-3952
web: www.nps.gov/oclp/

Spotted something that isn't quite right?

Let us know and we'll fix it for future reprints.
And as a thank you for your diligence, we'll
send you a free Sothis book of your choice.

publisher@sothis.press

This page intentionally left blank

Made in United States
North Haven, CT
01 September 2026

17811876R00314